MW00827316

Irene Eber
**Wartime Shanghai**

# New Perspectives on Modern Jewish History

—

Edited by Cornelia Wilhelm

## Volume 1

ISBN 978-3-11-048568-4
e-ISBN 978-3-11-026818-8
ISSN 2192-9645


**Library of Congress Cataloging-in-Publication Data**
A CIP catalog record for this book has been applied for at the Library of Congress.

**Bibliographic information published by the Deutsche Nationalbibliothek**
The Deutsche Nationalbibliothek lists this publication in the Deutsche
Nationalbibliografie; detailed bibliographic data are available in the Internet
at http://dnb.dnb.de.

© 2012 Walter de Gruyter GmbH & Co. KG, Berlin/Boston
Printing: Hubert & Co. GmbH & Co. KG, Göttingen
∞ Printed on acid-free paper
Printed in Germany

www.degruyter.com

Irene Eber

# Wartime Shanghai and the Jewish Refugees from Central Europe

—

Survival, Co-Existence, and Identity
in a Multi-Ethnic City

**DE GRUYTER**

To
Professor Paul Mendes-Flohr, Friend and Colleague
With Much Gratitude

# Acknowledgments

Many years were spent in writing *Wartime Shanghai and the Jewish Refugees from Central Europe*. The project began with the encouragement of Harold Z. Schiffrin, then chairman of the Department of East Asian Studies at the Hebrew University of Jerusalem. Eventually Avraham Altman, also of the department, joined the research project and we collaborated fruitfully for many years. I am grateful for their encouragement to persevere with this project, despite the lack of materials in Israeli libraries at the time. At an early stage of research and writing, when I enjoyed the hospitality of Harvard's Fairbank Center, my friends there helped me define this history as part of Holocaust history. The many good talks we had are a cherished memory.

I thank friends and colleagues who have read long portions of the text, Eli Joffe (deceased), Maisie Meyer, Yitzhak Shichor, Barbara Johnson and Paul Mendes-Flohr. To Paul Mendes-Flohr my debt of gratitude is boundless. Without his help and unfailing support this book would continue to languish in a dark corner. To him I gratefully dedicate this volume. My friends' useful comments were extremely helpful and I am grateful for the time they invested in reading these pages. Yitzhak Shichor especially saved me from a number of serious mistakes.

Among scholars who have sent me often much needed materials, special thanks are due to Hartmut Walravens and Knut Walf. Over the years Wolfgang Kubin has patiently listened to my tirades about Shanghai. Nitza Wu, translator and dear friend, never failed to inquire about my progress and did not miss an opportunity to cheer me on. A number of archives opened their doors in my search for materials and to these I express my gratitude. They include YIVO, Yad Vashem, the American Joint Distribution Committee, and the Central Archive for the History of the Jewish People.

Above all, I am grateful to Joan Hill and Itamar Livni. Joan Hill's research in Harvard's Widener Library has brought to light materials I did not suspect existed. Her help at every stage of writing is deeply appreciated. I am also vastly indebted to Itamar Livni, who read all of the chapters with a critical eye. He pointed out a number of crucial problems that needed correcting and clarification. He also prepared Appendix One of street names and Appendix Four of English and German language memoirs. He has my utmost gratitude for his friendship and his tireless help.

Last but certainly not least, I am deeply grateful to Dr. Albrecht Doehnert and to Professor Wilhelm, editor of this series of Modern Jewish History, for her kind words of support. Dr. Doehnert's encouragement to persevere has made possible the publication of this book. For Dr. Julia Brauch's unstinting encouragement and support I am more grateful than I can ever express. Her warm letters and sage advice accompanied me every step of the way in the process of seeing the volume into print. The skillful and painstaking copy editing by Ms. Marcia Rothschild has led to untold improvements of the text. Old friends and new – I owe all of them a huge debt of gratitude.

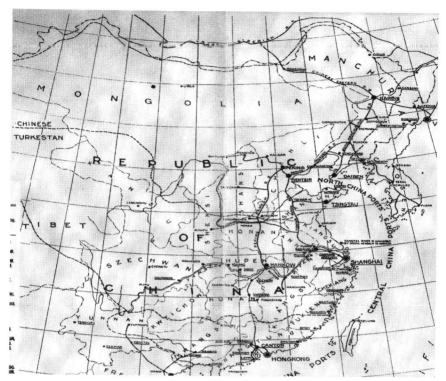

**Map 1:** "Republic of China". From Tess Johnston, Deke Erh, The Last Colonies, Western Architecture in China's Southern Treaty Ports, Hongkong: Old China Hand Press, 1997, frontis piece. By permission of Deke Erh.

# Table of Contents

# Abbreviations

| | |
|---|---|
| JDC | American Jewish Joint Distribution Committe |
| CP | China Press |
| DGB | Dagongbao |
| CAHJP | Central Archive for the History of the Jewish People |
| CAEJR | Committee for the Assistance of European Jewish Refugees |
| IM | Israel's Messenger |
| JT | Japan Times |
| JFM | Japan, Ministry of Foreign Affairs, 1868–1945, S Series Microfilm |
| JN | Juedisches Nachrichtenblatt |
| NAC | National Archives of Canada, Manuscript Division |
| NCH | North China Herald |
| PRO | Public Record Office |
| SEPM | Shanghai Evening Post and Mercury |
| SMP | Shanghai Municipal Police Investigation Files, 1899–1944, Records of the Central Intelligence Agency, Record Group 263 |
| SMC | Shanghai Municipal Council |
| XSB | Xin Shenbao |
| YVA | Yad Vashem Archives |
| YIVO | Yiddisher Wissenshaftlicher Institut |

# Introduction

Shanghai today is a city of nearly twenty million inhabitants. The largest urban center in China, it is a metropolis not only of skyscrapers, flourishing business establishments and shipping, but also of museums and many universities. At first sight, the traveler of six or seven decades ago, who arrived by ship at one of Shanghai's many wharves, would not find much today that is familiar. Yet, the old alleyways with their two- or three-story unique Shanghai-style houses can still be seen in various places; the city even then was a large metropolis of over four million people. Indeed, neither Paris nor London could rival Shanghai in size. In the 1930s the city was a metropolis, a cultural as well as an economic center, the like of which a European from Russia or Germany had not seen before. It should not come as a surprise that, in spite of China's political upheavals after the communist victory, Shanghai should be once more one of the great cosmopolitan cities of the world with a foreign population nearly as large as in the 1930s.

Among the earliest foreigners to arrive in Shanghai were the Sephardi, or Baghdadi Jews, who came with British traders in the 1840s. The Russo-Japanese War in 1904–1905 brought a new influx of Jews who opted to remain in China rather than return to Russia. Settling at first in Manchuria, they gradually moved south and to Shanghai. The second group, also from Russia, came after the Bolshevik revolution in 1917 and 1918. Finally, after Hitler came to power in 1933, a small trickle of German Jews began to arrive. This turned into a veritable flood by the end of 1938 and the first half of 1939 and included Austrian Jews as well. By the end of 1941 when the Pacific War broke out, there were nearly 30,000 Jews in Shanghai; approximately 1,000 Baghdadis; nearly 7,000 Russian Jews; and somewhat less than 20,000 Central Europeans.

Although we might be tempted to refer to them as a Jewish community, the fact is that Shanghai's Jews were a polyglot population consisting of several culturally and linguistically different communities. There were Sephardi and Ashkenazi Jews; religious and secular; old-timers and newcomers; German, English, Russian, Polish, and Yiddish speakers. Their dislike of one another increased during the war years, exacerbated by the Japanese occupation, which brought vital consumer shortages and general impoverishment.

My aim in these pages is to understand the Central European refugees within the Shanghai setting. To what extent were they aware that they arrived in the city that only a short time before had been subject to war and to partial Japanese occupation? It will be important, furthermore, to understand their uneasy co-existence with the established Baghdadi and Russian communities. Equally significant are the German foreign policy and economic considerations that brought them to these foreign shores in the first place. On this point many questions still remain. Major among these is the position of the *Yishuv*, or the Palestine Jewish community's attitude to saving lives of both young and old instead of selective emigration, that is of saving only the able-bodied young. Whereas the German Jewish leadership, on the whole, did not enthusiastically endorse the Shanghai escape route, the fact was that entire families, grandparents and small children came to Shanghai. Did the Yishuv never urge non-selective emigration and the saving of lives in Shanghai?

However, one must not be misled into thinking that Shanghai's ruling authority, the Shanghai Municipal Council, welcomed the thousands of Jewish refugees with open arms. Quite the contrary, they tried to stem the influx by all means available to them. This put considerable pressure on the wealthy Jewish businessmen who made their living within the British mercantile community. The dire destitution of their co-religionists, for this is how they were perceived by non-Jews, threatened to greatly impair their standing. Not only the British, but also the Japanese authorities believed that the established Jewish communities were responsible for impoverished Jews. Any discussion of relief efforts in Shanghai must, therefore, consider the dilemma, if not nervousness, of men whose expertise was in business and management and not social work.

The lengthy ocean voyage undertaken by the majority of the refugees on luxury ocean liners afforded them weeks of respite from the anxieties of departure. Leaving loved ones and friends behind, not to mention the comforting certainties of familiar surroundings, must have been a harrowing experience. But nothing prepared these middle-class businessmen and professionals and their families for the squalor, unsanitary and crowded facilities, disease and vermin-ridden living quarters of Shanghai. For these Central Europeans the weather was especially taxing: hot and humid in summer, cold and damp in winter. In addition, the primitive cooking facilities made life indescribably difficult. It must be remembered that by the time these men and women reached Shanghai, the horror and deprivation of wartime Europe with German deportations, ghettos, and work camps had not yet begun. At first, many may have regretted undertaking this journey into the unknown.

With this in mind, one cannot but admire the stamina and energy with which many of the refugees devoted themselves to creating a semblance of cultural life in their strange new world. In Hongkou, where most lived in rooming houses and converted schools, cafes, restaurants, and shops featuring familiar items appeared. There were newspapers in German and Yiddish as well as theatrical performances, variety shows, and eventually even radio broadcasts in German. The ingenuity and inventiveness these strangers brought to making a living was seemingly limitless. How to understand their exile condition is an intriguing question. Was it to recreate a minimal semblance to the places they had come from? Or was it simply to search for a livelihood with means that were familiar? More research is needed to better understand the meaning of exile for these individuals and groups.

How persons react to the unknown, what adjustments in thought and behavior they are able to make, is not easily reconstructed. In the case of Shanghai there are special difficulties. Not many diaries have survived the ravages of time and letters are practically non-existent after the outbreak of war in 1939. The literary record however, especially poetry written in reference to an event or situation, can be helpful in supplying an emotional dimension. Here the historian may find the emotional response of the moment needed to understand better how exile affected the individual, even if it is an outcry of pain or a statement of stubborn resistance.

The Japanese Proclamation of February 1943, confining those stateless refugees to a portion of Hongkou – the ghetto – was a major blow. It affected those Central Europeans who had arrived after 1937 when more than 15.000 people were crowded into an area of less than three square kilometers, which they could leave only after obtaining a pass from the Japanese. Conditions were harsh, made brutal by disease, a high mortality rate, and real hunger. The Russian Jewish community was spared the ordeal of the ghetto, and those Baghdadis who had British passports were interned in camps where conditions were even more intolerable. Yet most survived and saw the end of war in August 1945.

Although they no longer feared for their lives, not knowing what plans the Japanese invaders might have for them, the time of anxiety for the refugees was by no means over. News from Europe, when it finally came, told of the vast disaster that had decimated the Jewish communities wherever German armies had invaded. Therefore, only very few thought of returning to Russia, Germany, or Austria. Most wanted to settle elsewhere, far from the killing fields where once their homes had been. Even if some might have opted for remaining in Shanghai or elsewhere in China, the civil war that increasingly engulfed the country was hardly conducive to the settled existence they yearned for. Thus by the beginning of the 1950s Shanghai's Jewish Diaspora had come to an end.

The Shanghai story is part of Holocaust history that is often forgotten or ignored. It is neither sufficiently considered nor explored, but it is a story of survival, even of heroism, and of stubbornly defying fate. To be sure, the memoirs that have been appearing in recent years are important and useful, but they are not a substitute for historical research and for attempting to establish an historical record without mythologizing and without distortions. Stories of courage and survival are part of the history of those dark years and with the historian, Yosef Hayim Yerushalmi, I believe that it is better to remember too much than to forget. Like he, I fear forgetting[1]. This book is, therefore, not intended as a definitive history of the Shanghai refugee community. Rather it aims at establishing the context within which both arrival and survival in Shanghai were possible. It furthermore aims to show the kinds of strategies that could be pursued within the context of Shanghai to ensure cultural identities.

---

1 Yosef Hayim Yerushalmi, *Zakhor, Jewish History and Jewish Memory*, New York: Schocken Books, 1989, p. 117.

# Chapter 1:
# Shanghai

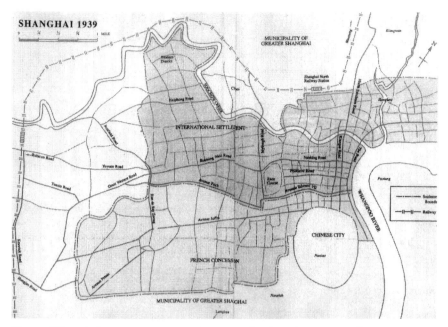

**Map 2:** "Shanghai 1939." From Tess Johnston and Deke Erh, *A Last Look, Western Architecture in Old Shanghai*, Hongkong: Old China Hand Press, 1993, frontispiece. By permission of Deke Erh.

The first Central European refugees in 1933 and even the later ones in 1938 were hardly aware of, nor especially curious about Shanghai's long and often important history. For most of them "their" Shanghai consisted of the International Settlement, the French Concession, both with their mixture of populations, and the busy (until the end of 1941) port installations. Few asked themselves when and how the foreign administrations began, why some of Shanghai's areas were under a Chinese administration, or who the Chinese were that they encountered daily, either as destitute beggars or prosperous businessmen, as rickshaw coolies, or as workers in the many factories. To most of them in their vague perception, this was China, and they did not realize that Shanghai was, in fact, like no other Chinese city. It was, as Frederic Wakeman remarks, "one of the most intricate and complicated urban societies in the world."[1]

---

1 Frederic Wakeman, Jr., "Policing Modern Shanghai," *The China Quarterly*, no. 115 (September 1988), p. 409.

Shanghai was a treaty port that grew by degrees from locally leased territory. Before becoming a treaty port, Shanghai had been a walled town, a third class county seat, under the jurisdiction of Nanjing, the provincial capital, and Songjiang, the prefectural capital. Its commercial prosperity had derived from the bourgeoning cotton trade of the Qing dynasty (1644–1912).[2] Far from being a mere fishing village, walled Shanghai boasted forty-nine bridges, six drawbridges at its six gates, and numerous bridges in the district. Canals crisscrossed the city.[3] Indeed, when Karl Friedrich August Gützlaff (1803–1851), the adventurer missionary, reached Shanghai in August 1831, he admired not only the prosperous town and its well-off inhabitants, but especially the thousands of junks lying at anchor for loading or unloading.[4]

## Beginnings of the Treaty Port

Much has been written about Shanghai and, except for some general observations, the history of the city's development into a thriving port city need not be repeated here.[5] First and foremost is the fact that the Opium Wars (1839–1842) between Great Britain and the Chinese empire resulted in the treaty system in favor of the British. The aim was, as John Fairbank succinctly states, to rid the China coast of the traditional tribute system, that is, to eliminate the Chinese restrictions on foreign trade. Thus, "The first treaties ... emerged as a charter of rights primarily for merchants." They included almost from the very beginning the principle of extraterritoriality, meaning consular jurisdiction over British nationals.[6] Shanghai was only one of five treaty ports opened to foreign trade between 1842 and 1844 (there would be others, among them

---

**2** Hanchao Lu, *Beyond the Neonlights, Everyday Shanghai in the Early Twentieth Century*, Berkeley-Los Angeles: University of California Press, 1999, p. 26.

**3** School of Oriental and African Studies, Library, the University of London, CCWM N6/10, Pams 6, "General Description of Shanghae [Shanghai] and Its Environs, Extracted from Native Authorities," Shanghae: Printed at the Mission Press, 1850, p. 161.

**4** H. Lang, *Shanghai Considered Socially, A Lecture*, Shanghai: American Presbyterian Mission Press, 1875, 2nd ed., pp. 22–24.

**5** Among works dealing with Shanghai I might mention William C. Johnstone, *The Shanghai Problem*, Stanford: Stanford University Press, 1937; Parks M. Coble, *The Shanghai Capitalists and the National Government, 1927–1937*, Cambridge: Cambridge University Press, 1980; Linda C. Johnson, *Shanghai: From Market Town to Treaty Port, 1074–1858*, Stanford: Stanford University Press, 1995.

**6** John K. Fairbank, "The Creation of the Treaty System," in D. Twitchett and J. K. Fairbank, eds., *The Cambridge History of China*, Cambridge: Cambridge University Press, 1978, Vol. 10, pp. 214, 217.

inland treaty ports like Changsha in Hunan and Harbin in Heilongjiang), but Shanghai's growth and increase in population was exceedingly rapid. In the mid-1840s, Shanghai had only around a dozen foreign firms and some one hundred foreigners. A decade later there were approximately seventy firms and more than three hundred foreign residents in Shanghai, in addition to eight consulates.[7] The increase in foreign commerce and population is also reflected in the number of foreign ships that made port in Shanghai. In 1844, forty-four foreign ships entered Shanghai. By 1849, this number grew to one hundred thirty-three and in 1863 to 3,400 foreign ships.[8]

While at first Protestant missionaries tended to locate their chapels in the walled city, foreigners generally preferred to live in the sparsely populated northern suburbs outside the city walls. This area later became the International Settlement (*gonggong zujie*) with its favorable location on the Huangpu River. Hongkou, initially an American settlement facing Suzhou Creek merged with the International Settlement in 1863; the French Concession, and the Chinese areas of Zhabei, Pudong, and Nandao, all developed outside the walled Chinese city.[9] This brings us to the second important fact about Shanghai, namely its growth as a Chinese city and as a city of immigrants. Hanchao Lu remarks that Guangdong and Fujian merchants came to Shanghai during the Qing period and that the encounter with outsiders was an everyday occurrence. Outside influence and the value of commerce caused Shanghai to be less conservative than most other Chinese cities and played a role in its becoming a modern city.[10] So were, no doubt, also the Ningbo and Zhejiang provincial merchants and workers, with their distinctive cultural traits and social habits, who flocked to Shanghai in search of a better livelihood.[11] Other Chinese outsiders came in the course of time, and the Taiping rebellion (1850–1864), which spread to the Shanghai countryside, brought numerous refugees to Shanghai in search of protection by the foreigners. By 1865, Lu writes, "The population of the British-American settlement had increased to 92,884. At the same time, almost 50,000 Chinese moved into the French Concession. By the end of the Taiping Rebellion well over 110,000 Chinese had moved into the foreign settlements."[12]

---

7 Ibid., p. 227.

8 Lu, *Beyond the Neonlights*, p. 27.

9 According to Betty Peh-T'i Wei, *Shanghai, Crucible of Modern China*, Hong Kong Oxford: Oxford University Press, 1987, p. 84, the wall around the Chinese city was demolished between 1912 and early 1914.

10 Lu, *Beyond the Neonlights*, pp. 36–37.

11 Yuen Sang Leong, "Regional Rivalry in Mid-Nineteenth Century Shanghai: Cantonese vs. Ningpo Men," *Ch'ing-shih Wen-t'i*, Vol. 4, no. 8 (December 1982), p. 31.

12 Lu, *Beyond the Neonlights*, p. 36.

The foreign settlements offered protection from the depredations of the Taipings as well as from other bands of marauders, including soldiers of the imperial army,[13] but the settlements also held the promise of order and the possibility of pursuing a livelihood with minimal interference. To be sure, the treaties signed with the Western powers were not to China's benefit, yet the Land Regulations of 1845, 1854, and 1869 for governing the International Settlement contributed greatly to tranquilizing the area.[14] In Shanghai then developed a "mutuality of Sino-foreign interests [which] became the secret of Shanghai's successful independence. By 1854 the ingredients of a new order were present and taking shape in new institutions," argues John Fairbank. He adds that, furthermore, "the result was less an exploitation of China in a colonial style ... than it was a privileged foreign participation in the attempted westernization of Chinese life."[15] Whether we would call this "westernization" is arguable; nonetheless, it is important to realize that the treaty system also served Chinese interests. This brings us to the third important fact about Shanghai, namely that it was not a colony in the sense of a colony established by the Western powers in Asia. The treaty port did not become the means of extracting profits from Shanghai or for providing jobs only for Western officials. Rather, it also served Chinese interests. In time Shanghai became a modern Chinese city, as will be shown below, and within the metropolis a Chinese middle class and a Chinese capitalist class developed. No doubt, Shanghai's favorable location was a factor. There were port facilities and a safe harbor on the Huangpu; it was at the crossroads of domestic and international trade and shipping; Shanghai could and did for a time serve as a shipping center for all of East Asia. In 1846 Shanghai was described as "not only a point of great trade in imports and exports, but also an emporium where there is an exchange of national and foreign commodities between the southern and northern parts of the empire."[16]

---

**13** Such was the occupation of the walled city by the Small Sword Society (*Xiaodao hui*) in 1853 and the arrival of the imperial army in 1855, ending with the so-called Battle of Muddy Flat. See "The Battle of Muddy Flat," pamphlet, Shanghai: Printed and Published at the North China Herald Office, 1904.

**14** The Land Regulations and their revisions were considered a "constitution" for Shanghai until 1943. Aside from its various regulations, deleted and amended in its several revisions, the Land Regulations also spelled out who was qualified to vote in municipal elections. The French Concession promulgated its own regulations, generally referred to as Règlement, in 1868.

**15** Fairbank, "Creation of the Chinese Treaty System," pp. 240, 263.

**16** "Notices of Shang-hai: Its Position and Extent; Its Houses, Public Buildings, Gardens, Population, Commerce, etc.," *Chinese Recorder*, Vol. 15, no. 9 (September 1846), p. 469.

Yet – and this is the fourth important fact about Shanghai – the city developed not as a unified urban complex, but as a fragmented collection of interlocking and interrelated areas with their own administrations. The Shanghai Municipal Council (SMC) was the governing body of the International Settlement, which in time was composed of British, American, Chinese, and Japanese officials. The SMC was, however, not a sovereign body and its responsibilities were merely administrative. The local authority for the SMC was the Consular Body which was responsible, in turn, to its respective governments. The French Concession was governed by the French Consul General, who had an advisory body, but whose authority was derived directly from the French government. The third governing body was the Chinese Municipal Administration, which governed the areas of Nandao, Pudong, Zhabei, Jiangwan, and Wusong. This administrative system was, in effect, set up only in July 1927 under Mayor Huang Fu (1880–1936), when the Nationalist government of the Republic of China assumed power in Nanjing.[17] Each area, furthermore, had its own police force: the Shanghai Municipal Police (SMP) in the International Settlement, the Frenchtown Concession Police, and the Nationalist Garrison Command Military Police in the Chinese areas. Despite having its own jurisdiction, each police force had to work in cooperation with the others on routine criminal cases. This was especially true in the 1930s when the power of Chinese gangs grew in the French Concession and the Chinese areas.[18] However, coordination in political cases was less common.[19]

But coming to Shanghai from other provinces – Zhejiang, Guangdong, or Jiangnan – did not automatically turn a person into a Shanghainese, a *Shanghairen*. Whether as villagers now turned workers, small merchants, clerks, or artisans, the new urbanites retained their native-place identities, in addition to assuming new ones. Native-place associations (*huiguan*) and the modernized forms that they developed, as well as the native-place networks, could lead to employment, but were also at the basis of later gangster organizations. Indeed, even Shanghai student organizations with their modernizing and patriotic aims were organized as native-place associations (*tongxianghui* ). While rejecting traditionalistic practices, "they did not reject the principle of organization accord-

**17** Robert W. Barnett, *Economic Shanghai: Hostage to Politics, 1937–1941*, New York: Institute for Pacific Relations, 1941, pp. 5–7. The Japanese were not part of the Treaty Powers, but had assumed increasing control over Hongkou (part of the International Settlement) after 1932, as will be discussed below.

**18** Wakeman, Jr., "Policing Modern Shanghai," p. 409.

**19** Bernard Wasserstein, *Secret War in Shanghai*, London: Profile Books, 1998, p. 62, observes that "the two neighboring police authorities ... frequently behaved more like enemies than allies." The SMP was often highly suspicious of the French police.

ing to native-place origin."[20] This combination of new forms and old patterns was characteristic of Shanghai in its growth into a modern metropolis. And it is this unique development, in addition to the city's treaty port status, as we shall see below, that provided the opportunity for the settlement of different Jewish communities.

**Fig. 1:** The Cathay Hotel built by Sir Victor Sassoon in 1929. Courtesy Tess Johnston and Deke Erh, *A Last Look: Western Architecture in Old Shanghai*, Hong Kong: Old China Hand Press, 1993, p. 96. By permission.

---

**20** Bryna Goodman, "New Culture, Old Habits, Native-Place Organization and the May Fourth Movement," in Frederic Wakeman, Jr., and Wen-hsin Yeh, eds., *Shanghai Sojourners*, Berkeley: Institute of East Asian Studies, University of California Press, 1992, p. 77; see also Frederic Wakeman, Jr. and Wen-hsin Yeh, "Introduction," pp. 1–14.

# Shanghai until the Sino-Japanese War of 1937

Hanchao Lu has argued persuasively in *Beyond the Neonlights* that Shanghai developed as a modern city under the Western impact, but beneath it or within this ever increasing modernity, a Chinese way of life for most of the population remained profoundly traditional. Or, to put it another way, the Chinese traditional way of life continued in Shanghai and changed in accordance with urban, not western demands.

Western style amenities were introduced into the concessions soon after the opening of the treaty port. Thus, Western-style streets began to appear as early as 1856, gas lighting in 1865, telephones in 1881, electricity in 1882, running water in 1884, automobiles in 1901, and tramways in 1908. The first tram ran on Nanking Road (today Nanjing Donglu), extending from the Bund (today Zongshan Dongyilu) to Tibet Road (today Xizanglu). The first horse race, the British sport for which Shanghai became famous together with its race course, was probably held in 1846.[21] However, the Chinese refugees who came at first, and most of the others, Chinese and Westerners alike, lived not on Shanghai's fashionable streets, but in the alleys and the alleyway houses (*lilong fangzi*), as did the majority of Central European refugees after they arrived in large numbers in 1938.

Alleyway houses began to be built after 1880, in accordance with a new, non-traditional, design. There were those that had modern amenities (flush toilets and gas) and those that did not. Both older and newer types were usually two- or three-story brick buildings (sometimes with gardens) and were built in rows along the alleys. Alleyways sprawled all over the city and its houses were inhabited by urbanites (*xiao shimin*), not the truly poor, who lived in shanty towns.[22] Coolies, of whom there were 100.000 or more by the 1930s in Shanghai, beggars, and people with unsteady incomes lived in the shanty towns, sometimes temporarily, when lack of income caused them to return to their native villages. Alleys formed neighborhoods for which stores carrying everyday needs were indispensable. There were the rice and coal stores, the sesame cake and hot water stores ('tiger stoves', *laohuzao*), which never closed.[23] In short, a person's life could be lived in the alley neighborhood

---

**21** Leo Ou-fan Lee, *Shanghai Modern, The Flowering of Urban Culture in China, 1930–1945,* Cambridge: Harvard University Press, 1999, pp. 7, 31.

**22** Lu, *Beyond the Neonlights*, p. 2.

**23** Hanchao Lu, "Away from Nanking Road: Small Stores and Neighborhood Life in Modern Shanghai," *The Journal of Asian Studies*, Vol. 54, no. 1 (February 1995), pp. 93–123.

without ever venturing into the westernized sections of Shanghai – the famous Bund with its foreign banks and Nanking Road and its department stores – or into those parts, like the western part of Bubbling Well Road (today Nanjing-xilu), where wealthy Westerners and Chinese lived.

> The city therefore was fragmented into numerous small communities wherein a life of moderate comfort could be obtained and maintained without venturing into the outside world – just a few blocks away. To many residents the few blocks around their homes were what the 'city' meant to them ... [24]

The wealthy, although a small percentage of the more than 3.5 million Shanghai population by the 1930s, were nonetheless an important elite segment of Chinese society. Hailing from diverse native place backgrounds, these urban elites were either self-employed or were active in modern banking, industry, communication and transportation. Shanghai was the seat of large trading firms – as many as twenty eight foreign banks had agents or head offices in Shanghai by 1919 – and major foreign cotton mills employed thousands of Chinese workers. As Marie Bergère writes, a major new urban class originated in Shanghai, an intelligentsia, a business, and a working class. Before July 1937, which marked the beginning of the so-called "undeclared war" (the Sino-Japanese War), fully half of China's modern factories were in Shanghai;[25] doctors of Chinese and western medicine, professionals of many kinds as well as investors, publishers and writers flocked to Shanghai. In the 1930s, the city was both a capitalist and a cultural center. Not to be forgotten are Shanghai's universities, of which the first Protestant missionary college (at the beginning more a high school than a college) was St. John's, founded in 1879.[26] Other institutions of higher education were founded after the turn of the century, until by 1934 Shanghai had twenty- five institutions of higher education (compared with Beijing's seventeen), private as well as public,[27] and 10,520 students.[28] Although Shanghai was not considered the intellectual center that

---

24 Lu, *Beyond the Neonlights*, p. 15.

25 Lu, *Beyond the Neonlights*, pp. 58–59.

26 Irene Eber, *The Jewish Bishop and the Chinese Bible, S.I.J. Schereschewsky (1831–1906)*, Leiden-Boston: Brill, 1999, pp. 133–137. For the important university that it became during the Republican period, see Ceng Xubai, "Sili Sheng Yuehan daxue (Private St. John's University)," in *Zhonghua minguo daxue shi* (Record of Chinese national universities), Taibei: Wenhua, 1952, Vol. 2, pp. 397–403.

27 Wen-hsin Yeh, *The Alienated Academy, Culture and Politics in Republican China, 1919–1937*, Cambridge-London: Council on East Asian Studies, Harvard University Press, 1990, p. 281.

28 Bergére, "The Other China," p. 20.

Beijing (then Beiping) was, neither was it solely devoted to business and money.

Not only did the universities and their active student bodies contribute to the lively atmosphere that characterized Shanghai in the 1930s, its large publishing industry and its extensive popular press, both foreign and Chinese, were an important element in the city's life. This is a large subject to which I cannot do justice in these pages except to point out several aspects worth noting. The Commercial Press (*Shangwu yinshu guan*, established in 1897), although best known, was only one of many hundreds of presses in Shanghai. Moreover, the city was famous for its bookstores, concentrated along Fuzhou and Henan Roads in the International Settlement. "No city in Republican China enjoyed more freedom of the press ..." writes Lu.[29] The first modern Chinese newspaper, *Shenbao* (Shanghai News) was published in Shanghai from 1872 on, as were such widely read journals as *Dongfang zazhi* (Eastern Miscellany) and *Xiaoshuo yuebao* (Short Story Magazine). In the first readers would find essays about other places and people and in the second, translations from Western literature.[30]

There were Chinese dailies, whether as morning or as evening papers, as well as the foreign press, especially English-language dailies like the first American newspaper, the *China Press* (founded in 1911) and the British, the *North China Daily News* (first appeared in 1850). Dailies provided not only all-important shipping news – the arrival and departure of ships necessary for business transactions – but also news about events in China and abroad. The Chinese and foreign press had a significant, if not revolutionary, impact on political and cultural life especially in the 1930s. So did even such short-lived weeklies as the *China Forum*, which aimed at creating a new awareness about China, its politics and culture, among Chinese and foreign readers.[31] Freedom of the press existed in the treaty port, yet the journalists and writers in these papers often endangered their lives, especially in the 1930s. They were not outside the political system, they had political roles which were often at odds

---

**29** Lu, *Beyond the Neonlights*, p. 60.

**30** A number of important writers and translators of the Republican period lived in Shanghai for longer or shorter periods of time. Among them Mao Dun (Shen Yanbing, 1896–1981), Yü Dafu (1896–1945), and Lu Xun (Zhou Shuren, 1891–1936). For a valuable discussion of the literary publishing scene, see Lee, *Shanghai Modern*, pp. 120–150.

**31** The *China Forum* was founded by Harold R. Isaacs (1910–1985) in January 1932. It ceased publication exactly two years later, January 1934, after thirty-nine issues, the last sixteen bilingually in Chinese and English. Harold R. Isaacs, *Re-Encounters in China, Notes of a Journey in a Time Capsule*, Armonk, N.Y.-London: M. E. Sharpe, Inc., 1985, pp. 13–26.

with those in power, or they ran afoul of censors.[32] Significant for our story is the fact that coming into this environment of publishing and printing, it is not surprising to find refugee entrepreneurs also engaged in publishing shortly after their arrival.

Aside from the print culture, Shanghai boasted a flourishing motion picture industry as well as a large number of movie theaters, located in various parts of the city. A foreigner could see the latest Hollywood productions as advertised in such papers as the *Shanghai Evening Post and Mercury*, or Chinese films produced in Shanghai's film studios and shown in theaters in Shanghai's Chinese sections. According to Leo Lee, "the movie theaters created both the material conditions and a cultural climate for movie going as a new habit of urban life, without which the development of the native Chinese cinema would have been impossible."[33] Although Shanghai's workers or coolies who eked out a meager living would not have been able to afford the price of a ticket, the foreign population and the growing middle class undoubtedly took advantage of the new art form. The production of Chinese films in Shanghai's studios and the fact that eight of some forty movie theaters were in the Chinese portions of the city, clearly indicates a substantial Chinese film audience.[34]

Yet, beneath the glittering facades of the banking houses on the Bund, fashionable department stores on Nanking Road, or the opulent mansions on Bubbling Well Road new forces were gradually taking shape that affected the foreign and the Chinese business communities. The prosperous foreign businessmen were now joined by a steadily increasing Russian refugee population which arrived in Shanghai after the Russian October Revolution of 1917. At the same time, the Japanese population also grew in size in the 1920s, settling for the most part in Hongkou. Unlike the destitute Russians, the Japanese were mainly small business and tradesmen, and both will be discussed below. Aside from the Japanese, although numerically far smaller, other Asians, like Indians, Koreans, and Taiwanese, also trickled into the treaty port in search of new opportunities. Europeans too were no longer only British, American, or

---

**32** Stephen R. McKinnon, "Toward a History of the Chinese Press in the Republican Period," *Modern China*, Vol. 23, no. 1 (January 1997), pp. 5–11.

**33** Lee, *Shanghai Modern*, p. 84.

**34** Ibid., p. 357, note 10. Chinese films included silent films and increasingly "talkies" in the 1930s. Some were based on traditional or current popular novels as, for example, *Lianai yu wuyi* (Love and Duty) by Luo Chen. The film dates from 1931, but the novel was a Chinese translation from French (?) and was written by a Jewish woman from Poland, named S. Rosenthal, then living in Beijing. I thank Professor Yomi Braester for making the film available to me.

French. They now came from many different countries and were often migrants from other parts of Asia or Africa. They engaged in what John Darwent calls "serial migration," an important element in European colonialism.[35] Many Europeans were no longer temporary residents, returning to their home countries after a tour of duty. On the contrary, they considered Shanghai home and planned to remain there. The treaty system and its denationalized order[36] suited many foreigners who referred to themselves as Shanghailanders, rather than as the nationals of the countries from which they had come.

Although the 1920s were years of unprecedented growth and prosperity as an international port and industrial center, Shanghai experienced its first challenge in March 1927, when Chiang Kai-shek's (Jiang Jieshi, 1887–1975) Nationalist troops entered Shanghai and when in the following month his troops broke the power of the leftist and communist labor unions, launching a ferocious campaign against Shanghai's workers.[37] In October 1928, Chiang established Nanjing as the capital of his Nationalist government. But the "Nanking decade," as it is known in Chinese history (actually only some nine years) affected the Chinese capitalists in Shanghai more than it did the Western businessmen. Nonetheless, these were turbulent years of ferment within China and of increasing friction and encroachments by the new East Asian power – Japan.

Yet, it would seem in retrospect that both the Chinese and Western businessmen failed to read and interpret the ominous signs. Only three years after the establishment of the Nanjing regime, which led to a large role for the Nationalist party bureaucrats in Shanghai affairs, the Japanese occupied Manchuria, China's three northeastern provinces of Liaoning, Jilin, and Heilongjiang. There was no resistance and on September 18, 1931, Japanese troops occupied the major cities of southern Manchuria within hours. Some weeks later, a puppet government was established in China's northeast.[38] On March 1, 1934, Henry Puyi (1906–1967), scion of the last dynasty, the Qing (1644–1912), was formally crowned emperor of the state of Manchukuo.

---

**35** John Darwent, "Afterword: A Colonial World," in Robert Bickers and Christian Henriot, eds., *New Frontiers, Imperialism's New Communities in East Asia, 1842–1953*, Manchester-New York: Manchester University Press, 2000, pp. 251–253.
**36** Bickers and Henriot, "Introduction," in *New Frontiers*, p. 5.
**37** The so-called Northern Expedition, of which Chiang's sweep into Shanghai was the aftermath, will not be discussed in these pages. For Chiang's break with the communists, see the documentary collection by C. Martin Wilbur and Julie Lien-ying How, eds., *Documents on Communism, Nationalism, and Soviet Advisers in China 1918–1927*, New York: Columbia University Press, 1956, and Jonathan D. Spence, *The Search for Modern China*, New York-London: W. W. Norton and Co., 1990, pp. 341–360.
**38** Parks M. Coble, *Facing Japan, Chinese Politics and Japanese Imperialism, 1931–1937*, Cambridge: Council of East Asian Studies, Harvard University Press, 1991, p. 11.

Manchuria was a long way from Shanghai and repercussions from the creation of the puppet state may not have been felt strongly in Shanghai. The
matter was entirely different, however, some months later when Japanese forces clashed with the Chinese Nineteenth Route Army in Shanghai's Zhabei
district at the end of January 1932.[39] During the fighting, which lasted until
March 3, 1932, large portions of Zhabei were laid waste; civilian casualties from
indiscriminate Japanese bombing were extremely high; the Commercial Press
together with its important library was destroyed; factories and universities
suffered partial or complete destruction.[40]

The final link in this chain of events was the outbreak of the Sino-Japanese
war in July 1937. First in the north, it was followed one month later by the
fierce battle for Shanghai. Parks Coble writes that "The bloody Battle of Shanghai would become the most intense conflict since Verdun in World War I."[41]
Although the International Settlement and the French Concession were largely
spared, Zhabei bore once again the brunt of the fighting, as did large areas of
Hongkou. The battle in and around Shanghai lasted well into the winter
months with a staggering cost of Chinese civilian and army casualties. To the
foreigners in Shanghai the bombardment of August 14, 1937, brought home the
fact that they were no longer as invulnerable as they might have thought.
According to an eyewitness, the Chinese attempt to bombard a Japanese war-
ship on that Saturday morning, went as follows:

> Suddenly there was a roar of aircraft as a half-dozen or so low-flying planes ap-
> peared ... dropping a number of bombs, which sent up a great fountain of mud and
> water but did not appear to hit any ships. All the Japanese warships opened up
> at the planes ... but although the air was full of bursts and flying pieces of metal ...
> miraculously nobody and nothing of importance on the river seemed to have been
> hit.

Civilians were not so lucky. In the afternoon of that same day, another forma-
tion of Chinese planes appeared and bombs fell on Nanking Road and a
crowded square on Avenue Edward VII outside the Great World Theatre. For

---

**39** Ibid., pp. 41–43. Coble describes the events that led up to what is usually referred
to as the Shanghai Incident. The Japanese, being vastly outnumbered by the Chinese
forces, had not expected the fierce resistance they encountered.

**40** Ibid., p. 48. See also He Pingsong, "Shangwu yin shuguan beihui jilue, (General
account of destruction by fire of the Commercial Press)," *Dongfang zazhi*, Vol. 29, no. 4
(October 16, 1932), pp. 3–9, who describes in detail the destruction of the library and
its works on January 28.

**41** Parks M. Coble, *Chinese Capitalists in Japan's New Order, The Occupied Lower
Yangzi, 1937–1945*, Berkeley–London: University of California Press, 2003, p. 11.

the next three months, Shanghai ports were closed to international traffic.[42] During this time, aside from the countless people made homeless during the bombardment, Chinese refugees from the surrounding countryside began arriving in overwhelming numbers in the International Settlement and, less than a year later, Central European refugees arrived by sea in ever increasing numbers. Before discussing the new difficulties created for the foreign community by the war and the refugees, I want to turn to some of the ethnic communities within Shanghai's foreign enclave.

## Baghdadi (Sephardi) and Russian (Ashkenazi) Jews

At its height more than fifty different nationalities were represented in Shanghai's foreign community, and among the earliest newcomers, British and American, were the Sephardi or Baghdadi Jews, though not all hailed from Iraq. They came mostly via Bombay where they had prosperous business firms, and their aim was to establish branches in the newly opened treaty port.[43] Elias David Sassoon (1820–1880) arrived in Shanghai as early as 1844 and eventually built up a commercial empire along the China coast. Other members of the Sassoon family followed, contributing to the various Sassoon enterprises and making this one of the wealthiest families in Shanghai.[44] By 1862 a small Jewish community had already come into being, necessitating the establishment of a cemetery. The cemetery was in use until 1919 when the need for a new one arose.[45] An early colorful personality on the Shanghai scene was Silas

---

**42** W.J. Moore, *Shanghai Century or "Tungsha Flats to Soochow Cree,"* Ilfracombe, Devon: Arthur H. Stockwell, Ltd., n.d., pp. 35–37. For an eyewitness account of the events of August 14, see also John B. Powell, *My Twenty-Five Years in China*, New York; The Macmillan Co., 1945, pp. 298–303.

**43** "List of Commercial Houses, Agents, etc.," *Chinese Repository*, Vol. 15, no. 1 (January 1846), p. 7. Eliahoo [Elias] D. Sassoon established a firm in Canton with Moses Dahood and A. d'Miranda, the latter probably as agents.

**44** For a detailed history of this important family, see Maisie Meyer, *From the Rivers of Babylon to the Whangpoo*, Lanham-New York: University Press of America, Inc., 2003, pp. 11–16; also Mendel Brown, "The Modern Jews of China – Shanghai – II," *Israel's Messenger*, Vol. 33, no. 9, December 4, 1936, p. 10.

**45** Brown, "The Modern Jews of China." Brown still saw this cemetery on Mohawk Road (today Huangpin Beilu) opposite the race course and its tombstones. He noted that the first burial took place in 1863 and was that of Joseph Rahamim (son of Isaac Reuben) who died at the age of 25. This cemetery and three others in Shanghai have since disappeared together with most of the tombstones after being moved to Qingpu county in the late 1950s. Tess Johnston was the first to alert readers to Jewish gravestones scattered in fields and villages. Tess Johnston and Deke Erh, *God and Country, Western*

Aaron Hardoon (1851?–1931), whose life is one of rags to riches. Arriving in Shanghai in 1874, he was employed by David Sassoon and Co. as a rent collector and watchman. Less than thirty years later Hardoon was on his way to becoming one of Shanghai's major landowners, and by 1916, according to Chiara Betta's account, he owned most of the properties along Nanking Road. At the time of his death he may have been the richest foreigner in East Asia.[46] Silas Hardoon was, however, not only known for his fabulous wealth. He and his wife, Luo Jialing (also known as Liza, 1864–1941)[47] supported and contributed to a variety of Chinese causes and institutions.[48] Although the Hardoons, no doubt, were more interested in China and the Chinese than most Jewish families, others too contributed to Chinese life. Among them the Kadoorie family is noteworthy. Sir Ellis Kadoorie (1854–1922) established six schools in Hong Kong, Shanghai, and Canton (Guangzhou), three of which were in Shanghai. The aim was to provide free education for poor Chinese that included Western (arithmetic, map drawing, etc.) as well as Chinese subjects.[49] Despite boasting more wealthy families than any other Jewish community in Shanghai – indeed, quite out of proportion, for the Baghdadis never numbered more than approximately 1,000 persons – there were also the less well-off and poor Baghdadi Jews. These tended to find employment in the firms of the affluent families. Class differences existed in the Baghdadi community that were also manifested in the extent of westernization, with the upper classes taking more readily to western ways in distinction to the poorer, lower ones.[50]

---

*Religious Architecture in Old China*, Hong Kong: Old China Hand Press, 1996, pp. 123–[125]. For more about the cemeteries and current efforts to recover gravestones, see below, ch. 4.

**46** Chiara Betta, "Myth and Memory. Chinese Portrayals of Silas Aaron Hardoon, Luo Jialing and the Aili Garden Between 1924 and 1925," in Roman Malek, ed., *From Kaifeng ... to Shanghai, Jews in China*, Sankt Augustin: Monumenta Serica Institute, 2000, p. 377. For a largely anecdotal account, see also Xu Zhucheng, *Hatong waizhuan* (Hardoon's unofficial biography), Hong Kong: Wuxing jishu baoshe, 1982.

**47** For the biography of Liza Hardoon, see Ephraim Selmanson, "Liza Hardoon, die Geschichte der reichsten Erbin Asiens," *Shanghai Morgenpost*, November 16, 1941, p. 7.

**48** Among these especially is the Patriotic School (Aiguo xueshe) in Shanghai, with which major personalities of the Republican period were associated. See Mary Backus Rankin, *Early Chinese Revolutionaries, Radical Intellectuals in Shanghai and Chekiang, 1902–1911*, Cambridge: Harvard University Press, 1971, pp. 61–69.

**49** Arnold Wright, ed., *Twentieth Century Impressions of Hongkong, Shanghai, and Other Treaty Ports of China: Their History, People, Commerce, Industries and Resources*, London: Lloyd's Greater Britain Publishing Co., Ltd., 1908, pp. 127–128.

**50** Chiara Betta, "From Orientals to Imagined Britons: Baghdadi Jews in Shanghai," *Modern Asian Studies*, Vol. 37, no. 4 (2003), p. 1019.

**Fig. 2:** Marble Hall, home of the Kadoorie family, completed in 1924, now the "Children's Palace." Tess Johnston and Deke Erh, A Last Look: Western Architecture in Old Shanghai, Hong Kong: Old China Hand Press, 1993, p. 17. By permission.

A study of the Shanghai tycoons and their far-flung business connections is still lacking, nor do we know, except for fragments, what their connections were to the Shanghai Chinese capitalists in the 1920s. Yet, clearly their adaptability to changing circumstances is admirable. The opium trade had initially attracted Baghdadi Jewish entrepreneurs to Shanghai and other treaty ports. The Sassoons even owned their own opium clippers,[51] but they soon branched out into other commodities and business ventures.

Baghdadi Jews settled for the most part in the International Settlement where they also had their businesses. Although their native tongue was Judaeo-Arabic, they rapidly acquired English as their major language, and their main organ, *Israel's Messenger,* published between 1904 and 1941, was printed in English.[52] Synagogue life developed but slowly and the magnificent structure

**51** Wright, *Twentieth Century Impressions*, p. 224, and Meyer, *From the Rivers of Babylon*, pp. 57–68.

**52** The journal was actually considered the official organ of the Shanghai Zionist Association and carried news of the several Jewish communities in China.
It suspended publication from 1910 to 1918. First published as a fortnightly, it became a monthly in 1921. See Meyer, *From the Rivers of Babylon*, p. 186.

of Ohel Rachel on Seymour Road (still standing on today's Sha'anxi Beilu Road) was consecrated only in 1921. At the same time the Baghdadi community also appointed its first rabbi, W. Hirsch. In 1927, Silas A. Hardoon donated the Beth Aharon synagogue in Hongkou on Museum Road (now demolished). Although the earlier prayer halls, Beth El on Peking Road (today Beijing Lu) and Shearith Israel on Seward Road (today Changzhi Donglu) had been important in providing meeting places for religious life, the new synagogues made possible a new solidarity, as Maisie Meyer remarks.[53] Jewish traditions and observances were maintained by the Baghdadis in Shanghai, but tended to weaken as time went on. This does not mean that the Baghdadis assimilated, or intermarried, becoming a part of the British environment. Rather, certain practices like the Sabbath closure of businesses were no longer strictly observed by all Baghdadis, yet they did not forget their Jewish antecedents nor, indeed, their identity as Sephardim. On the other hand, similar to some major businessmen in the treaty port, a number of Baghdadis had close connections to British governing circles and the Shanghai Municipal Council. After the outbreak of the Sino-Japanese war in July 1937 and the increasingly dominant role assumed by Japan in Shanghai affairs, these relationships exhibited new complexities. The political roles of the Baghdadis cannot, however, be explored in these pages.

The complex relations are especially evident in their support of charitable causes. Until the arrival of large numbers of refugees toward the end of 1938, when the burden became too heavy for the wealthy Sephardi families and when aid from abroad was required, the Sassoon, Kadoorie, Abraham, and Joseph families were the chief support of several Jewish charitable organizations, such as the Shanghai Hebrew Relief Society and the Free Loan Society. But by 1938 these barely scraped by on locally raised donations, as the minutes of the "Investigating Committee for International Sufferers" show.[54]

Later that year, in October 1938, therefore a new committee under Sephardi leadership was established during a meeting in the office of Sir Elly Kadoorie (Reuben Ezekiel) and Sons. "The Committee for the Assistance of European Jewish Refugees in Shanghai" (CAEJR) had a new organizational structure, first with Michel Speelman (1877–?) and later with Ellis Hayim (1894–1977) as chairman.[55] The Public Relations Committee of the new organization was of major

---

**53** Meyer, *From the Rivers of Babylon*, pp. 95–100.

**54** JDC, file 456, "Investigating Committee for International Sufferers," minutes of the 5th meeting, January 5, 1938.

**55** Speelman was a Dutch Jew, undoubtedly of Sephardi parentage. He was a prominent banker and was active in Nationalist government circles. There is a brief biography in George F.M. Nellist, *Men of Shanghai and North China. A Standard Biographical Work,*

importance and included R. D. (Reuben David) Abraham. It was this committee which was to be in contact with the SMC, the French Municipal Council, the Japanese authorities, as well as with the Joint Distribution Committee (JDC) in New York and Paris, the London Council for German Jewry, and other Jewish organizations.[56] The letter does not state, but it can be easily assumed, that the spokesmen for the refugees had to be English speakers (Speelman also spoke French). Furthermore, they had to be prominent members of the business community who were well known in official circles. Neither the refugees – though many may have held prominent positions in Germany and Austria – nor members of the Russian (Ashkenazi) community qualified on both counts. The letter also indicates that the attempt would be made to coordinate relief efforts and with the Relief Society for German Jews (Hilfsfond für deutsche Juden),[57] and the "International Committee" (both to be discussed below) as well as with the newly formed CAEJR. The amalgamated efforts never actually materialized, and I will have occasion to return to this subject later.

Let us now turn to the Russian Jewish community which in time became larger than that of the Baghdadis, numbering between 6,000–8,000 persons by the 1930s. The Russians, moreover, came to Shanghai well after the Sephardim were established there. As Ashkenazim and Russians, they were a different community both culturally and linguistically. A systematic history of this important community is lacking and perhaps impossible to write, due to the scarcity of materials. It will be discussed here in large outlines only. The earliest arrivals may have come to Shanghai after the Russo-Japanese war (1904–1905), but larger numbers, including Polish Jews, arrived only after the Russian October Revolution of 1917. However, by 1907 there were apparently enough Ashkenazim in Shanghai to form the congregation, Ohel Moishe, on the prem-

Shanghai: Oriental Press, 1933, pp. 496–501. For Ellis Hayim's biography, see pp. 209–210.

**56** JDC, file 458, Speelman, Hayim, Mendel Brown to M. Troper, JDC, Paris, December 14, 1939, 8 pp. This long letter does not state who was heading the other six committees established at the time.

**57** The Relief Society was established as early as December 1934 with Dr. Bernhard Rosenberg, Fritz Kauffmann, E. Lazarus, Dr. Karl Mosse and M. Neumann, to help refugees arriving in Shanghai. This information according to Ernst Pollak, "Menschen die uns halfen," *Shanghai Jewish Chronicle,* Special Number, March 1940 p. 6. By 1938, the "Relief Society" was under the direction of Dr. Kurt Marx. According to CAHJP, 76.1, Rundschreiben no. 365, January 1939, its name was changed to Relief Society for German and Austrian Jews. See also YVA, 078/58, Heinz Ganther, Günther Lenhardt, eds., *Drei Jahre Immigration in Shanghai*, Shanghai: Modern Times Publishing House, 1942, p. 14.

ises of the Sephardi Shearit Israel synagogue. In 1927, the Russian congregation moved to its own premises on Ward Road (now Changyang Lu) in the Hongkou section of the International Settlement.[58] The real growth of the community took place in the 1920s with the appointment of Rabbi Meir Ashkenazi, who came to Shanghai in 1926 from Vladivostok; the organization of a burial society in 1922; the acquisition of their own cemetery on Baikal Road (now Weiming Lu); and the establishment of secular clubs.[59] The Shanghai Jewish Communal Association (Ashkenazi) held its first general meeting in June 1931. In its constitution and by-laws, printed in English, Russian, and Chinese, the association declared that it was "the official representative of the Ashkenaz Jewish population in dealing with Municipal or Government institutions ..." Its activities were to include educational, charitable, and religious affairs.[60] At about the same time, in 1931 or 1932, the Jewish Club was founded that sponsored sports activities as well as theatrical performances. The younger generation participated in Zionist organizations, "Kadimah" and "Betar," the latter especially emphasized physical training and sports. Their model was Vladimir (Ze'ev) Jabotinsky (1880–1940).[61]

The Russian Jews lived for the most part in the French Concession where they engaged in import-export and were reasonably well-to-do businessmen and store owners. But wealthy individuals comparable to those in the Sephardi community did not exist among Russian Jews. Moreover, the Ashkenazi population that lived in Hongkou and Yangzipu – craftsmen, small store keepers, or boardinghouse owners – suffered great losses both in 1932, when Japanese bombs fell on Hongkou and Zhabei, and during the Sino-Japanese hostilities in 1937. The community was hard pressed during those years to find means of supporting newly destitute families in their midst,[62] who fled to the more se-

---

**58** David Kranzler, *Japanese, Nazis and Jews, the Refugee Community of Shanghai, 1938–1945*, New York: Yeshiva University Press, 1976, pp. 60–61.
**59** Ibid.
**60** "Constitution and Bye-Laws of the Shanghai Jewish Communal Association (Ashkenazi," Pamphlet, Shanghai: Nashe Zarya, 1931. Representatives of the association were: Dr. I. Rosenzweig, M. Vipkovsky, R. Poliak, H. Kammerling, E. Hirsch.
**61** Marcia R. Ristaino, *Port of Last Resort, The Diaspora Communities of Shanghai*, Stanford: Stanford University Press, 2001, p. 67 and Rena Krasno, "History of Russian Jews in Shanghai," in Malek, ed., *Jews in China*, p. 335.
**62** JDC, file 456, Rabbi M. Ashkenazi to Mr. Alkow, August 23, 1937. Ashkenazi was asking the JDC for support in this difficult situation. Also, JDC, file 456, excerpts from letter by Joe Hollzer, Shanghai, to Judge H. A. Hollzer, Los Angeles, December 25, 1937, mentions Russian Jewish emigrants whose poverty has reduced them "almost to savagery."

cure areas in the French Concession. Thus the Shanghai Jewish Communal Association could not be expected to render much help when the Central European refugees arrived in 1938.

The community took special pride in the large participation of Russians in the Shanghai Volunteer Corps (SVC). First formed in 1853, it eventually included volunteers and units from twenty seven countries, including a Chinese and Jewish company, and consisted of 2.300 men.[63] The Jewish company was formed in 1932 and 1933 and consisted of 120 former scouts and "Betar" members. N. S. Jacobs (died 1977) became its commander, R. B. Bitker (a decorated veteran of the Russian army) and M. Talan were the company's sergeants. The chaplain was Mendel Brown, the rabbi of the Sephardi congregation. On their uniform collars the Shanghai Volunteers wore a *Magen David* to identify them as a Jewish company. The SVC ceased to exist after the outbreak of the Pacific War and was officially dissolved in February 1942.[64]

The Russian community participated little, if at all, in the initial relief efforts on behalf of the Central European refugees set in motion in 1938. Nor did they found an organization of their own to help the new arrivals. As mentioned earlier, the lead to do so was taken by the Sephardi community.[65] The two major organizations that were active from the fall of 1938 in Shanghai were the Committee for the Assistance of Central European Jews in Shanghai and the International Committee for Granting Relief to European Refugees, also known as the International Committee (IC), or the Komor Committee. This committee was established in August 1938 by Paul Komor (1886–?), a Hungarian gentile, who had set up his own trading company in 1937. Much of the work of the IC consisted of registering the new arrivals and keeping individual records as well as cooperating with the SMP and the German Consulate Gen-

---

**63** J. V. Davidson-Houston, *Yellow Creek, the Story of Shanghai*, London: Putnam, 1962, p. 141.

**64** Benis M. Frank, "The Jewish Company of the Shanghai Volunteer Corps Compared with Other Jewish Diaspora Fighting Units," 1992, pp. 20–22. Unpublished paper, by permission of author. A. G. [probably Anna Ginsbourg], "Evrey-grajhdane i patrioty Shanghaia (Citizens and patriots of Shanghai)," *Nasha Zhizn*, June 6, 1941; Ristaino, *Port of Last Resort*, pp. 62–66, and I. I. Kounin, comp., *Eighty Five Years of the Shanghai Volunteer Corps*, Shanghai: The Cosmopolitan Press, 1938, pp. 215–216. I thank Benis Frank for making the book available to me.

**65** Kranzler, *Japanese, Nazis and Jews*, p. 94 states that the Sephardi and Russian Jews cooperated in establishing the "Committee for the Assistance of European Jewish Refugees in Shanghai," but there is no evidence in the letter, cited above, n. 57, that Russian Jews participated in the meeting.

eral whenever necessary.[66] The Relief Society (previously Hilfsfond), headed by Dr. Kurt Marx, continued its work under the auspices of the CAEJR until its dissolution in early 1939.[67]

In addition to the CAEJR and the IC, the HICEM (HIAS) branch in Shanghai, headed by Meir Birman (1891–1955), established its operation in fall 1939. HICEM did not duplicate the work of the other two agencies; its sole function – and a formidable task it was – was to bring as many endangered Jews as possible to the safe haven of Shanghai and move those who had visas – or were able to obtain them – to other destinations. Although Sir Victor Sassoon generously contributed to refugee relief work, the activities of the three relief associations were funded 90%–100% by the JDC from September 1939 on.[68] After the outbreak of the Pacific War in December 1941 and the conquest of all of Shanghai by the Japanese, the work of these organizations ended. The Japanese-sponsored Jewish aid organization, the Shanghai Ashkenazi Collaborating Relief Association (SACRA), was established in 1943 with Russian Jewish leadership. Its function will be discussed in a later chapter.

## Shanghai's Russian and Japanese Communities

By far the largest non-Jewish communities in Shanghai of the 1930s were those of the Russians and the Japanese. So pervasively noticeable were Russian refu-

---

**66** Ristaino, *Port of Last Resort*, pp. 104–105. See also JDC, file 457, "Report on Jewish Refugee Problems in Shanghai," by M. Speelman, Chairman of the Committee for the Assistance of European Jewish Refugees in Shanghai, June 21, 1939, Annex I. According to Speelman's report, written in Paris, the IC was established in July 1938.

**67** The motives of Kurt Marx for involving himself in relief work were, however, suspect to HICEM (the HIAS bureau, Far Eastern Central Information Bureau for Emigrants, known as DALJEWCIB, its telegraphic acronym) even before HICEM relocated in 1939 from Harbin to Shanghai. See copy of B.S. Barbash's letter to HICEM, Paris, JDC, file 456, August 16, 1938. Barbash's letter is dated July 19, 1938. As the Shanghai representative of HICEM, he accused Marx of fund raising to gain an income, thus bringing "chaos into our [HICEM's] work." In another letter, YIVO, HIAS-HICEM, MKM 15,57, File XV, A-17, Harbin to HICEM, Paris, August 16, 1938, Barbash wrote on July 29 that "Dr. Marx has scented rich soil for speculation," being offered by Kadoorie 300 dollars/month to organize immigration. See also JDC, file 456, no signature, letter from "Hilfsfond" to HIAS, Paris, October 1938, asking urgently for funds. According to Speelman, JDC, file 457, report dated June 21, 1939, Annex I, cited in note 67, the "Hilfsfond" had already been dissolved.

**68** JDC, 33–44, file 456, pages from a long report on organizations and disbursement, p. 172 and JDC, file 456, "Statement of Subsidies made by the J. D. C. April 24 Through March 1938." The JDC subsidized the Shanghai Jewish School once, in July 1926, and

gee peddlers on the streets that they even appeared in Chinese novels written long after the Russians had gone elsewhere.[69] The initial Russian population did not consist of refugees, but rather mostly traders and military procurement officials who arrived during WWI. By 1917, this population numbered around 700–800 persons,[70] and soon increased after several waves of White Russian refugees arrived following the civil war in Russia's far east between 1918 and 1923. The complicated history of the Bolsheviks, the Japanese, and the White forces during these years cannot be recounted here. Suffice it to say that the White Russian armies, including Cossacks, and sailors, eventually fled south-ward via Vladivostok. As described by Marcia Ristaino, "Refugees had been arriving in Shanghai from the north by train, on foot, by mule, or by ship since the Russian revolution had begun, most of them destitute."[71] More than 1,000 arrived each year and by 1929 there were more than 13,000 Russian refugees in the city. Thousands more came from Harbin after the establishment of Man-chukuo on March 1, 1932,[72] and by 1939 their number had grown to 25,000.

Although we speak here of a community, it must be remembered that the balance among the Russians was forever shifting between old-timers and new-comers. Those who had settled in Shanghai and even found a means of liveli-hood more often than not looked askance at the new arrivals. "White Russian refugees did not find in Shanghai a large Russian community able or willing to ease their accommodation into the city. Rather, in many cases, they were shunned by the established locals as 'poor relatives'."[73] The Russians settled at first in the cheaper housing of Hongkou and Zhabei. However, after the Japanese bombed these areas causing large scale destruction, most moved to

the Refugee Relief Committee in March 1938. In other years subsidies went to Harbin's Talmud Torah.

**69** For example, Cheng Naishan, tr. Britten Dean, *The Banker*, San Francisco: China Books and Periodicals, Inc., 1992, pp. 128–129.

**70** Ristaino, *Port of Last Resort*, p. 33. There was, of course also the Russian consular personnel since the Russian consulate, established in 1860, was not closed until 1920. Tsarist Russia also had banking interests in Shanghai. The Russo-Chinese Bank was established in December 1895, which may have further increased the Russian presence. See Rosemary Quested, *The Russo-Chinese Bank: A Multi-National Financial Base of Tsarism in China*, Birmingham: Birmingham Slavonic Monographs, 1977, p. 1.

**71** Ristaino, *Port of Last Resort*, p. 35.

**72** The Russian Diaspora generally in the 20th century is estimated between one and two million persons. The many cities in which the people settled for longer or shorter periods of time, including Harbin, are detailed in Karl Schlögel, ed., *Der grosse Exodus, die russische Emigration und ihre Zentren 1917 bis 1941*, Munich: C. H. Beck, 1994.

**73** Ristaino, "The Russian Diaspora Community in Shanghai," in Bickers and Henriot, *New Frontiers*, p, 195.

the French Concession, as did the Jewish Russians as well. Thus eventually the French Concession became the cultural as well as the political center of Russian life. Large class differences created divisions among the refugees. The numerous military men were joined by workers, clerks, managers, and the like from the Chinese Eastern Railway who found themselves unemployed when the railway was sold to the Japanese in 1935. There were erstwhile aristocrats, numerous musicians, writers, similar to the Paris Russian diaspora, as well as shopkeepers of many kinds. Most of them, as would be also the case for the Central European refugees at the end of the thirties, found it very difficult to secure employment. Some were able to continue in their military professions. The Russian regiment of the SVC absorbed one hundred fifty men with military background.[74] Others served as bodyguards, guards, or watchmen. The plight of women was especially severe. Respectable women did not work outside the home, and Russian refugee women, having no choice, were often forced to earn a living as waitresses, taxi dancers, entertainers, or prostitutes.[75]

Not only class differences, but ideological differences as well led to divisions within the community. The majority were, of course, uncompromisingly hostile to the Soviet regime, indulging in the nostalgia of a Russia that had ceased to exist and hoping for its return. Others, however, were susceptible to Soviet propaganda that urged the stateless Russians to obtain Soviet citizenship and return to the homeland. This division, though the pro-Soviet stand did not find many adherents, was exacerbated by the Japanese who sought to capitalize on the Russians' anti-Soviet sentiments.[76]

Just how heterogeneous the community actually was is obvious from the numerous organizations created to help the refugees and the largely futile attempts to unify them under one umbrella organization. The Russian Emigrants Committee, formed in July 1926, under the leadership of Victor Fedorovich Grosse (a former Russian Consul General in Shanghai) faced a daunting task.[77] When Grosse passed away in 1931, Charles E. Metzler, his vice consul, became head of the Emigrants Committee, but was murdered in 1940, having run afoul of his Japanese patrons. The third leader, Nikolai A. Ivanov, lasted nine months. He too was assassinated in September 1941.[78] Neither the Russian

---

**74** Kounin, *Eighty-Five Years*, pp. 242–248, provides considerable background, including photographs, about the Shanghai Russian regiment "C" Battalion.
**75** Ristaino, *Port of Last Resort*, pp. 88–94.
**76** Wasserstein, *Secret War in Shanghai*, p.286.
**77** Ristaino, *Port of Last Resort*, p. 50. Marcia Ristaino has contributed more than anyone else to our understanding of the problems of the extremely diverse Russian refugee community.
**78** Wasserstein, *Secret War in Shanghai*, p. 86; Ristaino, *Port of Last Resort*, pp. 165–173.

Emigrants Committee nor its leaders succeeded in unifying the refugee community, and they were unable to prevent the emergence of rival organizations, such as the Council of United Russian Public Organizations.

Despite the difficult conditions of refugee life, the infighting and rivalries, there was no lack of Russian culture. Similar to the Russian Jews, the White Russians established clubs and gave theatrical performances, but unlike Russian Jews they created a major publishing center of Russian literature in Shanghai. Books, literary journals, newspapers, patriotic and religious writings flourished. There were six dailies and a Russian bookstore on Avenue Joffre (today Huaihai Lu) as well as a lending library. There were several schools, several Russian Orthodox churches, including a Russian orthodox cathedral on Rue Paul Henri (today Xingle Lu).[79] Yet, no matter how prominent some may have been in Tsarist Russia, or how important a role they had in Shanghai's Russian community, these Russians were socially on the periphery of the foreign community. They never became part of the influential and mostly British business community, and no Russian had a significant role in the political structure of the treaty port.

The Japanese community was very different. First, it was not a refugee community and secondly, in the course of time the Japanese became the city's largest community of foreigners, despite being relative latecomers to the Shanghai scene. Unlike the British, Americans, and French, the Japanese never established a concession, but in Hongkou where the majority settled, they eventually reaped all the benefits a concession had to offer.

In 1870, three years after the Meiji Restoration, a Japanese mission was sent to China to conclude a treaty with privileges similar to those of the Western powers. Most significantly, it was to include a most-favored-nation clause and the right to trade and travel in the interior.[80] Concluded in 1871, the treaty, however, was disappointing because the privileges stipulating trade, purchase of land, and establishment of consulates, were limited to the ports already opened on the China coast.[81] It was only after China's defeat in the Sino-Japanese War of 1895 and the subsequent Treaty of Shimonoseki that Japan obtained the treaty rights she sought. That treaty and the 1896 Treaty of Commerce and Navigation gave Japan equality with the other treaty powers,

---

**79** Ristaino, *Port of Last Resort,* pp. 82–85. John Powell, *My Twenty-Five Years,* p. 60, mentions more than a dozen Russian orthodox churches, some richly decorated.
**80** Peter Duus, Introduction, "Japan's Informal Empire in China: An Overview," in Peter Duus, Ramon H. Myers, Mark R. Peattie, eds., *The Japanese Informal Empire in China, 1895–1937,* Princeton: Princeton University Press, 1989, p. xx.
**81** Ibid.

especially the right to establish a concession, which Japan did not exercise. Why they chose not to press a claim for an exclusive concession is not entirely clear, according to Mark Peattie. One plausible reason, he thinks, might be that to obtain a less conveniently located and a less developed area than Hongkou would not be to the advantage of Japanese interests.[82] Hongkou, though part of the International Settlement, may have seemed a logical choice for Japanese settlement, considering its proximity as well accessibility to the Huangpu river wharves. On the other hand, there is probably no single factor that can explain the Japanese preference of Hongkou over other areas. But then, the Japanese authorities may have been confronted with a *fait accompli*. The first Japanese traders had come to Shanghai (and presumably settled in Hongkou) in 1868; in 1870 there were three Japanese, and by 1894, there were one thousand.[83] Despite repatriations in times of conflict and fighting between Japanese and Chinese, the Japanese population soared to 15,551 in 1920, 24,207 in 1930, and 54,308 in 1939,[84] as business opportunities expanded. The Central European refugees settling in Hongkou after 1938 thus were unwittingly in close proximity to the Japanese population.

The Japanese were essentially a lower middle class community that did not reflect Japanese society at home. As Joshua Fogel remarks, "there were no rural Japanese farmers or a significant Japanese working class in Shanghai."[85] Unlike prosperous Westerners, they did not indulge in a "grand colonial life style" and they lacked the glitter of many Western communities in Shanghai. Above all, they were merchants and traders with few major industrialists who, in any event, appeared only after WWI.[86] Christian Henriot describes it as a self-contained community "with a strong tendency to preserve a large degree of autonomy vis-a-vis Westerners and the Chinese population. This created the

---

**82** Mark R. Peattie, "Treaty Port Settlement in China, 1895–1937," in Duus, Myers, Peattie, eds., *The Japanese Informal Empire*, p. 83. See also Joshua A. Fugal, "'Shanghai-Japan': The Japanese Residents' Association of Shanghai," *JAS*, Vol. 59, no. 4 (November 2000), p. 944, who suggests that Japanese hesitated alienating other foreign establishments.

**83** Christian Henriot, "'Little Japan' in Shanghai: An Insulated Community, 1875–1945," in Bickers and Henriot, *New Frontiers*, p. 148.

**84** Ibid. and Xu Jie, "Hongkou Ribanren juzhiqu shulun (Presentation of the Japanese quarter in Hongkou)," *Shanghai yenjiu luncong* (Papers on Shangha" studies), 10 (1996), p. 297.

**85** Fogel, "'Shanghai-Japan': The Japanese Residents' Association of Shanghai," JAS, 59, no. 4 (November 2000), p. 933.

**86** Peattie, "Japanese Treaty Port Settlements," in Duus, Myers, Peattie, eds., *The Japanese Informal Empire*, p. 193.

condition for the development of a full-fledged Japanese city that offered myriad jobs to people of almost any extraction." Being concentrated in one part of the city together with their shops, firms, and apartments, they lived in an insulated environment and were hardly in touch with Chinese realities.[87]

There were, of course, plenty of commercial and employment opportunities, which attracted Japanese immigrants to Shanghai. Major among these was the textile industry, which grew by leaps and bounds after WWI. Although at the end of the nineteenth and beginning of the twentieth centuries, the Japanese had not been eager to establish cotton manufacture in Shanghai – preferring to export cotton products to China – but when they finally did, manufacturing cotton proved immediately profitable. "By 1930, the Japanese owned more than 40 mills, or about one-third of the 127 mills then operating in China," writes Peter Duus. Two major reasons account for this. The first was the availability of capital for investment in Japan during WWI, when the wartime boom produced considerable profits. The other was the growth and expansion of the Chinese cotton industry and the dramatic increase of Chinese production. Japanese entrepreneurs were fearful that the Chinese production would cut into their profitable exports.[88]

This largely civilian middle class community was, however, deeply affected by Chinese workers' strikes and especially by the anti-Japanese boycotts which became a feature of Shanghai life from 1915 on. And much to the surprise of the Westerners in the settlements, the usually placid Japanese rioted in January 1932, attempting to force the Japanese authorities to take action against the Chinese. When a mob attacked policemen of the SMP and marched on the Japanese Consulate General, the *North China Herald* report called it an "extraordinary development in the Sino-Japanese situation which had hitherto failed to disturb the peace and security of the International Settlement ..."[89] The writer's surprise also reveals, however, the ignorance of Westerners about the mood in the Japanese community since 1927. Since that date, the Special Naval Landing Party had become a permanent fixture in Shanghai's Japanese areas and should have been noted due to its increasingly close ties with the Japanese community by means of para-military groups. After the 1932 hostilities, the Special Naval Landing Party erected permanent barracks in Hongkou that could hold up to 2,000 men, tanks, and armored cars. For the next five

**87** Henriot, "'Little Japan' in Shanghai," in Bickers and Henriot, eds., *New Frontiers*, pp. 156–157, 164.
**88** Duus, "Zaibabo: Japanese Cotton Mills in China," in Duus, Myers, Peattie, eds., *The Japanese Informal Empire*, pp. 79, 81, 84.
**89** "Serious Sino-Japanese Disturbances," *NCH*, January 26, 1932.

years, until the outbreak of the Sino-Japanese war in July 1937, it "ran Hong-kew [Hongkou] as if it were an exclusive Japanese concession."[90] In addition, the role of the Japanese Residents' Association as a link in the control of the Japanese community must not be overlooked.[91]

Like the other communities, the Japanese also established schools in Shanghai, including primary as well as vocational schools. These grew in number together with the population, until by late 1940 there were as many as 9,894 pupils enrolled.[92] Nor were religious institutions neglected. A Shinto shrine, much enlarged after the 1932 hostilities, served the community's spiritual needs. This, being a community of mostly families and unmarried soldiers, parks and their aesthetic appeal, played an important role in the lives of the people.[93]

I have discussed above four especially prominent communities in Shanghai, the Baghdadis, Russian Jews, White Russians, and Japanese. They were prominent either because of their size or because of their wealth, and they are notable because all four were organized as communities with communal and religious institutions. Each community would continue to play a role in treaty port affairs after the arrival of the Central European Jews, who also constituted themselves as several communities. Although dependent in large measure on the good will of their co-religionists, the Central European refugees asserted their separate identities on linguistic or religious grounds. Their increasingly accelerating arrival coincided with one of the most difficult periods in Shanghai's history: the aftermath of the outbreak of the Sino-Japanese war in July 1937. It is to this period that I want to briefly turn now.

## Aftermath of the 1937 Hostilities

A British consular report dated September 27, 1937, provides an excellent description of how the tension mounted in the International Settlement each day in August. On August 10, the Japanese 1st fleet arrived at Wusong, bringing the total to twenty eight Japanese ships at Shanghai. The Japanese garrison of 2,000 men was increased by an additional 1,000. On August 12, British subjects were warned to move inside the International Settlement. Firing broke out in the northern area on August 13, and on August 14, Chinese air raids, missing

---

90 Peattie, "Japanese Treaty Port Settlements," pp. 198–200.
91 See Fogel, "'Shanghai-Japan'," pp. 927–950.
92 Ibid., pp. 930, 939.
93 Peattie, "Japanese Treaty Port Settlements," pp. 195–198.

the Japanese ships, bombed the settlements. By August 17, as described earlier, people were being evacuated from the International Settlement to Hong Kong. The report adds that business was almost at a standstill, although ships seemed to move freely along the river.[94]

By year's end, the Japanese had retreated from Shanghai and the war moved toward Nanjing and Hangzhou. Nonetheless, as another consular report indicated, "a tense situation has arisen which, in some respects, is even more dangerous and harmful to foreign interests than the hostilities which preceded it." Increasingly, the Japanese asserted themselves and took control, to which the foreign powers saw no way out except to agree. Chinese government offices were closed by the Japanese, including the Chinese telegraph in November 1937; the wireless administration on January 5, 1938; the Chinese post office on March 8, 1938. The areas under Japanese control, Hongkou and Yangshupu, were temporarily closed to foreign and Chinese residence. Moreover, on December 5, 1937, the Japanese set up a new city government, *Dadao*, with the puppet mayor Fu Xiaoan (1871–1940), who under Japanese supervision assumed power in the Chinese areas of Shanghai.[95] But despite the seeming calm in the settlements, guerilla activity in the vicinity of Shanghai was common even in 1939, and firing could be heard in the foreign areas.[96] The immediate aftermath of the war led to the removal of Chiang Kai-shek's Nationalist government from Nanjing inland, first to Wuhan and then to Chongqing. After Wang Jingwei (1883–1944) defected from the Chongqing government in December 1938, he established a rival puppet regime under Japanese guidance in Nanjing in March 1940.[97]

Not only foreign interests, Chinese business interests, too, were badly affected by the hostilities. Industrial and warehousing facilities in Hongkou, Pudong and Yangshupu suffered enormous damage. Zhabei, together with its newly rebuilt civic center (severely damaged in 1932) was again nearly reduced

---

**94** PRO, FO 371/20985, no. 208, September 28, 1937. Report forwarded by the Consul General Herbert Phillips to the British Embassy in Beijing. The report was compiled by Consul J. A. C. C. Alexander.

**95** PRO, FO371/22129, "Political Report for the Shanghai Consular District for the Quarter Ended 31st December 1937," and Barnett, *Economic Shanghai*, p. 26.

**96** Barnett, *Economic Shanghai*, p. 17.

**97** Wang Jingwei continues to be controversial in modern Chinese history. Was he a traitor, an opportunist who made common cause with the enemy? Or was he a patriotic nationalist who sought to protect the Chinese people from brutal exploitation by joining the enemy? For a thoughtful exploration of Wang's position, see Lin Hansheng, "Wang Ching-wei and Chinese Collaboration," *Peace and Change*, Vol. 1, no. 1 (Fall 1972), pp. 17–35.

to ruin. More than that, both international and national trade suffered great losses. Cargo ships on their way to Shanghai were diverted to other Asian ports, straining warehousing facilities there. Import and export business suffered because credits abroad were withheld and cash withdrawals from Chinese banks were limited for several months after August. Shanghai was described as having "been dealt a staggering blow in physical destruction of property, and in losses in current and future business ..."[98] Although coastal shipping and passenger services, as well as shipping to Yangzi ports, which had ceased altogether in August and September 1937, had resumed on a much reduced scale, the Japanese continued to blockade the Yangzi for many months after the fighting had stopped.

The large scale destruction of various industrial installations led to considerable unemployment of Chinese workers, estimated at 600,000 people out of work.[99] This situation was exacerbated by the destitute refugees that poured into the settlements from outlying areas where fighting had taken place, especially the refugees of Shanghai itself who had been made homeless in the fighting. "Few villages within a 50-mile radius of Shanghai escaped attention and thousands of unfortunate non-combatants were bombed out of their homes. All these displaced persons sought refuge in the foreign settlements," writes Christian Henriot.[100] The aid extended by several organizations could hardly alleviate the suffering of tens of thousands of needy people. The refugee crisis lasted throughout 1938 as did the pressure of the Japanese on the Shanghai Municipal Council for concessions. When the Central European refugees started arriving at the end of 1938 in ever increasing numbers, it must have seemed like the last straw to the beleaguered SMC. Its adamant refusal to aid yet another refugee group (discussed below) must be understood as part of the difficult situation that had arisen as a result of the war. The Jewish arrivals, on the other hand, with little or no comprehension of Shanghai's situation and Chinese politics, deplored Chinese indifference to the suffering and death of the needy that they witnessed daily in the streets. They did not realize that the pictures of abject poverty were those of refugees made homeless in war.

Although the four years between the "undeclared war" and the outbreak of the Pacific War in December 1941 were years of increasing hardship in

---

**98** A. Bland Calder, "Shanghai Trade," *IM*, January 14, 1938, pp. 23, 18. Calder was the assistant American commercial attaché.

**99** Frederic Wakeman, Jr., *The Shanghai Badlands, Wartime Terrorism and Urban Crime, 1937–1941*, Cambridge: Cambridge University Press, 1996, p. 7.

**100** Christian Henriot, "Shanghai and the Experience of War. The Fate of Refugees," *European Journal of East Asian Studies*, Vol. 5, no. 2 (September 2006), pp. 218–219.

Shanghai, initially, at least, there were signs of a slight business recovery. Despite being surrounded by occupied Shanghai, the foreign settlements (now termed *gudao,* or solitary island) continued unoccupied by the Japanese for the next four years. Those Chinese entrepreneurs who could salvage their equipment in the industrial areas, gradually moved their installations into the settlements. The nine textile mills in the concessions in 1936 increased to twenty-three by 1940. Silk filatures, chemical plants, even paper mills sought the safety of the foreign settlements, as did regional banks. Despite losses, the banks of such cities as Hangzhou, Suzhou, and Wuxi moved to unoccupied Shanghai. According to Parks Coble:

> By fall of 1938, the solitary island had become a bustling center of economic activity. Though surrounded by a war-scarred and devastated hinterland, the Shanghai concessions experienced an economic flourishing fueled by the influx of capital and business. While total economic activity in the lower Yangzi suffered, within island Shanghai a boom of sorts occurred.[101]

The boom, however, was of short duration. Increasingly, the Japanese took over Chinese plants and inland shipping was drastically reduced. Although trade between areas occupied by Japan and "free China," the areas held by the Chiang Kai-shek's government, never ceased entirely, it is hard to say how much commerce between them actually contributed to Shanghai's economy.[102] In any event, by 1941 the boom had ended and production of many commodities dropped precariously as compared to 1936 levels. This situation was accompanied by ever increasing inflation, when both the Chiang government in Chongqing and the Wang Jingwei government in Nanjing began printing money. Inflation had increased at a moderate rate until mid-1939, now began to soar[103] and had a disastrous impact on the lower classes in the treaty port and the newly arriving refugees. Added to this were the waves of crime and terrorism that swept through Shanghai. Racketeering, gambling, the narcotics trade, prostitution – all of these flourished in Shanghai. As discussed by Wakeman in *The Shanghai Badlands,* assassinations, bombings, Chongqing and puppet sponsored, were a common occurrence between 1937 and 1941. The treaty port era ended, for all practical purposes, when the Pacific war broke

---

**101** Cobble, *Chinese Capitalists,* pp. 22–24.
**102** Lloyd E. Eastman, "Facets of an Ambivalent Relationship: Smuggling, Puppets, and Atrocities During the War, 1937–1945," in Akira Iriye, ed., *The Chinese and the Japanese, Essays in Political and Cultural Interaction,* Princeton: Princeton University Press, 1980, pp. 275–285. See also Wakeman, *The Chinese Badlands,* pp. 7–8, who estimates trade between the Japanese areas and Free China around U.S. $ 120 million.
**103** Cobble, *Chinese Capitalists,* p. 29.

out after the Japanese bombed Pearl Harbor and when the Japanese occupied the International Settlement and more or less controlled the French Concession.

## Shanghai-Harbin-Tianjin

It should not be assumed, however, that the Shanghai communities existed in isolation from other foreign communities elsewhere in China. This was especially true for the Russian Jewish community, which was connected with the two major communities in Harbin and Tianjin.

From the end of the 19th century until the collapse of Japanese military power in 1945, Manchuria developed rapidly, both economically and industrially. Together with it, Harbin grew from an insignificant frontier hamlet into a thriving social and administrative center. Located in present-day Heilongjiang province on the Sungari (Songhuajiang) river, the city also became a multi-ethnic transportation center.[104] The construction of the Chinese Eastern Railway (CER) by the Russians in 1898 was a major event that triggered the growth and development of Harbin. Running from Manzhouli through Hailar, Qiqihar to Vladivostok, Harbin was at the hub of the CER and the South Manchurian Railway (ceded to Japan after the 1904–1905 Russo-Japanese War) branching off to Lushun (Port Arthur).

Jews first arrived in Manchuria and Harbin together with the CER personnel. Their initial numbers were augmented after the Russo-Japanese War when Jewish soldiers, conscripted into the Russian army, decided to remain in Manchuria. Pogroms and finally the Russian Revolution of 1917 caused large numbers of both Russians and Jews to arrive. Some moved on to Tianjin and Shanghai, others remained in Harbin. The large number of Russians present in Harbin (200,000 according to one estimate) endowed the city with a distinct Russian character. This, together with its multi-ethnic population – consisting of Chinese, Koreans, Japanese, and various kinds of Europeans, including perhaps 13,000 Jews – made Harbin a lively cosmopolitan city in which bankers, merchants, entrepreneurs of many kinds, and professionals made their homes. In recent decades Harbin is remembered nostalgically in a variety of languages.[105]

---

**104** For an excellent description of the pre-WWI Russian role, see David Wolff, *To the Harbin Station, The Liberal Alternative in Russian Manchuria, 1898–1914*, Stanford: Stanford University Press, 1999.

**105** Thomas, Lahusen, "Remembering China, Imagining Israel: The Memory of Difference," *The South Atlantic Quarterly*, Vol. 99, no. 1 (Winter 2000), pp. 253–272.

As a whole, the Jewish community was relatively well-off. "With material success," wrote Boris Bresler, "came community and cultural institutions – synagogues, a cemetery, a home for the aged, support for the sick and for the poor, schools, youth organizations, clubs, publications, dramatic productions and lectures." Such publications as, *Sibir-Palestina*, a Zionist magazine and the later *Evreiskaya Zhizn* (Hebrew life) were avidly read.[106] Among the affluent families of the community were the Skidelskys, whose lumber interests along the CER lines and coal mining enterprise brought them enormous wealth.[107] Nor was the Kabalkin family far behind. Their wealth derived initially from export trade and in the 1920s from flour milling and the soybean trade.

Yet, the well-being of this thriving community was short-lived. The 1929 depression in America and Europe adversely affected business enterprises geared toward exports, setting in motion the exodus that was accelerated by subsequent events. The Japanese invasion of Manchuria in 1931 and the establishment of the puppet state, Manchukuo, resulted not only in the exodus of the Russian population southward and to Shanghai, Russian Jews left as well. Friends and families were reunited in Shanghai or Tianjin, and the community gradually declined in the next thirteen years. By the end of the war, 2,000 Jews remained in Harbin and most of these departed in the next decade as well for various destinations, among them the United States and Israel. By 1985 the lone survivor in Harbin was probably Hanna Agre, too old to leave the place she called home.

However, when the Jews went to Shanghai, they left behind friends and, no doubt, family members. Although we have no evidence so far, and this remains a topic in need of further exploration, some form of connection continued between members of the communities. In short, it is highly unlikely that families, or members of families, would cease to maintain contact with the place and the people among whom they had lived.

A similar assumption must be made about Tianjin. Although its Jewish community was much smaller than either Shanghai's or Harbin's, never numbering more than 2,500 persons, it consisted mostly of Russian Jews who for the most part had come from Manchuria. In 1917 Tianjin had fewer than ten

---

**106** Boris Bresler, "Harbin's Jewish Community, 1898–1958. Politics, Prosperity, and Adversity," in Jonathan Goldstein, ed., *The Jews of China*, Armonk-London: M. E. Sharpe, 1999, Vol. 1, p. 206.

**107** The great-grandson of Lev Shmulevich Skidel'skii has written a brief biography of his family when he visited China recently. See his, Robert Skidelsky, "A Chinese Homecoming," *Prospect*, (January 2006), pp. 36–41.

Jewish families, but within twenty years, and especially after the Japanese occupation of Manchuria, the Jewish community grew rapidly, in the process building religious and social institutions.[108]

Tianjin's Jews took pride in the Tientsin Jewish School, founded in 1925, under the able leadership of the community by Lev Gershevich (1878–1950). The school's medium of instruction was English and its curriculum was designed to have students continue their studies at European or American universities. Cultural activities were not neglected. Entertainment was provided in the Jewish club "Kunst," founded in 1928, and its library boasted presumably 5,000 volumes in Russian and Yiddish. From 1934 on, the Russian newspaper *Nashe Zarya* (Our dawn) twice monthly devoted one page to Jewish affairs. Finally, in 1937 the Jewish community began to build a synagogue.[109]

Like Shanghai, Tianjin had its foreign concessions, but unlike Shanghai, most of the Russian Jews lived and worked in the British Concession. Fur trade was by far the most lucrative enterprise, at least until the great 1929 depression. Chinese middlemen obtained pelts in the vast Manchurian forests, bringing them to Tianjin for sorting and processing. From Tianjin they were shipped to American and European markets. Although this luxury trade ceased for all practical purposes after 1929, Tianjin firms rapidly diversified, so that the community was spared the disastrous economic setback of Harbin.[110]

Japan's gradual military expansion into north China following the occupation of Manchuria seems not to have adversely affected the Jewish community. However, the Sino-Japanese war in 1937 brought the Japanese armies to its doorsteps and with it Japanese apprehension about communist activities among the Russian Jewish population. Unlike Shanghai, which experienced a massive Central European refugee influx, in addition to its own refugee problem, Tianjin largely escaped both calamities. On the one hand, Tianjin's Chinese sections did not undergo the bombardment Shanghai had. On the other, the Japanese authorities, fearful of communist infiltration, denied residence permits to most Central European applicants. As had been the case in Harbin and Manchuria where only a few Central European refugees were allowed to

---

108 Nehemia Robinson, *Oifleizung fun di Yidishe kehilos in Chine* (Dissolution of the Jewish communities in China), New York: Institute for Yiddish Affairs, 1954, p. 13.
109 A. Isgur, "Yevreskaya kolonia Tientsina za posliednia wiesyat lat (The Jewish colony in Tientsin in the last ten years)," *Nashe Zarya*, no. 3181 (April 7, 1938), pp. 1–7. [Clipping bound as pamphlet].
110 A substantial history of the Tianjin community is still lacking. This account is based on my brief essay in *Chinese and Jews, Encounters between Cultures*, London: Valentine Mitchell, 2008.

settle, a mere handful of refugees was allowed to come to Tianjin.[111] It is doubtful that these had close relatives or friends with whom to maintain contact. I am led to believe, therefore, that a network of relationships, however loose it may have been, connected the Russian Jewish communities of the three cities through their publications in Russian and other means available.

In this chapter I have described the beginning and development of Shanghai as a treaty port and the opportunities it offered to both Chinese and foreigners. Foreigners were few as compared with Chinese and, as Rudolf Wagner argues, state and society were clearly separated in Shanghai. Thus treaty port Shanghai provided the possibility for innovation not found elsewhere. Moreover, "The governmental institutions in the enclaves did not compete with the Chinese government for control over the entire country and thus posed no real colonial threat." Within this context of a "relatively independent public sphere,"[112] the communities described above developed. Linguistically very different from one another as well as from the Chinese, who were the majority in Shanghai, they were able to maintain their identities as distinct groups within the treaty port setting. But ultimately, not only politics but also the economy determined Shanghai's future. The gradual and final Japanese takeover of Shanghai spelled the end of the Baghdadi community, whereas the Russians, both Jewish and non-Jewish, continued to exist as communities as did the Central European refugees. In Shanghai, however, Japanese control over both foreign and Jewish communities became part of Japanese occupation policy. How to control and oversee the Jewish communities was an experience the Japanese gained in Manchuria, China's three northeastern provinces.

---

**111** As late as 1941, a German memorandum noted that questions of arrival and residence of J-passport holders (that is Jewish) in north China has not been clarified. Pol 4–5a, Akten der deutschen Botschaft in China, "Über Pass- und Aufenthaltsfragen jüdischer Emigranten aus Deutschland in Nordchina," July 9, 1941, signed Marks, consular secretary. I thank Professor Bernard Wasserstein for making a copy available to me.
**112** Rudolf G. Wagner, "The Role of the Foreign Community in the Chinese Public Sphere," *The China Quarterly*, no. 142 (June 1995), p. 442.

# Chapter 2:
# Germany's China Policy, Forced Emigration and the Search for Alternative Destinations

The German regime's obsessive preoccupation with the "Jewish Question" was indirectly related to its interests and policies in East Asia. Thus the fact that thousands of German and Austrian Jews were able to land in Shanghai between 1938 and 1939 has as its background the relationship between Germany and China on the one hand, and Japan on the other. Complex considerations involving Germany's economic relations with China, internal power struggles, international diplomacy, and attempts to rearm both in Germany and in China – all these played a role between 1933, when the first small group of Jews arrived in China, and 1938, when thousands more embarked on the journey. This chapter will do no more than merely outline some of the major issues in Sino-German and German-Japanese relations. To these considerations must be added the question of German dissatisfaction with the speed of Jewish emigration and the steps undertaken to bring about a more rapid departure of Jews, accompanied by the confiscation of their property. Together with these questions, I will also ask what other destinations in Asia were being sought by various sources.

## The First Jewish Arrivals in China, 1933–1934

Years of political instability characterized the Chinese scene after the successful Republican revolution in 1911 under Sun Yat-sen (1866–1925), and the establishment of the Republic of China in 1912. The country came to be, for all practical purposes, divided between competing strong men – the so-called warlords – none of whom could muster the military strength to unify the country and establish a government with sufficient authority. A major change occurred, however, in 1928, when Chiang Kai-shek (Jiang Jieshi, 1888–1975) brought large portions of south and central China under the control of his Guomindang (Nationalist) government with its seat in Nanjing. Although Chiang's authority continued to be challenged by contenders for power in the north as well as in several provinces,[1] his government was internationally

---

1 The communists were the most formidable among Chiang's adversaries. After their abortive revolution in 1927 and the several uprisings thereafter they established a number of bases in southern and central China. But by 1934, the year they embarked

recognized. Nanjing's consulates continued to function in many European countries throughout the 1930s, as well as after 1937, following Chiang's retreat into the interior.

The group of German-Jewish professionals who arrived in China shortly after Hitler had come to power in January 1933 would hardly have been aware of the problems facing China which, in any event, must have seemed less formidable compared to those they left behind. Moreover, professionals, like doctors and dentists, who attempted to pursue their calling, were obviously more visible than others were. They were the initial immigrants, having lost their positions in state institutions as soon as the Hitler regime came to power. It began with the boycott against them of April 1, 1933; next came the decree of April 7, 1933, which stipulated that officials of "non-Aryan" descent were to be retired. The definition of non-Aryan was issued as a regulation on April 11, 1933 and stated that a non-Aryan was anyone with a Jewish parent, grandparent, or who belonged to the Jewish religion.[2] Thus, well before the Nuremberg laws were drafted in the fall of 1935, which defined more concisely who in the Nazi regime's view was a Jew, numerous professionals had already lost their positions and livelihood. Not that leaving Germany was inexpensive even in 1933. The "tax for fleeing the Reich" (Reichfluchtsteuer) had been enacted in July 1933. Later other so-called taxes would be added causing many erstwhile well-off Jews to become paupers.[3]

The fact that twenty-six families, among them five well-known physicians, decided to go to Shanghai in the fall of 1933 in preference to some other country, was presumably because they had read in a Berlin newspaper about China's shortage of doctors.[4] Although these arrivals represented but a tiny

---

on the Long March to the Northwest, they were numerically and militarily too weak to challenge Chiang's better equipped army.

**2** Esriel Hildesheimer, *Jüdische Selbstverwaltung unter dem NS-Regime, der Existenzkampf der Reichsvertretung und Reichsvereinigung der Juden in Deutschland*, Tübingen: J. C. B. Mohr (Paul Siebeck), 1994, pp. 9–10; Raoul Hilberg, *The Destruction of the European Jews*, New York–London: Holmes and Meier, 1985, rev. ed., Vol. 1, p. 66.

**3** Research currently under way in Germany about the function of the Reich Finance Ministry should add considerably to our knowledge how confiscated Jewish money contributed to the German economy. See the extensive article by Rainer Hank, "Die Grosse Plünderung," *Frankfurther Allgemeine Sonntagszeitung*, no. 44 (November 7, 2010), pp. 42–43. I thank Professor Wolfgang Kubin for making this article available to me.

**4** SMP, D5422 (c), Police Report dated November 7, 1933. The five physicians were doctors Rosenthal, Loewenberg, Hess, Elchengrün and Keinwald. According to a letter from December 1933, thirty Jewish families had arrived from Germany by the end of the year. CAHJP, DAL 48, Braverman to HIAS-ICA-EMIGDIRECT, Paris, December 13, 1933

fraction of Jews leaving Germany in 1933 and 1934,[5] (even if their numbers had apparently grown to eighty physicians, surgeons, and dentists by spring 1934),[6] apprehensions about their presence in China were voiced in German diplomatic circles, seemingly not taking account of their government's policies. One, as stated by a Dr. Mohr of the Hamburg-Bremen East Asian Association (Ostasiatischer Verein Hamburg-Bremen E. V.) in August 1933, was that Jewish professors or physicians in China cannot represent Germany's best interests. After all, having been fired from their positions in Germany, they would hardly sing Germany's praises. Indeed, a Chinese student wrote Mohr, who had studied with a now dismissed Professor Kaestner, had advised him to go to China "where he would surely find a position and where he would be treated with the greatest respect."[7]

Furthermore, in December 1933 the German consulate in Beijing, sent a telegram warning of the influx of Jewish physicians.[8] Dr. Ludvig Rajchman, a financial and China expert, who was in contact with the Chinese Finance Minister T. V. Soong in summer 1933 when the latter visited Europe, was accused of being behind the idea of recruiting Jews for China.[9] Also, as stated by Oskar

---

(in Yiddish). Another Police Report, SMP, reel 17, file 5422 (c), November 11, 1933, is a list of thirteen doctors, dentists, and pharmacists, who arrived in Shanghai. Eight had visas from the Chinese Consulate General in Berlin, three from Hamburg, one from Paris, and for one the place of issuance is not stated. See also *IM*, Vol. 30, no. 9 (December 1, 1933), p. 10, which mentions their arrival on the Conte Verde on November 6, as well as doctors Max Dahl, Georg Glass, Horst Lange, Walter Neubauer who have already established themselves. A word of caution is added, however, namely that the influx of doctors ought to be regulated as not everyone's services may be in demand. A letter from the Reverend Brown in Shanghai in response to an inquiry the following year also suggests that would-be immigrants were not especially welcome. He stated that anyone coming to Shanghai must do so at his own risk and responsibility. CAHJP, DAL 24a, Rev. Brown to Far Eastern Jewish Central Information Bureau, Harbin, September 21, 1934. The concerns in Shanghai will be discussed more fully below.

**5** Werner Rosenstock, "Exodus 1933–1939: A Survey of Jewish Emigration from Germany," *Leo Baeck Institute Yearbook*, Vol. I (1956), pp. 373–390. 37.000 left in 1933 and 23.000 in 1934. Of the 37,000, only 8 % chose overseas destinations, others remained in European countries.

**6** *CP*, November 26, 1938, p. 3.

**7** YVA, JM 11701, Mohr to Altenburg, Foreign Office, East Asian Division, Berlin, August 8, 1933.

**8** The telegram, dated December 4, is mentioned in YVA, J4, JM57, M. Fischer, Peiping, to the Foreign Office, Berlin, March 17, 1934.

**9** YVA, JM 11701, Altenburg to the Minister of Foreign Affairs, August 11, 1933. Rajchman had a one-year appointment from the League of Nations as adviser to the National Economic Council, which was to coordinate technical aid to China, See also Paul W. Frey,

Trautmann, Ambassador to China, Jewish physicians can have a detrimental effect on the activities of German physicians and on German cultural work in China generally.[10] According to a German embassy report of March 1934, concerns were even voiced by the Chinese Nanjing government, which had been informed by the mayor of Shanghai (?) of extensive recent arrivals of Jewish doctors. Although the Chinese were more concerned about communist leanings of the new arrivals, they considered limitations on licensing them. Presumably, the Chinese government was, in addition, keeping an eye on Ezra (meaning no doubt the owner of *Israel's Messenger*, N. E. B. Ezra) who "was diligently working to find places for his race in China."[11] Thus by the beginning of 1934, the German Foreign Office had concluded that while dismissal was desirable, emigration was a mixed blessing. Immigration to China, it was admitted, could not be prevented. However, German consulates in China were requested to supply the Foreign Office with accurate data of immigrants working in hospitals, universities, and similar institutions. Moreover, Germany's position on Jews was to be explained abroad,[12] and anti-German sentiments, hostility to Germans and German interests were to be monitored.[13] Clearly, Foreign Office views, which supported trade with China, did not accord entirely with Nazi policies. As will be shown below, as late as May 1939, when the Foreign Office had already come under the control of Joachim von Ribbentrop (1893–1946), the issue of trade versus Jews would be raised again.

Meanwhile, in 1933 the Jewish presence in China was seen as distinctly threatening to German interests. There were the persistent calls to boycott German goods in Shanghai's Jewish paper, *Israel's Messenger,* and on May 13, 1933, a delegation of the China League for Civil Rights came to Shanghai's

---

*Faschistische Fernostpolitik, Italien, China und die Entstehung des weltpolitischen Dreieckes, Rom–Berlin–Tokio,* Frankfurt/Main: Peter Lang, 1997, pp. 177–178.

**10** YVA, JM 4857, Trautmann, German embassy, Peping (sic) to the Foreign Office Berlin, March 17, 1934. Trautmann also wanted to know how many passports were issued to Jewish physicians.

**11** YVA, J4, JM57, M. Fischer, Nanjing report to the German embassy, Peiping, March 14, 1934. This is a report about Fischer's conversation with Dr. I. Heng Liu, director of Chinese Health Services. According to a list in YVA, 078/73A, 25 physicians had arrived in Shanghai.

**12** YVA, JM 11701, Foreign Office circular to all diplomatic and consular representatives, dated April 30, 1933.

**13** YVA, JM 11701, Foreign Office, Stieve to the German embassy, Peiping, January 31, 1934. In view of these concerns it was rather embarrassing that the Foreign Office had written recommendations on behalf of twelve physicians who had applied for visas to the Chinese embassy in Berlin. YVA, 078/83, Oster, Foreign Office to the German embassy, Peping (sic), June 22, 1934.

German Consulate General with a letter, protesting anti-Jewish activities in Germany. The delegation was composed of well-known intellectuals, writers, journalists, and scholars, among them the only Jew, 23-year old Harold R. Isaacs (1910–1985). Aware, no doubt, that he was Jewish, Isaacs was the only one threatened in the German account of the visit, which specified, "We urgently advise him not to poke his fingers in German domestic politics … he is liable to easily burn them."[14] Other protests and declarations of solidarity with German Jews were also noted by the German consulates in Mukden and Harbin. Although these were organized by the Jewish communities and were significantly different from Isaac's protest, they too were perceived as a threat. When the Mukden Jewish community declared that they would do everything to support German Jews, it was understood as a contemplated boycott.[15]

## Germany's East Asian Politics between China and Japan

There is of course a contradiction between the Nazi Party's eventual attempts at forcing Jewish emigration, to be discussed below, and the Foreign Office's concern about the emigrants' anti-German sentiments. Other contradictions existed regarding foreign policy and economic interests, not because the Foreign Office's Nazi inclinations were weaker, but mainly because of differences in basic premises.

In China, the Foreign Office saw its aim as both diplomatic and economic. The two were closely intertwined and for both the Germans and the Chinese the major issue was military supplies. Indeed, as pointed out by Bernd Martin, in China in the 1930s, "Next to the diplomatic experts, the military and the economists were to the same degree involved in the formulation of German interests and their implementation."[16] German political and commercial inter-

---

**14** YVA, JM 11701, M. S. E., "Frau Dr. Sun Yat Sen auf dem deutschen General-Konsulat! Haende weg von der deutschen Innenpolitik!" *Deutsche Schanghai Zeitung*, May 16, 1933. The delegates were: Song Jinling, Sun's widow and head of the League; Cai Yuanpei, president of Academia Sinica and Yang Quan, the vice-president; authors Lu Xun and Lin Yutang; the reporter Agnes Smedley. I suspect that it was Harold Isaacs who had organized the protesters; he was a unique personality whose strong convictions about human and civil rights were expressed later in many books and articles. The delegation's visit was publicized in *IM*, Vol. 30, no. 4 (June 2, 1933), p. 7, and no. 5 (July 1, 1933), p. 4.

**15** YVA, JM 11701, signature illegible, German consulate to German embassy, Peiping, June 15, 1933.

**16** Bernd Martin, "Das deutsche Militär und die Wendung der deutschen Fernostpolitik von China auf Japan," in Franz Knipping und Klaus-Jürgen Müller, eds.,

ests in China had begun in the nineteenth century when Germany, too, was one of the colonial powers anxious to gain a territorial foothold in China.[17] Although Germany lost her colonial possessions after World War I, a decade of important military relations began during the Weimar Republic and after the government of Chiang Kai-shek assumed power in Nanjing.

After Hitler came to power these earlier contacts were continued with increasing vigor while the Foreign Office under Constantin Freiherr von Neurath (1873–1956) championed a strong pro-China and pro-Chiang Kai-shek foreign policy. This was partly for reasons of commerce and trade, but had the additional aim, as suggested by John Garver, of including China "in a chain of anti-Communist states on the periphery of the USSR."[18] Being aware of the Nazi regime's anti-Communism, some leading Chinese Nationalist figures and intellectuals, in turn, became seriously interested in fascism and the fascist theory of strong leadership. But a fascist movement never emerged in China; it was rather a vogue and was seen entirely from a Chinese perspective.[19] For this topic, therefore, merely the coincidence of ideological and military interests on the part of both regimes, which figured in these Sino-German short-lived though significant contacts, is important. Germany needed exports at the time of her foreign currency crisis to pay for imports and to launch her rearmament program. Chiang had also needed arms to destroy the Communist contenders for power in their several strongholds (or base areas) since 1931, and he needed a trained and disciplined army to ultimately confront the Japanese invader.

Despite concerted and generally successful efforts between 1933 and 1938, years during which German military missions went to China, Chinese diplomatic and economic missions went to Germany, together with increasing trade, the relationship gradually unraveled in favor of Japan. Four crucial events mark Germany's turn to Japan: the German-Japanese anti-Comintern Pact, signed November 25, 1936 (and joined by Italy a year later); the German an-

---

*Machtbewusstsein in Deutschland am Vorabend des zweiten Weltkrieges*, Paderborn: Ferdinand Schöningh, 1984, p. 191.

**17** For an overview of Germany's imperialist ambitions in China, see John E. Schrecker, *Imperialism and Chinese Nationalism. Germany in Shantung*, Cambridge: Harvard University Press, 1971. A detailed account of the entire period of German-Chinese contacts is Udo Ratenhof, *Die Chinapolitik des deutschen Reiches, 1871 bis 1945, Wirtschaft–Rüstung–Militär*, Boppard am Rhein: Harald Boldt Verlag, 1987.

**18** John W. Garver, "China's Wartime Diplomacy," in James C. Hsiung and Steven I. Levine, eds., *China's Bitter Victory, The War with Japan, 1937–1945*, Armonk–London: M. E. Sharpe, Inc., 1992, p. 5.

**19** William C. Kirby, *Germany and Republican China*, Stanford: Stanford University Press, 1984, p. 175.

nouncement of recognition of Japan-dominated Manchukuo on February 20, 1938 (Italy had extended *de facto* recognition in November 1937); the Tripartite Agreement between Germany, Italy, and Japan of September 27, 1940; Germany's recognition of the Japan-sanctioned Wang Jingwei (1883–1944) regime on July 1, 1941. I do not include here the outbreak of the Sino-Japanese War in July 1937 because at that point Germany was more interested in trying to mediate between the two contenders.[20]

Behind the scenes negotiations to bring Japan and Germany together in an anti-Communist pact had already begun in 1935, without the Foreign Office or its head, Konstantin von Neurath, knowing anything about it. The negotiations were the work of Joachim von Ribbentrop, whose rise to power began in 1933 when Hitler set him up in an advisory office on foreign policy. Ribbentrop had met Oshima Hiroshi (1886–1975), then military attaché in Germany, in the summer of 1935. Both men were interested in a German-Japanese alliance and the two began talks with the aid of Hermann von Raumer, who headed the Eastern section of Ribbentrop's "Dienstelle" at the time, and who had lived in Manchuria.[21] As neither the German nor the Japanese Foreign Offices had been consulted, the talks were shelved until the following year. However, the anti-Comintern Pact, when signed in 1936, marked the beginning of the end of Neurath's pro-Chiang policy and, indeed, of Neurath himself, who was replaced by Ribbentrop in February 1938.[22]

Chiang Kai-shek played down the importance of the new alliance. He optimistically asserted that Germany could not afford to ignore China's friendship.[23] There were, however, more cautious assessments. China would feel the effects of the anti-Comintern Pact, it was argued, although one could not yet

---

**20** See James T.C. Liu, "German Mediation in the Sino-Japanese War, 1937–1938," *Far Eastern Quarterly*, Vol. 8, no. 2 (February 1949), pp. 157–171.

**21** See Mark C. Elliot, "The Limits of Tartary: Manchuria in Imperial and National Geographies," *JAS*, Vol. 59, no. 3 (August 2000), pp. 603–646, for the complex history of the place name Manchuria, which is usually referred to as the Northeast (*Dongbei*) in Chinese sources. In these pages I will refer to the three northeastern provinces – Liaodong, Jilin, and Heilongjiang – as Manchuria before the Japanese conquest, and as Manchukuo (rather than the Chinese *Manzhouguo*) after 1932.

**22** Michael Bloch, *Ribbentrop*, New York: Crown Publishers, Inc., 1992, pp. 96, 81. See also Herbert von Dirksen, *Moskau, Tokio, London, Erinnerungen und Betrachtungen zu 20 Jahren deutscher Aussenpolitik, 1919–1939*, Stuttgart: W. Kohlhammer, 1949, p. 168. Dirksen, who was Germany's ambassador in Tokyo, claims that he first heard of the Ribbentrop-Oshima talks from a confidential Japanese source and then informed Neurath.

**23** Chiang's speech is quoted in, "Situation in Far East Unchanged," *NCH*, December 2, 1936, p. 346.

know what the consequences would be for the participants.[24] The *North China Herald* stated on its front page: "An effective offsetting of Russian influence must of necessity mean the strengthening of the Japanese position in Asia, and … tend not toward greater stability but plunge this country into ever greater difficulties."[25] With hindsight these words seem prophetic.

The reaction to Hitler's announcement in the Reichstag of Manchukuo's recognition on February 20, 1938 was not as equanimous as it had been two years earlier to the anti-Comintern Pact. The Chinese government, which had fled to Hankou after the outbreak of the Sino-Japanese war in July 1937, roundly denounced the announcement. "Germany's action in forsaking China's friendship and justice at this hour will never be forgotten by the Chinese," declared the *Dagong Bao*.[26] Sino-German relations, while not yet frozen, were becoming colder.

The events leading up to the Manchukuo recognition had been complex and took place within the German requirements for soybeans, needed for edible oils and animal fodder. According to a report of 1932, Manchuria produced 61% of the world's soybeans, and bean products were 86.6% of the total exports from Harbin alone.[27] Nonetheless, Germany was unable to obtain soybeans in sufficiently large amounts and a German trade mission in Japan in 1935, also conducted talks with Manchukuo early in 1936.[28] The results were unsatisfactory and the bean demand, no doubt, had a role in the 1938 decision. But despite having recognized Manchukuo, German firms were no more successful even one year later in obtaining larger imports, though it was apparently realized by then that Japan controlled the bean market and was not about to reduce its imports in favor of Germany.[29]

There were other considerations as well. Gerhard Weinberg writes that Manchukuo recognition was already discussed some years earlier, especially after Germany withdrew from the League of Nations in October 1933 and dis-

---

**24** "Ri De xieding yu Zhongguo (The Japan-German agreement and China)," *DGB*, November 27, 1936, p. 2.

**25** "That Agreement," *NCH*, December 2, 1936, p. 345.

**26** *DGB* quoted in, "Hankow Amazed by Fuehrer's Speech," *NCH*, February 23, 1938, p. 274.

**27** [Sakatani Yoshiro], *Manchuria*. A Survey of economic development, based in part on material prepared under the supervision of Baron Y. Sakatani. Revised by Grover Clark. Prepared for the Division of Economics and History of the Carnegie Endowment for International Peace. Preface by Yoshiro Sakatani, dated 1932.

**28** "Germany May Buy More Soya Beans from Manchoukuo," *JT*, February 24, 1936, p. 1.

**29** YVA, JM 2.040. This is a "strictly confidential" report by a delegation dispatched to Manchukuo in December 1939. Its report seems to be addressed to various firms and the cover letter is on I. G. Farbenindustrie Aktiengesellschaft stationary. Nonetheless, Manchukuo continued to be a major soybean supplier to Germany. See "Japan Supplies Food to Germany; Sends 1.500 Tons Daily Via Russia," *The New York Times*, June 4, 1941.

cussions about the soybean trade had begun.[30] Recognition may have been shelved at the time while the arms trade with the Nanjing government was getting underway and the influential military adviser, Hans von Seeckt (1866–1936), (about whom more below) visited China and became a staunch supporter of Chiang Kai-shek. Jeopardizing valuable and lucrative commercial contacts for soybeans was, no doubt, not in Germany's interests at that time. The outbreak of the Sino-Japanese war in July 1937, the subsequent fall of Nanjing, and the retreat of the Nationalist government to the interior, the elimination of the pro-Chiang faction from the German Foreign Office, and the appointment as foreign minister of the pro-Japanese Ribbentrop in February 1938 brought about a vastly changed situation.

Manchukuo, or the Northeast, had come to be considered an integral part of China after the establishment of the Qing (Manchu) dynasty in 1644.[31] Japan's invasion and occupation of Manchuria was, therefore, the invasion of Chinese territory. Japan's establishment of a puppet government in Manchuria, or what was now called Manchukuo, did not alter this fact, and German recognition of Japan's outlaw behavior as legitimate should have produced a rift between Chiang Kai-shek's government and the Nazi regime. But despite the fact that Germany and Japan were obviously moving closer, the break between Chiang and Germany came three years later.[32] In the interim, the conclusion of the Tripartite Pact, which brought Italy, Germany, and Japan into an alliance in September 1940, can be seen as one further step in cementing relations with Japan. In fact, it represented a rearrangement of political forces with Japan now firmly allied against the United States and Great Britain. But equally important, if not more so, was Germany's invasion of European countries earlier in the summer of 1940, which had raised concern in Japan over the status of these countries' Asian colonies, an issue that was dealt with in the Pact.[33]

Although the clouds of the impending cataclysm were clearly gathering – Germany had invaded Poland in September 1939 and Italy had joined the Ger-

---

30 Gerhard L. Weinberg, "German Recognition of Manchoukuo," *World Affairs Quarterly*, Vol. 28 (1957), p. 151. See also Theo Sommer, *Deutschland und Japan zwischen den Mächten, 1935–1940*, Tübingen: J. C. Mohr (Paul Siebeck), 1962, pp. 17–42, who explains the larger interest in the alliance in terms of the anti-Soviet plans of the Japanese military and Hitler's East European expansionist plans.

31 This process and the cartographic implications are ably described by Elliot, "The Limits of Tartary."

32 Italy had already begun rethinking her support for Chiang at the end of 1936 and the break came in the fall of 1937. See Frey, *Faschistische Fernostpolitik*, pp. 255, 262–263.

33 Johanna Menzel Meskill, *Hitler and Japan: The Hollow Alliance*, New York: Atherton Press, 1966, pp. 12–14; Bloch, *Ribbentrop*, pp. 303–306.

man war in June 1940 – reactions in China to this new alliance were mixed. It signaled, according to one Guomindang writer, that the Sino-Japanese conflict in China was part of the European conflict, although the Pact affected America, Russia, and England more than China.[34] It was also seen as a warning, "The alliance designed by Germany to paralyze the United States into immobility and hasten the attempted dismemberment of the British Empire, will have far-reaching effects on the future of the Far East."[35] But, on the other hand, the alliance was considered not to make much of a change in the international situation, its purpose being to improve relations between Japan and Russia.[36] Not obvious at the time, though, was the fact that Germany and Japan were never able to coordinate their policies, as Johanna Meskill astutely observed. The 1940 Tripartite Pact did not cement relationships, despite the 1936 anti-Comintern Pact; Germany did not welcome Japan's attack on China in 1937, and the 1939 Russo-German Pact had come as a shock to Japan.[37]

The final twists in the reshuffling of alliances came in 1941. First the so-called "neutrality" or "non-aggression" pact between Japan and the USSR in April 1941, stipulated that both parties would maintain strict neutrality in case either was attacked. Then, on July 1, Germany and Italy recognized the Wang Jingwei regime in Nanjing. The former would have an unintended benefit for the Russian-Jewish communities after the start of the Pacific war, putting them in the category of neutrals in the conflict. The latter brought Sino-German relations to the breaking point. The foreign minister of the Nationalist government, then in Chongqing, declared indignantly that both Germany and Italy "have committed a gross injustice to China and have thereby forfeited any claim to the friendship of the Chinese Government and people."[38] Although relations were not definitively severed until the outbreak of the Pacific war in December 1941, all three governments recalled their diplomatic personnel.

---

**34** 078/108A, Shanghai Municipal Archive, Zhang Zhongfu, *De Yi Ri sanguo tongmeng* (The German–Italy–Japan tripartite pact), n. p.: Guomin tushu chupanshe, 1940, p. 33.
**35** Joseph Griggs, "Japan Joins Axis in Military Pact," *SEPM*, September 28, 1940, pp. 1,3.
**36** "The Triple Alliance," *NCH*, October 2, 1940, pp. 5–6. Johanna M. Menzel, "Der geheime Deutsch-Japanische Notenaustausch zum Dreimächtepakt," *Vierteljahrheft für Zeitgeschichte*, 5 (1957), pp. 182–193. Menzel shows that the Pact left many open questions that demanded reexamination. Hence the secret notes, which, however, raised further perplexities. Frey, *Faschistische Fernostpolitik*, p. 303 adds that Italian diplomats were not even involved in the Berlin–Tokyo negotiations, since it was assumed that Italy would sign. See also Bloch, *Ribbentrop*, p. 306, who sees the Pact as a "bluff" intended to frighten the Americans into isolation.
**37** Meskill, *Hitler and Japan*, pp. 3–10.
**38** "Dr. Quo Tai-chi Condemns Axis Recognition of Wang," *SEPM*, July 3, 1941, pp. 1,3.

Wang Jingwei, Chiang Kai-shek's erstwhile ally, had established his puppet government in March 1940 in Nanjing with Japan's blessing,[39] and both Germany and Italy recognized his regime more than a year later. To be sure, Chiang had ceased to be a partner in trade; his control of several hinterland provinces was insignificant compared to Japan's control over most of China in 1941. Yet Japan's dominant position had not netted Germany appreciable gains and the Nazi regime's expectations for increased trade after the outbreak of the Sino-Japanese war in 1937 remained unfulfilled. Nor did the signing of the Tripartite Pact in September 1940 and Japan's increasingly dominant position in French Indo-China and Thailand later in 1940 lead to German access to Southeast Asian raw materials, including tungsten.[40] On the other hand, after Hitler's reshuffling of his government early in 1938, the departure of Neurath from the Foreign Office and the semi-retirement of Trautmann, there was no longer an active pro-China lobby.[41] Perhaps it was felt that recognizing Wang made little difference one way or another and would be seen by Japan as a good-will gesture. Recognizing Wang may also have been an attempt to enlist Japan (despite the neutrality pact) in Germany's war against the Soviet Union.[42] Or was recognition thought to be a gesture of appeasement to counteract Japan's tendency to desert the Axis partnership?[43] While Shanghai's thermometers registered a sweltering 95 degrees, and Spain, Rumania, Bulgaria, and Hungary rushed to follow Germany and Italy's recognition, and while diplomats were recalled from Chongqing, Berlin, and Rome by their respective governments, H. G. W. Woodhead, the popular British editorialist with a fine sense for the absurd, hoped that the Charlie Chaplin movie, "The Great Dictator," banned earlier by Chongqing, would now be shown after all.[44]

## Money, Trade, Arms, and Military Missions

The Sino-Japanese war had a major role in precipitating Germany's switch from a pro-China to a pro-Japan policy. However, the die was cast in neither 1937

**39** Sommer, *Deutschland und Japan*, p. 457, writes that Japan nonetheless hesitated in recognizing Wang's regime, still hoping to make peace with Chiang. Recognition was extended November 30, 1940.
**40** Ibid., pp. 482–485.
**41** Hjalmar Schacht, minister of the economy, resigned in November 1937 and was replaced in February 1938; that same month, Ribbentrop replaced Neurath, and Ambassador to China Trautmann went on indefinite leave.
**42** Martin, "Das Deutsche Reich," p. 367.
**43** *CP*, editorial, July 3, 1941, p. 10.
**44** *SEPM*, July 1, July 2, 1941; H.G.W. Woodhead, "As Briton Sees It," July 3, 1941, p. 7.

nor 1941, but in 1938.[45] In that year Hitler reshuffled his government and assumed full control over the armed forces and Japan was seen as the Asian ally in Germany's European expansion. It was also the year when forcing Jews out of the Reich moved into high gear (discussed below), and when confiscation of Jewish wealth and properties began at last to ease Germany's foreign currency shortages. To understand this better, let us look briefly at Chinese-German trade relations as an integral part of foreign policy.

As mentioned earlier, Chinese-German commercial relations had a considerable history, having been pursued prior to WWI as well as afterwards during the years of the Weimar Republic. German military visits and the dispatch of advisers had an important role in trade relations, starting with retired Colonel Max H. Bauer's (1875–1929) visit to China from November 1927 to March 1928 and again in November 1928. Bauer's visits were not officially sanctioned by the German Foreign Office, which looked askance at this and other visits by military men, but there was nothing it could do to prevent them.[46] The Nationalist government's attempts to acquire armaments and to build and outfit a modern army were welcomed by German industrialists,[47] who in turn were eager to rebuild Germany's shattered economy. However, after 1933 trade with China changed significantly and for the next five years became an important source in Germany's economic recovery and her efforts to rearm. Commercial relations thus paralleled political relations, as was pointed out above.

Bauer's visits to China were followed by two visits by General Hans von Seeckt in the summer of 1933 and again in 1934–35. A career soldier, von Seeckt was the architect of Germany's post-war army (Reichswehr) and he and Chiang Kai-shek got along well.[48] Whether by chance or design, von Seeckt's arrival in China in May 1933 coincided with Chiang Kai-shek's determination to launch his fifth and final campaign against the Communists entrenched in

---

**45** For the importance of that year in modern Jewish history, see Joseph Tennenbaum, "The Crucial Year 1938," *Yad Vashem Studies*, no. 2 (1958), pp. 49–77.

**46** John P. Fox, *Germany and the Far Eastern Crisis 1931–1938, A Study in Diplomacy and Ideology*, Oxford: Clarendon Press, 1982, reprint 1985, pp. 15–16.

**47** Martin, "Das Deutsche Militär," p. 192. Bauer's visits are discussed in some detail by Ratenhof, *Die Chinapolitik*, pp. 373–377.

**48** The German military establishment pursued similar interests in mineral-rich Guangdong (Kuangtung) province, which until mid-1936, was not controlled by Chiang's Nanjing government. Indeed, von Seeckt who, despite negotiating with Nanjing also kept his eye on the southern province, considered China as "Germany's only escape from its raw material plight." For Foreign Office fears that negotiations with the Guangdong generals would interfere with Nanjing negotiations, see Ratenhof, *Die Chinapolitik*, p. 427.

Jiangxi (Kiangsi) province.[49] In fact, von Seeckt had journeyed to Guling where Chiang had taken personal charge of the preparations.[50] No doubt, the two men at the time discussed the secret treaty they would sign the following year, in August 1934, which included provisions for supplying Germany with tungsten. To assure von Seeckt of an unimpeded supply from the Xihua (Hsi-hua) mountains mine in Jiangxi province, prudence might have dictated the urgent removal of the Communist base areas from their relative proximity to the mine.[51]

Be that as it may, it was during von Seeckt's second visit that a treaty was signed and major steps were taken to modernize Chiang's army by using German advisers, and to lay the foundation for a military-industrial partnership whereby Germany delivered weapons, industrial installations, and railway equipment in exchange for raw materials, especially tungsten, which was indispensable for steel production.[52] General Alexander von Falkenhausen (1878–1966) who succeeded von Seeckt and became Chiang's adviser in 1935 continued the work begun by von Seeckt until the outbreak of the Sino-Japanese war. Clearly, however, Germany, which by the summer of 1937 was increasingly trying to draw Japan into an alliance, could not continue supplying arms and advisers to the Nationalist government in its "undeclared war" against Japan. After mid-1937, therefore, the political unraveling described above was accompanied by Germany's economic retreat and finally by the withdrawal of the military advisers in mid-1938.

Before examining some of these points in greater detail, it should be pointed out that not only Germany, but Italy too was actively engaged in contributing to Chiang's rearmament effort by supplying planes and parts together with the dispatch of aviation missions to train Chinese fighter pilots.[53] But like

---

**49** Four campaigns between 1930 and 1932 had for various reasons ended in failure. See Keiji Furuya, Chung-ming Chang, *Chiang Kai-shek, His Life and Times,* New York: St. John's University, 1981, pp. 384–385, abridged English edition.

**50** Spence, *Search for Modern China*, p. 400.

**51** Approximately 60 % of the world tungsten supply was in Jiangxi and Guangdong, with Xihua Mountain close to the Hunan province border and the railway line to Guangzhou (Canton). Several of the base areas (Ruijin, Yudu, for example) were located in an approximately 100–150 km. radius from the Xihua range. My measurements are, however, highly approximate. For details of the base area locations, see Furuya, *Chiang Kai-shek*, pp. 381, 382, 419.

**52** Pao-jen Fu, "The German Military Mission in Nanking 1928–1938, a Bridge Connecting China and Germany," Ph.D. Dissertation, Syracuse University, 1989, pp. 109–127.

**53** Frey, *Faschistische Fernostpolitik,* pp. 85–105, 173.

in the German case, the political turnabout was accompanied by the economic one, although the Italians terminated their trade relations more abruptly. The Italian advisers left in December 1937, and weapons deliveries destined for China, which were already on the high seas in September, were turned over to the Japanese.[54] Italy's trade in war materials with China, like Germany's, lasted no more than five years.

Taking now a closer look at German and Chinese trade, the first significant point is the foreign currency shortage experienced by the Nazi regime. Just how crucial the foreign currency question was surfaced, for example, in a Foreign Office report of August 1938 sent to the Qingdao (Tsingtao) consulate, which stressed that Jewish capital transfers abroad must be forbidden "from economic considerations of our foreign currency interests."[55] Avraham Barkai has argued that a more aggressive export policy by Germany would have alleviated the problem, and German industrialists certainly supported more exports to offset the expense of consumer imports.[56] Others have argued, however, that a more aggressive export policy would not have solved the foreign currency crisis evident since 1934. Even hopes for weapons exports, permitted since November 1935, were exaggerated. Armaments were merely 1% of Germany's total exports and earned little foreign currency.[57]

In view of these general considerations, how important in fact were exports to China? In 1937, the year that exports to China were at their all-time high,[58] they brought in 82,788,600 RM. Moreover, 37% of Germany's total armament exports went to China, which meant that China was Germany's major weapons buyer.[59] Aside from arms, a number of large industries, like IG Farben, Krupp, Siemens, and Daimler-Benz, were doing business in China; there were several railroad projects; entire factories were shipped to China and steel and chemical industries made investments. In part, these German exports were

---

**54** Ibid., pp. 263–264.

**55** YVA, J4 JM57, Foreign Office, Berlin, August 13, 1938, p. 7. This document is a long report on the Evian conference.

**56** Avraham Barkai, *Das Wirtschaftssystem des Nationalsozialismus, Ideologie, Theorie, Politik 1933–1945*, Frankfurt/Main: Fischer Taschenbuch Verlag, 1988, pp. 164–165.

**57** Willi A. Boelcke, *Die deutsche Wirtschaft, 1930–1945*, Düsseldorf: Droste Verlag, 1983, pp. 100, 109.

**58** Ratenhof, *Die Chinapolitik*, table, p. 562.

**59** Karl Drechsler, *Deutschland–China–Japan 1933–1939, das Dilemma der deutschen Fernostpolitik*, Berlin: Akademie Verlag, 1964, p. 52; Bernd Martin, "Das deutsche Reich und Guomindang-China, 1927–1941," in Kuo Heng-yu, ed., *Von der Kolonialpolitik zur Korporation, Studien zur Geschichte der Deutsch-Chinesischen Beziehungen*, Munich: Minerva Publikation, 1986, p. 359.

paid for by the Chinese with foreign currency;[60] in part they came under a "barter agreement," concluded in 1936, whereby raw materials were exported to Germany. Most important among these was tungsten, of which in 1937 Germany imported 72%, or nearly all of China's exports.[61] Whereas barter agreements did not alleviate foreign currency shortages, at least by 1937 German exports exceeded imports. And, we should remember that even if Manchukuo did not provide Germany with larger soy imports, as discussed earlier, the barter agreement with the puppet state did not excessively drain foreign currency reserves either.[62] But in 1938 Germany discovered another solution to its foreign currency shortages: forced emigration and confiscation of Jewish property, with assets remaining in Germany.[63]

Despite some arguments to the contrary, the China trade was important to German industrialists and to the military establishment, especially after the initiation of Hermann Göring's Four-Year Plan of rearmament in 1936. The China trade, therefore, together with maintaining strong political ties to the Nationalist government in Nanjing were firmly supported by the Foreign Office. Although the topic of the Chinese destination for Jewish emigration will be taken up later, we might note here that when it was first mentioned in 1936, both the Foreign Office and the industrialists' interests may have had a role in the suggestion not being taken up at the time.[64] Political and especially economic considerations apparently still predominated. Nonetheless, 1938, a year after the outbreak of the Sino-Japanese war, was the turning point. The rela-

---

60 Ratenhof, *Die Chinapolitik*, pp. 420–421.
61 Martin, "Das Deutsche Reich," p. 359. Between 1936 and 1938, German tungsten imports had nearly quadrupled. See H. G. W. Woodhead, ed., *The China Yearbook 1939*, Shanghai: China Daily News, 1939, p. 64. The complex maneuvers in Guangdong by Hans Klein and HAPRO (Handelsgesellschaft für industrielle Produkte), of which he was director, need not concern us here. Suffice it to say that by 1936 HAPRO came under army control and the competition between Klein and the army ended. By 1936 also Jiangxi province, with reputedly the largest tungsten mine, had come under Chiang Kai-shek's control. Both events guaranteed the unimpeded flow of tungsten to the German army even after Germany had turned to Japan. 500 tons were still delivered in 1940 to Germany. See Ratenhof, *Die Chinapolitik*, pp. 445, 522
62 "German-Manchu Trade Accord Concluded," *NCH*, July 27, 1938, p. 153. However, German imports from Manchukuo continued to exceed her exports. See "Reich Manchukuo' Trade Ends Year Favorably for Puppets," *CP*, August 7, 1939, p. 7.
63 Barkai, *Das Wirtschaftssystem*, pp. 177, 211–213, See also YVA, J4 JM57, Foreign Office, Berlin, August 13, 1938 to the German consulate in Qingdao, p. 7.
64 "Report by Oberscharführer Hagen on Jewish Emigration, September 13, 1936," in John Mendelsohn, ed., *The Holocaust, Selected Documents in Eighteen Volumes*, New York–London: Garland, 1982, Vol. 5, pp. 40–57. Hagen was head of the SD.

tionship with China was terminated in favor of Japan and the major figures who had championed a pro-China policy were dismissed. Military shipments to China were ordered stopped in April 1938, and the military advisers were recalled in May. Meanwhile, the Nazi regime created new realities in Europe when the German army marched into Austria and into parts of Czechoslovakia in March 1938; when the first Austrian refugees were preparing to leave with no more than 20 RM in their pockets,[65] and when Kristallnacht (the Night of Broken Glass) was only six months hence. Once thousands of Austrian and German refugees started arriving in Shanghai, Japan, now Germany's East Asian partner rather than China, had to decide how to deal with this massive Jewish influx expelled by its none too trustworthy ally.

Ending military shipments to China meant foreign currency losses as well as abandoning a relatively lucrative market for German goods. On the other hand, by 1938 foreign currency losses were to some extent offset by foreign currency gains from confiscations of Jewish assets. Moreover, toward the end of 1937 those engaged in the China trade may have been persuaded that Japan was winning the war in China and that soon Germany would have new markets in Japanese-occupied territories. To these might be added Barkai's suggestion that economic considerations were, in any event, subordinated to ideological ones and that German foreign trade and foreign currency management were dictated by politics.[66]

## Forced Emigration

By the end of 1938 both the policy and the institutional basis for the forced emigration of Jews came into being. The annexation (Anschluss) of Austria to Germany was complete March 13, 1938. Three days later, March 16, Adolf Eichmann (1906–1962) arrived in Vienna, and soon thereafter set about creating what came to be known as the Central Office for Jewish Emigration (Zentralstelle für jüdische Auswanderung), which began to function in August 1938. On May 8, he had already written to Herbert Hagen (1913–1999), director of the Jewish Section of the SD, that the reorganized Jewish community organizations in Austria work toward the aim of emigration.[67] Eichmann did not exag-

---

**65** The first fifteen arrived on the Conte Biancamano in Shanghai on August 15, 1938, *IM*, 32, no. 6 (September 1938), p. 6.

**66** Barkai, *Das Wirtschaftssystem*, pp. 198–109, 170–171.

**67** Yitzhak Arad, Yisrael Gutman, Abraham Margaliot, eds., *Documents on the Holocaust*, Jerusalem: Yad Vashem, 1981, pp. 94–95, document no. 44.

gerate. The brutal persecution of Austrian Jews, aided by the successful anti-Semitic mobilization of the population; the "Aryanization," that is the expropriation of business enterprises; the confiscation of dwellings owned by Jews and their virtual pauperization within the short period of six to seven months, induced many to flee to more hospitable parts. Presumably 50.000 Austrian Jews had been forced to emigrate by October 1938.[68]

The Évian conference of July 1938, called by President Roosevelt to mobilize international support to solve the refugee crisis, further strengthened the conviction of the Nazis that the Jews must be expelled one way or another from Germany and Austria while revealing to Jews the hopelessness of their situation.[69] The United States was not prepared to increase quotas for German and Austrian Jews, but nearly all the countries present were unwilling to admit Jewish refugees without means. The Intergovernmental Committee, appointed subsequently to deal with ways and means of resettling refugees, neither offered hope nor led to concrete results. Emil Schumburg's report to Germany's foreign representations considered that the Évian conference had failed because it had not solved the two major problems of how to systematize emigration and its destination.[70]

Two events in the autumn of 1938 contributed significantly to making forced emigration a reality: the expulsion of Polish Jews from Germany to Po-

---

68 Herbert Rosenkranz, *Reichskristallnacht, 9 November 1938 in Österreich*, Vienna: Europa Verlag, 1968, pp. 13, 24–26; Gerhard Botz, "The Jews of Vienna from the Anschluss to the Holocaust," in Ivar Oxaal, Michael Pollak, Gerhard Botz, eds., *Jews, Anti-Semitism and Culture in Vienna*, London–New York: Routledge and Kegan Paul, 1987, pp. 185–204.

69 President Roosevelt had invited representatives from thirty-eight countries to Évian-les Baines. The countries represented included Australia, France, Great Britain, Canada, and Sweden, as well as South and Central American countries. The conference, which met from July 6 to July 15, was also attended by around three dozen Jewish organizations. For an extensive summary of the conference and the negotiations that followed, see Henry L. Feingold, *The Politics of Rescue, The Roosevelt Administration and the Holocaust, 1938–1945*, New Brunswick, N.J.: Rutgers University Press, 1970, pp. 22–68. For a recent evaluation of the conference, see "Der Fehlschlag von Evian," *Süddeutsche Zeitung*, no. 134 (June 14, 2005), p. 14. I thank Knut Walf for bringing this article to my attention.

70 YVA, JM 4857, from Schumburg, the Foreign Office to all diplomatic and consular representatives abroad, January 25, 1939, 14 pp. Schumburg coordinated all incoming secret information and by 1940 coordinated the entire Jewish policy of the Foreign Office. In the Foreign Office he was considered the representative of the SS and of RSHA. See Hans-Jürgen Döscher, *Das Auswärtige Amt im Dritten Reich, Diplomatie im Schatten der "Endlösung"* Berlin: Siedler Verlag, 1987, p. 131.

land on October 27 and 28, and Kristallnacht on November 9. The former revealed the ease with which Jews could be rounded up and in coordinated moves expelled. As pointed out by Trude Maurer, "It was the first large-scale deportation requiring coordination between the police, the Reichsbahn railway, diplomats, and financial authorities."[71] The latter confirmed the correctness of Eichmann's procedures in Vienna and that similar measures would have to be instituted in Germany itself, according to discussions held on November 12 under the chairmanship of Hermann Göring.[72] This was reiterated more forcefully in a Foreign Office circular of January 25, 1939, stating that Germany's Jewish policy was a "condition and consequence of foreign policy decisions in 1938;" that the aim was emigration, and the "means, ways, and destinations of Jewish emigration" would have to be developed.[73] Meanwhile, as was done in Austria and in the aftermath of Kristallnacht, Jews were systematically eliminated from the German economy, thus deprived of their means of livelihood,[74] and many Jewish men were arrested and incarcerated in concentration camps. Release could be obtained by producing evidence of speedy departure from Austria or Germany, in accordance with a directive by Reinhard Heydrich (1904–1942) which stipulated that a detainee had to be in possession of emigration papers.[75] One such victim, Howard (Horst) Levin, was arrested November 10, 1938 by the Berlin Gestapo when he sought to rescue his father who had been arrested earlier in the day. Howard was sent to Sachsenhausen concentration camp, but was released two months later when his sister showed the Gestapo a paid-up booking for Shanghai on the *Biancamano*.[76]

Meanwhile, the German machinery for forced emigration was gradually created. Prior to Hitler's assumption of power in January 1933 no single Jewish organization in Germany could speak for the various Jewish communities. Not

---

71 Trude Maurer, "The Background of Kristallnacht: The Expulsion of Polish Jews," in Walter Pehle, ed., *November 1938, from 'Reichskristallnacht' to Genocide*, New York: St. Martin's Press, 1991, p. 70. See also Rolf Vogel, *Ein Stempel hat gefehlt, Dokumente zur Emigration deutscher Juden*, München–Zürich: Droemer Knaur, 1977, p. 65.

72 Arad, *Documents on the Holocaust*, pp. 108–115, document no. 51.

73 Ibid., p. 126, document no. 58.

74 Ibid., pp. 115–116, document no. 52.

75 Copy of letter signed by Heydrich, January 31, 1939, in Mendelsohn, *The Holocaust*, Vol. 6, pp. 202–203.

76 YVA, 078/72, Eber interview with Howard Levin, Jerusalem, October 14, 1988, pp. 1–8. In Vienna, similarly, the engineer Hugo Dubsky sought his release from Dachau with a visa from the Chinese consulate in Amsterdam, and Siegfried Cohen claimed to have visas for his two sons from the Chinese Consulate General in Vienna. CAHJP, A/W2689, 4, letter to the Vienna Kultusgemeinde, February 16, 1939; A/W2689, 3, letter to the Vienna Kultusgemeinde, February 3, 1939.

until September 1933 was the Reich Representation of German Jews (Reichsvertretung der deutschen Juden) established and this organization was forced to
change its name after the passing of the Nuremberg Laws in September 1935
to Representation of Jews in Germany (Reichsvertretung der Juden in Deutschland). But just how representative the Representation was, in fact, is arguable
and it was challenged by other Jewish organizations.[77] The importance that the
Nazi establishment ascribed to emigration can be seen in Hermann Göring's
ordering the establishment of a Central Office for Emigration January 24, 1939,
after Kristallnacht. Reinhard Heydrich, chief of the Security Police (Sicherheits-
polizei) was to head it, and Heinrich Müller was to be the responsible manager
(Geschäftsführer). The Central Office commenced work February 11, 1939.[78] Although in February, if not earlier, a Jewish organization in place of the Reich
Representation was contemplated, the so-called Reich Association of Jews in
Germany (Reichsvereinigung der Juden in Deutschland) was not established
until July 1939.[79] By establishing the Central Office for Emigration first, it was
assumed that all Jewish emigration would be channeled through – and thus
controlled – by this office. Advice and instruction on how to go about emigrating would be available from the emigration section (Auswanderungsabteilung)
of the Reich Association. That this is not what happened and that the Nazis
never managed to control emigration will be discussed in Chapter 3.

As mentioned above, in 1936 Herbert Hagen, director of the Jewish section
of the SD from 1936 on, suggested China as one of the destinations for Jewish
emigration, claiming that a number of Jewish immigrants had already arrived
there. His suggestion was not taken up at the time, perhaps because of opposi-
tion from the Foreign Office and its pro-Chiang Kai-shek faction. Matters had
changed considerably two years later. Now it was Adolf Eichmann who, within
the context of forcing emigration, decided to vigorously pursue the China destination. Toward that end he sent Heinrich Schlie, head of the Hanseatic Travel
Office in Vienna,[80] to the Japanese and Chinese embassies to ascertain their

---

**77** Esriel Hildesheimer, *Jüdische Selbstverwaltung unter dem NS-Regime*, pp. 16–17. For
the proclamation of the Reichsvertretung's founding in September 1933, see Arad,
*Documents of the Holocaust*, pp. 57–59, document no. 21.

**78** Arad, *Documents of the Holocaust*, pp. 125–126, document no. 57; Rolf Vogel, *Ein
Stempel hat gefehlt*, p. 90.

**79** Arad, *Documents of the Holocaust*, pp. 139–143, document no. 62 and Hildesheimer,
*Jüdische Selbstverwaltung*, pp. 94–95, who remarks that it is unclear why the Gestapo
and other authorities continued to discuss plans toward the establishment of an
umbrella organization.

**80** Schlie owned another travel office in Berlin. He must have profited nicely from
Jewish emigration and prudently established a Swiss bank account. His name is on
the list of Swiss account holders published in *The Jerusalem Post*, July 25, 1997.

attitudes to Jewish emigration to China. Schlie reported to Hagen on February 17, 1939, that he had spoken to the Japanese about one week earlier:

> Generally speaking there is from the Japanese side no enthusiasm about Jewish emigration ... mainly because of many cases of Jewish immigrants making themselves available to the Chinese for spying. Other arguments that European artisans have a higher standard of living and [therefore] cannot compete with native artisans were also voiced.[81]

In a subsequent report, forwarded by Eichmann to Hagen, Schlie explained that the Japanese were also not keen about having Jewish refugees in cities other than Shanghai, claiming that matters had not sufficiently developed in them.[82] (In fact, in November 1938 Consul General Horinouchi had advised from Hsinking, the capital of Manchukuo, that Jewish refugees be prevented from leaving Shanghai for other parts of North China).[83] But, wrote Schlie, he had better luck with the Chinese. They were not opposed to bringing large numbers of Jews to Tianjin or Guangzhou – Schlie apparently did not realize that Tianjin was controlled by the Japanese and that Guangzhou had been under Japanese occupation since October 1938 – nor did the Chinese object to special refugee ships. Furthermore, Schlie was assured that Jewish refugees would receive *pro-forma* visas for illegal immigration to Palestine. The cost and bribe would be determined shortly in Berlin by the responsible chancellor in the passport office, but "absolute discretion is required. For this reason negotiations should take place between him [Schlie] and ... the chancellor under four eyes."[84] Apparently this offer was not taken up by Schlie.

At the same time, the Foreign Office sent a rather curious inquiry to the Central Office urging it to decide clearly about whether to support Jewish immi-

---

**81** YVA, 051/oSo/41, Schlie to Hagen, February 17, 1939.

**82** In a follow-up letter to the Japanese embassy Schlie reiterated that it would be a catastrophe for Shanghai and the immigrants if all came to the metropolis. Therefore, it would be best if they went to other places as well. Jews, moreover, he generously conceded, would be valuable for contributing to the rejuvenation of the economy in war-devastated areas. YVA, 051/OSO/41, copy of letter Schlie sent to the Japanese embassy, February 17, 1939.

**83** JFM microfilm Series S, reel 413, frame 771, Horinouchi to Foreign Minister Arita, November 26, 1938.

**84** YVA, 051/oSO/41, Report from Schlie, forwarded by Eichmann to Hagen, March 5, 1939. YVA, 051/oSo/41, Eichmann to Hagen, June 2, 1939, telegram, Eichmann added to Schlie's report that anyone with a German passport, no matter what his race or religion, can come to Shanghai. Eichmann, moreover, was clearly aware, and stated so, that the Chinese cannot stop immigration "because the Japanese sit in all Chinese ports."

gration to China. This must be decided, stated the inquiry, because, according to the Foreign Office's views, continued immigration could lead to the loss of the Chinese market. What is odd about this inquiry is that by the end of May, when the letter was sent, commercial relations with China had for all practical purposes ceased already a year.[85] Perhaps this missive reflects, as Dalia Ofer, remarks, the Security Service (Sicherheitsdienst) of the SS's attempts to expel Jews, not caring where they went, whereas the proponents of emigration in the Foreign Office considered the Jews' final destination of foremost importance.[86]

Being obviously aware of the limitations of shipping space (to be discussed later) Schlie paid a visit in June to Director Zar in charge of Italian shipping lines. Schlie's aim was to persuade Zar to take on additional Jewish passengers by converting accommodations on every ship sailing for Shanghai. Zar agreed that as many as two hundred per ship could be accommodated; however, Germany would first have to deal with its large debt to the Italian account.[87]

Even if Schlie's hopes to enlist more extensive Italian aid did not materialize, he did manage to charter a German merchant ship, the *Usaramo*, for exclusive Jewish use from the Deutsch-Ostafrika line. The ship arrived in Shanghai on June 29, 1939.[88] Both Schlie and Eichmann intended to follow up the *Usaramo* success with further chartered ships, capable of transporting 1.000 to 1.500 Jews. But here they encountered a major problem: foreign ships could not be chartered for Reichsmark, requiring payment in foreign currency. German ships, in turn, used imported fuel oil which also had to be paid for with foreign currency.[89] Schlie commented, "The North-German Lloyd was prepared to furnish one or two of its large ships for Jew transports to Shanghai. But the project failed because we could not raise the sum of 250.000 RM in foreign currency for the necessary fuel."[90] Clearly, Germany was not about to use its

---

85  YVA, 051/0So/41, Vermerk, Berlin, May 31, 1939.

86  Dalia Ofer, *Escaping the Holocaust, Illegal Immigration to the Land of Israel, 1939–1944*, New York: Oxford University Press, 1990, pp. 98–99.

87  YVA, 051/OSO/41, Schlie to Hagen, June 2, 1939.

88  *CP*, June 28, 1939, p. 2. According to the *China Press*, the Usaramo landed 339 passengers. According to SMP, D5422 (c), reel 18, Police Reports on Ship Arrivals, January–July 1939, 459 passengers landed. The Usaramo presumably had a capacity of 250 passengers in all classes, and usually carried 126 ship personnel. See Claus Rothke, *Deutsche Ozean-Passagierschiffe, 1919 bis 1985,* Berlin: Steiger, 1987, p. 47. Whether the Usaramo carried 339 or 459 passengers, there is no question that the ship was crowded beyond capacity. The *IM*'s report of May 1939 that three German vessels had been chartered to transport Jewish refugees is apparently erroneous. "Four Hundred Emigres Arrive Here Eve of Passover," *IM*, Vol. 36, no. 2 (May 5, 1939), p. 10.

89  YVA, 051/OSO/41, signature illegible, Vermerk from II 112, July 14, 1939.

90  YVA, 051/OSO/41, Schlie to Hagen, July 7, 1939.

scarce foreign currency reserves on behalf of Jews and, in the end, the *Usaramo* would be the only chartered ship transporting them to the safety of Shanghai.

Without knowing any of the details, Ernst Pollak wrote regretfully in 1940, "If double, triple, as many ships would have sailed, double and triple as many people would have come."[91] Neither Eichmann, Hagen, nor Schlie were interested in saving Jewish lives. To them, what mattered was carrying out Göhring's policy of forced emigration. That forced emigration was one way of saving lives was apprently not understood by the Jewish leadership abroad.[92] Nor was Shanghai considered by many a suitable place for Central European Jews. And Norman Bentwich of the British Council for German Jewry wrote, for example, that in 1938 German Jews were "dumped" in Shanghai.[93] But where else could Jewish refugees go in 1938 and 1939? Were there other destinations in Asia aside from Shanghai that were considered more favorable?

## Alternative Destinations: Manchukuo, the Philippines, Yunnan

Aside from the legal and illegal emigration to Palestine, described by Dalia Ofer in *Escaping the Holocaust*, a variety of schemes and plans were proposed for Jewish emigrants. Among these, a Jewish reservation was contemplated in Madagascar and was especially championed by the Nazis following the invasion of France.[94] Like Angola or British Guiana, Madagascar never materialized. More successful destinations were the Dominican Republic and Bolivia,[95] and

---

**91** Ernst Pollak, "Menschen die uns halfen," *Shanghai Jewish Chronicle*, special number, March 1940, p. 6.

**92** Instead of considering Japan as a life saving destination, Baerwald of the JDC suggested as late as October 1940 that Jews not be booked on Japan lines. They "were better off in Germany for the time being, than they would be in Japan." JDC, RG 33–44, File 59, "Meeting of the JDC Administration Committee," October 9, 1940.

**93** Norman Bentwich, *Wanderer Between Two Worlds*, London: Kegan Paul, Trench, Trubner and Co., Ltd., 1941, p. 278.

**94** For example, Philip Friedman, Ada J. Friedman, ed., *Roads to Extinction, Essays on the Holocaust*, New York–Philadelphia: The Jewish Publication Society of America, 1980, pp. 44–52; Hildesheimer, *Jüdische Selbstverwaltung*, pp. 185–192, and Christopher R. Browning, *Nazi Policy, Jewish Workers, German Killers*, Cambridge: Cambridge University Press, 2000, pp. 15–19.

**95** See Leo Spitzer, *Hotel Bolivia, The Culture of Memory in a Refuge from Nazism*, New York: Hill and Wang, 1998, p. 203, n. 2. Spitzer estimates that perhaps as many as 20.000 refugees arrived in Bolivia, a figure that he bases on a tally of immigrant tally

Martinique. Not exclusively meant for Jews, but for anti-Nazi intellectuals and artists, six ships landed on the island in early 1941. Significantly, in these and other cases, expulsion amounted to rescue, as Eric Jennings remarks.[96]

Several destinations in Asia were considered and among these only one, the Philippines, was moderately successful. Questions about Siam (Thailand) were raised, but nothing came of them.[97] In Shanghai, whether Manchukuo could be considered was explored with the Japanese Vice-Minister of Foreign Affairs as early as 1933, but the idea was abandoned the following year. Individuals could settle in Japan's recent acquisition, Mamoru Shigemitsu presumably replied, but a large-scale emigration was at present out of the question. When next the issue of 50.000 German refugees was raised with the Foreign Office in Tokyo, the answer was similarly negative.[98] James McDonald, Special High Commissioner of the League of Nations, moreover, indicated that the League could hardly approve settling refugees in a country conquered by Japan.[99]

Nonetheless, by November 1934, eight German Jewish physicians had opened practices in Harbin and by 1935 there were seventeen German refugees in Manchukuo.[100] Yet the Manchukuo consulates in European cities, like Rome, Berlin, or Hamburg, did not pursue a consistent policy. Visas might be ob-

---

sheets. But he adds that accurate figures are difficult to come by, and estimates vary widely.

**96** Eric Jennings, "Last Exit from Vichy France: The Martinique Escape Route and the Ambiguities of Emigration," *The Journal of Modern History*, Vol. 74, no. 2 (June 2002), pp. 289–324.

**97** YIVO, HIAS-HICEM, MKM 15.57, file D-1, May 26, 1939, memorandum on conditions in Thailand; file D-3, from James Bernstein, January 3, 1939 and January 23, 1939, in French about Thailand.

**98** "Dr. Yotaro Sugimura Discusses World Jewish Problems," *IM*, November 3, 1933, p. 9. The issue of settling 50.000 Jews in Manchukuo was raised peripherally as part of an interview with Sugimura who was unofficially in Shanghai, and "Manchukuo Fades as Centre of German-Jewish Settlement," *IM*, Vol. 31, no. 7, October 5, 1934, p. 8.

**99** "Manchukuo Fades as Centre of German Jewish Settlement," *IM*, Vol. 31, no. 7, October 5, 1934, p. 8.

**100** CAHJP, DAL 53, from Froomkin, Harbin, to Dr. Lurje, Frankfurt/Main, November 22, 1934, and, "Refugees from Germany Go to the Far East," *IM*, Vol. 33, no. 3 (June 5, 1936), p. 10. It would seem, however, that the Japanese presence in Manchuria prevented HIAS, Harbin, from making concerted efforts to settle refugees in Manchukuo. A sheaf of letters from DALJEWCIB, Harbin, written in September and November 1935 to various Jewish organizations in Hong Kong and Shanghai attest to the fact that Meir Birman and others were trying to settle refugees in Chinese cities rather than in Manchukuo, CAHJP, DAL 57 and DAL 52.

tained at one, while none were issued at another, even though the official policy presumably was that a visa could be issued upon evidence of a work contract, and there was no official prohibition on immigration into Manchukuo. For example, a Dr. Goldhammer arrived with a visa from Rome and was already working in January 1939, and another family received their visa in Hamburg.[101] Apparently there were also cases of Manchukuo visas being issued without special difficulties in Dalien (Dairen), if the person had a work invitation.[102] Clearly however, Manchukuo could not be counted on as a destination for large-scale Jewish immigration and, as reported in the *Shanghai Times*, Manchukuo "does not welcome Jewish mass immigration. Still, it will not discriminate against Jews due to their race or creed, even if Jewish immigrants may infringe on Japanese interests due to their "peculiar commercial ingenuity."[103] Also, in 1940 and 1941 the Jewish agencies both in Shanghai and in Europe were more concerned procuring Manchukuo transit visas rather than visas to the puppet state. Despite these difficulties, Lew Zikman, a Polish Jew and resident of Qiqihar (Tsitsihar), was persuaded in 1938 or 1939 to try to interest the Manchukuo authorities in settling 200 Jewish refugee families that were already in China. He suggested they establish a leather goods manufacturing plant with US money. Zikman would donate the land and an unfinished brick structure for that purpose.[104] Unfortunately, it is impossible to say how many Central European refugees eventually found a sanctuary in Manchukuo.

Although it is similarly impossible to say with any degree of accuracy how many refugees arrived in the Philippines, the case of the islands is quite different. In 1939, the Philippine islands were not an independent, sovereign state. Ceded to the United States in the Spanish-American War of 1898, they had become the Philippine Commonwealth under the Tydings-McDuffie Act of 1934, which stipulated that the U.S. would withdraw from it in 1945, at which time it would become the Republic of the Philippines. WWII intervened, however, and the islands were occupied by the Japanese in December 1941. Meanwhile,

---

**101** CAHJP, 76.1, Hilfsverein, Berlin to DALJEWCIB, Harbin, signed by Dr. Arnold Israel Horwitz, May 11, 1939; DAL 76, Birman to Swedish Mission, Mission Station, Vienna, January 26, 1939; DAL 76, DALJEWCIB to Vienna Emigration Section, signed Birman, January 25, 1939.

**102** CAHJP, 76.1, from DALJEWCIB to Hilfsverein, February 18, 1939. See also CAHJP, 86.2, Memorandum from CAEJR to Far Eastern Jewish Central Information Bureau, Harbin, September 7, 1939 with a cable from the Dairen Hebrew Society, "Abstain from sending here refugees destination Harbin, Tientsin."

**103** "Jewish Influx Being Studied by Japanese," *Shanghai Times*, May 24, 1939.

**104** Japan FM, reel 414, frames 1158–1160, from Lew Zikman to?. The first page of this document is missing.

in 1935, Manuel Quezon was elected the first president of the Philippine Commonwealth, and the islands received its first U.S. high commissioner.

Jews had arrived in the Philippines during the period of Spanish rule, but an actual community did not come into being until after WWI, when the Temple Emil Congregation was formally incorporated and when a synagogue was constructed in Manila in 1924. A Jewish Refugee Committee was established in 1937 and a rabbi and cantor were hired from among the German refugees, who began arriving at the end of the 1930s.[105] There was some interest in supporting immigration to the Philippines, as there was "no direct law" forbidding it, which presumably depended on the American consul in Manila, and it was especially tempting because after five years residence a person could immigrate to the U.S. without coming under a quota.[106] Accordingly, in January 1937, information on the Philippines was sent to Paris which estimated the Jewish community at perhaps 800–1000 people of various nationalities: American, French, Baghdadi, Dutch, German, British, and Eastern European.[107] By July 1938, forty-some families had made their way to the Philippines on their own initiative, and plans were under way to allow 200 families to settle.[108]

IIere, however, problems developed. Although the high commissioner was informed by Washington that "victims of German and Austria anti-Semitism" were to be admitted, a meeting at Temple Emil in Manila decided that at first only one hundred families were to be allowed to come, and these should be professionals. Visas were to be obtained in Washington upon presentation of a letter of invitation from a permanent Philippine resident.[109] But apparently the initiative to have one hundred families come was not that of the Manila community. It had been proposed by High Commissioner, P. V. McNutt, at whose request "these assimilated American and foreign Jews assembled to discuss this problem of immigration of refugees."[110] It is difficult to know whether

---

**105**  John W. Griese, "The Jewish Community in Manila," MA thesis, University of the Philippines, 1955, pp. 25–27.
**106**  YIVO, HIAS-HICEM, I, MKM 15.57, file XV, D-1, Shapiro, Manila to Birman, Harbin, December 24, 1936.
**107**  YIVO, Ibid., from Birman to HICEM, Paris, January 15, 1937.
**108**  YIVO, Ibid., from HIAS, New York to HICEM, Paris, July 19, 1938.
**109**  YIVO, Ibid., From Birman, Harbin to P.S. Frieder, Temple Emil Congregation, Manila, July 5, 1938.
**110**  YIVO, Ibid., from Philippine Islands to HICEM, Paris, July 8, 1938. Twenty physicians, twenty-five nurses, and five dentists were selected who were to arrive in three groups. According to CAHJP, 76.1, Horwitz to DALJEWCIB, December 24, 1938, forty-two persons altogether were approved. See also YIVO, Ibid., James Bernstein, Paris to HIAS, New York, September 6, 1938, who writes that McNutt acted on the personal advice of President Roosevelt.

the high commissioner or the Manila Jews was to blame for the indifferent attitude to the refugee crisis. Meir Birman in Harbin commented that not a single letter of invitation was received from the Philippines, concluding that Jews live there wealthy and happy, without worry, far from the troubles across the ocean. The Philippine Jews "do not feel" that they want to care for the Nazi victims.[111] Later in fall, Layzer Epstein commented that the Manila Refugee Committee did not want to invite too many Jews "as they are under the impression that it may affect their own status."[112]

Nor was there sufficient encouragement from abroad. The Assistant Secretary of the Refugee Economic Corporation Bruno Schachner's insistence that people be selected for the Philippines was counterproductive when saving people's lives was the issue.[113] Moreover, President Manuel Quezon's offer in February 1939 to resettle 10.000 Jewish refugees on the islands of Mindanao or Polillo came too late and may have been half-hearted. Possibly, Quezon's offer was the reason why the Germans evinced some interest in the Philippine option, though they indicated that a large Jewish emigration might endanger the local economy.[114] The German Consulate General in Shanghai gleefully indicated that, despite American negotiations in Manila, Philippine leaders fear that the Jews will not take to agriculture, but instead will monopolize coffee and rubber production as well as buy up land and become landowners.[115] In the end, only 750–900 Jewish refugees may have arrived in the Philippines.[116]

The influx of large numbers of Jewish refugees into Shanghai was also seen as inherently unproductive and possibly dangerous by the Chinese Nationalist authorities who, it will be remembered were, however, no longer in control of the city in 1939. A plan was apparently discussed in Chongqing early in 1939 to settle Jewish refugees in China's south- or northwest, Yunnan, Guizhou, Sichuan, and Xikang being mentioned.[117] Possibly as a result of these discus-

---

**111** YIVO, Ibid., Birman to Isaac L. Asofsky, July 8, 1938 (in Yiddish).

**112** YIVO, Ibid., Epstein to HIAS, October 10, 1938.

**113** YIVO, Ibid., from Bruno Schachner to HIAS-ICA Emigration Association, Paris, August 1, 1938.

**114** Quezon's plan is mentioned by Griese, "The Jewish Community of Manila," p. 28. The German response to a report from Manila is YVA, 051/oSo/41, from Reichsstelle für das Auswanderungswesen signed by Schmidt in place of Dr. Müller, March 15, 1939, with a cover letter from the Gestapo, March 31, 1939, signature illegible.

**115** YVA, JM 3/155, German Consulate General, "Judentum in Shanghai," Report to the Foreign Office, Berlin, June 30, 1940, p. 5, signature illegible.

**116** Griese, "The Jewish Community of Manila," p. 24. More research is needed to better understand the Philippine option and its failure.

**117** "China Plans Special Area for Emigres," CP, March 1, 1939. Holington K. Tong, vice-minister of propaganda in Chongqing, sent a cable to that effect to Speelman.

sions, Mr. Dijour, secretary of the HIAS bureau in Paris, went to see Chinese Consul General Huang Tianmai on April 22, 1939. According to Dijour's report of the conversation, which lasted more than two hours, Huang told him that he had taken the initiative of proposing to Chiang Kai-shek a concrete plan for organizing immigration to China. Specialists such as doctors, mining engineers, architects, and capitalists who would create industries or exploit mines came under consideration. Huang mentioned Ningxia and Qinghai provinces in China's northwest and Xikang province in the south.[118] Significantly, Dijour reported that the Chinese offer was not made solely for altruistic reasons:

> The Consul General admitted to me that besides the purely practical considerations which prompted the Chinese authorities to make us such proposals, they also expected to be able to interest the influential Jewish centers of the democratic countries and the United States to the lot of China, who, as a victim of Japanese totalitarianism, has the right to expect the sympathy from the democratic countries.

The Jews, Huang argued in conclusion, would make a large contribution to the reconstruction of China once there was peace.[119]

Nothing came of Huang's proposal. And upon closer examination, it was neither particularly generous nor did it sufficiently consider the kind of immigrants who would be coming to China. Ningxia, Xikang, and Qinghai were established as provinces only in 1928, when the Nationalist government assumed power in Nanjing. Qinghai and Xikang are mountainous borderlands at the ascent to Tibet with sparse populations and Ningxia is part of Inner Mongolia. Qinghai was then and still is an arid region of deserts, grazing lands, and severe cold. There was little irrigated land, and even in 1949 the area lacked major roads.[120] Huang's proposal may have reflected (as had the earlier notice in the *China Press*, mentioned above) discussions that were held between February and May by the Nationalist government in Chongqing about resettling Jews in China, the area of settlements, and their legal status. On March 7, 1939,

---

**118** The transcription is not always clear and I was unable to identify "Houel-Chow," also mentioned by Huang, which may be Guizhou in the south.

**119** YIVO, HIAS-HICEM I, MKM, 15.57, file XV, C-4, from D.J. Bernstein to HIAS New York, April 27, 1939. English translation of report of conversation with the Chinese Consul General, Huang Tianmai, April 22, 1939. The cover letter for the English translation by Dijour emphasizes that the matter is in its very beginning.

**120** See George B. Cressey, *China's Geographic Foundations, A Survey of the Land and Its People*, New York-London: McGraw-Hill Book Co., Inc., 1934, pp. 53, 58, 268, 390, and Clifton W. Pannell and Laurence J. C. Ma, *China, The Geography of Development and Modernization*, New York: John Wiley and Sons, 1983, Tables 6–1, p. 119. and 6–5, p. 135, maps, pp. 105, 120, 169.

Sun Fo (1891–1973), Sun Yat-sen's son and president of the Legislative Yuan, proposed settling Jews in the southwest border region, that is Yunnan province which was one of the regions under Nationalist control, to alleviate the "unregulated entry into Shanghai." Sun Fo said that "the Jewish people have a strong financial background and many talents," and that settling them in Yunnan province would gain a favorable attitude for China from the British and Americans. The proposal was then discussed by several ministries (Interior, Foreign Affairs, Military, Treasury, Economics, Education, and Transportation), and having passed the fifth discussion, the report was submitted by Kong Xiangxi (H.H. Kung, 1881–1967) for "official endorsement."[121] There are no further documents to show whether and in what form the resolution was ever endorsed.

A similar proposal by Jacob Berglas was probably made in response to the Chongqing deliberations, which began early in 1939, whereas Berglas's plan was first noted several months later, in May or June, but definitely after the Chongqing deliberations were concluded.[122] Berglas, a 52-year old German refugee (it is not entirely clear that he was, in fact, a refugee) in Shanghai, had been a banker and textile industrialist. He apparently had contacts with persons in Chongqing and in Yunnan and, having first visited China in 1935, had

---

**121** [Di Jin, Diane Rabinowitz and Michael Rabinowitz, trans., Bi Chunfu and Ma Chendu, eds., "A Plan to Settle Jewish Refugees in China," *Sino-Judaica Occasional Papers*, Vol. 2 (1995), pp. 67–84. The documents were published in Chinese in *Minguo dang'an shiliao* (Historical materials from the archives of the Nationalist period), Vol. 3 (1993), pp. 17–21. Courtesy of Anson Laytner and Al Dien. I read the final sentence of the Chinese document by Kong Xiangxi as submitting the resolution for "consideration" rather than for endorsement. See also Peter Merker, "Israel in Yunnan – zu den Plänen der GMD-Regierung, in Südwestchina ein jüdisches Siedlungsgebiet einzurichten," *Newsletter, Frauen in China*, no. 9 (August 1995), pp. 10–12, where Merker summarizes these documents. See also Xu Xin, "Sun Fo's Plan to Establish a Jewish Settlement in China During World War II Revealed," *Points East*, Vol. 16, no. 1 (March 2001), pp. 1, 7–8. Xu Xin introduced and translated Sun Fo's proposal only and stated that the plan was approved. See also Xun Zhou, *Chinese Perceptions of the 'Jews' and Judaism, A History of the Youtai*, Richmond: Curzon, 2001, p. 122, who states that the Nationalist government in Chongqing accepted Sun's proposal. It was not put into practice because China was at war and the government was short of funds.
**122** Ristaino, *Port of Last Resort,* pp. 117–118 assumes to the contrary that the Chinese government acted upon Berglas's plan. A Chinese version of the plan is in the Shanghai Municipal Archive and is dated May 26, 1939. It is a handwritten document, but beyond stating "Chinese Government" (Zhonghua Minguo), there is no mention of the document's provenance. It is labeled "Yizhi Zhong Ou Youtairen lai Hua zhih jihua (The Plan to Colonize China by Means of European Jews coming to China)," YVA, 075/107, 5 pp.

gone to Shanghai four times since then.[123] Bernhard Kahn, of the New York
JDC, who had several conversations with Berglas when he was in New York in
the autumn, added some further details. There were four Berglas brothers and
two sisters, but the Berglas family "is not conspicuous in social work in Germany." The Berglas's had investments abroad and a factory in England; Berglas said that he was in China "at the invitation of the Chinese government to
be their financial adviser in some activities."[124] These scanty bits of information do not tell us much about the man.

The Berglas proposal, as revealed at a press conference in Shanghai's elegant
Cathay Hotel, envisioned a planned society with a planned economy for 100.000
refugees both Jewish and "any victims of current circumstances who were without a home." He had tentatively selected Kunming with its 300.000 inhabitants
as the location for the colony which would be an extension of the city. Each immigrant would need initially three British pounds per month support but within
one to two years he would be able to establish himself in his vocation and would
be self-supporting. Funds in RM could be obtained from blocked accounts in Germany. A portion of the funds the refugees would bring along could be used for
industrial development. However, war industries would be absolutely excluded.
Berglas proposed the establishment of a cooperative bank and a transportation
company responsible for bringing immigrants from port to city, and he stressed
Kunming's favorable location; the Saigon (Vietnam, then Indo-China)-Kunming
railway is under construction, he said; about 10,000 km of highways will be
ready in 1940. The Yunnan provincial government is in favor of the plan and the
Chinese government is presently discussing it.[125]

The plan was widely commented on in Shanghai's foreign press. John Ahlers wrote in the *China Weekly Review* that Yunnan was chosen because it was
remote from hostilities and the Japanese were unlikely to invade it. Yunnan,
however, is extremely conservative and the Nationalist government is only
partly in control. General Lung Yun[126] and his conservative administration are
the chief powers in the province. Jewish refugees could not hope for special

---

**123** YVA, 078/106, "Berglas Publishes Plan for Settling 100.000 Jewish Refugees in
China," August 5, 1939, p. 305. There is no indication where the plan was published.
**124** JDC, file 458, B. Kahn, "Memorandum on Conversation with Mr. Jacob Berglas of
China," November 15, 1939.
**125** "One Hundred Thousand Jews May Find Home in China," *IM*, Vol. 36, no. 4 (July 14,
1939), p. 14; JDC, 1/033, file 458, from Berglas to JDC, Paris, June 15, 1939, 4 pp. The
last is a printed version of the plan, "Immigration to China," but consists of only two
pages with the last two pages missing.
**126** Lung Yun (1888–1962) was governor of Yunnan from 1928 to 1945, when he was
deposed.

privileges, and "Zionist experiments could [not] be carried out anywhere in China." Small groups might find a home there; doctors might be in demand, but not merchants.[127] The *North China Daily News* was in favor of settling refugees in Yunnan "irrespective of nationalist, creed or political affiliation",[128] and the *Shanghai Evening Post and Mercury* thought that "The plan does not impress as impossibly utopian."[129] But an editorial in the *China Press* considered bringing 100.000 refugees to Yunnan as extremely ambitious. Moreover, the problem of political loyalty of such a large number of people was a paramount problem.[130] *Israel's Messenger* was cautiously optimistic, but warned that the Yunnan plan was not a substitute for Zionism; it was at best a temporary expedient.[131]

The *Gelbe Post* gathered the views of a number of China experts in Shanghai on the feasibility of the plan, to which reactions were mixed with some outright negative, others non-committal and a few in favor. Thus the chief editor of the *Shanghai Times*, E. Morley, believed that the economic collapse of a colony of strangers in China's interior was inevitable, whereas the businessman, Eduard Kann, was certain that neither Jewish farmers nor workers could succeed because there was no arable land and because they could not compete with Chinese labor. The chief editor of the *Shanghai Evening Post* thought that immigrants to Yunnan would have to be selected in accordance with their abilities.[132] A thoughtful contribution by Julius R. Kaim pointed to the pleasant climate and the often spectacular scenery, but also to the problematic relationship between the Han Chinese and the native minorities. He concluded that European immigrants must always remember that they are in Inner Asia which is as remote as Tibet.[133]

There were other reactions. A Chinese businessman in Hong Kong was not only negative, but also repeated several prevalent anti-Semitic statements. He wrote that such a venture will not be profitable for China, for Jews are looking

---

**127** YVA, 078/106, John Ahlers, "The Proposal to send 100.000 German Jewish Refugees to Yunnan Province," *The China Weekly Review*, July 22, 1939, pp. 226–227.
**128** SMP, roll no. 18, D-544 (c), "100,000 Emigrants to Settle Yunnan Province," *North China Daily News*, June 21, 1939.
**129** "A New Homeland in China," *SEPM*, June 26, 1939.
**130** *CP*, August 1, 1939, p. 10.
**131** "Yunnanfu: A Refugee Haven," and "One Hundred Thousand Jews May Find a Home in China," *IM*, Vol. 36, no. 4 (July 14, 1939), pp. 14–15, and *IM*, Vol. 36, no. 5 (August 16, 1939), p. 9.
**132** *Gelbe Post*, no. 2 (May 16, 1939), pp. 27–28, and no. 3, (June 1, 1939), p. 62.
**133** Julius R. Kaim, "Neugierig auf Yunnan," *Gelbe Post*, no. 6 (end of July 1939), pp. 122–123.

for quick profit, using the money to invest in industry in Shanghai, or to purchase stocks abroad. Better to be subjugated by other nations than by Jews and, comparing Jews to bacteria, he concluded significantly that it is best not to introduce bacteria into a sick body. Once the bacteria are in the person he dies a slow and painful death. There is no medicine.[134] Yet there is also another letter, apparently from Shanghai, which considers the Berglas plan a very sensible one. Although the letter writer cannot be identified – there is no signature – he writes that he only now returned from Chongqing where he discussed the plan with Dr. Francis Liu and Director General Li. He suggests that 2,000–3,000 trucks and 500 buses be purchased for the transportation company in Germany. Half of the money for these will come from the immigrants' accounts. "I have no doubt," he concluded, "that the plan ... will be a sensational success for China and the emigration."[135]

Undaunted by the negative and hesitant reactions, Berglas next headed for New York and Washington to present his plan and to raise funds. Arriving in Vancouver in September 1939 aboard the *Empress of Canada*, he stated in an interview that he was about to organize a committee of international leaders to launch the immigrant colony. Each person would bring along about $ 250, enough for one year, after which the immigrant would become self-supporting. Still maintaining the uniqueness of a planned and cooperative society and economy, he now optimistically envisioned solving the jobless and émigré problem by providing a home for anyone regardless of creed, race, or religious belief.[136] But the New York JDC had been already forewarned in August that the Berglas scheme was "of questionable practicality."[137] As reported by Bernhard Kahn, of the New York JDC, Berglas spoke in generalities, the figure of 100.000 refugees was most certainly exaggerated since experts believe that

---

**134** YVA, 075/107, from Chen Dewen (?), Hong Kong to Liusien, May 26, 1939. The letter is in German on stationary of the Kien Gwan Co., India, Ltd., which had branches in China, Southeast Asia, and London, 8 pp. Although the signature is not entirely clear, the content of the letter indicates that it was written by a Chinese who was apparently influenced by Nazi propaganda.

**135** YVA, 075/107, to Mr. Chu Cha Chua, June 4, 1939. This letter too is in German. I have been unable to identify Drs. Cha and Francis Liu as well as director general Li.

**136** "N.Y. Committee Planning for Jewish Colony in West China," *CP*, September 22, 1939, p. 3.

**137** JDC, 1/035, file 458, from Stephen V.C. Morris, Acting Chairman, Departmental Committee on Political Refugees to George L. Warren, Executive Secretary, President's Advisory Committee on Political Refugees, August 18, 1939. The letter mentioning the cable from Shanghai was forwarded by Warren to Joseph C. Hyman of the JDC.

at most 1.000–2.000 persons could be settled, and Berglas only discussed a transportation company.[138]

Did Berglas see Edward Warburg, as he told Kahn he wanted to? Did he confer with the Chinese division at the State Department in Washington, as was his intention? We do not know, for Berglas fades from the historical record. That a small number of Jewish refugees managed to reach Yunnan is clear, however, although we know nothing about them or how long they remained there. In August 1940, for example, several people received permission from the Chinese consulate in Berlin to travel to Yunnan. Presumably there was air travel between Alma Ata and Kunming, and the refugees were to leave September 11, 1940.[139] A Max Kanner ended up in Kunming (address: POB 1600) as did Michael Nothman (address: POB 159), and Dr. Viktor Karfunkel, a physician.[140] Nonetheless, neither the ambitious Berglas plan nor, for that matter, any other plan to save lives, succeeded. Whether it was human failure or indifference, the fact is that both the Jewish and non-Jewish establishments made no response to the gravity of the human plight.

As I tried to show, the small beginnings in 1933 and the large exodus of Jewish refugees in 1938 and 1939 had wider ramifications. They included Germany's international and commercial relations with China and Japan and the creation of a unified domestic approach to the "Jewish Question." Ethnic cleansing, to be sure, was part of Nazi policy throughout the years under discussion, yet it could not be instituted as forced emigration as long as other problems had not been resolved. By no means a predetermined process, it was not obvious in, say 1934 or 1935, that Germany would forsake China in favor of Japan, or that Chiang Kai-shek would not be able to withstand the onslaught of Japan's armed might. Nor was Nazi power as monolithic in 1934 and 1935 as it would be in 1938. The events of that year – the Austrian Anschluss, the expulsion of Polish Jews from Germany, and Kristallnacht – were instrumental in making Shanghai an option for flight to safety. Unfortunately, the Jewish leadership in Europe and America, in casting about for alternative destinations, did not seem to grasp just how grave and immediate the threat to Jewry in Germany and Austria was. That the several attempts to find Asian destinations ended in failure is perhaps less surprising than that nearly 20.000 Jews found a haven in Shanghai.

---

**138** JDC, 1/037, file 458, B. Kahn, "Memorandum on Conversation with Mr. Jacob Berglas of China," November 15, 1939.

**139** CAHJP, 86.3, Birman to Reichsvereinigung, August ?, 1940.

**140** CAHJP, 99, Birman to HICEM, Marseille, August 1, 1941. Marseille asked Birman to locate Max Kanner so that he could help his ex-wife, Herta Kanner, who was incarcerated in Gurs to reach Kunming. For a brief history of the Karfunkel family, see Appendix 5.

# Chapter 3:
# "To Suffer a Martyr's Death Rather than Perish in Shanghai" or to "Die as Free Men in Shanghai"[1]

**Fig. 3:** Yuya Ching Road in the 1940s. Courtesy of H. P. Eisfelder Photography Collection (4801-4648). Now housed at Yad Vashem Archives, Jerusalem.

Until October 1939, when the Permit System was instituted (the revised system went into effect in July 1940), arrival in Shanghai by ship required no more than a valid passport, the price of a steamship ticket, and a visa from the

---

1 Statements by Dr. Julius Seligsohn and Frank Foley. Seligsohn quoted by Abraham Margaliot, "Emigration – Planung und Wirklichkeit", in Arnold Pauker, ed., *Die Juden im national-sozialistischen Deutschland, 1933–1943*, Tübingen: J. C. B. Mohr, 1986, pp. 303–316; Foley, PRO, FO 371/24079 (22652), British Consulate General, Hamburg, to British Embassy, January 10, 1939.

Chinese authorities. In the absence of passport controls at the port of entry, the latter was not always a requirement and depended on the steamship company's insistence to produce a visa before issuing tickets.

Five phases in the refugee exodus by sea, the subject of this chapter, can be distinguished. (1) The slow beginning of mostly German professionals who, deprived of their livelihood after Hitler came to power in January 1933, decided to start new lives in China. (2) Increasing numbers left after the Austrian *Anschluss* in March 1938, together with German Jews when a concerted anti-Jewish economic campaign began and when decrees, including those against professionals, were enacted.[2] (3) The actual flood of German and Austrian refugees leaving for China occurred between November 1938 and September 1939, when probably something under 20.000 refugees arrived, of whom the vast majority remained in Shanghai for the duration of WWII. (4) Smaller but still considerable numbers of refugees left Europe for China after the outbreak of war until June 1940, when Italy entered the war. (5) Flight by ship nearly ceased thereafter, and only a very small number of refugees were still able to sail from Marseilles. In this chapter I will discuss the refugee flight by sea and the difficulties which the refugees eventually encountered. The special concern will be with their reception in Shanghai by the Jewish communities, the attempts by the Shanghai Municipal Council (SMC) and the Japanese authorities to stem the influx of the destitute refugees, and the creation of the permit system.

## The Journeys

As mentioned earlier, a number of physicians had already come to China in autumn 1933. They were joined by others in 1934. Until December 1933, Jewish

---

**2** The decree against physicians dates from July 25, 1938, the decree against lawyers was enacted September 27, 1938. The addition of Sara and Israel to first names dates from August 17, 1938, and on October 5, 1938 Jews were required to turn in their passports in order to receive the large "J" (Jude) in new ones. Martin Broszat and Norbert Frei, eds., *Das Dritte Reich im Überblick, Chronik, Ereignisse, Zusammenhänge*, Munich-Zurich: Piper, 1989, pp. 246–247. See also, Saul Friedländer, *Nazi Germany and the Jews, Vol. I, The Years of Persecution, 1933–1939*, New York: HarperCollins, 1997, pp. 257–263. The "J" requirement was instituted at the request of the Swiss on October 4, who wanted to limit the influx of Jewish refugees, p. 264. See, however, also Reinhard Wolff, "Hässliches Mobiliar im schönen Volksheim, *Taz-mag* (Tageszeitung, Berlin), February 5/6, 2000, pp. 4–5, who writes that the "J" was instituted at the request of both the Swiss and Swedish. I thank Professor Wolfgang Kubin for this reference.

physicians were able to obtain visas from the Chinese embassy in Berlin upon presenting a recommendation from the German Foreign Office. Although after that date the Foreign Office no longer made such recommendations, Chinese consulates outside Germany made visas available to anyone wanting to emigrate[3], and the Witting family, for example, obtained its visa for China in London.[4] As He Fengshan (1901–1997), Consul General in Vienna in 1938, wrote in his memoir, China did not have a uniform policy toward issuing visas to Jews even in 1938. Indeed, he received instructions at the time from the Ministry of Foreign Affairs (*Waijiaopu*) not to refuse issuing visas.[5] Meanwhile, recommending Jews, or vouching for their professional competence once they had arrived, continued to trouble German consulates in China, since Jews as German citizens, apparently turned to German consulates for such documents. Even in spring 1939, the German Foreign Office still considered it necessary to send a letter to consulates and missions warning them not to recommend Jewish physicians, pharmacists and lawyers, and not to help them when they encountered difficulties. Not all the doctors, dentists and other professionals who came singly or in small groups to China after 1933, remained in Shanghai. Two partial lists show that they also went to Guangzhou (Canton), Tianjin (Tientsin), Nanjing, Central China (which may have been Wuhan) and Qingdao (Tsingtao).[6] China's interior did not hold out much promise for European medi-

---

**3** YVA, 078/83, Foreign Office, signed Oster, to German Embassy Peping (sic), June 22, 1934. The Foreign Office claimed to have written only twelve recommendations.

**4** YVA, 078/1, Annie Witting letter, May 1939, on board the "Conte Verde", p. 3.

**5** He Fengshan, *Waijiao shengya sishi nian* (My forty year diplomatic career), Hong Kong: The Chinese University Press, 1990, p. 75. Douglas Davis, "Ho Fengshan: The Chinese Oskar Schindler", *The Jerusalem Post*, February 20, 2000, p. 2, seems to have gotten matters confused when he writes that Chen Jie, ambassador to Germany, ordered He to stop issuing visas. His reason was, according to Davis, that to continue would damage Chinese relations with Germany. Chen did not present his credentials until November 16, 1938, and by then Sino-German relations were already in cold storage, a fact that Chen Jie would surely have known. It is, therefore, highly doubtful that Chen ordered He to desist.

**6** YVA, 078/83, list of physicians for whom the Foreign Office wrote recommendations, and 078/73A, attachment to Beijing report, no. 259; Bracklo, German Consulate, Jingtao to the Foreign Office, April 14, 1934. This communication concerned Dr. Rosemarie Pfeil, a dentist and married to a non-Jew, and Wolf Dubinski, a medical doctor. The three decided to settle in Qingdao after not finding anything suitable in Shanghai. See also, CAHJP, DAL 86.4, Birman to Reichsvereinigung, November 12, 1940, according to whom only ten to fifteen immigrants were able to settle in Qingdao. See, however, also the list compiled by Professor Wilhelm Matzat, according to which there were 18 families in Qingdao in 1939. Several single people still arrived in 1940 and 1941. Personal communication to Avraham Altman.

cal practitioners, however, and Dr. Richard Mayer, who was active at the Guangxi Provincial Medical College (*Guangxi xian li yixueyuan*) in Nanning, would have been among a mere handful in such far flung regions.[7] Most seem to have remained in Shanghai, however, and a later account mentions eighty refugee physicians, surgeons and dentists, who had arrived by spring 1934.[8] But refugees other than these professionals began to arrive as well, usually in small groups, in which men predominated and in which there were very few children. One such group, on October 18, 1938, for example, had nineteen men, five women and one child.[9] By November 26, an estimated five hundred refugees were in Shanghai alone, all having arrived before *Kristallnacht*. A sharp increase occurred when the *Conte Verde*, a Lloyd Triestino luxury liner, brought 187 refugees on November 24.[10] It was this and the following month's even larger contingent that began to worry the Shanghai Municipal Council (SMP) and that led the council and others to search for means to limit or stop the influx, as will be discussed later.

What was a sea voyage like for these travelers? The Eisfelder family – Hedwig, Louis and their two sons – was among the *Conte Verde* passengers who landed in Shanghai on November 24. Mrs. Eisfelder's letters, written on board ship and posted along the way, allow us glimpses of their journey. Traveling economy class, the family boarded the ship on October 29, in Trieste, where they had spent a few days sightseeing. The following day, in Venice, they went to San Marco, looked at palaces and marveled at the city's beauty. Once on board ship, Hedwig gradually became acquainted with her fellow passengers, most of whom were from Berlin and Vienna, with a few Indians, Japanese and Englishmen among them. In Brindisi she saw her first palm trees, but found the city unimpressive. On November 2, they reached Port Said. There, despite it being night, stores were open and they went shopping in a large department store, their baggage not having yet caught up with them. It began to get warmer in the Suez Canal and became oppressively hot as they

---

7 CAHJP, Dal 24a, Mayer to Far Eastern Jewish Central Information Bureau, Harbin, January 26, 1936. Mayer's letter is in response to an inquiry from Harbin about employment for Jewish physicians in South China.

8 *CP*, November 26, 1938, p. 3. According to a German account, Shanghai by mid-1939 was "inundated" with physicians, dentists, and chemists. YVA, 051/0So/41, Security Service Leader of the SS Oberabschnittes North-West to Sicherheitshauptamt, Zentralabteilung II/1, Re: Jewish Emigration to Shanghai, June 21, 1939, signature illegible.

9 "More Jewish Refugees Reach Shanghai from Germany and Austria", *CP*, October 19, 1938, p. 3.

10 "Reich Emigres in Shanghai Placed at 500", *CP*, November 26, 1938, p. 3.

sailed into the Red Sea. After Suez, where she admired the gardens and a spectacular sunset behind a mountain range, the journey became tedious. But entertainment was provided on ship (movies, a concert, a fencing match) to relieve the boredom. On November 6, they arrived in Aden and small boats took the Eisfelders ashore. It was their first encounter with heavily veiled women, "I realize increasingly", she wrote, "that we are making a 'world journey'". The shock of reality reached them in Bombay on the 12th while reading in the newspaper about Kristallnacht. "Only now are we completely aware how fortunate we are to sail on the ocean and we say to ourselves, no matter what may await us in the new world, we are lucky to be outside", she wrote to her family. Although worried about those left behind in Germany, and increasingly suffering from the unaccustomed heat in economy class, they nonetheless enjoyed Colombo on November 16, its grand buildings; mosques; and the banana, pineapple and rubber trees in Victoria Park. With a keen eye for feminine attire, she noted that European women were elegantly dressed but were not wearing hose. The following day they would be in Singapore and eight days later in Shanghai, where the temperature of 53 °C would strike them as cold and where, she noted in her last letter, "the seriousness of life begins again.[11]"

At a time when Jews were increasingly excluded from contact with non-Jews in public places, ship space was not always considered a problem and discrimination was rare. Ernest Heppner sailed on the *Potsdam* on March 3, 1939. He recalls in his memoir that "no sooner would I pick a deck chair to sit in for a moment than a steward would be at my side, offering hors d'ouvres and drinks.[12]" Mrs. Annie Witting, sailing on the *Conte Verde* May 9, 1939, reported at length from on board ship:

> Our ship is ... many stories high. The director of the ship received us and led us to our cabins, where he handed us over to the cabin steward. We are in a luxury cabin with private bath and a first class cabin with shower for our children. Our cabin has wall-to-wall carpeting and white wood walls; beds, closets ... all are white lacquer; there is direct and indirect lighting, two windows, a large mirror ... After a bath, we were taken to a wonderfully appointed dining room, where we had our welcoming dinner ... We have our own table steward who served us especially attentively, we have our room steward and stewardess, and a Chinese boy.

Like Hedwig Eisfelder, Annie was enchanted on seeing Suez and like Hedwig experienced the tedium of the hot journey via the Red Sea. Although not al-

---

11  YVA, 078/20, Annie Witting letter, 10 pp. Her account breaks off in Colombo and there are no further letters.
12  Ernest G. Heppner, *Shanghai Refuge, A Memoir of the World War II Jewish Ghetto*, Lincoln–London: University of Nebraska Press, 1993, p. 32.

lowed to leave the ship in Bombay, they made up for it with sightseeing in Colombo. Unable to take money out of Germany, the Wittings were virtually without funds, however she quickly learned that items like watches or cameras could be sold. When they arrived in Singapore on May 29, the sale of a Swiss watch allowed them to rent a car for sightseeing with another family. It was the zoo and the botanical garden in particular that caught their attention, "Everything is so different", she wrote, "and perhaps therefore so uniquely beautiful and unforgettable for us". The journey was like a dream and, like all dreams, she knew that it must end. Yet, she was optimistic. Somehow they would manage in Shanghai, their new home.[13]

But Wilhelm Deman, in his memoir, remembers a decidedly unpleasant crossing. Sailing on the *Guilio Cesare* in second class accommodations, the Deman family and the 450 passengers – nearly all Jewish – were treated with contempt by the crew, who had dubbed the liner the "criminals' ship" (Verbrecherschiff). The Demans had crossed the Austrian border April 12, 1939, on their way to Genoa, where they boarded the ship April 20. Similar to the recollections of others, they had few complaints until they sailed into the Red Sea. Thereafter, the extreme heat, the tedium of the journey and, especially on the *Guilio Cesare*, the meals increasingly deteriorated. Meat was no longer served when the cooling system broke down and the ship sailed directly to Shanghai without stopovers, arriving May 15.[14]

As is obvious from the accounts cited, ship routes varied little. Italian ships sailed from either Trieste or Genoa and, with brief stopovers in Venice or Naples and occasionally in Brindisi, sailed on to Port Said and the Suez Canal. The ships might anchor briefly in either Masawa, Aden, or both on the way to Bombay, and from Bombay generally sailed to Colombo, Singapore, Manila, Hong Kong and Shanghai. German ships left from Hamburg and might take different routes to Genoa via Bremen, Rotterdam and Southampton. Some German ships stopped at Antwerp, others at Barcelona. Japanese ships sailing from Hamburg took various routes until Port Said, stopping over generally in Antwerp, London, Gibraltar, Marseilles and Naples. From Port Said the route was the same as that of Italian and German ships.[15] But after September 1939 German ships, of course, no longer sailed to Shanghai and Italian shipping ceased as well in June 1940 when Italy joined the war.

---

**13** YVA, 078/1, Annie Witting's letter on board the "Conte Verde", May 1939, pp. 1–5.
**14** YVA, 078/56A, Wilhelm Deman, "Ein verlorenes Jahrzehnt, Shanghai 1939–1949, Tagebuchblätter eines Heimatvertriebenen", pp. 56, 59, 61–62.
**15** Ship routes were detailed in the *CP* together with the announcement of the ship's arrival.

# The Refugee Flood and its Cessation

According to the Nazi regime, encouraging Jews to emigrate by curtailing or depriving them of their livelihood did not have the desired results. Jews were unwilling to depart voluntarily in sufficiently large numbers. The solution, short of outright expulsion, was forcing their emigration, which was made possible by two major events in 1938: the annexation of Austria in March and *Kristallnacht* in November.

While the Nazis were readying the organizational structure for their version of "ethnic cleansing" in Germany and Austria, concern turned to near panic in Shanghai's SMC when on December 20, 1938, 524 refugees arrived among the *Biancamano*'s 767 passengers.[16] Now there were over one thousand refugees in Shanghai alone and more were said to be on the way by month's end.[17] For the next eight months Italian, German and Japanese ships continued to arrive at an alarming rate – as many as three and four, and in the end even eight per month – each bringing hundreds of refugees. In January 1939, the German luxury liner *Potsdam* and the Italian *Conte Rosso*, *Conte Verde* and *Victoria* docked with approximately 1,100 refugees. The *Biancamano* arrived in February with 841, and the *Conte Rosso* and *Oldenburg* brought over 400 in March.[18] The numbers increased as spring turned to summer; between July 3 and 31 alone, eight ships docked – four Japanese, one Italian and three German – with 1,315 refugees.[19] In August eight more ships arrived, among them two from Marseilles, bringing the number of refugees in Shanghai to 17,000.[20] According to police reports, between April 24 and September 12, 1939, thirty-five German, French, Japanese, and Italian vessels arrived in Shanghai carrying 7,097 refu-

---

**16** "562 German Emigres Due in Port Today", *CP*, December 20, 1938, p. 1, and "524 German Emigres Land in Shanghai", *CP*, December 21, 1938, p. 1, which describes the refugees as a "cheerless group." The 562 in the December 20 issue was a misprint. 526 persons had actually sailed, but two left ship either in Manila or in Hong Kong. See also CAHJP, DAL 76, Birman, DALJEWCIB to Hilfsverein, January 16, 1938, who had estimated the number of refugees in Shanghai between 1,300 and 1,400 at the beginning of the year.

**17** "1,400 Emigres to Greet New Year in City", *CP*, December 31, 1938, p. 2.

**18** "New Emigre Group of 400 Arrives Here", *CP*, January 1, 1939, p. 1; "250 Jewish Emigres Due Here Today", *CP*, January 15, 1939, p. 1; *CP*, January 31, 1939, p. 2; *CP*, February 23, 1939, p. 3; *CP*, March 6, 1939, p. 2.

**19** Reel 17, SMP D54422 (c), Police reports dated July 3, 7, 9, 15, 24, 31, 1939. Japanese ships usually brought anywhere between 60 and 80 refugees.

**20** CAHJP, DAL 86.4, Birman to HIAS, Warsaw, February 5, 1940. This figure is corroborated by reel 17, SMP, D5422 (c), Police report, August 12, 1939.

gees[21], and the German General Consulate in Shanghai, which monitored the Jewish influx, noted that after a brief hiatus in fall 1939, Jews continued to arrive in Italian, Dutch, and Japanese ships throughout the spring of 1940. But there were far fewer now, and by June only 1,900 Jews had arrived.[22] The splendid luxury liner *Conte Verde* docked on June 6 at the Shanghai Hongkou Wharf with 586 passengers, among them 263 refugees.[23] It was also her last journey. Unable to return to Italy, the crew eventually scuttled the ship September 9, 1943.[24] The *Conte Biancamano*, having sailed from Genoa August 16th, brought the last large contingent of German Jewish refugees to Shanghai on September 12. The passengers did not seem overly surprised by the outbreak of war in Europe, reported the *China Press*, and were probably much relieved to have at last reached the safe haven of Shanghai.[25] After neither German nor Italian ships any longer sailed to East Asia, Jews fleeing Europe increasingly used the land route via what was then the Soviet Union to either Dairen or Vladivostok and then made their way by ship to Shanghai. Some refugees, after managing to reach Moscow overland, apparently sailed on Japanese steamers from Russia. Unfortunately, the correspondence only supplies the names of the ships and does not specify the ports of departure.[26] Although thoughts were enter-

---

**21** Reel 17, SMP D5422 (c), Police reports dated April 24 through September 12, 1939. The Shanghai Municipal Police apparently dispatched men to the docks to take a head count.
**22** YVA, 078/73B, German General Consulate, Report to the Foreign Office, June 30, 1940, and Report to the Foreign Office, February 2, 1940. See also, for example, "Emigre Colony Entertains New Arrivals" *CP*, February 23, 1940, p. 4, among the Biancamano's 720 passengers were only 65 German and Austrian refugees; "Latest Batch of 100 Jewish Emigres Lands on Conte Verde", *CP*, April 5, 1940, p. 3, among its 900 passengers were only 100 refugees. CAHJP, DAL 87, Birman to Speelman, May 30, 1940, 163 refugees arrived on the "Conte Rosso".
**23** *CP*, June 7, 1940, p. 2. A number of refugees almost did not make it when they were turned back at the Italian border due to Italy's preparing to join the war. "Jew Arrivals Describe Detainment", *CP*, June 8, 1940, p. 3.
**24** I thank Ralph Hirsch for supplying the date. Salvaged by the Japanese, the *Conte Verde* continued to operate until 1951. Hirsch's information is based on Roger W. Jordan, *The World's Merchant Fleets 1939, The Particulars and Wartime Fates of 6000 Ships*, Annapolis: Naval Institute Press, 1999. A slightly different account is supplied by John Powell, who writes that the Japanese intended to take the ship to Japan for repairs after she tipped over September 8. But an American plane dropped several bombs on the "Conte Verde" which sank in the muddy river. John B. Powell, *My Twenty-Five Years in China*, New York: The Macmillan Co., 1945, p. 407.
**25** "Last Group of German Jewish Refugees Brought to Shanghai", *CP*, September 13, 1939, p. 3.
**26** CAHJP, 86.4, Birman to Reichsvereinigung, October 7; October 14; October 21; December 16, 1940.

tained of having refugees sail on Soviet steamers bound for Shanghai – either bringing Soviet officials or anchoring there for repairs – the scheme never materialized.[27]

Finally, considerable numbers of refugees took the French Messageries Maritime line from Marseilles, either directly to Shanghai or, more frequently, via Saigon, especially after German and Italian ships were no longer available. Moreover, by the end of 1940, French vessels apparently no longer sailed to Shanghai[28], and refugees had no choice but to travel via Saigon. By summer 1941 this route too became uncertain and Meir Birman reported in September that very few French steamers were still going to Saigon.[29] But in the summer of 1940, when the Germans invaded France, the journey became an odyssey for some. Josef Schwarz with his wife and son left from Marseilles June 7, 1940. Five days later France fell, and the ship was ordered to remain in Equatorial Africa. For the next seven months they sailed to Dakar, Casablanca and Madagascar, eventually reaching Saigon. From there via Manila they made their way to Shanghai, arriving January 28, 1941.[30] Probably among the very last refugees to reach Shanghai by way of Saigon were Edgar Rosenzweig and Dr. Michael Langleben who landed in Shanghai November 26, 1941 on the *Marchal Joffre*.[31]

Timing – how to keep ahead of events that forever threatened to overtake a person – was crucial. Decisions had to be made hurriedly; their consequences unforeseeable. One example will illustrate this. Käthe Keibel's Jewish husband had sailed ahead of her to Bangkok. She had an entry permit for Siam (Thailand), a Japanese transit visa and, as a non-Jew, a passport without a "J". Käthe got as far as Japan, but in the spring of 1940 could go no further. Ships to Bangkok stopped at French or British ports where she, as an enemy national, would have been interned.[32]

## Factors Limiting Sea Travel

That no more than approximately 20,000 refugees were able to reach Shanghai is due to a variety of factors in which both political events and the German

---

**27** CAHJP, 95, Birman to Reichsvereinigung, March 27, 1941. The letter was not sent.
**28** CAHJP, DAL 93, Birman to HICEM, Lisbon, December 20, 1940.
**29** CAHJP, DAL 99, Birman to International Migration Service, Geneva, July 28, 1941, "However, in view of the present situation we doubt whether this will be possible in the future", wrote Birman; Birman to HIAS, New York, August 13, 1941; Birman to International Migration Service, Geneva, September 5, 1941.
**30** CAHJP, DAL 94, Birman to HICEM, Marseilles, February 6, 1941.
**31** CAHJP, DAL 101, Birman to HICEM, Marseille, November 28, 1941.
**32** CAHJP, DAL 86, Birman to Jewish Community in Kobe, May 9, 1940.

conquests that increasingly engulfed Europe had a role. Before discussing these together with the major reason – lack of ship accommodations – let us briefly consider who these refugees were and why they came. Some were well-off families, such as the already mentioned Wittings or Eisfelders, who decided that the time had come to pull up stakes and leave. Families were, however, far fewer than single men and women, and men outnumbered women.[33] The reason for the preponderance of men is close at hand: Jewish men, as family providers, were increasingly eliminated from both Austrian and German economy. In Austria, even before Kristallnacht, between April and September 1938, more than 4,000 men were sent to the Dachau and Buchenwald concentration camps.[34] This number increased massively during the November 1938 pogrom when thousands more were incarcerated. The release of these Jewish men was ordered in January 1939, if they were in possession of emigration papers[35], which could be either a visa to another country or a ship booking.

Obviously the scramble for visas and tickets by the desperate families of the incarcerated men helped to disseminate information about China as an option for gaining their freedom. No doubt the grapevine, rather than an organized information campaign, most likely increased awareness of Shanghai as a destination.[36] Conversely, lack of information, unfortunately, may have contributed (though it was not a major reason) to limiting the number of Jewish arrivals in Shanghai. Wilhelm Deman, quite by chance, heard about Shanghai from a woman who came to his office. Convinced that Jews would be allowed

---

**33** For example, YVA, 078/73B, German General Consulate Shanghai to Foreign Office, Report, January 11, 1940, p. 2. The report has a figure of approximately 10.000 people between mid-August 1938 and May 1939, among them 5.200 men, 3.800 women and 1.000 children. Telling figures are also, for example, "Biancamano with 841 Jews Due Tomorrow", *CP*, February 21, 1939, pp. 1,4, where 532 men and 263 women are listed. See also Appendix 6, which briefly analyzes the composition of the Jewish population of one police precinct.

**34** Herbert Rosenkranz, *"Reichskristallnacht", 9. November 1938 in Oestereich*, Vienna: Europa Verlag, 1968, pp. 13, 24–26; Gerhard Botz, "The Jews of Vienna from the *Anschluss* to the Holocaust", in Ivar Oxaal, Michael Pollak, Gerhard Botz, eds., *Jews, Antisemitism and Culture in Vienna*, London–New York: Routledge and Kegan Paul, 1987, pp. 185–204.

**35** Copy from the Gestapo, signature illegible, January 31, 1939, in John Mendelsohn, ed., *The Holocaust, Selected Documents in Eighteen Volumes*, New York-London: Garland Publishing Inc., 1982, Vol. 6, pp. 202–203.

**36** Where figures of emigrants and their destinations are available, they are revealing. See, for example, *300 Jahre Juden in Halle, Leben. Leistung, Leiden, Lohn*, Halle: Mitteldeutscher Verlag, 1992, pp. 235–249, which lists 584 emigrants from Halle, 93 of whom went to Shanghai.

neither to remain nor to work in Vienna, she was about to depart for Shanghai.[37] Alfred Dreifuss was told by a fellow Buchenwald prisoner that a Vienna branch of a Dutch organization was managing immigration to Shanghai.[38] On the other hand, when the Eisfelders turned to the Jewish organizations for information about Shanghai, which was certainly available by autumn 1938, they were unable to obtain much-needed facts about the metropolis.[39] Many, like Inge Deutschkron, did not consider going to China – about which she knew nothing except that it was a country always at war and a place of "indescribable poverty.[40]" Others felt that the Shanghai option was not the worst. Günter and Genia Nobel, Communist Party members, were arrested in a Gestapo sweep in 1936 and jailed for three years. When released on August 1, 1939, they were given the choice of leaving Germany within four weeks or being taken to a concentration camp. But with a criminal record, the only places they could go to were Palestine or Shanghai. According to the Nobels' account, they decided on Shanghai for ideological reasons because they opposed the establishment of a Jewish state at the expense of the Palestinian people.[41]

The Nazis had many complaints about the quality of the work of the Jewish organizations and "the lack of popular and impressive propaganda" that would induce Jews to emigrate.[42] In June 1939 the suggested German remedy was to imprison in concentration camps all Jews whom the Jewish authorities considered undesirable for one reason or another. Because Jewish organizations made special efforts to have prisoners released and on their way across the German border, or so the argument went, these "undesirables" would have no choice but to emigrate.[43] Indeed, a somewhat similar method was tried when Jewish

---

**37** YVA, 078/56A, Deman "Ein verlorenes Jahrzehnt", p. 15.

**38** Alfred Dreifuss, "Shanghai – eine Emigration am Rande", in Eike Midell, *Exil in den USA*, Leipzig: Verlag Philipp Reclam jun., 1983, pp. 555–556.

**39** YVA, 078\21, H. (Peter) Eisfelder, "Chinese Exile, My Years in Shanghai and Nanking, 1938–1947", as recollected by H. (Peter) Eisfelder, July 1972, p. 9.

**40** Inge Deutschkron, *Ich trug den gelben Stern*, Köln: Verlag Wissenschaft und Politik, 1978, p. 51.

**41** Günter and Genia Nobel, "Erinnerungen, als politische Emigranten in Schanghai", *Beiträge zur Geschichte der Arbeiterbewegung*, Vol. 21, no. 6 (June 1979), pp. 882–894. This in retrospect; the term "Palestinian people" did not come into general use until sometimes in the 1960s.

**42** YVA, 051/oSo/41, "Toward Jewish Emigration", undated and unsigned document.

**43** YVA, 051/oSo/41, SS captain of the Security Main Office to Section II, 112, June 2, 1939, signature illegible. The letter, in fact, accuses the Jewish organizations of sabotaging emigration.

men who had police records, even for the most trivial reasons, were rearrested and sent to concentration camps. In June 1939, the police netted some 10,000 to 15.000 prisoners, according to one account, and arrests were made even in almshouses. The prisoners were released from concentration camps only upon showing documents for leaving Germany.[44] But clearly the Jewish organizations had no way of taking charge of emigration. Many, if not most, of those who landed in Shanghai had gone there on their own. As stated succinctly by Horwitz of the Relief Organization (Hilfsverein) in December 1938, "You must consider that especially from Berlin a large number of emigrants undertake the journey to the Far East without our support". We have only control, he wrote, over those who need support from us, or who require our help.[45]

The organizations that handled emigration were not to blame for the fact that Jews did not go to Shanghai in greater numbers. To be sure, if given a choice most Jews would have preferred to depart for the United States. People feverishly searched for long-out-of-touch American relatives who might be willing to send the much coveted affidavit, vouching for their financial solvency. And William Shirer, American correspondent in Berlin, learned in February 1939 that 248,000 names – fully half of Germany's Jewish population – were on the American consulate's waiting list.[46] Still, unable to enter the U.S., many were prepared to go to any country that would have them and Jewish leaders in Berlin argued that whatever colonization schemes were being studied in London "might come too late for a very great part of German Jewry". "Please trust us", stated a letter of February 1939, "when we tell you that we are unable to diminish the emigration from Germany ...[47]" More telling even than this letter is the report of a secret conference Pell[48] had with Berlin's Jewish leaders:

---

**44** YVA, 078/40, "Germany no. 2 (1939), Copy of Papers Concerning the Treatment of German Nationals in Germany, 1938–1939". Presented by the Secretary of State for Foreign Affairs to Parliament by Command of his Majesty, 1940, pp. 27–36. Rearrests also occurred in February 1937. See Friedländer, *Nazi Germany and the Jews*, p. 204.
**45** CAHJP, DAL 76, Arnold Horwitz, Hilfsverein to DALJEWCIB, December 20, 1938.
**46** William L. Shirer, *Berlin Diary, the Journal of a Foreign Correspondent 1939–1941*, New York: Alfred A. Knopf, 1941, p. 292, entry February 27, 1940.
**47** JDC, 33/44, file 457, from Hilfsverein der Juden in Deutschland to JDC, Paris (forwarded to JDC, New York, by Morris Troper), February 10, 1939, signed A. Prinz, F. Bischofswerder, V. Loewenstein. Copy in CAHJP, DAL 76.1, sent to HICEM, Harbin.
**48** This is, no doubt, Robert T. Pell, who handled State Department issues connected with the Intergovernmental Committee on Refugees, established by the Évian Conference in 1938, See David S. Wyman, *The Abandonment of the Jews, America and the Holocaust 1941–1945*, New York: Pantheon Books, 1984, p. 137.

They are, of course, very nervous and jumpy ... They are quite frank about the shiploads of their co-religionists which they are heading in various directions such as Shanghai ... They said that they had to get their people out, whether there was an easing of tension or not. At any moment an incident might occur which would endanger the very lives of their people. They could not afford to take chances, with the consequence that they were ready to yield to the pressure of the secret police and enticements of the shipping companies ... I pleaded with them that they were doing more harm than good ... that they were defeating our efforts to open up places ... but they laughed in my face. After six years of dealing with the problem they are very hard. They do not believe in promises.[49]

But, as the Evian conference had clearly demonstrated, few countries were willing to open their gates to the masses of desperate people.[50] Thousands more would have gladly left for Shanghai, not because of its desirability, but out of necessity. Unfortunately, they were prevented from doing so by the lack of available ship space.

The difficulty of securing bookings was frequently mentioned. Bookings on German and Italian liners to East Asia were completely sold out as much as six and seven months in advance as early as January 1939.[51] Bribes or connections sometimes helped to obtain bookings. Ernest Heppner, for example, mentions that his mother turned over two Impressionist paintings to the shipping agent in return for two tickets on the *Potsdam*.[52] Willy Frensdorff, who had designed the *Scharnhorst*'s electrical installations, used his connections to get four tickets for the ship's last sailing on July 10, 1939.[53] Obviously, in their eagerness to expel as many Jews as possible in the shortest time possible, the Würzburg district authorities (and possibly others) were authorized to permit the use of non-German shipping lines. These included several Dutch, Nor-

---

**49** JDC, RG 33/44, file 457, letter from Theodore C. Achilles, Chairman, Departmental Committee on Political Refugees, Department of State, to George L. Warren, March 31, 1939. Pell's letter is dated March 8.

**50** See Henry L. Feingold, *The Politics of Rescue, the Roosevelt Administration and the Holocaust, 1938–1945*, New Brunswick N.J.: Rutgers University Press, 1970, pp. 22–68 for an extensive summary of the conference and the negotiations which followed. For a discussion of the Evian conference, see Ch. 5.

**51** PRO, FO 371/24079, L.M. Robinson, British Consulate General, Hamburg, to Sir George Ogilvie-Forbes, British Embassy, Berlin, January 10, 1939; PRO, W 9840/519/ 48, W 9840, 90, H. Bullock, Consulate, Bremen, to British Embassy, Berlin, June 22, 1939, who mentions continued waiting lists; CAHJP, 71.6, Horwitz to Birman, December 28, 1938; see also, Werner Rosenstock, "Exodus 1933–1938, A Survey of Jewish Emigration from Germany", *Leo Baeck Institute Yearbook*, Vol. 1 (1956), p. 386, who writes that getting to Shanghai was limited by "shipping difficulties".

**52** Heppner, *Shanghai Refuge*, pp. 28–29.

**53** Claudia Cornwall, *Letter from Vienna, A Daughter Uncovers Her Family's Jewish Past*, Vancouver-Toronto: Douglas and McIntyre, 1995, pp. 62–63.

wegian, Swedish, Japanese and U.S. lines. Meanwhile, the Gestapo urged the local authorities to pursue Jewish emigration even more vigorously, despite the war.[54] Of interest here is the degree of control the Gestapo exercised over the ousting of Jews and, notwithstanding assumptions in other German quarters, the Jewish organizations responsible for emigration had a limited function.

Lack of ship space was thus a major factor in preventing more refugees from reaching Shanghai. Attempts by Schlie of the Hanseatic Office to charter additional ships after the *Usamaro* came to naught, as we saw in the previous chapter, over the issue of foreign currency. Although it may indeed have been too late in summer 1939, clearly I cannot help but conclude that a singular opportunity for saving lives by major organizations in the democracies was lost earlier, in spring 1939, when the Nazis searched for ways and means to ship out large numbers of Jews. Nor was the ship charter plan a secret. Men at the British Embassy in Berlin were well aware of the attempts to charter ships and it was conjectured that one would sail from Danzig as well.[55]

As pointed out earlier, the Nazi policy had been from the start to cleanse Germany and, after the *Anschluss* in March 1938, Austria of its Jews. Therefore obtaining a passport presented no special difficulties. Aside from the passport, a "statement of good conduct" (Führungszeugnis) was required from the police. It stated that the emigrant had no police record, had not offended social order, is not abnormal and is not a beggar.[56]

Concerning Chinese visas, as far as can be ascertained, some emigrants made efforts to obtain them while others did not, the still prevalent view being that a visa was not required for Shanghai. The facts of the case were, however, somewhat different. Despite the political changes in China due to the Sino-Japanese war and the Nationalist retreat to China's interior, embassies and consulates of the Nationalist government continued to function throughout

---

**54** YVA, M.1 DN221, Administrative District President to the Administrative Authorities, including Police, Würzburg, December 13, 1939, January 6, March 11, July 17, 1940, and letter from the Würzburg Gestapo to the police, various mayors, other Gestapo offices and the Security Service, May 4, 1940.

**55** PRO, FO 371/24079, F. Foley, British Consulate, Bremen, to Chancery, May 26, 1939; PRO, W 8663/519/48, Foreign Office to Sir A. Clark Kerr, Shanghai, telegram, June 12, 1939.

**56** I thank Peter Witting for furnishing a photocopy of his father's conduct statement. He also had a "Heimatschein", which was valid for one year and which testified to his being a German citizen. An additional document from the Jewish community stated that he did not owe them money. It is not clear whether all the refugees were required to obtain these three documents. Heppner, *Shanghai Refuge*, p. 27, mentions needing only the conduct document.

Europe, issuing visas to refugees planning to settle in Nationalist controlled areas and to those who went to Shanghai.[57] Indeed, the *Shanghai Times* stated quite clearly, "Chinese consulates in Europe are granting visas to all those applying with their passports for permission to come to Shanghai ..." This was in accordance with the agreement between China and the Powers whereby Shanghai had become a treaty port.[58] Moreover, a letter to Lisbon and New York mentions clearly that the Chinese consul in Stockholm is granting visas without difficulties.[59] But there is much confusion regarding this question. Some booking agents but not others may have required a Chinese visa, or there may have been rumors of a sudden visa requirement. An article in the *China Press* of February 26, 1940, for example, stated that visas were now required for Shanghai, implying that none had been earlier. Memories are uncertain here. What is certain, however, is the absence of passport control upon docking in Shanghai.

Because of the unique political situation in Shanghai, neither the Chinese nor any foreign country was sovereign in the metropolis after 1937. While Chiang Kai-shek's Nationalist government was in power, the Chinese controlled passports at the port, although it was a mere formality (more a source of revenue than anything else) since Chinese officials had no jurisdiction over extraterritorial foreigners. Still, as long as there was a legal Chinese government, British subjects were advised to obtain visas from Chinese consulates as a courtesy[60], and quite likely other nationals followed the British example. But after the 1937 hostilities, the Nationalist passport office ceased to exist. The British ambassador in Shanghai, Sir Neville Henderson, explained to the Foreign Office that in the changed circumstances, the Japanese could not very well be asked to assume this function for the benefit of British interests. "And

---

57 According to his daughter, Chen Jie presumably believed that He Fengshan, who was appointed to Vienna in May 1938, was issuing too many visas in Vienna. Rumor had it in Berlin, furthermore, that he was selling them which turned out to be groundless. In his memoir, He explained that he had instructions from the Chinese Foreign Office not to refuse visas to Jews. He, *Forty Year Diplomatic Career*, pp. 75–76. Chen Jie was new to the job, having replaced the previous Chinese ambassador in November 1938. Misgivings by the Chongqing government about the Shanghai destination, mentioned earlier, may have been fresh in Chen Jie's mind. The visas which I examined were for Shanghai only, and not for China. Yad Vashem named He a "Righteous Gentile" in February 2001.

**58** YVA, 078/85, Shanghai Municipal Archive, clipping, *The Shanghai Times*, February 5, 1939.

**59** JDC, RG 33–44, File 732, letter from I. Valk, Vilna to HICEM, Lisbon and HIAS New York, October 7, 1940.

**60** PRO, FO 371/24079 W8663, from Sir Neville Henderson to Foreign Office, May 31, 1939.

in any case we would not wish to encourage the institution of passport control measures by the Japanese and so add to the many vexatious restrictions under which our people are already suffering.[61]" Using even stronger language, Michel Speelman, the important Shanghai businessman and Jewish community leader, wrote that the Japanese "could do so [exercise passport control] only at the unanimous request of the whole Consular body. Such a request is entirely out of the question.[62]" Thus it was unrestricted entry due to the absence of passport control, rather than a visa non-requirement, that enabled refugees to land without difficulty.

Preservation of the status quo seemed the best policy in order not to give the Japanese authorities an excuse for assuming passport control functions. When in June 1940 officers of the SMP, acting on a tip received from the Hong Kong police, boarded two British vessels, the *SS Santhia* and the *Ming San*, to inspect passports of refugees, there was an immediate outcry. The Japanese Harbour Master, Y. Sugiyama objected, stating that his office should have been notified. And the River Police accused the SMP of usurping the function of a Passport Bureau.[63]

Neither passports, nor legal documents, nor visas limited travel to Shanghai. But was money – the cost of ship fare and expenses – added on later? Figures are hard to come by, but one that was mentioned is 2,000 RM on a German ship. A more reliable sum is recorded by Willy Frensdorff, who paid 6425,70 RM for four tickets on the *Scharnhorst*.[64] It is not clear whether these were first class tickets, because another source mentions over 2,000 RM for a first class ticket.[65] If it is true that the North-German Lloyd line also required a money deposit in case a person had to return, the price of a ticket could certainly skyrocket.[66] Still, as long as tickets could be purchased with RM, they were affordable by many. The problem became formidable when, beginning

---

**61** PRO, FO 371/24079, W8663, Henderson to Foreign Office, May 31, 1939.

**62** JDC, RG 33–44, file 457, Michel Speelman, "Report on Jewish Refugee Problem in Shanghai", Paris, June 21, 1939.

**63** Reel 18, SMP D5422 (c), W.C. Woodfield, Chief of Police, June 27, 1940; Report, D. S. I. Pitts; Special Branch, letter, signature illegible, July 3, 1940. The SMP's justification was that incoming refugees supplied the police with valuable information.

**64** Cornwall, *Letter from Vienna*, p. 63.

**65** Personal correspondence from Ralph B. Hirsch, who cites Monika Richarz, ed., *Bürger auf Wiederruf: Lebenszeugnisse deutscher Juden 1780–1945*, München: C. H. Beck, 1989, p. 500.

**66** PRO, FO 371/24079, L. M. Robinson, British Consulate General, Hamburg, to Ogilvie-Forbes, January 10, 1939. See also YVA, 078/73B, German General Consulate, Shanghai, Report, June 30, 1940, p. 2, signature illegible, where, in comparison, the cost of 2nd class overland travel, Berlin–Shanghai, is given as 490 RM.

on June 1, 1939, passage on Italian, Japanese, Danish and Norwegian lines had to be paid in foreign currency.[67] But there was another factor that no doubt limited refugee flight: the so-called permits, or immigration certificates instituted by the SMC in early fall 1939 as a response to the refugee influx between December 1938 and August 1939

## Responses in Shanghai[68]

The first group of fifteen Austrian refugees, victims of the *Anschluss*, arrived on the *Biancamano* early in September 1938. They were soon followed by increasingly larger groups. The reporter who covered the arrival of 187 refugees on the *Conte Verde* was moved to write, "Everywhere the tragedy of people torn out of their familiar setting and removed to a remote, strange country thousands of miles away is apparent.[69]"

The SMC response to this new Shanghai crisis was less charitable, especially when 524 more refugees arrived on December 20, again on the *Biancamano*.[70] Initially, the SMC asked the Jewish organizations in Europe, England and America to prevent refugees from coming to Shanghai in view of the many Chinese refugees already being sheltered there. G. Godfrey Phillips, SMC secretary cabled the JDC in New York,

> Municipal Council of International Settlement Shanghai is gravely perturbed by abnormal influx of Jewish refugees. Shanghai is already facing most serious refugee problem due to Sino-Japanese hostilities. It is quite impossible to absorb any large number of foreign refugees. Council earnestly requests your assistance in preventing any further refugees coming to Shanghai ...[71]

But a threat was appended, namely that the "Council may be compelled to take steps to prevent further refugees landing in International Settlement.[72]"

---

**67** PRO, FO 371/24079, F. Foley to the Chancery, May 26, 1939.

**68** The account in this section relies in great measure on the joint article by A. Altman and I. Eber, "Flight to Shanghai, 1938–1940: The Larger Setting" *Yad Vashem Studies*, 28 (2000), pp. 65–82.

**69** *IM*, Vol. 35, no. 6 (September 20, 1938), p. 6; *CP*, November 26, 1938, p. 3.

**70** See above, note 9. The lavishly appointed liner had cabin space for 1.864 passengers. See Nicholas T. Cairis, *Era of the Passenger Liner*, London–Boston: Pegasus Books, Ltd., 1992, p. 134.

**71** 71JDC, RG 33–44, file 456, Phillip to Joint, New York, December 24, 1938.

**72** YVA, 078/85, Shanghai Municipal Archives, G. Godfrey Phillips, SMC secretary and commissioner general, to German Jewish Aid Committee, London; Hias-ica Emigration Association, Paris; AJDC, New York, December 23, 1938.

How to maintain the refugees was an issue, but so were housing and employment.[73] The newly created Committee for the Assistance of European Jewish Refugees in Shanghai (CAEJR) was, however, also concerned about the influx. Its honorary treasurer, Michel Speelman, acknowledged to the SMC and French Concession authorities the "danger of an unlimited influx of refugees to Shanghai.[74]" Exactly what he meant by "danger" is not clear, but the fact was that Speelman and the committee suddenly confronted the monumental task of having to feed and house hundreds of destitute refugees. That his and others' anxieties were real is beyond doubt. Shanghai winters are unpleasantly damp and chilly. Daytime temperatures hover in the mid-thirties to mid-forties Fahrenheit in January and February. Europeans, for the most part from more than comfortable circumstances, would have been unable to endure hardships similar to those of Chinese refugees who crowded the International Settlement and the Chinese areas of Shanghai. The two Jewish communities, the Baghdadi and the Russian, had neither the organizational framework nor the experience needed to care for large numbers of destitute persons after the outbreak of hostilities in the summer of 1937.

The SMC had made it quite clear that it would not contribute any funds whatsoever toward maintenance of the refugees. "There is no Poor Law or public system of relief in China, and consequently none in the International Settlement", the SMC minutes stated. Relief has always been a private affair. Therefore, the burden cannot be assumed by the Shanghai ratepayer and the Jewish organizations must deal with it.[75] Funds for caring for the refugees had to come from Europe and America and, Speelman wrote, unless they were received he would have to tell the Municipal Council and the Consular body of "our inability to continue to succor refugees.[76]" The implications of the sentence were clear: an admission of this sort by a successful and respected businessman would cast a bad light not only on Shanghai Jewry but on British

---

**73** YVA, 078/85, Shanghai Municipal Archives, December 23, 1938; December 25, 1938; December 31, 1938.

**74** JDC, RG 33–34, file 457, "Report on Jewish Refugee Problem". Speelman's communication does not have an exact date. It is, therefore, not clear whether it preceded the SMC's December 23 communication or followed it. For the organization of this and other charitable Jewish bodies, see Chapter 1.

**75** PRO, minutes, first page missing.

**76** YVA, 078/85, Shanghai Municipal Archives, Speelman cable to ?, January 6, 1939. It must be remembered here that the Shanghai Jewish communities had not requested funds from the JDC since 1926. See JDC RG 33/44, file 456, "China, Statement of Subsidies Made by the J.D.C. April, 24 Through March, 1938".

Jewry as well. The loss of face was unthinkable. Moreover, when even by April insufficient funds had been received from London, the British suspected that the local organizations would turn to the German Consulate General, asking them to "assume responsibility for their Jewish nationals.[77]"

Beneath British fears over expenditures was, however, a far greater apprehension over the Japanese reaction to the refugee influx. "There is a definite risk that unless this emigration is checked without further delay Japanese authorities will institute passport inspection generally at Shanghai which would be damaging to British interests and foreign interests", read a January 1939 communication from the British Foreign Office.[78] Indeed, according to a police informant, rumors had it that the Japanese authorities were discussing measures for establishing passport examination on ships docking in Shanghai, due to Japanese concerns over the presence of communist and pro-communist elements among the refugees.[79]

Looming in the background was the specter of anti-Semitism in Shanghai. This was first pointed out in a confidential communication to Sir Herbert Phillips, British Consul General. "It seems to me that a large influx of refugees would have most certainly upsetting results here, and we certainly do not want anti-Semitic problems added to our Shanghai problems.[80]" British fears were by no means groundless. The Japanese actively supported militant fascist and pro-Japanese elements among the White Russian population which was not known for its pro-Jewish sentiments. Anti-Semitic leaflets in English were appearing, according to the British Consular report from Shanghai, which attacked "by name certain of the most influential and wealthy 'native' Shanghai Jewish families", both British and Iraqi. Also, a campaign against admitting more Jews had started in the Japanese-controlled Russian and Chinese press, labeling Jews "bearers of the Communist virus.[81]" Not only are Jews depriving

---

77  PRO, FO 371/23510 (27385), Report, quarter ending March 31, 1939, April 24, 1939.

78  PRO, FO 371/24079 (22652) W519, 5, Foreign Office cable to the Ambassador in Shanghai, January 10, 1939.

79  Reel 17, SMP, D5422 (c), Police Report, December 13, 1938. The Japanese also explored, according to the report, instituting certificates of "political reliability".

80  YVA, 078/85, Shanghai Municipal Archive, unsigned to Sir Herbert Phillips, December 28, 1938.

81  PRO, FO 371/23509, Political report ending December 31, 1938; see also *CP*, October 2, 1938, p. 2, which describes the anti-Semitic content of one such pamphlet; police report in SMP, D-5422C, translation from the *Russian Voice*, January 7, 1939. Marxism, Bolshevism, and Jews were coupled even earlier in Shanghai's German newspapers. See SMP, Reel 25, D-6961-6964, translation from the *Deutsche Schanghai Zeitung*, September 6, 1935.

Russians of jobs, it was claimed in the daily *Xin Shenbao*[82], a Jewish capitalist takeover in China is in the making. Thus the Jewish problem has also become an East Asian problem. Those Jews who came to Shanghai earlier, according to the article, have already established themselves in business and amassed capital. It is, therefore, entirely possible that within twenty-five years the wealth of China's economy will gravitate into Jewish hands. Not only will Jews then be able to control China, they oppose Japan now, and Jewish capital is behind British designs. One might say, the article concluded, that "Shanghai is the Jews' market.[83]" For different reasons, but with equal anxiety, the Japanese Special Naval Landing Party watched the ever growing refugee numbers. But the Japanese were caught on the horns of a dilemma. Notwithstanding the red "J" stamped in their passports[84], the refugees arrived with valid German passports. Not allowing entry might cause friction in the Japanese-German alliance. The policy formulated by the Five Ministers Conference in Tokyo on December 6, 1938, pointed the way to a formal solution. It had been agreed upon, among others, that, while Jews would be treated impartially like other aliens wishing to enter Japan, Manchukuo and China, no positive steps would be taken to harbor Jews expelled from Germany. Yet, to discriminate against Jews, as Germany was doing, would contradict the oft-stated Japanese principle of racial equality and might endanger the inflow of foreign capital needed for economic reconstruction as well as exacerbate Japanese-U.S. relations.[85] On the surface, therefore, Jewish refugees would not be discriminated against, but, by the beginning of December 1938, the Special Naval Landing Party was said by the Japanese consul general in Shanghai to be limiting their entry into Hongkou.[86]

---

**82** "Chise Youtairen lai Huhou, bai E shangji beiduo (After red Jews come to Shanghai, White Russians are deprived of their livelihood)", *XSB*, December 18, 1938, p. 2. The *Xin Shenbao*, or New Shenbao, one of the most respected of Chinese newspapers, started by Japanese journalists in imitation of the original *Shenbao* began publication in 1938.

**83** "Zhongguo he Youtairen wenti (China and the Jewish problem)", *XSB*, September 29, 1939, p. 2. See also Chen Jian, "Shijie dongluan yu Youtaizhi guoji yinmou (World disorder and the Jewish national conspiracy)", *Chongguo Gonglun*, Vol. 2, no. 5 (February 1940), pp. 13–24.

**84** See note 2, above.

**85** JFM, S Series microfilm, Reel 415, frames 2561–2562, December 6, 1938, for text of the document. The document has been sometimes misunderstood as expressing a pro-Jewish policy, as, for example, in David Kranzler, *Japanese, Nazis & Jews*, New York: Yeshiva University Press, 1976, p. 224 ff. The five ministers were the prime minister, the army, navy, finance and home ministers.

**86** JFM, Reel 413, frames 797–798, Consul General Hidaka, Shanghai, to Arita, December 7, 1938.

Although one would have expected a certain degree of relief on the part of the Jewish organizations in Europe and America over Shanghai as a refuge – especially after the Evian conference – this was not the case.[87] Joseph C. Hyman, of the JDC, wired Berlin not to send more refugees to Shanghai, and was thanked by Max Warburg.[88] Many among Jewish leaders did not support Shanghai as a viable option. At the end of 1938, some countered the panic to escape with the warning not to travel blindly abroad. "It is more honorable to suffer a martyr's death in Central Europe than to perish in Shanghai", Dr. Julius Seligsohn, member of the governing body of the Union of Jews, is quoted as saying. He and others resisted German pressure to transport Jews on "Jewships" (Judenschiffe).[89] Norman Bentwich of the British Council for German Jewry wrote in 1938 that German Jews were "dumped" in Shanghai.[90] As late as January 1941, when Josef Loewenherz, head of the Vienna Kultusgemeinde, desperately pleaded for immigration to Shanghai, he encountered resistance from the JDC. Its representative argued that Japan's rule in Shanghai might endanger Jews as much as German rule. At a meeting in Lisbon, he had to plead for a limited budget toward the $400 financial requirement of "show money" (to be discussed below), even if it was acknowledged at the time that getting Jews out was a question of life and death and that they must leave "before the 'final accounts are in'".[91]

Professor Nathaniel Peffer of Columbia University, eminent expert on Asia, too lent his voice to those who clamored for a cessation of Shanghai immigration, declaring that the influx must be shut off at any cost. His argument was based on the depressed conditions in Shanghai since the hostilities of 1937.

---

**87** Until 1938, Jewish organizations did not encourage emigration from Germany, except of some selected groups to Eretz Israel. See Abraham Margaliot, "The Problem of the Rescue of German Jewry during the Years 1933–1939; The Reasons for the Delay in Their Emigration from the Third Reich", in Yisrael Gutman, ed., *Rescue Attempts during the Holocaust*, Proceedings of the Second Yad Vashem International Historical Conference, Jerusalem, April 8–11, 1974, Jerusalem: Yad Vashem, 1977, pp. 247–265. The Jewish leadership, moreover, continued to hope of bringing about an orderly and planned emigration. See Abraham Margaliot, "Emigration – Planung und Wirklichkeit", in Arnold Pauker, ed., *Die Juden im National-Sozialistischen Deutschland*, Tübingen: J. C. Mohr, 1986, pp. 303–316.
**88** JDC, RG 33–44, file 456, Max Warburg to Joseph C. Hyman, December 29, 1938.
**89** Abraham Margaliot, "Emigration – Planung und Wirklichkeit", pp. 303–316.
**90** Norman Bentwich, *Wanderer Between Two Worlds*, London: Kegan Paul, Trench, Trubner and Co., Ltd., 1941, p. 278.
**91** Bauer, *American Jewry and the Holocaust*, p. 61; JDC, RG 33/94, file 440, Herbert Katzki, Lisbon, to Troper, "Confidential Memorandum", January 23, 1941, pp. 13–14, 17.

He saw no prospect for the refugees, "except degradation to a kind of Occidental coolie status until they die of deprivation or shame.[92]"

In comparison, Frank Foley's humane and compassionate stand in his "Minute" which he appended to his letter to the British Embassy in Berlin is moving:

> It is useless to talk to the German Government whose declared object is to destroy these people [the Jews] body and soul; it makes no difference to them whether destruction takes place in Germany or in Shanghai. I rather think preference would be given to the Far East as their shipping companies are paid for the freight. One has to remember that the declared wish of the N.S.D.A.P. is that Jews should *verrecken* ... It might be considered humane on our part not to interfere officially to prevent Jews from choosing their own graveyards. They would rather die as free men in Shanghai than as slaves in Dachau.[93]

In January 1939, however, when Foley wrote this, the British were determined to halt the refugee traffic at its source. For the next nine months, British embassies and consulates in Europe were requested to prevail on the governments of the countries to which they were posted to curtail and even stop the refugee traffic. The consuls in Shanghai also agreed to contact their respective governments.[94] Meanwhile it was feared that Danzig's Jews, who had been given an ultimatum to leave by April 1, 1939, would also end up in Shanghai.[95]

---

**92** JDC, RG 33/34, file 457, Nathaniel Peffer, Department of Public Law and Government, Columbia University, "Memorandum to Professor J. P. Chamberlain", n. d. [April 1939].

**93** PRO, FO 371/24079 (22652), Foley, British Consulate General, Hamburg, to British Embassy, January 10, 1939. Foley was posthumously named a "Righteous Gentile" by Yad Vashem, *Ha'aretz*, February 28, 1999, p. 8a. We might also note the comment of the minister of the American Church in Berlin, who wrote shortly after returning to the U. S., "The German objective was extermination of the Jews and their method was murder". Stewart W. Herman, Jr., *It's Your Souls We Want*, New York-Boston: Harper and Brothers, 1943, p. 234.

**94** PRO, FO W519/519/48, Walter Roberts, Foreign Office to Norman Bentwich, Council for German Jewry, January 20, 1939; FO W2061 to Ambassador at Shanghai, February 4, 1939. This was duly noted in the Japanese controlled Chinese press, "Youtai nanmin rujing wenti, benshi ponan rongua, geguolingshi yicheng zhengfu (The Jewish refugees are a regional problem, the city has considerable difficulty accommodating them, consuls of other countries have already notified their governments)", *XSB*, no. 479, February 19, 1939, p. 7.

**95** PRO, FO 371/24085, W5285, Sir G. Ogilvie-Forbes, Berlin, to Foreign Office, March 25, 1939. For details about the Danzig deportations, see Joshua B. Stein, "Britain and the Jews of Danzig, 1938–1939", *The Wiener Library Bulletin*, Vol. 32, nos. 49–50, n.s. (1979), pp. 29–33.

Like the earlier efforts of getting Jewish organizations to stop the exodus, these moves too produced no results. The Germans claimed that they could not control the ultimate destination of Jews leaving Germany, although they later conceded "that it is essential that all Jews must leave Germany as soon as possible". They also claimed they could not deter Jews from emigrating "if they so desire". The Italians protested that they did everything in their power, that shipping companies were not selling tickets to anyone who did not have proper documentation and, lying blatantly, that few if any refugees have sailed on Italian ships to Shanghai.[96] When the British Foreign Office next tried to prevail on its own shipping companies not to engage in the refugee traffic to Shanghai, it met with similar failure. Even an appeal to British patriotic sentiments, namely that the refugees endanger British interests, led nowhere, and on June 1, 1939, someone in the Foreign Office noted laconically, "There is not much more which the F. O. could do to stop this emigration to Shanghai.[97]"

Others had reached the same conclusion. Sir John Hope Simpson wrote in his general summary on the refugee problem that China is "a most unsatisfactory place of refuge ... Nevertheless, in despair of escaping anywhere else, large numbers have gone to Shanghai ...[98]" Thus a letter sent by the Jewish leadership in Berlin to the London Council for German Jewry underscored the lack of faith in promises:

> We have now the very greatest misgivings whether those [colonization] plans[99] which the Sub-Committee in London is studying now might not take such a long time for preliminary work that the practical realization might come *too late for a very great part of German Jewry* [underlining in original]. Please trust us when we tell you that we are unable to diminish the emigration from Germany ...[100]

---

**96** PRO, FO 371/24079, W3341/519/48, N. Henderson, Berlin, to Foreign Office, February 23, 1939; W9863/519/48, Henderson to Foreign Office, June 26, 1939; W4253/253/519/48, Earl of Perth, Rome, to Foreign Office, March 6, 1939.
**97** PRO, FO W5686, Mercantile Marine Department, Board of Trade, London, to Foreign Office, Under-Secretary of State, April 4, 1939; W5868/519/48, A. W. G. Randall for Lord Halifax to the Secretary of the Board of Trade, May 16, 1939; W8638/519/48 W8638, 72, Home Office (Aliens Department), unsigned to ?, June 1, 1939.
**98** John Hope Simpson, *Refugees, A Review of the Situation Since September 1938*, New York: Oxford University Press, 1939, p. 47.
**99** According to Bentwich, *Wanderer Between Two Worlds*, p. 288, these "overseas settlement" plans included British and Dutch Guiana, Northern Rhodesia, the Philippines, San Domingo, and Ecuador.
**100** CAHJP, DAL 76.1, Hilfsverein to the Rt. Hon. Viscount Samuel, The Council for Germany Jewry, February 10, 1939, signed by Dr. Victor Israel Bischofswerder, Dr. Arthur Israel Prinz, Victor Israel Löwenstein. Copies were sent to Mr. Stephany; Mr. Otto Schiff, AJDC, Paris; Hicem, Paris; Refugee Economic Corporation, New York.

While the Jewish leaders in Germany were becoming increasingly desperate and the British increasingly discouraged, the Japanese in Shanghai were not idle. They, too, searched for a solution to the refugee influx, especially because most of the refugees were finding asylum in Hongkou, which was under Japanese control, north of Suzhou Creek, where rents and food were cheaper. The first steps were taken in April 1939, when a three-man committee representing the Foreign Ministry, the army, and the navy was set up to investigate the "Jewish problem" on the spot in Shanghai. The committee was given a wide-ranging brief, which indicated the political, economic, and military setting in which the Japanese viewed their problem. It was instructed to propose how to deal not only with the Jewish refugees, but with all the Jews in China.[101]

The committee began work on May 9 and formulated its proposals into a top-secret report consisting of two parts: (1) a strategy for winning the support of Shanghai's Jewish capitalists for Japan, primarily the Sassoon interests and, through them, of American Jewish influence on the U.S. government; and (2) measures to keep the Jewish refugee community in Shanghai under the Japanese thumb. The report was discussed on June 3 at a meeting of local army, navy, Foreign Ministry, and Asia Development Board representatives.[102] This meeting was followed by nearly three months of examination of the document and of proposals for amendments and revisions.[103] The final text of the Joint Report stated that the number of refugees to be allowed into Hongkou had to be limited and that their financial capabilities carefully scrutinized to ensure that they not become a liability. Measures taken now, it was stressed, were to be provisional, until the final plans – among them the postwar reconstruction of Shanghai in a Japanese-ruled China – were worked out.[104]

---

**101** JFM, Reel 414, frames 1168–1171, Arita to Miura, Top Secret. The three committee members were Ishiguro Yoshiaki, a consul in the Shanghai consulate general; Col. Yasue Norihiro, the head of the Dairen Special Services Agency who controlled the Manchukuo Jewish community, and Navy Captain Inuzuka Koreshige, who was attached to China Area Fleet HQ for the duration of the investigation. The latter two were considered experts on the "Jewish problem".

**102** The Asia Development Board, the Koain, was a cabinet agency established in December 1938, to coordinate all government activities related to China, apart from formal diplomacy; *Kodansha Encyclopedia of Japan,* Tokyo: Kodansha, 1983, Vol. 1, p. 102b.

**103** Although a good half of the report dealt with strategy vis-à-vis the well-to-do Jews in Shanghai and, through them, with the Jews in the United States, the views on these proposals were not recorded in the available documents. The discussions dragged on for three months, probably due to disagreements among the participants.

**104** "A Joint Report of Research on the Jews in Shanghai", Top Secret, July 7, 1939, JFM, Reel 414, frames 1235–1281. For discussions of the report and proposed changes:

Some weeks later, on August 4, Arita instructed Ambassador Oshima Hiroshi (1886–1973) in Berlin to ask the German government to stop sending Jewish refugees to Shanghai and all other areas occupied by the Japanese armed forces. Arita also informed Oshima that, on August 10, acting consuls general Enno Bracklo (1886–1963) and Farinacci were to be told to have their governments take "all steps within their power to prevent Jewish refugees from coming to Shanghai."[105]

Also on August 10, Ellis Hayim, the CAEJR chairman while Speelman was abroad, was summoned to a meeting at the Japanese consulate general. There he faced, in addition to Ishiguro, Inuzuka and one Tanii, a staff officer in Third Fleet HQ. However, an army representative was notably absent. Hayim was handed a memorandum in English stating that the Japanese authorities had decided to call a "temporary" halt to further "European" immigration to Shanghai, because "an influx of refugees in exceedingly large numbers will have a direct bearing ... on the plan of reconstruction of the war-torn areas". So crowded was Hongkou that "even the return of the Japanese to the area is not permitted unrestrictedly, not to mention the free return of the Chinese". The memorandum went on to claim that "it was made clear that the Jewish leaders among the Refugee Committee wished to see, for the benefit of the refugees already arrived in Shanghai, that further influx be discouraged in some way or other ..."

Hayim was ordered to have the CAEJR register the refugees living in Hongkou by August 22. Only those so registered would be allowed to remain. Hayim was also ordered to have the CAEJR inform Jewish organizations in England, the United States, France, and Germany of the Japanese decision. Thereupon, under duress, he sent off a cable to the Council for German Jewry saying, "Further immigration to Shanghai must cease and be prevented. Inform Paris New York Cairo Speelman". In another cable, to the JDC office in Paris, he asked that Berlin and Vienna also be informed.[106]

---

Reel 414, frames 1102–1104, 1219–1220, 1227–1233, 1285–1290, 1293–1296, 1321, 1354, 1397–1404, 1458–1469. I thank Professor Avraham Altman for making these and the following materials available to me.

**105** The communications to Bracklo and Farinacci, both dated August 10, 1939, are in JFM, Reel 414, frames 1414–1418 and frames 1421–1423.

**106** The two cables, the first dated August 14, 1939, and the second August 16, 1939, are in JDC, RG 33–44, file 458, Troper to JDC New York, August 18, 1939. The meeting at the consulate general is detailed in JFM, Reel 414, frames 1419–1420, Miura to a list of senior military recipients and the Liaison Sections of the Central China Fleet Expeditionary Force HQ and of the Asia Development Board, Secret, August 11, 1939. The text of the memorandum, dated August 9, 1939, is in Reel 414, frames 1424– 1426. For the Chinese text, see "Youtai nanmin xuxiang Ri, shenqinghou ke juliu, fouze

In fact, the SMC had been forewarned earlier that the Japanese were planning some kind of closure. A note transmitted to an unspecified addressee stated that Captain Matsubara, Chief of the Shanghai Naval Rehabilitation Corps, had informed the sender of the note that, "... in future the right of residence of these refugees will be controlled in favor of Japanese interests and also in favor of those Chinese desiring to return to that area.[107]" Thus the subsequent unilateral SMC decision to close the International Settlement altogether to European refugees might have been contemplated for some time.

The SMC's reaction to the Japanese closure two days later in August was to decide unilaterally and without consulting the Consular body "that the Council is compelled to forbid any further entry into International Settlement of refugees from Europe". All steps will be taken, according to the Council, to prevent further immigration, although refugees already embarked on ships or on the high seas would still be allowed to land.[108] As reported in the press, the SMC decision was taken August 11, 1939, in "parallel but independent action" with the French, who did not sign until August 14. The SMC secretary denied that the decision was related to the Japanese closure. However, if the Japanese lift the embargo, he declared, the SMC might also consider finding homes for the 5000 Jews already "booked for Shanghai.[109]" Having decided and informed the members of the Consular body, the secretary of the SMC held a meeting on August 17 with the Japanese and the French Consuls General, at which time they determined that refugees who sailed after August 18 from European ports would not be permitted to land.[110]

---

lingqi tuichu jingbeiqu (Jewish refugees must now request from the Japanese to live in the special area, otherwise they will be ordered to leave it)", *XSB*, No. 671, August 12, 1939, p. 7. For the English text, see YVA, 078/86, Shanghai Municipal Archives, "Memorandum". This is an unsigned copy of the memorandum.

**107** YVA, 078/85, Shanghai Municipal Archive, signature illegible, July 3, 1939. The letter from Matsubara was dated June 28.

**108** PRO, FO 371/24079, W12030, ? addressed to the British Ambassador, Shanghai, August 15, 1939. See also PRO, FO W12030/519/48, telegram from Sir H. Phillips, Shanghai, to the Foreign Office, August 15, 1939, informing the Foreign Office of the Japanese move and the Council's decision to forbid entry of refugees to the International Settlement.

**109** "All Shanghai Now Closed to Emigres", *CP*, August 15, 1939, pp. 1,8. See also, *Evreiskaya Zhizn*, no. 38, September 6, 1939, pp. 4–6, where the Japanese authorities are quoted as reiterating that they will not interfere with the arrival of Jews in Shanghai, but that Jews must settle in districts other than Hongkou.

**110** PRO, FO 371/24079, W14479, ? addressed to the British Ambassador, Shanghai, September 1, 1939.

The German and Italian consulates and, surprising to the British, also the Portuguese consulate, swiftly lodged protests. In their view, the Council's decision was not legal, as it was taken without the full agreement of the consular body. But the protest was, in fact, only a formal gesture, for both the German and Italian consuls included a paragraph in their letter stating that in the current situation they accept the SMC's decision. Each added a condition: the Germans, that relatives be allowed to join family members already in Shanghai; the Italians, that the Council's decision be confirmed by the consular body.[111]

The announced closure created a major problem for the shipping lines. They above all wanted to make certain that those refugees already on the high seas would be allowed to land. But they were also concerned over how to distinguish refugees from non-refugees, since both traveled with valid passports. What documents are required, asked the North-German Lloyd Bremen agent in Shanghai, to prove that a person is not a refugee? And the Lloyd Triestino agent wondered who is to be considered a refugee. Their worries were justified. By mid-August, the Lloyd Triestino line alone had over 900 refugees on the high seas who would arrive at the end of August and in September; another 120 were about to board the *Potsdam* in Germany.[112] No doubt, many hundreds more had also already booked passage.

Realizing that these questions demanded answers, and having meanwhile reached a consensus in private talks with the Japanese and French consuls general on not admitting any more refugees, Phillips undertook the initial step toward limiting the refugee flow. He informed the local representatives of nine shipping companies that regulations would be promulgated in the near future regarding the entry into Shanghai of European refugees. Pending this action, Phillips asked the companies to "avoid taking any bookings for Shanghai from persons who may possibly come within the ambit of any proposed regulations.[113]"

---

111  PRO, FO 371/24079, W14479, E. Bracklo, Acting Consul-General for Germany to Poul Scheel, Consul-General for Denmark and Senior Consul, August 19, 1939; G. Brigidi, Acting Consul-General for Italy to Poul Scheel, August 16, 1939; J. A. Ribeiro de Melo, Consul-General for Portugal to Poul Scheel, August 18, 1939.

112  YVA, 078/86, Shanghai Municipal Archive, A. Bonetta to G. G. Phillips, August 16, 1939; Melchers and Co. to [Phillips] Secretary and Commissioner General, SMC, August 16, 1939. Also YVA, 078/87, Norddeutscher Lloyd Bremen to the Secretary and Commissioner General, SMC, November 15, 1939. At the outbreak of war, the German "Coburg" with its contingent of refugees sought refuge in Massowah. The agent hoped that the refugees would be allowed to land when they arrived on a Lloyd Triestino ship, since they had departed prior to the closure.

113  JFM, Reel 414, frame 1474, G. G. Phillips to shipping companies, August 17, 1939.

At the same time, the committee on the definition of a refugee, the Refugee Admittance Committee, consisting of Eduard Kann, vice-chairman of the CAEJR; Japanese consul S. Ishiguro; French vice-consul M. G. Cattand; E. T. Nash of the SMC, began its deliberations.[114] In the draft documents circulated among the members of the committee, the word "Jew" or "Jewish" was never mentioned, as it would also not be in the final version.[115] Stressed were rather the economic and social problems and lack of employment opportunities that a large influx of immigrants in Shanghai would cause. Thus the draft "Preliminary Regulations for the Entry of European Refugees into Shanghai" stated in the first paragraph that, "'Refugee' has application irrespective of race, nationality or religious faith; having a purely economic connotation". And the second paragraph defined a refugee as a "non-Asiatic foreigner.[116]" That limitations on entry into Shanghai applied only to passport holders with a red "J" was successfully hidden and in subsequent years the SMC persistently refused to state this fact in writing.[117] Defining who was a refugee entailed, of course, also defining who would be permitted to land in Shanghai. The permit system that subsequently came into being, therefore, had its genesis in the unilateral Japanese decision to close Hongkou to the refugees, on the one hand, and to the SMC reaction, on the other. But the permit system was destined to be as ineffective as the Japanese and the SMC steps. Ultimately, it was events in Europe – the start of WWII, Italy's entry into the war, and Germany's invasion of the Soviet Union – that ended sea travel and the refugee influx into Shanghai

## The Permit System

Despite the agreement of the three partners on immigration restrictions, they soon disagreed on their implementation, and in the end decided to implement them independently of one another. The regulations for Shanghai entry, issued October 22, were published in the *Municipal Gazette* of October 27, 1939. They

---

**114**  "Committee Formed for Jew Problem", *NCH*, August 23, 1939, p. 325.
**115**  According to the "Rules for Refugees", the *NCDN*, October 6, 1939, carried a report from the *Tairiku Shimpo* from October 5, that it was decided at the meeting to drop the term "Jewish refugee" in favor of "Central European Refugee".
**116**  YVA, 078/86, Shanghai Municipal Archives, "Provisional Arrangement Regarding Entry into Shanghai of European Refugees", n. d., signature illegible; "Suggested Regulations re Admittance into Shanghai of European Refugees", E. Kann, August 25, 1939; "Prohibition of Entry of European Refugees into Shanghai", no signature, August 1939.
**117**  CAHJP, DAL 96, Birman to Hicem, Marseilles, October 27, 1941.

stated that a person could land if he or she had the required sum of $400 per adult and $100 per child, which travel agents or shipping companies were to verify. Instead of money, a person could also land with an SMC entry permit, which had been granted if the person was an immediate relative of a financially secure refugee in Shanghai, intended to marry a Shanghai resident, or had an employment contract. Entry permits were to be obtained from the Council through the CAEJR, and the Special Branch of the Police Department would investigate each application. An appended note stated that these regulations were valid only for the International Settlement south of Suzhou Creek; those wishing to reside north of the Creek had to apply to the Japanese authorities.[118] The French Concession is not mentioned in the note, but it was understood that arrangements with it would have to be made separately. The French financial requirement differed from the SMC's and demanded $300 for the first and $200 for every additional person, including children.[119] By the time the regulations came into effect, Germany had invaded Poland, WII had begun, and German ships no longer sailed to Shanghai.

Before many months had passed, however, the Shanghai Municipal Police discovered a serious loophole in the regulations. Refugees who managed to secure bookings on non-German vessels generally preferred showing possession of money, rather than wasting precious time waiting for permits, and shipping companies were often lax in enforcing possession of funds. Among the ninety refugees who arrived on April 4, 1940 on the *Conte Verde*, only eighteen had permits, while seventy one landed with money.[120] According to the police report of May 23, 1940, of the 213 refugees arriving on the *Conte Rosso* on May 2, only 47 had permits. The October regulations, stated the report, were therefore not stopping the influx and, "Any Tom, Dick, or Harry can land here provided he has the necessary funds and as many as a shipload can arrive with each and every steamer". The police verdict was that permits alone, and not money, would "act as a brake". Even members of the Jewish community agree, the report went on, that immigration be either forbidden or limited to a few "desirables from time to time.[121]"

---

118  YVA, 078/88, "Entry of European Refugees", dated October 22, 1939. For the aftermath of the closure, see also JDC, RG 33/44, file 458, E. Kann, "Report on the Problem of Immigration into China on the Part of European Refugees", November 11, 1939.
119  CAHJP, 86.3, Birman to Reich Association, May 13, 1940. The French procedure was also somewhat different.
120  CAHJP, 86.4, CAEJR to Daljewcib, April 8, 1940.
121  YVA, 078/88, Shanghai Municipal Archives, Police report sent to the SMC Secretary and Commissioner General, May 24, 1940.

Meir Birman also realized that permits did not deter immigrants: if a person can show the required sum of money, permits are easily obtained on arrival, he wrote.[122] While the SMC undertook the revision of the permit regulations, the Jewish leadership in Shanghai too wanted to introduce a change in the financial arrangements. According to the October regulations, the "show money" (Vorzeigegeld, as it was considered by the Jewish organizations) was paid to the shipping companies, which gave the money to the passengers upon arrival. Not all arrivals had used their own funds, and those who had received money from the Jewish organizations were expected to return it to the HICEM office in Shanghai. Unfortunately, some refugees – penniless arrivals, it must be remembered – refused to part with the funds, which led to considerable unpleasantness between the Jewish authorities and the refugees, as neither HICEM nor anyone else had the authority to collect the money from a recalcitrant refugee. A Mrs. Baden, for example, requested and was given "show money" by two different offices[123], and arrived in Shanghai with double the amount needed, which she refused to return. Other refugees were said to be sending the money to their relatives in Germany to enable them to come, instead of returning it or using it in Shanghai.[124] Several months later, Birman still recalled the embarrassment the refugees' untrustworthiness had caused. Even the Japanese got wind of it, he said.[125]

Therefore, both the SMC regulations and the financial regulation were also revised. Henceforth funds were to be paid into Speelman's account with the Hongkong and Shanghai Banking Corporation, and the CAEJR was to send a letter to the Settlement police that the money was indeed on deposit.[126] The revised regulations, dated June 1, 1940, were published in the *Municipal Gazette* of June 28, effective as of July 1, 1940. They stated that refugees must have entry permits as well as money, which was to be deposited with the CAEJR. Shipping or travel agents must verify the possession of the permit at the time of booking passage, and permits were valid only for four months. Similar to one year earlier, these regulations applied to the International Settlement south of Suzhou Creek and not to other areas.[127]

---

**122** CAHJP, DAL 86, Birman to the South African Fund for German Jewry, May 3, 1940.

**123** CAHJP, 86.2, Birman to Speelman, May 30, 1940.

**124** YVA, 078/88, Shanghai Municipal Archives, Shanghai Municipal Council to Members of the Council, May 29, 1940, signature illegible.

**125** CAHJP, 86.4, Birman to Reich Association, November 21, 1940.

**126** YVA, 078/88, Shanghai Municipal Archives, Nash to Kann, June 19, 1940; CAHJP. 86.3, Birman to Reich Association, June 27, 1940. The bank was changed later in the month to the Chase Bank because it belonged to a neutral power.

**127** YVA, 078/88, Shanghai Municipal Archives, *Gazette* copy. CAHJP, 86.4, Birman to Reichsvereinigung, November 11, 1940, the SMC has agreed to issue permits for six

Although generally referred to as "permits", the actual document was labeled a "Certificate", which stated: "This is to certify that there is no objection to the entry into the International Settlement of Shanghai South of the Soochow Creek", followed by the name of the person. This careful wording had political reasons and reflected the SMC's delicate relationship with the Japanese, and the continued question of the measure's legality that the Japanese might want to turn to their advantage.

Clearly, the Japanese were pursuing their own policy in regard to the refugees and the SMC was unwilling, or considered its position too vulnerable, to challenge it. Perhaps this is the reason why Assistant Secretary E. T. Nash felt compelled in July 1940 to put himself and the SMC on record. "By understanding reached with the Japanese, we are exercising assumed powers to prohibit certain Jewish parties from 'entering' Shanghai", wrote Nash. The SMC, however, had no such powers; it had no passport office, and it was not empowered to authorize entry to anyone. Therefore, the permits only stated that there are 'no objections' to entry into the International Settlement. Nowhere was either "permission to enter" or "Shanghai" referred to. However, should the Japanese not permit entry into Shanghai, the letter continued, "on the strength merely of our certificate of 'non-objection', we should refrain from challenging their decision". On the other hand, if the Japanese authorities refused entry to qualified Jewish refugees, such information would probably have been conveyed to the Consular body, who could raise the matter with the Japanese if they wished.[128]

There were other problems. The SMC tried to control the continued, though much smaller, refugee influx on Japanese ships arriving from Dalian. A Mr. Nakashima from the Dairen Kisen Kaisha Line was requested to prepare lists of refugees and to collect their passports for members of the Jewish committee who met the ships. But Nakashima was uncooperative. The ships' crews were

---

instead of four months; DAL 99, Birman to International Migration Service, Geneva, September 5, 1941, Japanese permits continued to be valid for only four months, but none have been issued since a year ago; DAL 87, Birman to Hicem, Paris, June 5, 1940, unlike the SMC and the French, the Japanese did not have a money requirement. See also, Efraim Zuroff, *The Response of Orthodox Jewry in the United States to the Holocaust, the Activities of the Vaad-Ha-Hatzala Rescue Committee, 1939–1945*, New York: Yeshiva University Press, Hoboken, N.J.: Ktav Publishing House, Inc., 2000, p. 147, notes 13, 15, p. 165. Some manipulation of the permit system was apparently possible. When the Shanghai Ashkenazi Jewish Communal Association provided guarantees for $ 30 maintenance per person for 300 Polish refugees in March 1941 the SMC agreed to issue permits for them.

**128** YVA, 078/88, Shanghai Municipal Archives, Nash to R.W. Yorke, July 10, 1940.

unable to do these extra chores, he declared, nor was he willing to post a notice advising refugees to remain on board until they were met by a member of the committee.[129] The SMC was also attempting to control the arrival of refugees with expired permits as the shipping companies seemed to pay no attention to their expiration dates.[130] Finally, refugees with criminal records, who had been imprisoned, were said to be arriving in Shanghai. This was in fact so. Not only had Jews been arrested and rearrested, but among them were also Communist Party members, as mentioned earlier. These staunch communists held meetings and engaged in, to use their term, educational activities.[131] They may not have escaped the notice of police spies who were active among the refugees.[132]

A new and at first puzzling development meanwhile took place in spring 1940. Whereas to the British the refugees were a worrisome nuisance, to the Japanese they looked potentially useful in their bid to gain greater power in Shanghai politics. By the middle of April 1940, Meir Birman noticed a sudden increase of permits issued by the Japanese Consulate General since the beginning of the month. Compared to the Settlement's 800 permits issued by February 1940, there had been only around fifty or sixty by the Japanese.[133] In the first two weeks of April, however, the Japanese issued around 200[134], and by May apparently as many as 800 or 900 had been obtained by the refugees.[135] An irate Eduard Kann penned an angry letter to Japanese consul Ishiguro,

---

**129** YVA, 078/88, Shanghai Municipal Archives, Nash to Dairen Kisen Kaisha Line, June 4, 1940; Police memorandum (?), unsigned, June 26, 1940.

**130** YVA, 078/88, Shanghai Municipal Archive, Police memorandum (?), unsigned, May 30, 1940.

**131** Gerd Kaminsky, *General Luo genannt Langnase, das abenteuerliche Leben des Dr. med. Jacob Rosenfeld*, Vienna: Löcker Verlag, 1993, p. 48, mentions weekly meetings of German Marxists with Gregory Grzyb alias Heinz Shippe, members of the German Communist Party.

**132** Dreifuss, "Shanghai – Eine Emigration am Rande", p. 575, mentions around twenty-five party members; Nobel, "Erinnerungen", pp. 885–886; see also SMP, Reel 17, D-5422 (c). D. S. I. Gigarson, a Russian, for example, was watching and reporting on Jewish activities.

**133** CAHJP, 86.2, Birman to Braun, Reich Association, February 22, 1940.

**134** CAHJP, 86.3, Birman to Braun, Reich Association, April 15, 1940. Birman, by then, was well aware of the reason for the increase, but called it a "special occasion".

**135** CAHJP, DAL 87, Birman to HIAS, New York, June 6, 1940. According to a letter from Birman to the Vienna Kultusgemeinde, June 14, 1940, the Japanese issued 900 permits. However, according to a letter from the Japanese Consulate General by May 27 only 874 permits had been issued. SMP, Reel 17, D5422 (c) 70, M. Shibata to E. T. Nash, May 27, 1940.

strongly objecting to the issuing of "1,000 immigration permits for Hongkew residence". Without mentioning in so many words the reason for the Japanese authorities' munificence, Kann wrote that applications for permits "were submitted without the intermediary of our Committee, so that the latter was not enabled to investigate the bona fides of the applicants, nor could we examine the prospects of the new arrivals to make a living in Shanghai". And he added pointedly, "Recently the Electioneering Association, consisting of refugees, a body without juridical standing, has inaugurated a campaign for the issue of immigration permits. We have no desire whatsoever to either criticize, nor to interfere in any way with the decisions of your Consulate General in this respect". Kann nonetheless wanted it on record that his committee could not be responsible for persons whose background had not been examined.[136]

The Japanese suddenly issued a large number of permits because of the April 10–11, 1940, elections for members of the Municipal Council on which the Japanese wanted to increase their representation. Instead of their traditional two members, they put up five candidates. Elections were based on the so-called "rate-payers' principle".[137] Hongkou's large refugee population, where many met the rate-payers' requirement, thus became a valuable pool of votes. When, in addition, the Japanese promised to issue permits in return for refugee votes, it seemed a foregone conclusion that the Japanese would get their five council members.

Paul Komor, head of the I. C., Ellis Hayim, and others were horrified. On the one hand, they took pains to assure the Japanese that they would in no way influence immigrants to vote one way or another. But, on the other, they stressed that refugees should abstain altogether from voting, having been advised on arrival not to engage in political activities.[138] Whether the refugees would heed this advice was anyone's guess because in the meantime the Japanese opened a canvassing office in which two Japanese and four refugees busily wooed potential voters.[139]

The Japanese were not pleased with the advice to the Jews to remain aloof. On April 8 the Japanese confiscated all issues of the German-language emigre

---

**136** PRO, FO/371/24696, no. 364, Kann to Ishiguro, April 25, 1940. (Copy of Kann's letter).
**137** Eligibility to vote was based on taxes paid. Property owners as well as tenants who paid a certain assessed value were entitled to a franchise.
**138** "Refugees Urged to Remain Neutral", *NCDN*, April 4, 1940, p. 2. This had been stated in a meeting on March 29.
**139** "Japanese Bribing Emigres for Votes, Relatives Getting Landing Permits", *SEPM*, April 3, 1940, p. 2.

newspaper, *Gelbe Post*, whose lead article proffered similar advice.[140] At the same time, Shanghai's foreign community realized that their fate might very well be decided by these newcomers who had no stake in Shanghai's future, as they saw it. Under the screaming headline, "Emigres deciding S'hai's Fate, British-American Bloc Votes Equal Japanese; Jewish Holding Balance", the *SEPM* article went on to say, "Leaving their homelands within only the past year or so, German and Austrian Jewish refugees today hold the destiny of the International Settlement ... in their hands". Under its thinly disguised anti-Semitism, the article repeated the charge that the Japanese were bribing the refugees with permits for their relatives when, in fact, they "know nothing of the history of Shanghai" and its foreign investments.[141]

Fortunately, the huge turnout at this "most momentous municipal election that the city has seen", assured the maintenance of the status quo. As in previous years, two Japanese, two Americans, and five British were elected to the council. In spite of having received permits, overwhelmingly large numbers of refugees apparently did not vote for the Japanese candidates. According to a newspaper report, many were seen voting not at the Hongkou market, where there would have been greater Japanese surveillance, but at the Shanghai Volunteer Corps Drill Hall in the International Settlement.[142]

The defeat of the Japanese candidates may have prompted Inuzuka of the Japanese Naval Landing Party to write an insolent and threatening letter to Speelman and his committee in August. In it he reminded Speelman that a country admits aliens provided they exert themselves "to enlarge the prosperity of the country". Japan has admitted refugees into that portion of Shanghai which is under occupation, therefore,

> In view of the sweeping anti-Semitism which it is feared might spread to and be aggravated in the Far East, it would appear to be to their own interest ... to endeavor at all times to make the best possible impression upon ... [the Japanese authorities].

He also reminded Speelman that the Harbin Jews had adopted a resolution at the Far East Jewish Congress to cooperate with Japan. And he indicated that it behooves Jews living in the Japanese-occupied territory of Shanghai to do likewise.[143] Inuzuka may have regretted that by then many hundreds of permits had become available for the areas under Japanese control, although we have

---

140 "Japanese Seize Jewish Paper", *NCDN*, April 9, 1940, p. 2.
141 *SEPM*, April 5, 1940, p. 3.
142 *SEPM*, April 12, 1940, p. 1; "Election and War Fevers Compete in Shanghai", *NCDN*, April 11, 1940, p. 1.
143 PRO, FO/371/24684, K. Inuzuka to Speelman, August 27, 1940.

no way of knowing how many of these were eventually used. Inuzuka wrote still another letter, this time to Ellis Hayim, advising him and the I. C. to write to the United States government expressing "their gratitude and appreciation for 'the kindly attitude of the Japanese authorities to the Refugees.'" When Hayim refused, Inuzuka accused him of being more English than Jewish.[144] Pressure was also brought on Speelman to write to American Jewish leaders how indebted they were to the Japanese. Speelman proved more cooperative than Hayim and wrote to the JDC secretary, "We ... wish to place on record that the Japanese Authorities have always made it a point to treat our refugees ... in a very sympathetic and humane manner, which is greatly appreciated.[145]"

These letters, and there may have been others, brought home no doubt to Shanghai's wealthy Jews how precariously poised they were between protecting their privileged status with the British while somehow attempting to avoid Japanese pressure to do its bidding. They identified their interests with those of the British; it was in their interest to support British attempts to limit the refugee influx. And they, like the British, had no desire to antagonize the Japanese. Yet, men like Hayim, Speelman, and Kann, must have also realized that they were Jews in the eyes of the British as well as the Japanese, part of a world-wide Jewish community.

While the new regulations went into effect and Nash worried about the Japanese, world events intervened once again in the refugee flight. In June 1940 Italy joined Germany at war thus ending the Italian participation in the refugee traffic. Henceforth only French and Japanese ships would be available. Before long, however, these too would no longer leave from Europe for Shanghai. By the end of June 1940, the few Japanese liners that still sailed from Europe were generally fully booked with Japanese returnees.[146] In October 1940, the JDC discussed discontinuing bookings on Japanese liners due to the strained U. S.-Japanese relations, and in November 1940, Japanese ship travel from Lisbon to East Asia was suspended.[147] French ship space had never been plentiful and, after Germany oc-

---

**144** PRO, FO/371/24684, A. H. George, Consul-General to the Ambassador, Shanghai, September 5, 1940.

**145** JDC, RG 33–44, file 460, Speelman to JDC secretary, September 9, 1940.

**146** YVA, 078/73B, German General Consulate, Shanghai, Report, "Jews in Shanghai", to Foreign Office, Berlin, signature illegible, June 30, 1940, p. 1.

**147** JDC, RG 33/44, file 59, "Meeting of the Administration Committee of the Joint Distribution Committee", October 9, 1940. Although knowing full well how dangerous the situation had become for Jews in Europe, Morris C. Troper supported discontinuing use of Japanese ships by arguing that Jews sailing on Japanese liners might get stuck indefinitely in Japan and would then require JDC support; CAHJP, 86.4, Braun to Daljewcib, November 11, 1940.

cupied France in June 1940, dwindled even more. Moreover, the French Concession had issued very few permits since October 1939 and by May 1940 stopped issuing them altogether.[148] The advantage of French permits, however, was that they had no expiration date, so that recipients could at least continue to sail from Marseilles to an Indo-China (Vietnam) port provided they were able to obtain a booking. Indeed, Shanghai was increasingly less frequented by international shipping and by August 1941, Meir Birman remarked on the mostly local, Asian, traffic in Shanghai harbors. Three months later, a growing sense of isolation was evident in Birman's letters when he wrote that, "Shanghai is cut off from many countries, South and Central America. Trans-ocean traffic has been suspended by the Japanese lines.[149]"

Finally, Nationalist consulates abroad were apparently not informed of the permit requirements in Shanghai. Rene Unterman, stranded in South Africa after the German invasion of Antwerp and in possession of a Chinese visa which he had obtained in Lisbon, turned to the Chinese consulate when he was unable to book passage for Shanghai. Considering it probably no more than a mere procedural matter, Consul General F. T. Sung simply requested a permit from the SMP, receiving, in turn, no more than a frosty reply from Nash.[150]

## Legitimate and Forged Permits

The permit system as conceived in 1939 and revised in 1940 involved only the SMC, the French, and the Japanese Consulate-General. If the question arose whether the Chinese Municipal Government had the authority to issue permits, it is not mentioned in any of the documents. Yet, by mid-September 1940, permits issued by the Bureau of Social Affairs of the City Government of Greater Shanghai (*Shanghai tebieshi shehui ju* ...) suddenly came to Birman's attention, and were, according to Braun of the Reich Association, honored by the Japanese consulate in Berlin.[151] Eduard Kann, whom Birman consulted, was told by the Japanese consul that the people of the Bureau of Social Affairs were not trustworthy. But apparently he did not indicate that permits from the

**148** CAHJP, 86.3, Birman to Reich Association, April 1, 1940.
**149** CAHJP, DAL 99, Birman to Settlement Association, Dominican Republic, August 24, 1941; DAL 101, Birman to Polish Relief Committee, Melbourne, November 6, 1941.
**150** YVA, 078/88, Shanghai Municipal Council, F. T. Sung to The Chairman, SMC, November 19, 1940; Nash to F. T. Sung, January 30, 1941. Unterman had been Honorary Consul for Rumania in Antwerp.
**151** CAHJP, 86.3, telegram from Berlin to Hicem, September 18, 1940.

Chinese were not acceptable.[152] In fact, the Japanese consul had become aware of the permits – with seal and signature of a Yao Keming – already one month earlier, and had noted that these permits were circulating for several months. He considered them counterfeit (something he seems not to have wanted to admit to Kann), and he wondered if they were produced by officials of the Social Affairs Bureau on their own initiative.[153]

Despite the Japanese consul's hints that something unsavory was afoot, Meir Birman expressed cautious optimism about the appearance of the Chinese permits. In his view, "Although the issuing of permits for Greater Shanghai is not sufficiently organized and therefore not as significant ... meanwhile the Nanjing regime, to which the Greater Shanghai authorities are subordinate, was recognized by both Manchukuo and Japan.[154]"

There is no way of knowing how many such permits were actually in circulation, or how many people arrived with them in Shanghai. But counterfeit permits also circulated, and various individuals began to sell either genuine or counterfeit permits.[155] A Dr. Herbert Frank, an attorney in Shanghai, claimed to be able to get Japanese permits[156], and three German Jews were imprisoned in August 1940 for promising to get Japanese Special Naval Landing Party permits, having acquired in the process the tidy sum of $2000.[157] A Heinrich Haas, who had arrived in Shanghai in 1938 and was said to live with a Japanese woman, produced counterfeit municipal permits[158], and according to Birman,

---

**152** CAHJP, 86.3, Birman to Reich Association, September 19, 1940.

**153** JFM, Reel 415, frame 2304, Miura, Consul-General to Matsuoka, Foreign Minister, August 12, 1940; frame 2305–2306, Miura to two Army and Navy addresses in Shanghai, August 12, 1940. See also Japanese Foreign Ministry, Foreign Relations Archive, telegram, August 18, 1940, from Japanese ambassador Kurusa in Berlin to foreign minister Matsuoka. The ambassador had discovered four cases of permits issued by the Bureau of Social Affairs which he considered to be forged permits. The permits are labeled "Certificates", like those from the SMC, and the text reads, "This is to certify that the permission for entry into Shanghai is granted to", followed by name of person. It is signed Bureau of Social Affairs City Government of Great (sic) Shanghai. The signature for the English text is illegible, the Chinese text is signed by Yao Keming. A copy of this permit is reproduced in Inuzuka Kiyoko, *Yudaya mondai to Nihon no kosaku* , Tokyo: Nihon kogyo shinbunsha, 1972, p. 369.

**154** CAHJP, DAL 93, Birman to Reich Association, December 12, 1940.

**155** CAHJP, 86.3, Birman to Reich Association, March 28, 1940. This is the first mention in the correspondence.

**156** CAHJP, 86.2, Birman to Speelman, July 15, 1940; 86.3, Birman to Reich Association, August 8, 1940, Birman vigorously denied that Japanese permits are available through middlemen, they can be only obtained by a person living in Hongkou.

**157** *NCH*, August 14, 1940, p. 258.

**158** JFM, reel 415, frame 2312, Miura to two Army and Navy addresses in Shanghai, August 17, 1940.

some people actually managed to arrive in Shanghai with counterfeit permits.[159] Not all were that lucky. The Japanese Consul-General in Hamburg reported seizing one Japanese counterfeit permit in July and two in August.[160] Still other refugees arrived with permits obtained from "middlemen", for between $25 and $50.[161] Con games with permits did not turn out so well. Abraheim (sic) and Erich Schrangenheim were arrested when they defrauded Martin Bandman of 50 British pounds, by promising to obtain a Japanese permit for him.[162] Max Jacobi was arrested for taking $450 from three refugees to obtain permits.[163]

A Polish attorney and one-time police commissioner, Gabriel Lax, attempted to get SMC permits by forging the Shanghai Municipal Police stamp and two signatures on an application to the Jewish Immigration Committee. The forged signatures were those of two people who promised to provide employment for a family from Germany. Unfortunately, the forgery was discovered and Lax was convicted in court, but given a suspended sentence.[164] Nothing more is heard about counterfeit permits in 1941. Either the forgers were caught, or else decided not to press their luck.

The available data does not enable me to estimate how many permits were issued or how many were ultimately used. Presumably, between July 1940 and the beginning of 1941, the CAEJR had reviewed 3,700 applications for approximately 6,000 persons. 55% of these applications were for Japan-controlled Hongkou, 40% for the International Settlement; 5% for the French Concession. Altogether 2,500 applications for 4,000 persons were approved by the SMC.[165] The Japanese had issued more permits than the French, but only because they tried to buy the refugees' votes in the SMC elections, discussed

---

**159** CAHJP, 86.3, Birman to Reich Association, September 2, 1940.

**160** JFM, reel 415, frame 2321–2322, Kawamura to Foreign Minister Matsuoka, August 23, 1940.

**161** CAHJP, 86.3, Braun, Reich Association to Daljewcib, August 3, 1940. Braun adds that he has seen a number of "successful" cases. Emigres on their initiative made contact with the middleman and received certificates. These forged permits were, therefore, apparently produced in Germany.

**162** "Two Arrested in Fake Pass Count", *SEPM*, August 13, 1940, p. 2. They each received a two year prison sentence. *CP*, September 11, 1940, p. 3.

**163** "Refugee Held in Fake Pass Charges Here", *SEPM*, October 10, 1940, p. 2.

**164** *CP*, June 9 and June 16, 1940, p. 2; see also CAHJP, DAL 87, Birman to Reich Association, June 10, 1940. See also JDC, 33/44. file 460, clipping from the *Shanghai Jewish Chronicle*, n. d., which discusses the various counterfeit permits in circulation.

**165** YVA, 078/73B, German Consulate General, Shanghai, Report, "Jews in Shanghai", to Foreign Office, Berlin, signature illegible, February 2, 1941, p. 1.

above. The SMC had issued by far the largest number of permits, but in the spring of 1941, the waiting periods were long and the conditions ever more stringent.[166] Aside from the lack of ship facilities, the permit system was undoubtedly the next most important factor in preventing refugees from reaching Shanghai. Permits were crucial documents that refugees had to produce when applying for emigration and booking passage on steamers and trains. But due to the cumbersome system of obtaining and mailing them to recipients, these life-saving documents reached many too late. Let me cite several cases. There was the tragic example of Paula Laufer from Vienna. Her brother Moritz Laufer in Shanghai had managed to get her a permit sometime in 1939, but she was told in 1940 that permits issued prior to the outbreak of war were no longer valid. Another permit, issued April 28, 1941, was not acceptable to the German authorities because it was submitted without the envelope in which it had arrived. September 14, 1942 Paula Laufer was deported to Minsk.[167] Klara Lewin had left her two children in a Berlin orphanage. After reaching Shanghai, she requested permits for them from the Japanese. She never received them.[168] In May 1940, permits arrived in Warsaw for the Sonnenfeld, Goldman, Szmulewicz, Grynspan, and Jakubowski families, but they were unable to use them because Jews were no longer allowed to leave the German-occupied portion of Poland.[169] Permits for over fifty people still arrived in Warsaw in June 1940. On

---

**166** CAHJP, 72.4, Birman to Rosovsky and Epstein, Kobe, March 31, 1941; DAL 93, Birman to E. J. London, Washington D.C., December 26, 1940. See also JDC, RG 33/34, file 459, February 1, 1940. The SMP could deal with only thirty applications a week, while twice that number was received by the CAEJR. CAHJP, 86.4, Birman to Reichsvereinigung, November 7, 1940, at the Japanese consulate general there were presumably 4,000 requests for permits, which apparently were never dealt with.

**167** YVA, Dokumentsarchiv des österreichischen Wiederstandes, 16230, from Moritz Adolf Laufer to Modern Millinery LTD., January 15, 1940; Auslandbriefprüfstelle Berlin to Paula S. Laufer, June 13, 1941; W. Guttman of the U. K., Search Bureau for German, Austria, and Stateless Persons from Central Europe to Mrs. Josefine Bauer, n. d.

**168** CAHJP, DAL 86, Birman to Reichsvereinigung, May 3, 1940.

**169** CAHJP, 86.4, JEAS [acronym for Hias] to Birman, May 22. 1940, and cable from JEAS, also May 22; John Mendelsohn, ed., *The Holocaust, Selected Documents in Eighteen Volumes*, Vol. 6, pp. 234–236. A May 8, 1940 telegram from Kirk informed the Secretary of State, Washington, that, although no formal prohibition regarding emigration of Jews from the General Government exists, the Germans believe that allowing Polish Jews to leave would retard emigration from the Reich and Austria. The formal order prohibiting Jewish emigration is dated October 25, 1940. Tatiana Berenstein, A. Eisenbach, A. Rutkowski, comps. eds., *Eksterminacja Żydów na ziemiach Polskich w okresie okupacji hitlerowskiej* (Extermination of Jews on Polish soil during the Hitlerite occupation), Warsaw: Żydowski Instytut Historyczny, 1957, pp. 55–56.

September 6, 1940, Dr. J. Morgenstern of JEAS cabled Shanghai that all emigration from the General Government had been stopped since April 1, 1940.[170] Finally, there is the tragic case of Dr. Franz Spitzer and his wife Louise, who had come to Shanghai, having left their two children, aged fourteen and ten, in southern France. By the time they secured permits in August 1941, which had been sent to the children's uncle in Limoges with the necessary travel funds, it was already too late. Four months later, after Pearl Harbor, Birman returned the money to the parents.[171] In February 1941, Birman estimated that more than 2,000 Jews with SMC permits waited in various European cities.[172] For all these and many more it was already too late.

## Overland Routes

In order to reach Shanghai from Germany or Austria overland, a person required not only a permit from one of the three international bodies in Shanghai, but also two transit visas: one for the Soviet Union and the Trans-Siberian railway in Moscow[173], and another for Manchukuo to travel to Dalian (Dairen), and from there hopefully book ship passage to Shanghai. In order to avoid the Manchukuo transit visa complication, some travelers went to Vladivostok, hoping to find passage to Shanghai from there. But Vladivostok, as we shall see below, was hardly a solution because few Soviet ships (for the most part cargo ships) sailed from Vladivostok to Shanghai. A slightly different overland route was taken by a group of Polish refugees who had fled to Lithuania when the Germans invaded Poland September 1, 1939. Consisting of rabbinic school (yeshivoth) students and their rabbis as well as secular journalists, writers, poets, and actors, these people first obtained end visas from the Dutch consul,

---

**170**  CAHJP, 86.4, JEAS to Daljewcib, June 14, June 17, September 6, 1940. Morgenstern's terse sentence tells it all, "Jedwede Auswanderung aus dem Generalgouvernment ist seit April 1 J. eingestellt ..."

**171**  CAHJP, DAL 101, Birman to Margolis, December 22, 1941. A year earlier, December 16, 1940, Spitzer had written to Komor on behalf of his two and twelve other teenagers in France to prevail upon the French Consul General to allow the children to enter the French Concession. Spitzer's appeal produced no results. SMP, Reel 17, D-5422 (c)-10, 2–8.

**172**  CAHJP, DAL 94, Birman to Montreal, February 12, 1941.

**173**  The Trans-Siberian left four times per week from Moscow. Before arriving at the Manchukuo border, the line separated. Twice weekly the train traveled to Dalian, and twice to Vladivostok. YVA, JM/3155, Deutsches Generalkonsulat Shanghai, "Judentum in Shanghai", June 30, 1940, p. 2. Sinature illegible.

Jan Zwartendijk (1896–1976), in Kovno for Curaçao, a Dutch colony.[174] On the basis of the end visas, Sugihara Chiune (1900–1986), Japanese consul in Kovno, issued Japanese transit visas, allowing the refugees to go by Trans-Siberian railway to Vladivostok and to sail from there to Tsuruga on the Japan coast.[175] But instead of leaving for Curaçao, their supposed destination, they remained in Kobe until shipped to Shanghai in 1941 by the Japanese. [176]

The sources do not mention special difficulties in obtaining Soviet transit visas or exit permits, provided they were in possession of permits to enter Shanghai once the permit system had gone into effect. The Manchukuo transit visas for travel to Dalian were, however, a different matter, and the problems in obtaining them will be described below. Nonetheless, if they had not done so earlier, it was singularly important not to arrive at the Soviet border without a Manchukuo transit visa because at the Otpor station passengers had to obtain a Soviet exit visa. Once having left Soviet territory and entered Manchukuo territory without the proper documentation, a person could not re-enter Soviet areas nor, of course, could he remain in Manchukuo.[177] Whereas most refugees used the overland route after sea travel was no longer possible, groups of

---

174  Samuel N. Adler, *Against the Stream*, Jerusalem, 2001, p. 30 writes that Zwartendijk did not actually issue visas but wrote in the passports, "No visa is necessary for the admission of foreigners to Surinam and Curaçao". For details of Zwartendijk's granting of so-called visas and especially the motivation for doing so, see Jonathan Goldstein, "Motivation in Holocaust Rescue: The Case of Jan Zwardendijk in Lithuania, 1940", in Jeffry M. Diefendorf, ed., *Lessons and Legacies VI, New Currents in Holocaust Research*, Evanston: Northwestern University Press, 2004, pp. 69–87. See also Hillel Levine, *In Search of Sugihara, The Elusive Japanese Diplomat who Risked His Life to Rescue 10,000 Jews from the Holocaust*, New York-Singapore: The Free Press, 1996, p. 232 who corroborates this account.

175  Presumably Sugihara was to issue transit visas to Polish refugees only, but when many Jews from elsewhere came as well, he did not refuse. How many visas he ended up issuing – after all he wrote transit visas only from August 11 to August 31, 1940 – is not certain, as will be discussed below. Ewa Pałusz-Rutkowska, Andrzej T. Romer, "Współpraca, Polsko-Japońska w czasie II Wojny Światowey", *Zeszyty Historyczne*, no. 110 (1994), 43 pp. (English translation, "Polish-Japanese Co-operation during World War II", *Japan Forum*, Vol. 7, no. 2 (Autumn 1995), pp. 285–316.

176  Quite probably the Japanese decision to send the Jews to Shanghai was taken after JOINT money from America ceased. This had followed the freeze of Japanese assets on July 25, 1941 in retaliation for the Japanese move into Indo-China (Vietnam). See Joseph C. Grew, *Ten Years in Japan*, New York: Simon and Schuster, 1944, p. 408. See also Pamela Rotner-Sakamoto, *Japanese Diplomats and Jewish Refugees, A World War II Dilemma*, Westport-London: Praeger, 1998, p. 141.

177  JFM, reel 413, frames 775–778, Acting Consul Matsuda, Manchouli, to Foreign Minister Arita, December 1, 1938.

refugees mainly from Austria had begun using the rail link as early as November 1938.[178] Reaching Moscow was, however, often a problem after the start of WWII, when a person had to cross from German-occupied to Soviet-occupied areas of Poland. Some refugees opted, therefore, for air travel to Moscow, not realizing that transit visas for ground travel were not valid for air travel.[179]

But once on the Trans-Siberian, travelers often succumbed to the enchantment, the majesty of the vast and sparsely populated landscape that they confronted in the week-long journey of around 10,000 kilometers.[180] Four or five years earlier, in 1935, Meylekh Ravitch (Zekharia Khone Bergner, 1893–1976), the well-known Yiddish poet, penned a long poem about this journey on the Trans-Siberian railway.[181] In 1940, Leo Adler, when seeing Lake Baikal, wrote similarly, though perhaps less poetically:

> One sees snow, and only snow. The only interruption of this scene is an occasional train station. The scenery at the Baikal Lake was beautiful. The train travels for hours around the lake. The surface of the lake is the only thing not covered by snow. On the other side of the lake are the mountains. Since the train travels in a half circle around the lake, one sees the previous train stations light up like in an ocean of stars. This truly was a beautiful landscape.[182]

But this stretch of the journey was only a short reprieve from the realities that awaited travelers in Manchukuo or Vladivostok.

Much of the information they had was based on hearsay or contradictory facts. Thus, for example, (contrary to Japanese information), Birman believed in December 1938 that transit visas could be obtained at the Manzhouli border crossing. In November 1939 Manchukuo transit visas were presumably not available. In January 1940 the American Express thought that transit visas must be requested in Harbin. According to Birman in February 1940, transit visas were only issued against Japanese permits from Shanghai, and in March Manchukuo citizens had to act, it was said, as guarantors.

No doubt, because of the Shanghai Municipal elections in May 1940 transit visas were issued against SMC as well as French Concession permits. But by June 1940, no more Manchukuo transit visas were issued, and in March 1941

---

**178** *Evreiskaya Zhizn*, nos. 15–16, April 14, 1939, English section, p. 3.

**179** CAHJP, 86.3, Birman to Reich Association, August 15, 1940.

**180** The monotony of the landscape and its few high points are captured by Harmon Tupper, *To the Great Ocean, Siberia and the Trans-Siberian Railway*, London: Secker and Warburg, 1965.

**181** Meylekh Ravitch, *Kontinentn un okeanen: lider, baladn, un poeme* (Continents and oceans: songs, ballads and poems), Warsaw: Literarishe Bleter, 1937, pp. 24–26.

**182** Adler, *Against the Stream*, p. 37.

Birman reported 94 people stranded in Manzhouli with SMC permits and no hope of transit visas.[183] The frustration engendered by these prevarications was expressed by Dr. Arnold Horwitz in Berlin when he wrote to Harbin, "The information supplied by the Manchurian embassy is never consistent and changes from case to case. Ever new requirements are demanded, and when one succeeds to fill the requirement, still no visas are granted for one reason or another.[184]" Yet the overland route was attractive to many and seemed to solve at least one problem because it did not have to be paid with foreign currency until Manzhouli on the Heilongjiang border, or until Harbin, as Birman indicates.[185]

Turning now to the Vladivostok-Shanghai or Japan question, we find that despite the fact that ships frequently called on Vladivostok – leaving every 5th, 15th, and 25th of each month for Tsuruga[186] – there was much uncertainty about whether a person would be allowed to leave for the continued voyage to Japan or get stuck in Vladivostok or – worst of all – be sent back to an unknown destination. Moreover, Birman's inquiry at the Shanghai Intourist agency yielded the information that Soviet authorities were unlikely to permit travel via Vladivostok, thus contradicting the information that Braun in Berlin had, namely that the Soviets created no difficulty of travel via Vladivostok. Notwithstanding these uncertainties, an enterprising Herbert Braun advertised the help of his travel office in arranging the Vladivostok-Shanghai voyage for 100 Japanese yen. According to Birman, this sum was exaggerated for the run should cost no more than 65 yen.[187]

Whatever the truth of the matter, the fact was that there was no passenger traffic between Vladivostok and Shanghai, and only once, in May 1941, did 52 Polish and Lithuanian refugees arrive on the Russian freighter *Arctica*.[188] Unlike Dalian, which had a Jewish community and was prepared to care for refugees whose continued travel had been delayed, Vladivostok had neither a Jewish community nor facilities to care for persons waiting for passage. Nonetheless, and especially because the vexing Manchukuo transit visa defied solution, Birman decided to explore chartering a ship for the Vladivostok-

---

**183** Summarized from CAHJP, 76.1, 86.2, DAL 86, DAL 87, 86.3.

**184** CAHJP, 76.1, Arnold Horwitz, Hilfsverein, Berlin, to Daljewcib, Harbin, May 11, 1939.

**185** CAHJP, 86.3, from Braun, Reich Association to Birman, March 20, 1940 and 86.4, from Birman to Reich Association, June 17, 1940.

**186** CAHJP, DAL 87, Birman to Reich Association, June 10, 1940. The ships were handled by the Kitonihon Kisenkaisha Company.

**187** CAHJP, DAL 86.3, Birman to Reich Association, May 6, 1940.

**188** CAHJP, DAL 99, Birman to HIAS, New York, August 17, 1941, and Birman to Polish Relief Committee, Tokyo, September 8, 1941.

Shanghai run. This was especially tempting, provided it could be worked out, because then SMC and French permits could be used. Several problems had to be solved, however. The ship had to fly a neutral flag, several hundred people had to be brought in a short time to Vladivostok, and provisions as well as eating utensils had to be brought on board.[189]

Negotiations proceeded throughout the fall of 1940 and Birman finally turned to the French Messageries Maritimes which had two freighters in Vietnam harbors. The French company was willing, according to Birman, to make port in Vladivostok toward the end of the year, arrange accommodations for women and children, and take on food and dishes for the seven to eight day voyage. Yet to make plans under the tense circumstances in Shanghai seemed almost foolhardy. According to Birman:

> The only thing that worries us is the completely unclear situation ... everyone is nervous, and no one knows what will happen here. Today French steamers can still come to Vladivostok; they can also dock in Settlement and French Concession ports. But what will happen in the next weeks or months no one knows, of course, in the present situation.[190]

Let me now turn to the last large group that came overland, the Polish refugees who had left Lithuania after the Soviet armies marched in. Instead of trying to reach Shanghai from Vladivostok, they went to Tsuruga on the Japan coast and from there to Kobe. The refugees who embarked on this voyage had almost exclusively arrived from Lithuania with Japanese transit visas, which most of them had obtained from Chiune Sugihara on the basis of Jan Zvartendijk's Curaçao visas or permits, as mentioned earlier.[191] Precisely how many refugees eventually came to Kobe, how many left on American and other visas, and how many remained to end up in Shanghai will be, no doubt, always a matter of conjecture. Similar uncertainty surrounds the composition of the refugee group: how many Polish yeshiva students and their teachers were there, how many secular Polish Jews, and how many German refugees who had somehow made their way to Kovno and Vilna?

---

**189** CAHJP, 86.3, Birman to Reich Association, September 2, 1940, September 5, 1940, and September 12, 1940.

**190** CAHJP, 86.4, Birman to Reich Association, October 10, 1940.

**191** The story of the odyssey of the Polish group, from Warsaw to Vilna and Kovno, from Kovno by train to Vladivostok, by ship from Vladivostok to Tsuruga, from Tsuruga by train to Kobe, and seven or eight months later by ship from Kobe to Shanghai is not well known. Two excellent documentary films on this topic can be highly recommended. See Appendix 3 for their description.

We need to be also careful about distinguishing the number of transit visas issued and the number of people who actually arrived in Japan with transit visas. Another possibility may have materialized and a person, after obtaining a Japan transit visa, may have opted for a different destination. To be sure, there are lists, but one cannot be certain that they are accurate or complete. Hillel Levine admits in a note that Sugihara's saving of 10,000 Jews is only a "reasonable estimate.[192]" A list compiled at the time indicates that 4.413 refugees arrived in Japan between July 1, 1940, and May 30, 1941. This figure included 2074 German refugees, 2040 Polish ones, and 299 from other countries.[193]

Assuming that this is a trustworthy list, the figure of over 4,000 is also corroborated by Layzer Kahan who wrote shortly after his arrival in Shanghai in 1941 that between 4,000 and 5,000 refugees came to Japan.[194] At first glance a suspiciously large gap of time seems to exist between Sugihara's consular activity in Kovno and the arrival of the Jews in Japan. Sugihara was in Kovno between mid-October 1939 and the end of August 1940[195], the brief eleven months of Lithuania's independence, and the months during which he issued transit visas, whereas more than half of the refugees arrived in Kobe at the beginning of 1941.

To understand this gap of time, we must consider that the refugees had no reason to move on before the arrival of the Soviet armies. According to Kahan's often lively account, it was the threat of the Russian takeover of Lithuania and the anticipated closure of the consulates that sent the "Jews with their healthy feelings [of survival] ... to maps and globes to diligently learn geography". The road to America, they learned – and where most wanted to go – led over Japan, hence the attempt to procure end and transit visas.[196] People would have tried to obtain these only after the Soviet army arrived in the summer of 1940. Meanwhile, the Red army had marched into Lithuania in June 1940 and it took some time to apply for and receive Soviet exit visas.[197]

---

192  Levine, *In Search of Sugihara*, pp. 285–286, note 7.
193  YIVO Institute, HIAS-HICEM I, MKM 15–57, 15-B22, "Movement of refugees through Japan from July 1, 1940 till May 30, 1941". Earlier lists from 1940 and 1941 show the arrival of fewer refugees from Poland and more from Germany. See also CAHJP, 72.4, HICEM, Kobe [Epstein] to HICEM, Lisbon, July 31, 1941, who mentions the same figure of 4.413 arrivals by June 1, 1941.
194  Layzer Kahan, "Nisim oif unzer vanderveg (Miracles on our journeys)", *In Veg*, November 1941, p. 7.
195  Levine, In Search of Sugihara, pp. 130, 125.
196  Kahan, "Miracles on our journeys", pp. 5–6.
197  The exact reasons why the Soviet authorities allowed Jewish refugees to depart may never be known. For some interesting views why Soviet exit visas were granted, see Goldstein, "Motivation in Holocaust Rescue", pp. 81–82.

Presumably the majority of the Polish refugees departed Lithuania during January and February 1941 – the peak months of arrival in Japan were February and March 1941 when first 785 and the next month 624 Polish Jews arrived.[198]

The refugee flow did not always proceed smoothly and people were often stuck in Vladivostok. Shoshana Kahan worried in March 1941 about the fate of Raya Zomina, J. Rapoport (more about them in the next chapter) and others since they were not allowed into Japan.[199] The crossing from Vladivostok to Tsuruga was also often highly unpleasant, as confided by the outspoken Shoshana Kahan to her diary, "When I saw the ship, I saw black. An old broken-down boat. Small and tight, I wanted to run away. But where to?" In the end, 550 Jews were packed into the ship. Then they encountered a violent storm and everyone was terribly seasick. The journey, instead of lasting 36 hours, took 60 hours.[200]

Jews, escaping the Nazi scourge, confronted formidable obstacles in their search for a safe haven. For the Central Europeans, whether from Poland or Germany, the distance between Europe and China or Japan defied imagination. Added to this were the bureaucratic requirements: permits, visas, transit visas, good conduct certificates, exit permits, not to mention money in currency they were perhaps accustomed to, or more likely in strange local currency. As described above, arranging the sea voyage was simple and uncomplicated when compared with the overland flight. Still, it is difficult today to imagine what it was like for entire families, whether by ship or by train, to leave behind the comforting certainty of a familiar home for an unknown exile in strange parts of the world. Only in retrospect and from the distance of more than half a century can we say that those who left hearth and home chose life over certain death. At the time those who departed could not be certain that they would arrive. Not only that, they could not be certain that they would have the inner strength to create a cultural life on Chinese soil, that they would be able "to conserve their own integrity if their social, political and legal status is completely confused", as Hannah Arendt wrote in 1943.[201] That this is indeed what happened is as much due to the resilience of the human spirit as it is due to the nature of the Shanghai metropolis that the refugees encountered upon arrival.

---

**198** YIVO Institute, HIAS-HICEM, MKM 15.57, 15-B22, and Kranzler, *Japanese, Nazis, and Jews*, p. 312.

**199** CAHJP, HICEM, Kobe [Epstein] to HICEM, Lisbon, July 31, 1941 and Kahan, *In fajer un flamen*, p. 269, entries for March 10, 29, 1941.

**200** Kahan, *In fajer un flamen*, pp. 263, 266, entry for March 3, 1941.

**201** Hannah Arendt, "We Refugees", in Marc Robinson ed., *Altogether Elsewhere*, San Diego–London: Harcourt Brace and Co., 1994, p. 116.

# Chapter 4:
# Strangers in Shanghai

Too little is known about the first steps a person took upon arrival in Shanghai. Surely a Baghdadi Jew coming from Bombay or Calcutta to the port city in the 1840s or even the 1850s would not have put up at a Chinese inn, considering it no doubt beneath his station. Shanghai being an important junk port must have had numerous inns where itinerant Chinese merchants could lodge. But by the end of the nineteenth century Shanghai had changed greatly. Hotels catering to Westerners, such as the Astor close to Nanking Road (now Nanjing-dong Lu), were now available. By then employees arriving to work in the Jewish firms would have names and addresses and were probably provided with accommodations by their employers. In the early years of the treaty port few, if any, married men brought their wives and such distant postings were considered temporary.[1] Still at the turn of the century entire families had settled in what had become a modern, westernized city and these would have helped single men who came in increasing numbers.

Nothing much, if anything, is known about where Russian Jews and later Russian refugees turned upon arrival. Many of them destitute, they would hardly have gone to hotels, of which there were quite a few by the teens and 1920s. Unlike the Baghdadis, who came by ship, the Russian Jews came overland, which despite train travel on the Trans-Siberian and the Chinese Eastern Railway, was a tiresome and long journey. What were the first steps they took to find accommodations? How did they go about procuring food or cooking it? To be sure, Chinese vendors sold ready-to-go food, but most of the Russian Jews had little or no money. Like the Baghdadis, those who came later, say in the 1920s, were more fortunate in having earlier newcomers to turn to for advice and possible help.

By the end of the 1930s when the Central European refugees arrived, the Baghdadi and Russian communities were for the most part comfortably settled in the International Settlement and the French Concession. Some like the Hardoons and Kadoories lived in large mansions that still stand today, though others made do with more modest domiciles. Whereas most Russian Jews were not well-off, and in many instances were poverty stricken, wealthy families were not lacking among them either. Judith Ben-Eliezer described her protected childhood in a large house in the International Settlement. "On our side were

---

1 The loss of the Shanghai cemeteries is especially vexing in this connection, for some clues might be had from gravestones about nineteenth century burials. The earliest burial of a woman in Hong Kong's cemetery is 1860 of Rachel Hagiora. I thank Mrs. Judy Green for making this information available.

four houses, all more or less with same size grounds, a front garden large enough to contain several tennis courts and a vegetable garden at the back."[2] The Tukaczynski (Tekoah) house was perhaps less sumptuous, but as described by Shoshana Kahan, "It has been a very long time since I enjoyed a home as much, a dear Jewish house ... full of light and Shabbat-like. This is Shanghai's aristocracy."[3]

A great deal more is known about the process of arrival and settling in of the Austrian and German refugees who came at the end of the 1930s. Increasingly, they are publishing memoirs and, even if these are written from a great distance in time, they nonetheless afford glimpses of the painful adjustments their authors had to make. In addition, we have some very rare letters, the occasional diary, and a variety of documentary and newspaper materials from the 1938–1941 years, the years of their arrival and their attempts to somehow make a living in Shanghai.

In this chapter more attention will be paid, therefore, to the large Central European refugee community in Shanghai and, where indicated, their interaction with the settled Baghdadi and Russian communities. The seven years, 1938–1945, under consideration divide naturally into two periods: 1938–1941, before the Pacific War and the Japanese occupation of the Chinese portions of Shanghai, and 1942–1945 when the Japanese controlled the entire city. The war years will be discussed in the next chapter. All three communities were faced in the latter period with a new reality by the occupation and each had to adjust differently to the painful circumstances of wartime conditions. Whereas the first period can be discussed in some detail, the three and a half years of the Pacific War will unfortunately be fragmentary. Although unquestionably of great interest, the more detailed accounts furnished in a number of sources about the earlier period are lacking for the war years. One of the remarkable aspects of these seven years as a whole, however, is that individuals coped as best they could with adversity, trying and not infrequently succeeding in leading productive lives.

## Getting Settled: Flats and Heime

The refugees who landed in Shanghai before the large onslaught in 1939 had an easier time adjusting and sometimes had successful new careers for a time,

---

**2** Judith Ben-Eliezer, *Shanghai Lost, Jerusalem Regained*, Israel: Steimatzky, 1985, pp. 24–39.
**3** R. Shoshana Kahan, *In faier un flamen, tagebukh fun a Yidisher shoishpilern* (In Fire and Flames, Diary of a Jewish Actress), Buenos Aires: Central Association of Polish Jews in Argentina, 1949, pp. 287–288. Entry for November 7, 1941.

**Fig. 4:** One of the shelters (Heime), 1940s, where refugees came to live on arrival in Shanghai. Courtesy of H. P. Eisfelder Photography Collection (4801-4648). Now housed at Yad Vashem Archives, Jerusalem.

at least. To this must be added, however, a certain number of lucky coincidences and a great deal of daring, and their willingness to take chances.

The Eisfelder family is a case in point. The family of four arrived in Shanghai in November 1938 before the large influx began. Their steamer was met by members of the Komor Committee (I. C.) and they were given the address of their accommodations on 125/3 Wayside Road, actually in a lane off the main street. The house in which they were assigned a room, like many others, belonged to a Russian (or was perhaps leased by him), who then rented rooms to make a living. By chance, Mr. Eisfelder was introduced some time later to a Mr. Kammerling, a Russian Jew of Turkish origin, who in his later years devoted himself to helping the Jewish community. Fortunately for the Eisfelders they had left Germany while still able to take funds along and, having passed a course in cake baking in Berlin, they leased with Kammerling's assistance an apartment on 1255 Bubbling Well Road (now Nanjing Xi Lu). They hired a Chinese staff of bakers, pastry cooks, and a waiter, and on February 11, 1939 the Café Louis opened for business. The café, also a restaurant, served lunches and dinners, as well as cakes and handmade chocolates. Café Louis continued as a thriving business until February 1943, when stateless Jews were forced to move to the so-called "designated area," or ghetto. Dr. Cohn, head of the newly created S.A.C.R.A. Committee, bought the café and later handed it over to the Japanese.[4]

The Zunterstein family, too, prospered, though in a different field of endeavour. Also in November 1938, Al Zunterstein arrived in Shanghai together with his aunt and uncle and their son. Unlike the Eisfelders, they did not go immediately to a flat, but were sent to a *Heim*, or shelter – the aunt and uncle to one for married couples, the two youngsters to one nearby for bachelors.[5] Within only a few days his relatives rented a flat in the French Concession. Several months later, Al's parents and sister arrived and the family was reunited. Meanwhile Al had found a job with a trucking company. As he remarks in his perceptive memoir, "When we arrived only very few refugees had pre-

---

**4** YVA, 078/21, Horst "Peter" Eisfelder, *Chinese Exile, My Years in Shanghai and Nanking*, Victoria (Australia): Makor Jewish Community Library, 2003, 2nd rev. ed., pp. 8–17, 18, 54.

**5** *Heime*, or homes, were actually large buildings rented or bought for the refugees and quickly reconstructed as dormitory facilities. Until the end of 1938, only a floor of the Embankment Building was available and there was a place for bachelors on Whashing Road (Xuchang Lu). Then, in January 1939, the first dormitory was arranged for 1000 newcomers at 16 Ward Road (Changyang Lu). Others were opened later at 680 Chaoufoong Road (Gaoyang Lu), a school at 150 Wayside Road (Haoshan Lu), another school on Kinchow Road (Jingzhou Lu), a building at 66 Alcock Road (Anguo Lu), and a factory complex at 1090 Pingliang Road (Pingliang Lu). Heinz Ganther, Günther Lenhardt, eds., *Drei Jahre Immigration in Shanghai*, Shanghai: Modern Times Publishing House, 1942, p. 17. According to SMP report, reel 17, file 5422(c)7, September 5, 1939, another Heim was at 138 Ward Road and at 100 Kinchow Road, housing an additional 1,375 persons. See also CAEJR, 86.4, CAEJR report to Daljewcib, Hicem, November 11, 1940, which in addition supplies the addresses of the various offices concerned with refugee affairs. However, the available data does not allow for an accurate estimate of how many people lived at any one time in the shelters.

ceded us, so it was easy for us to find jobs from sympathetic and helpful fellow Jews."

Late in 1939, Al's father rented a garage and a sewing machine. A Chinese tailor was soon found and he sewed samples of work clothes for hospital employees. This was a lucky turn because work clothes came to be in demand, and his father was able to rent two small houses in the International Settlement, one for the business, the other for living quarters. Like the Eisfelders, the Zuntersteins also had to move to the designated area in February 1943. A Chinese acquaintance who had a house at 800 Tangshan Road, lane 818, with a toilet and a roof garden, helped out and a deal was made.[6]

Howard (Horst) Levin, though a single youngster and only seventeen years of age, but similarly innovative and enterprising, was preparing himself for making a living while still sailing on the *Biancamano* to Shanghai in December 1938. On board ship he had met an Indian Bombay-based tool businessman whose Shanghai office was not functioning due to the Sino-Japanese war. Howard offered to help him out and shortly after his arrival received by mail a package of samples as well as addresses of Shanghai companies. He began life in Shanghai in one of the shelters, but according to his account, stayed only a few days and soon rented a room from a Chinese family.

Selling tools proved to be fairly lucrative and Howard soon received a sizeable commission from his Bombay acquaintance. He next tried his hand at selling advertisements for the newly established *Shanghai Woche*. The editor, Wolfgang Fischer (1898–1075),[7] encouraged Howard to report on cultural events, which he did most enthusiastically. Finally, an introduction to Roy Healey (Halley or Hilley), manager of the American radio station XMHA, affiliated with NBC, landed him a job as a radio programmer. The German language broadcasts began May 2, 1939 at 4 o'clock in the afternoon and ran for ninety minutes each day except Sunday. The broadcasts consisted of news, music and commercials.[8]

With the support of Fischer and the newspaper's staff, Howard also broadcast special programs from various coffee houses. These programs were very popular and many were humorous, such as the benefit evening for the hospital

---

6 YVA, 078/70, "Shanghai 1938–1949," Al Zunterstein tape, pp. 3, 5, 14.,

7 For a brief biography of Fischer (1898–1975), see Herbert A. Strauss, *International Biographical Dictionary of Central European Emigrés 1933–1945*, Munich: K. G. Saur, 1983, Vol. II, p. 301.

8 YVA, 078/72, Howard (Horst) Levin interview with I. Eber, October 14, 1988, pp. 10b–12, 13–17, 18–24. Levin reviewed his activities as broadcaster, "2 Jahre," *Shanghai Jewish Chronicle*, Vol. 2, no. 119 (May 2, 1940), p. 7, stating that his broadcasts had been running since May 3, 1939 and, since the station also used shortwave, the German language broadcasts could be heard in areas remote from Shanghai.

fund on June 25, 1941, which he broadcast from the roof garden of the Mascot Café, or the various informative lectures on topics important to refugee life.[9] Howard Levin's career as a radio personality came to an end with the outbreak of the Pacific War when the American radio station shut down.

The Deman family of four, Wilhelm Deman, his wife and small daughter, and his wife's mother, Berta Antal, arrived in Shanghai May 15, 1939, and were assigned a place in one of the shelter facilities. However, Deman, a resourceful and successful businessman in his native Vienna, had sent approximately 100 letters to the United States asking that no more than $1.00 be sent to Shanghai as he was allowed only 10 RM per person to take abroad. And indeed, when he checked at the post office a packet of letters was waiting for him with the grand total of $160. Having come into this unexpected fortune, the Demans at once rented a garden apartment of three rooms and a porch from a Russian named Grebneff, who in turn had leased the building from a Chinese or from Sir Victor Sassoon. Deman writes that Grandmother soon sat in a rocking chair on the porch looking at the garden with two palms and flowers. By the time their lifts arrived with their office and household goods, they had been able to hang out their shingle advertising translations and correspondence services.

The Demans's enterprising spirit, together with good luck, led by January 1940 to a position for Wilhelm as director of the Junior Club of the Shanghai Jewish Youth Association (S.J.Y.A.) in the Kinchow Road School, the so-called Kadoorie School.[10] When in September 1941 the club had to vacate the premises, the Demans took over the well-known Gregg School of Business on Yuen Ming Yuen Road (now Yuan Ming Yuan Lu),[11] moving its contents to their own building on 9 Monkhams Terrace. But then Mr. Grebneff sold the building to a Japanese forcing the Demans to relocate both their school and themselves to yet another address. Unlike other refugees, they did not have to move again after February 1943 when stateless Jews who had arrived after 1938 had to move into the designated area. The address at which they now lived, 369 Kwenming Road (now Kunming Lu), was already within its borders.[12]

More examples could be cited of families and persons who, with initiative and luck, escaped the shelter facilities after a short time, managing somehow

---

**9** YVA, 078/42, Howard (Horst) Levin radio broadcast XMHA. This is the text of the "Mascot" broadcast together with a brochure of advertisements. YVA, 078/43, XMHA broadcast texts of various lectures. Typed manuscript.

**10** YVA, 078/56A, Wilhelm Deman, "Ein verlorenes Jahrzehnt, Shanghai 1939–1949, Tagebuchblätter eines Heimatvertriebenen," typed manuscript, pp. 119, 131,133, 135–136, 174.

**11** The director of the Gregg School, a Mrs. Carole M. Stewart, was returning to the United States in September 1941.

**12** YVA, 078/56B, Deman, "Ein verlorenes Jahrzehnt," pp. 125, 135–137.

to regain a measure of independence. Perhaps because he was optimistic by nature, Deman was able to remark in retrospect, "Shanghai was not a destination but a way station. At what time a destination for us and for others would become available was unfathomable. From this the conclusion should be drawn that the time of transition must be utilized as best one can."[13] Yet the large number of Central European refugees who arrived in 1939 vegetated in the Heime without any hope of gainful employment or of a measure of independence. They ate the largely unpalatable and generally unvarying food served to them from the kitchens. In November 1940, when there were four such shelters housing around 2,200 inhabitants, although many more – approximately 9,000 refugees – received meals in the kitchens.[14] This number increased greatly during the war years. Of course, provided they had the money to do so, refugees could supplement their meager kitchen diets with other provisions such as hot tea and bread, even sausages, which were sold at small tables in front of the dormitories by refugee peddlers.[15]

In contrast to the writers of the memoirs, discussed above, who remained in one of the facilities for only a short time and who put the memory of their unpleasant stay quickly behind them, the authors of several letters written at the time tell a grim story about these places. The letters were written by Mr. or Mrs. Hirschberg, most of them to their son Hans, who had left earlier for the kibbutz Ein Harod in what was then Palestine. The Hirschbergs and their young daughter Lilly arrived in Shanghai June 4, 1939, remaining in one of the shelters until November. After a pleasant crossing on the Italian liner *Conte Verde*, the shock of Shanghai, heat and mosquitoes in the dormitory, the refugee crowds, and the unpalatable food overwhelmed them. In one of the letters Mr. Hirschberg wrote:

> An income is not to be had here. We are housed in a totally bombed out section of town, in the midst of ruins, Chinese dirt, and vermin. An immigrant makes his living off [other immigrants] ... and if this does not work [he lives] by stealing and cheating. We have, thank God, food and a roof over our heads ... [but as to food] in the morning a piece of dry bread and a little tea. At noon, hot soup, 9/10 water, together with a piece of dry bread. In the evening, a piece of dry bread and two bananas or two tiny hard boiled eggs. This is repeated unchangingly ... [16]

---

**13** Ibid., p. 135.

**14** Ganther, *Drei Jahre Immigration*, p. 17, mentions one enterprising refugee who brought warm meals from the kitchen to over 100 refugees on a handcart that he had acquired for that purpose. The Committee eventually put an end to his business venture.

**15** YVA, 078/56A, "Ein verlorenes Jahrzehnt," p. 121.

**16** Letter from Samuel S. Hirschberg to his son Hans, July 10, 1939. This and other letters from her parents are in the possession of Mrs. Lilly Flis, their daughter. I thank Mrs. Flis for making these letters available.

Mr. Hirschberg notes the difference between those who are in charge and the helpless refugees; if someone complains, he is told that, after all, he was not invited to come to Shanghai. Relationships among refugees also left much to be desired. In another letter, Mr. Hirschberg wrote that there are ugly scenes and daily fights among the refugees. Indeed, these sometimes become physical battles and the previous night two couples had fought with knives. He added that Jewish criminals who have been released from jail also arrive in Shanghai and come to live in the shelters.[17] There were those refugees who later described their encounter with Shanghai as extreme culture shock. They were appalled by the poverty and the unsanitary conditions. Although, to be sure, for the younger generation the experience of exile had something positive to offer, many older people thought Shanghai deplorable.[18]

But not all later arrivals ended up in the Heime. The Polish refugees from Japan who came in the summer and early fall of 1941 were a special case. The actress, R. Shoshana Kahan and her husband Layzer who landed from Kobe in October 1941, were able to move at once into a room on Seward Road rented for them by friends. One month later they found a room in the French Concession and happily left Hongkou. In her diary, she ascribed this to the fact that the Polish and Lithuanian refugees refused to lower themselves as the Germans had done.[19] But the matter of the 1,000-odd refugees from Japan may have been more complex, as a letter from Ellis Hayim indicates. Three hours before the *Asamaru Maru* docked with 350 Polish refugees, Inuzuka Koreshige informed Captain Herzberg, executive officer of the Committee for the Assistance of European Jewish Refugees in Shanghai (CAEJR) that "under no circumstances would the Japanese Landing Party allow the Polish refugees an asylum in Hongkew." Among the various reasons that Inuzuka gave was that no one was allowed to reside in Hongkou without a permit.[20] To this Hayim replied in a meeting with Inuzuka that the Japanese N. Y. K. company had disobeyed government orders, which required refugee passengers to have a permit, by accepting these 350 without proper documents.[21] What kind of compromise was eventually worked out be-

---

**17** Letter from Samuel S. Hirschberg to his son Hans, August 1, 1939.
**18** Helga Embacher and Margit Reiter, "Schmelztiegel Shanghai? – Begegnungen mit dem Fremden," *Zwischenwelt*, Vol. 18, no. 1 (February 2001), pp. 40–50.
**19** R. Shoshana Kahan, *In faier un flamen*, pp. 283, 285–286, 288, entries for October 26, October 30, November 7, 1942.
**20** The problem was, however, more complicated than that. Apparently the Home Ministry in Japan was anxious to send the refugees to Shanghai, but Shanghai was not eager to have them, a fact that the Foreign Ministry ignored. See Sakomoto, *Diplomats and Jewish Refugees*, p. 151.
**21** SMP, reel 17, file 5422 (c)10, Ellis Hayim to G. Godfrey Phillips, September 4, 1941. Actually, this was not the first time Kobe Jews were shipped to Shanghai without permits.

tween the Japanese authorities in Hongkou and the CAEJR is not known. The fact is, however, that none of the Polish refugees from Japan became shelter residents. They settled in as best they could in rented rooms and apartments.

For many refugees, room or flat living did involve a different set of problems. Those lucky enough to have found accommodations with indoor plumbing considered themselves fortunate, even if they usually had to share toilet and washing facilities with several families. Others had to manage Chinese style with a bucket and the "honeypot," a wagon pulled by a coolie who came each morning to collect the refuse. Hot water had to be bought from the alley water seller and water for drinking had to be boiled. Nor was cooking a simple matter. Most apartments or rooms were not equipped with a coal cooking stove, and Europeans were not accustomed to charcoal cookers, or *hibachis*, as Shoshana Kahan called them, that had to be lit in the alley because of the smoke. She also hated the tea stored in a thermos which, she wrote, had a strange taste and was not hot.[22]

Shopping for food improved in time as Hongkou's refugee commercial center developed on East Seward and Chusan Roads (now Changzhi Dong Lu and Zhoushan Lu). Until 1942, at the market on Chusan Road, increasingly more stands appeared, operated by refugees, where housewives could buy fruit and vegetables and even kosher meat. Ollendorf's hot dog stand was famous. In the spring of 1939 jams, honey, and cakes had already become available. Money was needed for such purchases and few refugees had enough, especially with increasing inflation. Second-hand stores sprang up where those who had still managed to bring possessions were able to sell them.[23] Chinese peddlers were eager buyers of Western goods and on Ward and Chusan Roads many a transaction was concluded.

The fact that most of the Central European refugees did not have marketable professions was a major problem. A list of professions compiled in 1940 shows that the majority were merchants, 1,100 in all. Next were musicians numbering 260, physicians 220, and dentists 180. Other professionals, such as photographers, cooks, mechanics, or carpenters would hardly find employment in Shanghai.[24]

---

A report SMP, reel 17, *file 5422 (c)10*, from Pitts, August 22, 1941 discusses the imminent arrival of 300 refugees. Pitts complained about the lax attitude of D.K.K. line officials as early as January 1941, SMP report, reel 17, *file 5422 (c) 10*, 2–8, January 10, 1941.

**22** Kahan, *In faier un flamen*, p. 287, entry for November 1, 1942.

**23** Ganther, *Drei Jahre Immigration*, pp. 128, 116, 127.

**24** YVA, JM/3155, Deutsches Generalkonsulat, Shanghai, "Judentum in Shanghai," June 30, 1940. Appendix, no. B.389.

Despite the general poverty, coffee houses and various kinds of eateries were doing a brisk business. By 1942 there were more than fifty establishments including bars catering to refugees.[25] Many advertised in the German Jewish press, such as Café Munter and La Boheme on Ward Road; the garden cafe Ostro on Wayside Road or Picadilly Garden on East Seaward Road; the roof gardens Thal and Mascot also on Wayside Road.[26] Whereas on special occasions the more affluent might have gone to more elegant establishments like the White Horse (*zum Weissen Roessl*), many of the single men without cooking facilities would have frequented the cheaper eateries. Going out for an afternoon coffee to Café Hauser as, Mrs. Deman's mother, Mrs. Antal, was in the habit of doing was probably rare.[27]

## Entertainment

The variety of plays, concerts, movies, and shows available in Shanghai is amazing, especially since China was at war since mid-1937 and the economic situation was far from favorable. Depending on a person's financial resources, the latest Hollywood productions could be seen in one of the Settlement or Concession movie theaters, such as the Capitol on Museum Road (now Hu Qiu Lu) or the Rialto on Kweichow Road. In May 1940, for example, the Eastern Theatre was showing Cecil B. de Mille's classic *The Sign of the Cross* with Charles Laughton and Claudette Colbert.[28] Shanghai's famous night clubs, catering to an international clientele, were located in the Settlement and the Concession. Well-off Russian Jews would have frequented the DD night club on Avenue Joffre (now Huai Hai Zhong Lu), which served Russian cuisine, or the night clubs on Yu Yuen Road (now Yu Yuan Lu), such as the Roy and the

---

**25** Dr. Seeger, German General Consulate, Shanghai, report February 2, 1941, p. 3. Courtesy Bernard Wasserstein. See also Ganther, *Drei Jahre Immigration*, pp. 130–131 who writes that in Hongkou were approximately 200 tea rooms and "Imbissstuben." A list of restaurants and cafes together with brief biographies of some of the restaurateurs and/or businessmen is in the *Shanghai Woche*, no. 17, October 3, 1942. I thank Hartmut Walravens for making the newspaper available.

**26** Café Munter advertised in *Die Laterne*, June 21, 1941 as the place to regain one's health in its shady garden. La Boheme announced a café like in Paris, pleasant and reasonable prices, *JN*, December 27, 1940. Café Ostro too had reasonable prices as well as radio transmission and the Thal roof garden was open all day, *JN*, no. 11, May 20, 1941, p. 1. The Mascot roof garden promised good music and excellent cuisine, *JN*, August 30, 1940. YIVO Library, reel Y-2003-1854.

**27** YVA, 078/56A, Deman, "Ein verlorenes Jahrzehnt," p. 145.

**28** Advertisement in *Shanghai Jewish Chronicle*, Vol. 2, no. 119, May 2, 1940, p. 6.

**Fig. 5:** Rooftop Café Roy over the Broadway Theater, 1944. Courtesy of H. P. Eisfelder Photography Collection (4801-4648). Now housed at Yad Vashem Archives, Jerusalem.

Bolero.[29] But these were upper class establishments, not frequented by visiting soldiers and sailors, who were more likely to go to joints in the vicinity of the harbour, especially the street Chu Pao San, nicknamed "Blood Alley," with its night clubs and taxi dancers.[30]

A number of both Russian and Central European musicians had come to Shanghai. They never managed to form an orchestra, some becoming music teachers while others, more fortunate, joined the Shanghai Municipal Symphony Orchestra. According to Michael Philipp, as many as fifteen refugee musicians played at one time with the municipal orchestra.[31] Still others taught at the Shanghai Conservatory of Music.[32] Some performances were given in the

---

29 Advertisement in *Nasha Zhizn*, no. 4, May 23, 1941, p. 7, and *Shanghai Evening Post and Mercury*, no. 105, May 1, 1940.

30 *Gelbe Post*, Vol. I, no. 2, May 16, 1939, p. 42.

31 Michael Philipp, "Exiltheater in Shanghai 1939–1947," in Frithjof Trapp, Werner Mittenzwei, Henning Rischbieter, eds., *Handbuch des deutschsprachigen Exiltheaters, 1935–1945*, Munich: K. G. Saur, Vol. I, pp. 460–461.

32 Alexander Knapp, "The State of Research into Jewish Music in China," in Roman Malek, ed., *Jews in China, From Kaifeng ... to Shanghai*, Sankt Augustin: Monumenta Serica Institute, 2000, p. 506.

Shanghai Jewish Club to which both refugees and old timers came. For a time a group performed chamber music and were accorded an enthusiastic reception,[33] but this ended with the outbreak of the Pacific War.[34] Musicians of classical music did not find a fruitful field in Shanghai and most could not make a living from music. They needed additional jobs to provide an income. Furthermore, no doubt, the lack of a proper stage prevented the staging of operas. But even light opera was not that frequently performed. More popular by far were cabaret, variety shows, and solo performances. These could be staged in coffee houses, and even when performed in theatres no large scale organizational problems were involved.

The arrival in 1941 of a number of Jewish-Polish actors from Kobe who performed in Yiddish brought new life to the Yiddish stage in Shanghai. Shortly after she came to Shanghai, Shoshana Kahan together with her husband Layzer, J. Rapoport and Raja Zomina, a gifted singer who had been in Shanghai since May, appeared in a variety show in the elegant Jewish Club on Bubbling Well Road.[35] Regarding another one of her performances a reviewer wrote that "until now [audiences did] not have an opportunity to hear Yiddish artists of this caliber," hence their great interest.[36] But a mixed reaction greeted serious theater. A performance of *The Dybbuk* by S. An-ski (pen-name of Solomon Seinwil Rapoport, 1863–1920),[37] despite Raja Zomina's inspired performance and an excellent production by Boris Sapiro (about whom more below) in the Lyceum Theater, was poorly attended.[38] On the other hand, a performance of *Mirele Efros* with Shoshana Kahan was described by her as a great success.[39] But the performance of plays was a problem: Time was needed for rehearsals, money for costumes, settings, etc., and plays could be performed only once,

---

**33** "Konzert Albach-Adler-Loewit," *JN*, no. 4, February 21, 1940, p. 3. The performance included Mozart and Schubert songs.

**34** Martin Hausdorff, "Das Musikleben der Emigranten," *Shanghai Herald*, Sondernummer, April 1946, p. 16.

**35** Kahan, *In fayer un flamen*, p. 287, entry for November 6, 1941. She remarks that it was a very successful evening and the actors remained among the Shanghai Jews for a long time after the performance. According to Wolfgang Fischer, "Raja Zomina," *Shanghai Woche*, no. 2, June 6, 1942, Zomina captivated audiences with her performance of Yiddish songs.

**36** *Undzer Lebn*, no. 28, November 14, 1941.

**37** A dybbuk is the soul of a sinner that after death transmigrates into the body of a living person from where it must be exorcised.

**38** Review in *Undzer Lebn*, November 28, 1941. It is not clear in which language *The Dybbuk* was performed.

**39** Kahan, *In fayer un flamen*, p. 290, 290–293, entry for February 20, 1942. The play was also announced in *Undzer Lebn*, no. 40, February 6, 1942, but was not reviewed.

as she remarks, because audiences were too small for additional performances. Variety shows presented fewer problems and Shoshana and others appeared in these to considerable acclaim.[40] Critical voices were also heard, however, and J. Rottenberg wrote that despite increased cultural activity in Yiddish, theatre performances were not always up to standard. He suggested the establishment of a theatre society,[41] and may have had in mind a society similar to the one founded by the German refugees.

Yiddish theatre experienced a severe setback when in November 1942 the luxurious premises of the Jewish Club on 722 Bubbling Well Road were taken over by the Japanese authorities for the Press Office of the Army and the Jewish Club had to move to the Masonic Hall on 163 Avenue Road (now Beijing Xi Lu). "The removal of the Club from its own building was made voluntarily ..." reported *Our Life* laconically.[42] But, according to Shoshana Kahan, the Masonic Hall was in a dreadful Chinese area and Yiddish entertainment thereafter took place but rarely.[43] She did not exaggerate. By summer 1943, it was obvious that Yiddish theatre was severely curtailed.[44]

In contrast, German language theatre had an earlier start and proved remarkably popular. Several reasons may account for this. Between 1939 and 1946 there was in Shanghai an uncommonly large number of actors and actresses, singers, and musicians as well as persons who in one way or another were connected with the stage. Although exact numbers cannot be established, Michael Phillip counts around 200 persons.[45] Another reason may be that Shanghai's German-speaking population was much larger than its Yiddish-speaking one. Moreover, the several theatre companies usually presented comedies and light theatre their public liked best and was willing to pay for. In short, those who went to the theatre wanted to be entertained and the actors

---

40 These were reviewed in *Undzer Lebn*, no. 9, January 30, 1942, no. 45, March 13, 1942; review of Raja Zomina's performance, no. 55 (3), May 21, 1942.

41 J. Rottenberg, "Vegn a Yiddish teater in Shanghai (About a Yiddish theater in Shanghai)," *Undzer Lebn*, no. 78 (26), October 30, 1942.

42 "Jewish Club Removed to New Premises," *Our Life*, no. 25, December 11, 1942, and *Nasha Zhizn*, no. 90, January 22, 1943. The first Jewish Club had opened in August 1932 at 1321 Rue Lafayette, in October 1941 it had moved to its own building on Bubbling Well Road.

43 Kahan, *In fajer un flamen*, p. 297, entry for December 6, 1942 and p. 326, entry for November 21, 1944.

44 "Annual General Meeting of Shanghai Jewish Club," *Our Life*, no. 54, July 16, 1943.

45 Michael Philipp, *Nicht einmal einen Thespiskarren, Exiltheater in Shanghai 1939–1947*, Hamburg: Hamburger Arbeitsstelle für deutsche Exilliteratur, 1996, pp. 38–39.

obliged. The *Juedisches Nachrichtenblatt* put it succinctly: The public prefers cheerful to serious works.[46]

The problems encountered by Yiddish theatre – money for costumes and settings, time for rehearsals when actors had to hold down jobs to earn a livelihood – were also common to the German language theatre. But there were other problems as well. One was the scarcity of scripts. Neither actors nor directors had brought a sufficient number or variety along, nor, of course, could scripts be purchased in local book stores.[47] For this reason a number of plays were written by refugee dramatists in Shanghai. Another was the problem of an adequate stage, mentioned earlier. Due to the lack of European-style theatres, plays were performed in movie houses where stages were too narrow. Initially, variety evenings were performed on the small stages of the shelters, most of which were converted school buildings. In exceptional cases, facilities of the British Embassy were used, where, for example, the controversial play *The Masks Fall* (Die Masken Fallen) was performed in November 1940.[48]

On the initiative of Ossi Lewin, the owner and editor of the *Shanghai Jewish Chronicle*, the Artists Club, as an association of artists, was established in spring 1939 with about fifty persons. Less than a year later, in January 1940, the Artists Club became the European Jewish Artist Society (EJAS). Its president remained Ossi Lewin and the secretary continued to be Alfred Dreifuss (1902–1993), an important personality in Shanghai's artistic and cultural life.[49] EJAS, too, ceased to function in spring 1941, in part perhaps because by then Dreifuss had resigned as secretary, although in 1946 he claimed that the organization had run out of money.[50]

Several other theatre organizations were active aside from EJAS. Among these was the Sapiro-Bühne, established by the actor-director Boris Sapiro, who also presented Yiddish plays, some of which he had written himself.[51] The Ensemble, a company headed by the actor Fritz Melchior (1897–?) presented serious drama. Continuing to function during the war, his *Pygmalion* at the

---

**46** "European Jewish Artist Society," *JN*, no. 7, November 1, 1940, p. 7.

**47** Philipp, *Nicht einmal einen Thespiskarren*, p. 54.

**48** Ibid., pp. 53–54, 101, and Alfred Dreifuss, "Theater in Shanghai," *Aufbau*, August 16, 1940, p. 13. Presumably the actors were not allowed to perform the plays in the International Settlement and the British Embassy, as extraterritorial territory, made its premises available.

**49** For a brief biography of Dreifuss, see Phillip, *Nicht einmal einen Thespiskarren*, pp. 162–163.

**50** Dreifuss, "Unser Theater," p. 13.

**51** Philipp, *Nicht einmal einen Thespiskarren*, pp. 124–125, 75.

Eastern Theatre, despite the problems of the stage, had a glowing review.[52] According to David Kranzler, altogether more than sixty plays were performed in Shanghai, a fairly large number, which may have been even larger had not thirty three plays been prohibited by the Japanese censor during wartime.[53] Included in the repertoire were such well known European playwrights as Shaw, Molnar, Strindberg, as well as twenty six original plays by Shanghai refugee writers.[54] Unfortunately, the scripts of the latter either no longer exist or are not available, except two that are of special interest because they deal with political material.

The two plays were written by Hans Schubert (Hans Wiener, Hans Morgenstern, 1905–1965) and Mark Siegelberg (1895–1986) and are *Foreign Soil* (Fremde Erde) and *The Masks Fall*. The second drama is undisguisedly anti-Nazi and reflects one of the author's concentration camp experiences while he had been incarcerated in 1938. When performed in 1940, it raised a controversy in the *North China Daily News*, with Michele Speelman stating that provocative subjects like these should be avoided in Shanghai.[55] *Foreign Soil* is different and has as its subject the Shanghai refugees. The brief synopsis below cannot do justice to this powerful drama that evokes the difficulties of Shanghai existence, "getting by" attitudes as contrasted with petty bourgeoisie prejudices, sacrifices and sensitivities, and the mistaken assumption that even love can be purchased like a commodity. A refugee doctor wants to buy a practice, but has no money. If his wife were to sell her pearl necklace, it would suffice for the purchase. He does not know that his wife has already sold the necklace to the couple who manage to manipulate all situations to their advantage, and since she does not tell him, she desperately tries to obtain the needed sum. The wife works in a bar, entertaining guests. A Chinese client falls in love with the woman and gives her the needed sum. Eventually, of course, the story unravels, the husband discovers the affair, the wife leaves him, but in time husband and wife are reconciled, and decide to leave Shanghai to work in the interior in an epidemic infested area.[56]

---

**52** *Our Life*, no. 72, November 26, 1943.

**53** David Kranzler, *Japanese, Nazis, and Jews, The Refugee Community of Shanghai, 1938–1945*, New York: Yeshiva University Press, 1976, p. 369, and Dreifuss, "Unser Theater," p. 14.

**54** Phillip, *Nicht einmal ein Thespiskarren*, pp. 198–199.

**55** Hans Schubert/Mark Siegelberg, Michael Phillip and Wilfried Seywald, eds., *"Die Masken Fallen" — "Fremde Erde," Zwei Dramen aus der Emigration nach Shanghai 1939–1947*, Hamburg: Hamburger Arbeitstelle für deutsche Exilliteratur, 1996, p. 16. "The Masks Fall" was performed a second time in Shanghai in 1946. By then Schubert was still in Shanghai, but Siegelberg had managed to sail for Australia in 1941.

**56** Ibid., pp. 86–137.

The drama operates on several levels, but its central motifs are questions of bourgeois morality and genuine love of a married couple. Nor do the authors condemn the couple who take the easy way out, unhampered by moral issues. The Chinese man who tries to buy the love of a woman is also not portrayed unsympathetically. To the contrary, one feels sorry for him for he seems genuinely in love with the doctor's wife. To what extent did this play raise issues the refugees preferred not to touch? How many women had to earn money one way or another while their husband's self-image as bread winners was increasingly tarnished? How to deal with European-Chinese relations in an environment where prejudice and dated notions of middle-class morality predominated?

It is certainly significant that the play was performed only twice and, unlike *The Masks Fall*, was not staged again in the post-WWII era. The problems of politically engaged theatre and specifically Jewish theatre are pertinent here, and politically engaged drama was not popular with Shanghai audiences. As an ideologically motivated Marxist, Alfred Dreifuss believed that art must serve politics and Shanghai theatre ought to take an unequivocally anti-Fascist stand. To demand of theatre, however, to become an instrument of anti-Fascist propaganda when refugee audiences wanted no more than a few hours of entertainment and forget their present hardships seems unrealistic under the circumstances. Moreover, the question of Jewish theatre was for most artists an existential one. Had they not lost their native homes and livelihood because they were Jewish? Yet, their identity as actors was not, in fact, with Jewish drama but with drama from many countries. Also, which Jewish theater should be considered, western or eastern European? And if it is to be the latter, it would have to be Yiddish theater which was foreign to both the German-speaking actors and to the audiences. Dreifuss's insistence that émigré theatre must have a cultural message seems misplaced.[57]

Whether refugee theater had high standards or not is a question that will most likely never be answered. Immigration is not artistically creative, argued one critic, but seeks to conserve. Its goal is to preserve those artistic aspects that it has brought along, perhaps add to them, yet mainly to make certain that artistic elements are not lost and can be carried forward after emigration ends.[58] Much of the blame for the low level of Shanghai theater must be ascribed to the audience, wrote Dreifuss, its taste was too cheap, and actors were

---

**57** Philipp, *Nicht einmal ein Thespiskarren*, pp. 123–124.
**58** Lothar Brieger, "Emigration und kuenstlerische Produktivitaet," *The Shanghai Herald*, Sondernummer, April 1946, p. 18.

never able to develop their own style.[59] But then Dreifuss was often overly critical. Shanghai was not Berlin or Vienna. Conditions were too difficult and the outbreak of the Pacific War in December 1941 put severe limitations on all cultural
life. That first-rate actresses and actors like Lily Flohr and Herbert Zernik – to
name only two – carried on against all odds is to their credit, their stamina and
determination, and to a spiritual resilience not many were able to muster.

## Litigation

Crime was pervasive in Shanghai in the twenties and thirties, ranging from
petty theft to murder, to racketeering, and especially after the outbreak of the
Sino-Japanese war in July 1937, to terrorism. Gangsters, racketeers, and terror-
ists (to which must be added the effects of collaboration with the Japanese
invader) as well as the futile attempts by the several police forces to bring
about a semblance of law and order have been described in several excellent
works,[60] and the dismal picture need not be repeated here. Suffice it to say,
that the narcotics trade and gambling were major factors and in both Japanese
and Chinese political figures had a large stake.[61] There is no evidence that
Jews, wherever they hailed from, participated in organized crime.

The court system up to the Pacific War in December 1941 and thereafter,
when the Japanese occupied all of Shanghai, was complex and several court
systems functioned simultaneously in the city. Under the terms of extraterritoriality, foreign nationals were subject to the laws of their own countries and
cases were heard in their countries' consular courts. The Shanghai Mixed Court
consisted of a Chinese magistrate and a foreign consular co-judge who shared
the judicial function. This court handled cases between Chinese and Chinese
and foreigners.[62] In addition there was a system of Special District Courts, set
up under an agreement between the Consular Body and the Chinese government ten years earlier.[63] Whereas the Central European refugees would have

**59** Dreifuss, "Unser Theater," p. 13.
**60** Among these are, Frederick Wakeman, Jr., *Policing Shanghai,* Berkeley: University
of California Press, 1995; Brian G. Martin, *The Shanghai Green Gang: Politics and
Organized Crime, 1919–1937*, Berkeley: University of California Press, 1996; Bernard
Wasserstein, *Secret War in Shanghai*, London: Profile Books, 1999.
**61** Frederic Wakeman, Jr., *The Shanghai Badlands: Wartime Terrorism and Urban Crime,
1937–1941*, New York: Cambridge University Press, 1996, pp. 11–14, 108–110.
**62** John K. Fairbank, Edwin O Reischauer, Albert M. Craig, *East Asia, The Modern
Transformation*, Boston: Houghton Mifflin, 1965, p. 341.
**63** "German Jews Reported Setting up Own Court on Alcock Rd.", *CP*, November 13,
1939, pp. 1, 5.

few occasions to engage in legal action against one another in court, there was no absence of litigation.

For example, Mr. Henry Bachrach filed a suit for damages against Louis Eisfelder, owner of the Café Louis in First Special District Court because his wife's coat had disappeared from the cloakroom. Bachrach's lawyer pleaded that, according to the Chinese Civil Code (article 697?) a café owner was responsible for the items entrusted to him. Mr. Eisfelder's attorney argued, on the other hand, that she should have kept the coat at her table.[64] This case brings into focus the fact, as Heinz Ganther states, that the refugees did not know Chinese law and that they did not understand Chinese, the language of judicial proceedings.

More serious was the case of the Canadian and Oriental Exporters Company brought also before the Special First District Court in July 1939. The company had promised to renovate housing on Tungshan Road, requiring of the prospective tenants key money and advance rental payments. When the company requested additional money, and when it was discovered that the houses were, for all practical purposes, ruins, the people demanded return of their funds and went to court. The company, it turned out, was run by two Russians and a German refugee, Julius Mayer, who was the liaison man with the victims.[65]

Whether it was due to immigrant initiative or the result of a decision taken elsewhere, in the summer of 1939 Kurt Marx decided to establish an Arbitration Court, which would hear legal cases between immigrants and would attempt a compromise. At about the same time, the Komor Committee (IC) organized a similar court,[66] until eventually the two organizations merged and an arbitration court of the Committee for the Assistance of European Jewish Refugees in Shanghai (CEAJR) was established. The drawback was that none of these had the power to enforce its decisions. In some instances, writes Ganther, the Komor Committee used the threat of withdrawing support to force one or the other party to compromise, but threats were highly unacceptable.[67]

---

**64** "Emigre Court Here Rapped by Tribunal," *CP*, February 22, 1939, pp. 1, 3. The case is also mentioned in another connection by Marcia R. Ristaino, *Port of Last Resort, The Diaspora Communities of Shanghai*, Stanford: Stanford University Press, 2001, pp. 136–137.

**65** "Jewish Refugees Swindled of $ 10,000 by Bogus Company," *North-China Daily News*, July 12, 1939.

**66** Heinz Ganther, *Drei Jahre Immigration in Shanghai*, p. 103.

**67** Ibid., p. 104. Ganther's information seems not entirely accurate. The SMP report, reel 17, file 5422 (c), November 13, 1939, states that the CAEJR established the Arbitration Court on October 12, 1939 and not the Komor Committee.

Both Chinese and European lawyers objected to the arbitration court at once. The Chinese attorneys charged that it violated and undermined Chinese sovereign rights. The German government had relinquished extraterritorial right in China and therefore "Germans were not entitled to rights similar to those of other nationals here." (It must be remembered that German Jews did not lose their citizenship until October 1941). Moreover, the code drafted by the court, among others, makes Chinese law inapplicable to Jews, forbids Jews to take their cases to Chinese courts, and allows only lawyers registered with the court to appear before it. Thus the arbitration court infringes "directly on the jurisdiction of the First Special District Court."[68] An article in the *Hwa Pao* charged, in turn, that "the establishment of a Court constitutes an act of an organized group. A Court can be established only when there exists a national law for its observance." And the refugees had neither a country nor a national law.[69] The European lawyers claimed that the court would be ineffective. Some of them may have been disaffected by being excluded from the list of recognized lawyers.[70] Finally, Dr. A. Grossman, the legal advisor, considered it necessary to explain publicly that the court was an arbitration court operating in accordance with Chinese law and local customs, when the sum in question exceeded $ 500.[71] However, the Arbitration Court was short-lived. After the Japanese occupation of all of Shanghai in December 1941, the CEAJR court relinquished its function (under duress?) to the Jüdische Gemeinde and to the lawyers who were acceptable to the Japanese authorities.[72]

What was a member of the Shanghai Municipal Police to make of a report he had received about criminal activities committed in Germany by Jews who had come to Shanghai? There was Arthur Rosenbaum who had been charged in Luenen with forgery of public documents; Walter Fraenkel was charged in Schneidermühle with the offense of adulterating food, operating a slot machine, and rape; and Siegfried Levy from Altona, Hamburg, was guilty of high treason and sexual offenses between Jews and Aryans.[73] Would he assume that these were trumped up charges or would he draw conclusions about increased

---

**68** *CP*, November 13, 1939, pp. 1, 5. The code was published in the *Shanghai Jewish Chronicle*, February 18, 1940, but the issue was unfortunately not available.

**69** SMP translation, reel 17, file 5422 (c), November 14, 1939.

**70** "Tribunal Set Up by Jewish Emigres Hit," *CP*, November 14, 1939, p. 3 and Ristaino, *Port of Last Resort*, p. 136.

**71** "Local Jewish Refugee Court Explained," *CP*, November 15, 1939, pp. 1, 3, and his letter, p. 10.

**72** SMP report, reel 17, file 5422 (c) 11, April 6, 1942. The report adds that since the court deals with civil cases it is of no special interest to the police.

**73** SMP report (confidential), reel 17, file 5422 (c), April 27, 1939, signed by D. S. Pitts.

crime problems in Shanghai? A report by D. S. Pitts is revealing about assumptions held among the police. According to him, "a certain number of bad characters" are bound to be among the refugees.

> [Although] there is no reason to infer that crime will manifest in large degree among the newcomers, but with the number of refugees always growing ... such a development cannot be overlooked. In fact the potential factors for an increase in crime are already established ... Already two concrete instances have come to the notice of this office in regard to the attempts by young German Jews to secure money by fraudulent means.[74]

A random sampling of cases brought before the Special First District Court in August and beginning of September 1940 and reported to the press confirms that fraud was, indeed, the most common offense. Siegfried Pinkus, Isidor Director, and Hans Rechtling were arrested and brought before the court for passing counterfeit $ 5.00 bills. Kurt Mucha was similarly convicted for counterfeiting Chinese banknotes.[75] Ernst Rosen stole beer in the value of $ 1,000 from the shop where he was a salesman and Hans Selig stole an autographed picture of Enrico Caruso from a stationery shop.[76] More serious fraud was committed by Victor Siedler, who borrowed money from another refugee and gave him forged receipts.[77] Bernhard Meyzel defrauded three refugees of $ 4,973 for presumably being able to get Japanese permits for them.[78] The court looked askance at all forgeries and especially those involving the Shanghai Municipal Police. In a widely publicized case, Gabriel Lax, a Polish lawyer and one time police commissioner in his native Poland, was convicted of forging SMP seals and the signatures of two refugees offering a family of German Jews employment in Shanghai.[79] Lax's well-intentioned deed badly backfired. Murders among the refugees were practically unheard of and when they occurred tended to be crimes of passion.[80]

On the whole, however, and considering the impecunious condition of most of the refugees, petty crimes were few, even if it is assumed that more actually occurred without reaching the court. A police report emphasized,

---

74 SMP report, reel 17, file D5422 (c), March 15, 1939, signed by D. S. Pitts.

75 *CP*, August 16, 1940, p. 2, and *CP*, September 7, 1940, p. 2.

76 *CP*, August 17, 1940, p. 2 and *CP*, September 4, 1940, p. 2.

77 *CP*, August 24, 1940, p. 2.

78 "Emigree Jailed for Fraud Here," *SEPM*, October 21, 1940, p. 2.

79 *CP*, June 9, 1940, p. 2 and *CP*, June 16, 1940, p. 2.

80 Such, for example, was Inge Vasen's murder by L. Heyman, who he found had taken another lover. "Refugee Sentenced for Murder," *North-China Daily News*, October 20, 1939, p. 9.

It is a fact that the majority of refugee criminals are residents of the Hongkew area but their crimes have been invariably petty ones whilst taking into consideration the Jewish refugee population in Shanghai the number of criminals is an extremely small one.[81]

That fraud, embezzlement, and theft increased as conditions worsened during the years of war should be, no doubt, assumed. But after December 1941 the courts no longer functioned and the Japanese police together with its informers assumed an increasingly more powerful role. In the several memoirs that are available, questions of litigation are not raised and thus the war period remains largely undocumented on the subject of crime, although as stated earlier, the Arbitration Court of the Jüdische Gemeinde continued to function during the war years.

## Publishing

The abundance of Jewish publishing should not come as a surprise, considering the prevalence of large and small presses in Shanghai, the large number of Chinese and foreign language newspapers, journals, and book printings. To be sure, many papers were short-lived. Often weeklies changed to monthlies, or changed hands and/or names. Nevertheless, Russian,[82] German, Yiddish, or English readers, even Polish readers of *Echo Shanghajskie*, had access to news, provided they could afford the price of a newspaper.

One of the oldest English language journals was *Israel's Messenger*, which served almost exclusively the Sephardi community with news about Jewish social life in Shanghai and events in Palestine.[83] The Russian Jewish paper, *Nasha Zhizn* (Our Life) did not commence publication until 1941, eventually adding a Yiddish page and a year later an English page. The paper ceased publication in 1946.[84] Agudat Yisrael published two Yiddish journals, *Dos Vort*

---

**81** YVA, 078/88, Shanghai Municipal Archives, Report from Richardson, Special Branch, August 6, 1941.
**82** Shanghai's Russian language publications were especially numerous, with at least six daily newspapers. Ristaino, *Port of Last Resort*, p. 84.
**83** Founded in 1904 by Nissim Ezra Benjamin Ezra, *Israel's Messenger* was published as a fortnightly. The journal was suspended between 1910 and 1918 when it resumed publication as a monthly until 1941.
**84** *Nasha Zhizn* began as a weekly, but was frequently irregular during the war. Its editor was David B. Rabinovich. See Rena Krasno, "History of Russian Jews in Shanghai," in Malek, ed., *Jews in China*, pp. 336–337 who mentions several other Russian Jewish publications in English.

(The Word) in 1941 and *Di Yidishe Stimme fun Vaytn Mizrakh* (The Jewish voice from the Far East) in 1942. There was even a Hebrew paper, *Me'or Torah* (Torah light), published between 1944 and 1946, in which legal questions raised in the Talmud and raised again in Shanghai, were discussed. Most of the articles were written by rabbis from the Mir Yeshivah. Most numerous by far, however, were the German language papers. The longest run was that of the bilingual daily, *Shanghai Jewish Chronicle*, which began publication in January 1939 and continued until October 1945. Under Ossi Lewin (1905?–1975?), the paper even appeared during the war years because its publisher apparently cooperated with Japanese censorship. Presumably the paper would have succumbed to the competition, stated an article in 1946, had it not been saved by the Pacific War when other papers were closed down.[85] The weekly, *Shanghai Woche*, edited by Wolfgang Fischer also appeared in 1939 changing a few months later to the *8-Uhr Abendblatt*, a daily that ceased publication in 1941. It started up once more in 1942 under its first title.[86] For the more intellectually inclined reader there was the *Gelbe Post*, which appeared between May and November 1939, owned and edited by Adolph J. Storfer (1888–1944)[87] until bought by Ossi Lewin.

A number of papers were short lived, surviving barely a year, like *Der Queerschnitt*, published in 1939, *Der Mitarbeiter* between 1940 and 1941, or *Die Laterne* in 1941. The *Juedisches Nachrichtenblatt*, edited by Philipp Kohn, was the paper of the German Jewish Community and together with the *Shanghai Jewish Chronicle* was the only paper published during the Pacific War.[88] Finally, mention should be made of at least three medical journals that were published between 1940 and 1943. Among these the *Shanghai Medical Journal*, edited by Th. Friedrichs, was in English, German, and Chinese.

---

85 La France (Ladislaus Frank), "Die Presse der Emigration," *The Shanghai Herald*, German Language Supplement, Sondernummer, April 1946, p. 11.

86 In the first issue of May 28, 1942, Fischer writes on p. 1 that the paper appears again as a weekly after a lengthy interruption. The last issue that I have seen is dated January 9, 1943.

87 For more about the paper and its editor, see Francoise Kreisler, "Ein Journalist im Exil in Shanghai: Adolph Storfer und die *Gelbe Post*," in Malek, ed., *Jews in China*, pp. 511–524.

88 This brief overview is based largely on an unpublished chart of 46 Jewish papers in all of China in the YIVO archive, prepared by Asher Rozenboim, "Di Yidishe presse in Chine, 1937–1947 (The Jewish press in China, 1937–1947)." Unfortunately, accurate and complete data on the runs of the various papers is not available. A useful survey of German language papers is Wilfried Seywald, *Journalisten im Shanghaier Exil 1939–1949*, Salzburg: Wolfgang Neugedauer, 1987. See also the nearly complete listing of newspapers and journals in Appendix 2.

**Fig. 6:** Front page from the first issue of *Jüdisches Nachrichtenblatt*, published by the Juedische Gemeinde, August 2, 1940. Reel Y-2003-1854.9, YIVO Institute for Jewish Research.

The papers provided the opportunity for the many professional journalists to continue their journalistic careers as well as earn a livelihood. Advertisements were an important feature of the papers, offering services and especially information on stores where goods might be obtained. For readers this was important information and for the papers a source of income. Hence, as noted earlier in the case of Howard Levin, selling advertisements was another way to supplement small incomes. Once the papers closed down due to the Pacific War, incomes disappeared and writers and journalists were one of the hardest hit groups. In 1943, Anna Ginsbourg made an impassioned plea on behalf of these unfortunates writing that "some have already reached the limit of mental depression and physical exhaustion."[89]

---

89 Anna Ginsbourg, "The Well of Despair," *Our Life*, no. 68, October 29, 1943.

**Fig. 7:** Front page from the first issue of *Yedies*, November 1941. Harvard College Library (4071, reel 1).

What did the papers publish? Local news was of major importance, such as announcements of events, concerts, performances, or publishing events. The difficult lot of the Central European refugees was frequently discussed in the pages of *Our Life* and the means of assisting them.[90] Criticism of local efforts were, however, also voiced, and Wolfgang Fischer wrote, "We have not forgotten that for the new Jewish Club in Bubbling Well Road a sum of a million was raised overnight, while thousands of our impoverished, hungry co-religionists received only small amounts [of money] from the immensely rich local Jews."[91] The *Gelbe Post*, in contrast and in addition to local news, tried to

---

**90** For example, "Let us Come to the Assistance of German Refugees," *Our Life*, no. 10, August 28, 1942.

**91** Wolfgang Fischer, "Wir und Shanghai's Judenschaft," *Shanghai Woche*, no. 9, August 1, 1942, p. 1.

inform its readers about Chinese culture and China's political situation. There were articles, for example, about the Jews of Kaifeng, Chinese peasants, the warlord Wu Beifu, how to translate Chinese poetry, and the nature of Chinese music.[92]

Poetry was featured in a number of papers. These might be pious verses around holiday time, poems composed as a nostalgic look backward, or poems depicting the local scene. A satirical touch was not lacking such as in the long poem by Egon Varro, "Well, That is Shanghai." I translate one verse below.

At the Bund they ask: "parlez vous Francais?"
Around the corner a Berliner yells: "Ach nee!"
The press greets us: "How do you do?"
Uncomprehending the coolies look to.
In the bus, that's bursting full
a voice is heard: "hablo Espanol?"
At last come three Viennese
they want to know from an Italienese
if the Chinese post office is nearby.
Well, that is Shanghai.[93]

Whereas in Varro's German poem the Chinese are only silent background against Shanghai's wild cosmopolitanism, in Yosl Mlotek's Yiddish poem they become the subject of a bitter outcry.

Shanghai –

The city beckons
with a thousand passionate eyes.

Neon lights dazzle
a marvellous rainbow.
Changing colors, moving
glittering mercury.
Up and down, down and up –

**92** *Gelbe Post*, no. 1, May 1, 1939; no. 3, June 1, 1939; no. 5, July 1, 1939; no. 6, end July, 1939; no. 7, November 1, 1939.

**93** Egon Varro, "Ja, das ist eben Shanghai," *Shanghai Woche*, no. 1, March 30, 1939, p. 3.

an electric thunderstorm.
"Buy, buy these cigars
the brand 'Two times F'!
Women don't be fooled
silks, socks, the brand 'Blef'."

On houses
roofs
chimneys
and still higher
Buy! Buy!
Signal lights,
message,
call and pull, allure
remind and caress
Buy! Buy!

And at the side
runs
a man in harness – a horse
feet barely touch the ground.
Behind him – hauling, hundreds more
run, hurry, noisily.

\* \* \*

And outside
"Merciful Sir
we have not eaten so long ..."
They stand at the wall:
"Master, food ... food ..."

Above – jazz music
and drunken laughter.
Below a tight cluster
China's daughters.

Stand at the wall
together with their mothers.

\* \* \*

Shanghai
Nanking Road
the city screams
from thousand throats
and from thousand eyes.
Ever louder, shriller
shouts resound
Scream China! Scream Shanghai![94]

An angry poem by E. Simkhoni (Simkha Elberg) expressed his dismay about landing in Shanghai after fleeing his native Poland. In his poem, "Three Countries Spat Me Out," he wrote that first Poland spat him out, then Lithuania,

As one who is tubercular spits
his last drop of blood.

Finally:

On a humid day,
when Japanese tie up their nose
and step with wooden feet
Japan spat me out
into Shanghai.[95]

Book publishing was not as vigorous, nor was there a large book-buying public. Nonetheless, books in Russian and Yiddish and especially Hebrew religious works for the students of the rabbinic schools who had arrived from Japan, appeared in print. Prayer books, Talmud portions and Bibles had deteriorated from heavy use and there were not enough to go around. A Chinese printer who was able to reproduce books by lithography was found, causing *Undzer Lebn* to jubilantly report that, "Shanghai will enter history together with such

---

94 Partial translation of Yosl Mlotek, "Shanghai," *Undzer Lebn*, 38, January 23, 1942. My partial English translation first appeared in "Bridges Across Cultures: China in Yiddish Poetry," in Christina Neder, ed., *China and Her Biographical Dimensions, Commemorative Essays for Helmut Martin*, Wiesbaden: Harrassowitz, 2001, pp. 282–284. The full translation is in Eber, *Voices from Shanghai*, pp. 78–80.
95 E. Simkhoni, "Drei lender hobn mikh oisgeshpign," *Undzer Lebn*, 20, September 1941, partial translation in Ibid., p. 282 and the full translation is in *Voices from Shanghai*, pp. 59–60.

cities as Amsterdam and Vilna. For the first time a Gemarrah [book of the Talmud] is printed here ..."[96] The number of religious books reprinted by lithography or otherwise is uncertain. These included books of the *halakha* (law), portions of the Babylonian and Jerusalem Talmud, Mishnah, the *Shulchan Aruch*, philosophical treaties, and Hasidic works.[97] A later writer compared the volume of Shanghai publishing with that undertaken in Europe after WWII.[98] Whereas most religious books were reprinted, at least one was written in Hebrew by Rabbi Layzer Briks of the Pinsk Yeshiva and was a collection of articles on Talmudic themes.[99]

The Jewish Book Publishing Company, located in the French Concession, began its work in the spring of 1942, bringing out books for the most part in Russian and also some in Yiddish. J. Rapoport (1895–1971), for example, was particularly eager to see works by major Yiddish writers in print and as soon as a year later, five books had appeared with stories by such great writers as Sholem Ash, Sholem Aleichem, and I. L. Peretz, and poetry by N. Bialik.[100] *Selected Short Stories of Jewish Authors* was published in English with an introduction by J. Rapoport, and E. Simkhoni published a Yiddish collection of his poetry entitled *Vander Veg* (Journeys).[101] Apparently few if any novels were written in Shanghai, and the novel, *Schutzhaftjude 13877* (Jewish prisoner 13,877), by Mark Siegelberg, which appeared in 1940, is a rare exception.[102]

---

**96** "Shanghaier Yidn drukn a Gemarrah – a matanah fun di yeshivot (Shanghai Jews print a Gemarrah – a present from the Yeshivoth)," *Undzer Lebn*, 52, May 1, 1942. Amsterdam and Vilna had been major Jewish book publishing centers. "Nidpas beShanghai (Printed in Shanghai)," *Undzer Lebn*, 54, May 15, 1942, hailed it a "historic event."
**97** Over one hundred volumes (and "Periodicals") appear on a list by Fishburn Books, London. Many were printed during the war years by the printing establishment of J. M. Elenberg, 718 Avenue Joffre. I thank Dr. Maisie Meyer for making the list available to me.
**98** Avishai Elboym, "Defusei Shanhai ve'she'arit hapelitah' (Shanghai printing and 'refugee remnants')," *Hama'ayan*, 1999–2000, pp. 78–79, 81–83, also David Kranzler, *Japanese, Nazis and Jews, the Jewish Refugee Community of Shanghai*, pp. 433–434.
**99** "First Talmudic Book Published in Shanghai," *Nasha Zhizn*, no. 23, October 10, 1941, p. 8.
**100** A.G. [Anna Ginsbourg], "Jewish Authors in English," *Our Life*, no. 34, February 12, 1943, p. 1.
**101** A.G. [Anna Ginsbourg], "Know Thyself," *Our Life*, no. 50, June 18, 1943, p. 1, and "A ney zamlung lider fun Dr. E. Simkhoni dershaynt in Shanhai (A new collection of poems by Dr. E. Simkhoni appears in Shanghai)," *Undzer Lebn*, no. 56, May 29, 1942.
**102** The novel is listed in Trapp, Mittenzwei, and Rischbieter, *Handbuch*, Vol. 2, p. 869.

Another such rarity is the woodcut collection, *Huangbaoche* (Rickshaws), by David L. Bloch, published by Taiping Shuju in 1942.[103]

Further research is needed to do justice to Shanghai's publishing activities. Nonetheless, the market for books on Jewish subjects was clearly circumscribed. Also the writing of longer works was a luxury few could indulge in. Siegelberg was able to publish a novel in Shanghai because he wrote it (or the bulk of it) in the course of his ocean voyage to China. Shorter pieces that could be dashed off, published quickly in newspapers or journals, and bring in money were, therefore, preferable. For those who craved reading among the German-speaking refugees there were lending libraries – nine of these during wartime in the designated area that had English and German books. Most had existed since 1939, the largest being the "Lion" at 381 Ward Road One of the most popular was the "Travelling Bookcart" at 139 Ward Road.[104] Of course, these too would have had limited reading matter, being mainly dependent on books refugees had brought along and now sold, rather than the latest works of popular authors. These were, furthermore, business establishments, lending books for money, not public libraries.

Aside from a practically non-existent book market and the straitened circumstances of would-be authors, one other limitation on the writing of longer works must be mentioned. This is that German-speaking intellectuals, uprooted from the cultural world they knew and confronted by the radically different Shanghai environment, were traumatized by this experience. Is it that they had neither distance nor perspective to deal with or to take stock of this new place and themselves as part of it? On the other hand, why was it that no major writer or novel emerged from within the Baghdadi and Russian communities? Were both so divorced from the Chinese intellectual scene, caught in a kind of colonial provincialism, and therefore unable to see the creative potentialities of their existence? Where Chinese writers in the 1930s, before the outbreak of the Sino-Japanese war, explored the infinite variety that was Shanghai,[105] Baghdadis and Russians were for all practical purposes silent.

---

103 A larger edition of Bloch's Shanghai woodcuts was published by Barbara Hoster, Roman Malek, Katharina Wenzel-Teuber, eds., *David Ludwig Boch, Holzschnitte, Woodcuts, Shanghai 1940–1949*, Sankt Augustin: China-Zentrum and Monumenta Serica Institut, 1997.

104 Paul Wieraszowski, "Lending Libraries in the Designated Area," *Our Life*, no. 95, May 19, 1944, p. 2.

105 To mention only two, several of Mao Dun's (Shen Yanbing, 1896–1981) novels have Shanghai and its middle class as their setting. Before departing for Yanan and beginning a different literary life, Ding Ling (1904–1986) wrote a number of well known short stories on Shanghai and its middle class.

# Institutional Development:
# Synagogues, Burial Societies and Cemeteries,
# Hospitals and Schools

Cultural institutions, theatre and publications as well as religious institutions, cemeteries and burial societies (*hevra kadisha*) separated the Jewish communities one from the other. Each community maintained its own institutions and comingling occurred to some extent only in schools. The Baghdadis established their first synagogue, Beit El, in 1887 on Peking Road and a splinter group founded Shearit Israel in 1900 on Broadway (now Dong Daminglu). The temporary prayer houses on rented premises were eventually replaced by two beautiful structures: Ohel Rachel in 1920 on Seymour Road (now Shanxi Beilu) and Beit Aharon in 1927 on Museum Road (now Huqiulu). Sir Jacob Elias Sassoon financed the first, Silas Hardoon the second. At first the Russian congregation used the Shearit Israel premises, but in 1927 the Ohel Moishe congregation moved to its own premises on Ward Road in Hongkou.[106] There it remained until 1941 when a splendid new structure was built, the New Synagogue, on rue Tenant de la Tours (now Xiangyang Nanlu) in the French Colony.

In congregational life Baghdadis, being Sephardic Jews, and Russians and Central Europeans, as Ashkenazi Jews, did not mix. The latter consisted of Jews whose religious persuasions can be characterized as conservative, orthodox, or liberal. To these should be added the various religious schools (yeshivas), ultra-orthodox rabbis and students, who arrived from Japan and who kept apart from the (merely) orthodox. A generally conservative congregation came into being in 1939, celebrating its first holiday at the Broadway Theatre at *Shavuoth* (Weeks) in spring 1939. By mid-1940 the liberal Jewish congregation was founded, at first as a private undertaking, which used instrumental music and a mixed choir. This congregation had its Friday evening and Saturday morning services at various restaurants, until able to rent a hall on the first floor of the Broadway Theatre.[107] Aside from these two, weekly services were conducted at the Ward Road shelter until the fall of 1941 when the first refugee synagogue was founded on MacGregor Road (now Dong Yuhan Lu) in Hongkou,[108] receiving the name Emet Ve'shalom. Both this synagogue and Beit Aharon were demolished in 1985.

---

**106** Tess Johnston, "Jewish Sites in Shanghai," March 15, 1990, unpublished ms. states that the original congregation was founded in 1907 at an unknown location.

**107** According to Kranzler, *Japanese, Nazis and Jews*, pp. 414–415, this congregation ceased after the outbreak of the Pacific War.

**108** Ganther, *Drei Jahre Immigration*, pp. 49, 52.

It was not always easy to find rabbis for the Sephardi and Russian communities who were familiar with their respective liturgies and languages. Moreover, a rabbi would have to come from abroad as there were no rabbinical schools in China that offered rabbinical training and ordination. The Baghdadis never solved their problem satisfactorily, and eventually the Rev. Mendel Brown was recruited to serve as unofficial rabbi of the Ohel Rachel Synagogue. He was active in various capacities, especially educational matters, but was not empowered to make *halakhic* (legal) decisions.[109] The Russian Jews were luckier. In 1926, they recruited Rabbi Meir Ashkenazi who had served in Vladivostok, and he became the Russian community's spiritual leader for the next twenty-one years.[110] Although several refugee rabbis arrived in Shanghai, the religious divisions created complexities in forming congregations. Rabbi Willy Teichner (died 1942) was a popular educator and orator, but he was liberal[111] and did not attract the several factions.

Most important among communal organizations were burial societies. The earliest was the Baghdadi one, established in 1862, probably at the same time as the cemetery on Mohawk Road (now Huang Beilu). The Russian community organized its burial society only sixty years later, using throughout the years a separate section of the Mohawk Road cemetery and later one on Baikal Road (now Huiming Lu).[112] The refugees organized their burial society in 1940 and that same year acquired their own cemetery on Columbia Road (now Fanyu Lu).[113] Due to the high mortality rate among the refugees it was necessary to add a second cemetery in 1941 on Point Road (now Li Ping Lu).[114] Unfortunately, the Chinese authorities moved the four cemeteries between 1957 and 1959 and they have since disappeared.[115]

---

**109** The problem of Sephardi rabbis is discussed in detail by Meyer, *From the Rivers of Babylon*, pp. 100–108.

**110** Kranzler, *Japanese, Nazis and Jews*, p. 60.

**111** Ibid., p. 413.

**112** Ibid., p. 425. According to Kranzler, the Baikal Road cemetery was Ashkenazi. It would, therefore, be a cemetery of the Russian and not the Baghdadi Jews.

**113** However, according to Johnston, "Jewish Sites," the Columbia Road cemetery was acquired in 1926.

**114** I thank Ralph B. Hirsch for making available the list "Central European Refugees Who Died in Shanghai, 1940–1945." The list consists of 1.433 names. See also YVA, 078/96, list of correspondence between December 1939 and March 27, 1941, concerning Jewish cemeteries. These are letters between Ellis Hayim and the Council and Health Commission and a Dr. Jordan about burial of indigent Jewish refugees. The last letter is dated July 24, 1942 about rights to cemetery lands to be transferred from the Jewish Refugee Committee to the Jüdische Gemeinde.

**115** JDC, RG 33/44, File 487, letter from P. Udelevich to Igud Yotsei Sin, October 27, 1958 and P. I. Yudalevich to Henri Elfenbein, AJDC, Geneva, January 6, 1960. According

**Fig. 8:** The Jewish Hospital on Route Pichon (now Fenyang Lu), established in 1943. Tess Johnston and Deke Erh, *A Last Look, Western Architecture in Old Shanghai*, Hong Kong: Old China Hand Press, 1993, p. 60. By permission.

Chinese and foreigners alike were susceptible to illnesses prevalent in Shanghai. Extremes of temperature, intense heat and humidity in summer, cold in addition to rain and flooding in winter, were difficult even for the most robust persons. Not only the climate, but also the crowded and largely unsanitary conditions under which large segments of Shanghai's population lived, together with vermin and mosquitoes that spread disease made escaping illness difficult. Not enough is known about epidemics, such as dysentery, cholera, typhoid, or malaria that threatened Shanghai's population, especially in summer. Vaccines against typhus and cholera were available, but the population apparently was not routinely vaccinated. Added to this were the deplorable practices of unscrupulous fruit vendors who, according to Samuel Didner, injected oranges and watermelons with river water so that people were imbibing polluted water, even though they boiled drinking water.[116]

Shanghai had several hospitals for its Jewish and non-Jewish population. Under ordinary circumstances, the B'nai B'rith Polyclinic run for Sephardi Jews

---

to Dvir Bar-Gal, he has so far collected 85 headstones of these lost cemeteries that had been put to various domestic uses in villages west of Shanghai. "Carved History," ArtSea Studio and Gallery, 2004 (Pamphlet).

**116** Samuel Didner quoted in James R. Ross, *Escape to Shanghai, A Jewish Community in China*, New York: The Free Press, 1994, p. 67.

and the Shanghai Jewish Hospital in the French Concession had a sufficient number of beds. There was also no scarcity of doctors, especially after 1933 when German-Jewish physicians opened practices in Shanghai. However, once the large influx of Central European refugees, who rapidly succumbed to all sorts of infectious diseases, began, available hospital facilities proved soon inadequate.

A clinic was set up at the Ward Road shelter as early as January 1939 and outpatient clinics were set up shortly thereafter at the various dormitory facilities.[117] But the outbreak of scarlet fever among the refugees in May 1939 alerted both the Public Health Department of the SMC and the International Committee to the threat of a widespread epidemic. In a meeting of May 11, 1939 with officials of the SMC, Komor said, "that the disease had fallen like a bombshell with no previous warning" and that on the suggestion of the Public Health Department an isolation Hospital had been created on the premises of Medhurst College on Chaoufoong Road. Eventually that facility, said Chief Inspector Self, would be able to accommodate 300 patients. During a subsequent meeting on May 25, it became clear that the epidemic had been contained with 124 cases under treatment by May 22.[118]

Due to the small number of cases reported among the Chinese population and the large number among foreigners, it was assumed that the disease was introduced into the treaty port by European arrivals. The recently docked *Biancamano* was held responsible, but Triestino agents hastily denied these allegations, claiming that sanitary regulations were observed aboard ship.[119] Be that as it may, the scarlet fever scare brought into focus the importance of sufficient hospital facilities. These were eventually created when the Emigrant Hospital was established in the summer of 1940 in the Ward Road Heim with 100 beds, in place of the Whashing Road hospital which had only sixty beds. Surgical cases continued to be referred to the Shanghai General Hospital and some emigrant doctors were able to send patients there as well as to care for these in the hospital. Howard Levin, for example, who had an extreme case of pleurisy and emphysema, was taken at once to the Shanghai General Hospital in the International Settlement for an emergency operation.[120]

Not everyone among non-surgical cases, however, opted for an emigrant or Jewish hospital. Annemarie Pordes contracted polio in Shanghai and was

---

117  Kranzler, *Japanese, Nazis and Jews*, p. 299.
118  YVA, 078/85, Shanghai Municipal Archives, Shanghai Municipal Council to Members of Council, Report, May 19, 1939, p. 2. There is mo cover letter for the second report.
119  *Gelbe Post,* Vol. 1, no. 2 (May 16, 1939), p. 45.
120  YVA, 078/72, Howard (Horst) Levin interview with I. Eber, October 14, 1988, p. 28.

moved to the isolation ward in the Russian Hospital in the French Concession. The care she received there was probably as good as any she might have received elsewhere. Yet, the nurses were all Russian speakers and Annemarie did not know that language at all.[121] Layzer Kahan, the actress Shoshana's husband, took out a loan in order to go to the hospital in the French Concession (she does not say which) where he expected to get better care.[122] Difficult as the situation for the ill apparently was, it became much worse during the Pacific War, especially after February 1943 when the stateless Jews had to move to the designated area in Hongkou.

Turning now to elementary and high school facilities, there were no major problems until the arrival of the refugees. In the early years of the Baghdadi community more affluent parents tended to send boys to the secular British public schools. Religious instruction was generally provided by home tutors, but a Hebrew School (Talmud Torah) was established as early as 1902. This school developed rapidly and the Shanghai Jewish School, as it was called, in time became an institution for children of both the Baghdadi and Ashkenazi communities, serving mainly the less prosperous segments of Jewish society. Its curriculum included religious and secular subjects; instruction was in English.[123]

Initially refugee children attended the Shanghai Jewish School, but overcrowding soon made it imperative that a school be provided for their use. Attendance had rapidly increased when numerous refugee families arrived, and the Shanghai Jewish Youth Association, S. J. Y. A. or Kadoorie School, began to function in October or November 1939 with 280 children at the Kinchow Road shelter. Lucie Hartwich was the headmistress and Horace Kadoorie supplied the financial backing. By mid-1941 the school had more than 700 pupils. Problems developed, however, in 1940. Since the building had been originally a Chinese school and had been leased by the SMC to the Committee, the facilities had to be returned when the Chinese returned to the area. This is indeed what happened when the lease was terminated by summer 1940.[124] Attractive new premises were eventually found in January 1942 on Chaoufoong Road (or East Yuhang Road).[125]

---

121 YVA, 078/105, Memoir of Annemarie Pordes, p. 42.
122 Kahan, *In fayer un flamen*, p. 318. Entry for July 31, 1944.
123 Meyer, From the Rivers of Babylon, pp. 118–130.
124 JDC, RG 33–44, file 459, Speelman to Troper, February 21, 1940, and file 460, Secretary of SMC to Ellis Hayim, May 30, 1940.
125 YVA, 078/54, *Almanac Shanghai 1946–1947*, Shanghai Echo Publishing Co., n. d., p. 62. Kranzler, *Japanese, Nazis and Jews*, pp. 390–392 writes that the school was on East Yuhang Road, as does Deman, YVA, 078/56A, "Ein verlorenes Jahrzehnt," p. 260.

Like in the Shanghai Jewish School the language of instruction was English and both secular and religious subjects were taught. While the school was located on Kinchow Road, the Demans ran a popular "Vocational Training Center and Junior Club" in the school, also sponsored by Horace Kadoorie, that Deman believes was the forerunner of ORT, discussed in the next chapter.[126] Twelve-year-old Peter Witting's report from December 1940, for example, shows that he received grades in Hebrew, composition, recitation, dictation, arithmetic and history. He was also learning to write Chinese and Japanese in transliteration.[127] Mrs. Hirschberg was quite satisfied with the progress her daughter Lilly was making in English and wrote to her son, "In any event, she speaks English very well and reads English books as easily as German ones."[128] Despite the enthusiastic essay about the Kadoorie School, published in December 1940,[129] not all the children, now adults, have fond memories of their time there. Peter Eisfelder thinks that neither the teaching nor the discipline was great, and he writes, "I cannot claim to have derived any benefits by the time spent at this school."[130] Sigmund Tobias remembers how as a ten-year-old he pleaded with his reluctant parents to allow him to drop out of the Kadoorie School to attend the Mir Yeshiva where he felt accepted and more comfortable.[131]

Not much is known about several other educational establishments. The Freysinger Jewish Elementary and Middle School founded in April 1941, by Dr. Ismar Freysinger, was a small private school, catering no doubt to the more affluent. It functioned throughout the war years.[132] There were several kindergartens, some or all private, including one in the French Concession, run by Mrs. Pordes, who even received permission from the Japanese authorities in 1943 to continue outside the ghetto area.[133] This kindergarten catered most likely to more prosperous foreigners rather than refugees.

Religious instruction for boys who attended secular schools was provided in the afternoon by the Talmud Torah in the Ohel Moishe Synagogue. For boys

---

See also, Ganther, *Drei Jahre Immigration*, p. 67, according to whom the new school building was on Chaoufoong Road.

**126** YVA, 078/56A, "Ein verlorenes Jahrzehnt," pp. 174, 210.

**127** YVA, 078/15, Shanghai Jewish Youth Association School, Peter Witting Report, December 25, 1940. For Chinese and Japanese he had a special exercise book.

**128** Mrs. Hirschberg's letter to her son, Hans, May 25, 1941. Courtesy Mrs. Lilly Fleese.

**129** "Die Kinder von Hongkew," *Der Mitarbeiter*, no. 5, December 20, 1940, p. 11.

**130** YVA, 078/21, H. (Peter) Eisfelder, "Chinese Exile," p. 16.

**131** Sigmund Tobias, *Strange Haven, A Jewish Childhood in Wartime Shanghai*, Urbana-Chicago: University of Illinois Press, p. 56.

**132** YVA, 078/54, Almanac Shanghai 1946–1947, p. 63.

**133** YVA, 078/105, Annemarie Pordes Memoir, p. 76.

of the Russian community a Talmud Torah was at last established in October 1942 on Avenue Joffre, in the French Concession. A year earlier, in May 1941, a Yeshiva was opened for the Baghdadi community in the Museum Road Synagogue. The festivities were attended by many personalities.[134] Religious refugee girls could receive instruction in a Beit Ya'acov school, though it is not clear whether this was only an afternoon or a full time school. In addition, the several rabbinic schools that had arrived in Shanghai from Kobe continued educational work for their members. Unfortunately, we have no way of knowing how many boys, girls, or older students were enrolled in the various religious institutions. But clearly, illiteracy was non-existent among the Jewish population. Whether religious or secular, youngsters did receive a basic education. Opportunities for vocational training too were had in Shanghai. But the major and most popular institution, ORT (Society for the Encouragements of Handicraft), only developed during the war years.

## To Leave Shanghai

It would be erroneous to assume that leaving Shanghai prior to and at the beginning of the Pacific War was impossible. To be sure, it took luck, ingenuity, and enterprise, but some individuals did manage to travel to Tianjin and Qingtao, others ended up in Australia, and still others were on their way to Palestine via India.

Apparently refugees were settling in Tianjin illegally and the Tientsin Hebrew Association wrote to Birman not to allow refugees to go to Tianjin without explicit permission from the local authorities.[135] This had not always been the case. Until spring 1940, at least holders of a Da Dao passport (actually a Russian Emigrant passport), which some refugees had managed to obtain, could go to Tianjin without a special permit.[136] But Rudolf Hennenfeld who had been

---

**134** "Talmud Torah Inaugurated in French Concession," *Our Life*, no. 18, October 23, 1942, and *Undzer Lebn*, no. 5, May 30, 1941.

**135** CAHJP, 86.2, Tientsin Hebrew Association to All Shanghai Committees, December 8, 1940.

**136** CAHJP, DAL 86, Birman to Tientsin Hebrew Society, May 1, 1940. For the short lived Da Dao or Great Way government, see Timothy Brook, "The Great Way Government of Shanghai," in Christian Henriot and Wen-hsin Yeh, eds., *In the Shadow of the Rising Sun, Shanghai Under Japanese Occupation*, Cambridge: Cambridge University Press, 2004, pp. 157–186. The Great Way puppet government was inaugurated December 5, 1937 and ceased April 28, 1938, though its name continued in popular use for some years thereafter.

a medical student in Vienna, sailing via Marseille to Shanghai in March 1939, chose a rather original path to leave Shanghai. Unable to make a living, he joined the Foreign Legion in Saigon, Vietnam. In May 1941, he returned to Shanghai, having received a military passport and, provided he could obtain a work contract, the Japanese authorities were willing to give him a visa to Tianjin.[137]

In fact, permission had to be obtained from the Japanese authorities for settling in all areas of North China under their control, which is probably the reason why only between ten and fifteen immigrants were actually in Qingdao[138] – and these might have come earlier, in 1933 or 1934. As early as February 1939, Daljewcib in Harbin had indicated that it was not easy to relocate from Shanghai to other places. "With regard to Tientsin and Tsingtao [Qingdao], in order that refugees may enter, our representatives there have to solicit the local authorities for special entrance permits."[139]

Leaving Shanghai for destinations abroad was a different matter. How the journalist and publisher, A. Storfer, and the playwright, M. Siegelberg, sailed to Australia at the end of 1941 is unclear, as is the question of whether other Shanghai refugees were booked on the same ship. Tadeusz Romer (1894–1978), the Polish ambassador to Japan who, having closed the Polish embassy in Tokyo, had come to Shanghai with his staff at the end of October, was probably the source of the Australian visas.[140] But by November 1941, which is the approximate time they left, only Dutch liners were able to sail to Australia via Batavia.[141] This may have been the reason that the sixty-five Australian visas he had been promised were reduced to forty-five and finally to eighteen.[142]

To leave Shanghai by sea for other countries required proper papers, a visa, and money. Most refugees lacked one or all of these. Still, some Polish

**137** CAHJP, DAL 99, Birman to Valentine, 128 Victoria Road, Tianjin, July 25, 1941.

**138** CAHJP, 86.4, Birman to Reich Association of Jews in Germany, November 12, 1940.

**139** CAHJP, 76.1, from Daljewcib, Harbin, February 20, 1939.

**140** CAHJP, DAL 101, Birman to HIAS, New York, November 19, 1941. See also NAC, Manuscript Division, reel C-10451, File 1. Romer, Shanghai to London, November 5, 1941. Romer states in the telegram that he has made arrangements to obtain Australian visas for the refugees. See also file 19, Romer, Tokyo to London, October 26, 1941, in which he informs the Ministry of Foreign Affairs in London that he has finished liquidating the embassy and is leaving for Shanghai with his personal archives and complete codes, and October 4, 1941, where it is stated that the Japanese embassy in Warsaw is closed as of October 4.

**141** CAHJP, DAL 101, Birman to Polish Relief Committee, Melbourne, November 6, 1941.

**142** NAC, MG 31, o–68, Vol. 2, file #3, 3 pp., reel C-10451. Tadeusz Romer, "Uchodzcy żydowscy z Polsku na dalekim Wschodzie (Jewish refugees from Poland in the Far East).

Jews arrived from Kobe with Palestine Certificates and these people Birman tried to dispatch as quickly as he could, even if they had to sail on Chinese ships as far as Bombay or Calcutta. According to Birman, by mid-November 1941 he had sent seven groups of pioneers (*halutzim*) to Palestine, although they were apparently stranded in Bombay and unable to continue their voyage. It is not clear whether they remained in India until the end of the war or were able to leave earlier. In any event, the distraught Polish consul in Bombay wired both London and Shanghai, pleading for an end to the emigrant flood.[143] To his friend in Tianjin, Birman confided his distress. War was looming and it was imperative to send out from Shanghai as many people as possible, especially those who had visas for the United States. But at that point it was the JOINT representative in Shanghai, Laura Margolis, who refused to accede to his request.[144]

Finally a group of Polish refugees was able to leave Shanghai, apparently with Romer's help, after the start of the Pacific War. Shoshana Kahan had hoped that her husband Layzer would also be among the fifty places reserved for Poles on the evacuation ship *Kamakura Maru*. Regretfully this did not happen, she noted in her diary.[145] The ship sailed August 17, 1942 for Lorenzo Marquez (in Portuguese South Africa) with several Jews aboard, among them, at least, one student from the Mir Yeshiva.[146]

Baghdadis, Russians, or Central Europeans, all were strangers in Shanghai. But, for that matter, so were many, if not most, Chinese who hailed from various provinces and who considered their native villages or towns home. Yet

---

**143**  CAHJP, DAL 101, Birman to HICEM, Lisbon and HIAS, New York, November 17, 1941. Sometimes there were also stowaways on these ships. Szepsel Lewin and Gerszel Apfelbaum were caught on the "Hunan" and handed over to the Hong Kong police.

**144**  CAHJP, DAL 101, Birman to Sam Bleviss, Tianjin, November 27, 1941. The letter is in Yiddish.

**145**  Kahan, *In fajer un Flamen*, pp. 294–295, entries for July 20 and July 25, 1942. She noted that already April 16, 1942, p. 292, Layzer went with a delegation of writers to Ambassador Romer who told them that he hoped to bring about an evacuation of writers.

**146**  *Undzer Lebn*, 15 (67), August 14, 1942, and no. 17 (46), October 16, 1942. A cable was received on the latter date that the ship had safely reached Lorenzo Marquez from where the refugees traveled on to several destinations. The HICEM official, Layzer Epstein, wrote a long letter on board the "Kamakura Maru," in which he stated that among the British, Dutch, Norwegian, and Belgian passengers were also 43 Polish citizens. I assume that most of these were, however, not Jewish. YIVO Institute, MKM, 15.57, XVB-26, Epstein to HICEM, Lisbon, September 1, 1942, 4 pp. Arc. 4°, 410. Yehoshua Rapoport Diary, Jewish National and University Library, Jerusalem, entry July 23, 1943. Rapoport mentions yet another evacuation that was to take place at the beginning of October. Apparently it never took place.

despite China at war, Shanghai crime, the pervasive opium problem, abject poverty and ostentatious wealth, the strangers in Shanghai were not solitary and alienated urbanites. Individuals were part of groups – be they ethnic, cultural, linguistic in origin – made possible by the mosaic nature of Shanghai. Added to this was the absence of a unified political authority capable of enforcing uniformity on the polyglot population, at least until the outbreak of the Pacific War and the occupation of all of Shanghai by Japanese forces.

The cultural and institutional life of the several Shanghai Jewish communities, and especially of the refugee community, described in these pages, obscures to a large extent the real misery, destitution, and abject loneliness experienced by many. I have highlighted the success stories of adjustment of the very few. I have also tried to show, however, that despite sudden poverty and dislocation from a known into an alien environment, some people coped remarkably well. How much help the established Jewish communities extended to the newcomers, to what extent individuals or groups furnished models for emulation, are and will remain subjects of controversy. That the Central European refugees were not welcomed with open arms seems in retrospect only natural. At the time though, it was clearly one more insult added to their battered sensibilities.

Although the British and others probably identified them (and one would like to know more about that) as "co-religionists," the fact is that neither Baghdadis nor Russians had much in common with the newcomers, except that they were all Jewish. But the Judaism of the Jews, as I tried to point out, was by no means monolithic, and the Baghdadis had not much in common with the Russians either. All the same, to both groups Shanghai had become home, whereas to the Central Europeans Shanghai was a way station to elsewhere, a temporary and often none-too-friendly haven. Another major difference between the Baghdadis and Russians, on the one hand, and the Central Europeans, on the other, was the latter's status as expellees, of people driven out from their native homes. "Once we were somebodies about whom people cared, we were loved by friends ..." wrote Hannah Arendt, and "Man is a social animal and life is not easy for him when social ties are cut off. Very few individuals have the strength to conserve their own integrity if their social, political and legal status is completely confused."[147] During the war years the confusion of status would become even greater.

---

147 Hannah Arendt, "We Refugees," in Marc Robinson, ed., *Altogether Elsewhere*, San Diego–London: Harcourt Brace and Co., 1994, pp. 115, 116 (first published in 1943).

# Chapter 5:
# Years of Misfortune: 1941–1945

For Shanghai 1941 was not an auspicious year. The economic recovery, which had followed the outbreak of war in 1937 and the abandonment of Chinese Shanghai to Japanese occupation, was winding down. Although it seemed like business as usual in the foreign settlements because many Chinese business-men had fled there, bringing their business with them, rampant inflation and the increasing scarcity of raw materials resulting from the Japanese army's restrictions on the movement of goods, were increasingly felt. Moreover, in July 1941 the British and American governments froze Japanese assets in their countries and terminated commercial relations with Japan and the territories under its occupation. When the Japanese banned the export of products con-sidered essential to the war effort, foreign currency coming into Shanghai was much reduced.[1]

Fig. 9: "Wood carburetor and manpower." From Barbara Hoster, Roman Malek, Katharina Wenzel-Teuber, eds., David Ludwig Bloch, Holzschnitte, Woodcuts, Shanghai 1940–1949, Sankt Augustin–Nettetal: Steyler Verlag, 1997, p. 36. Courtesy Lydia Abel. Used by special permission of David Ludwig Bloch / Lydia Abel; all rights reserved.

---

1 Christian Henriot, "Shanghai Industries under Japanese Occupation, Bombs, Boom, and Bust (1937–1945)," in Christian Henriot, Wen-hsin Yeh, eds., In the Shadow of the Rising Sun, Shanghai under Japanese Occupation, Cambridge: Cambridge University Press, 2004, p. 36.

**Fig. 10:** "Horsepower," From Barbara Hoster, Roman Malek, Katharina Wenzel-Teuber, eds., David Ludwig Bloch, Holzschnitte, Woodcuts, Shanghai 1949–1949, Sankt Augustin–Nettetal: Steyler Verlag, 1997 p. 38. Used by special permission of David Ludwig Bloch/ Lydia Abel; all rights reserved.

The economic problems, ever more obvious in 1941, were exacerbated by energy shortages. Due to the Japanese invasion, Shanghai could no longer rely on domestic coal from North China, and the growing imports from Southeast Asia dwindled after the summer of 1941.[2] As emphasized by Henriot, Shanghai's existence was dependent on foreign markets for selling manufactured goods and on its hinterland for obtaining raw materials. This was still possible in 1940, yet during 1941 – and certainly after Pearl Harbor – both the foreign markets and the hinterland were no longer viable.[3]

The Jewish population, old-timers and refugees alike, may not have been aware of the dire economic situation, but businessmen like Michel Speelman or Ellis Hayim could not ignore the warning signals. Their problems were compounded by the thousands of Jewish refugees in Shanghai who had to be housed and fed and the fact that more were on their way from Kobe Japan. These were not the pliable, if not docile, German and Austrian refugees. They were for the most part Polish Jews who had fled to Lithuania when the Germans marched into Poland in September 1939 and among them were quite a few demanding and rebellious individuals. How to maneuver between the ever growing demands of the refugees, maintain their respected positions in Shanghai's commercial world while not antagonizing the Japanese conqueror had become a major though unspoken consideration for these wealthy businessmen.

---

**2** Ibid., p. 38 and n. 98.
**3** Ibid., p. 41.

# Eastjewcom, Laura Margolis, and the Polish Jews

Some twenty rabbinic schools (yeshivoth), among them a small number of secular Yiddishist intellectuals, had fled to Vilna at the outbreak of war, where they were supported by the American Joint Distribution Committee.[4] After the Soviet army marched into Lithuania, most of these managed to arrive in Kobe, as discussed earlier. They might have hoped to remain in Kobe for the duration of war, but in the early months of 1941 it became clear that their journey had not ended. The next destination was Shanghai. As Inuzuka Kiroshige explained some months later, the Japanese authorities were forced to evacuate the Jews because (1) they had remained in Kobe far too long on transit visas, and (2) as a result of the freezing of currency the Joint had ceased sending funds to Japan for their upkeep.[5]

In response to this new situation the Committee for Assistance of Jewish Refugees from Eastern Europe (Eastjewcom) was organized March 14, 1941 by Layzer Szczupakiewicz and Zorach Wahrhaftig for the purpose of raising additional funds to support the refugees.[6] At the beginning of April the two men came to Shanghai, ostensibly to inform the Committee for the Assistance of European Jewish Refugees (CAEJR) that the Polish refugees would be arriving from Kobe.[7] Speelman did not entirely trust them, believing that the two men were not "very reliable," trying to bring refugees to Shanghai without observing the necessary formalities and creating difficulties for refugees already in Shanghai.[8] By formalities Speelman was referring to the fact that the Kobe refugees had neither permits for Shanghai, nor show money as required by the Municipal Council. Indeed, he was quite annoyed because apparently Szczupakiewicz and Wahrhaftig had first gone to Boris Topas, chairman of the Russian Ashkenazi Community, and it was from him and Bitker that Speelman learned of the impending Polish problem, and that the refugees had permits to leave Kobe, but had none allowing them to land in Shanghai. Clearly expressing his frustration with this new development, Speelman wrote to Troper in New York:

> You cannot imagine how we are troubled with this Polish question and we have enough troubles already as it is with the Austrian and German refugees. There is

---

4 JDC, RG 33–44, file 739, "JDC Aid to Refugee Yeshivoth Students and Rabbis from Poland."

5 "Japanese Authorities Explain Policy of Emigrants in Hongkew," *Nasha Zhizn*, September 12, 1941, p. 11.

6 JDC, RG 33–44, file 462, letter from A. Oppenheim to Speelman, October 2, 1941.

7 JDC, RG 33–44, file 461, Speelman to Troper, JDC, April 5, 1941.

8 JDC, RG 33–44, file 461, Speelman to Troper, JDC, April 7, 1941.

great dissatisfaction at present among these people ... Now on top of all this comes the Polish problem.[9]

Unlike Speelman, the Kobe refugees were not concerned with Shanghai's problems. Their major concern was twofold: they absolutely refused to live in the shelters (Heime) as did most of the German and Austrian refugees. Secondly, they rejected (particularly the large group of 451 yeshiva students and their rabbis) eating the food prepared in the shelter kitchens as it was deemed not kosher. In short, they demanded separate accommodations and sufficient funds for preparing their own meals,[10] and they insisted on preferential and better treatment than was accorded the other refugees.

Their demands were not entirely unreasonable. Letters that they had received from Shanghai described the deplorable conditions there. R. Shoshana Kahan wrote after four days in the city in her diary:

> Now I understand why everybody has fought with all their strength to remain longer in Japan and not to go to Shanghai ... now I understand the terrible letters that we received from those that had the misfortune to be sent as the first to Shanghai. A dirty, disgusting city ... Hongkou [where most of the refugees lived] is the poorest and dirtiest part of Shanghai.[11]

Unlike Shoshana Kahan, Yehoshua Rapoport did expect Shanghai to be an improvement over Kobe. After all, he wrote, there was a Jewish community. But it took no more than the reception in Shanghai to shatter his illusion:

> We arrived in the middle of the night ... without having had warm food, and the Jewish community in Shanghai did not even receive the fifty refugees in their homes. They took us to the Jewish Club where we spent the night on chairs. The rabbi arranged a place for the Yeshiva students and the rabbis, but for the Jewish writers and the simple Jews there was no room. The next day we were thrown into the Pingling shelter; a pigsty, without tables or chairs ... It was difficult to get a few dollars for rent. The Jews [of Shanghai] were upset: why are you better than the German Jews? They can live in the shelters and you can't?[12]

---

**9** Ibid., April 5, 1941.

**10** JDC, RG 33–44, file 461, a flurry of telegrams were dispatched between March 22 and March 25, 1941 from Kobe to New York, signed by a number of dignitaries and demanding "minimal human living conditions."

**11** R. Shoshana Kahan, *In fajer un flamen, tagebukh fun a Yidisher shauspilerin* (In fire and flames, diary of a Yiddish actress), Buenos Aires: Central Publisher of Polish Jews in Argentina, 1949, p. 283, entry for October 26, 1941.

**12** Yehoshua Rapoport, Diary, Arc. 4°, 410, Jewish National and University Library, entry for May 12, 1941. I thank Dr. Shalom Eilati for preparing a typed copy of Rapoport's Yiddish handwritten diary.

An outsider, J. Epstein of Hias-Hicem, wrote, "There are no words which would describe the very bottom of misery that these people [the German refugees] live in. It is simply horrible."[13] And elsewhere he wrote in rather quaint English:

> It is difficult to state what are these sad conditions accounted for. As a matter of fact, our refugees fear to go to Shanghai in the most panic way which does not seem unreasonable especially as the possibilities of earning for the life in Shanghai are also not easy ones.[14]

And even the generally understated *American Jewish Yearbook* declared that "The situation of the refugees there is deplorable."[15]

Considering the amount of correspondence between New York, Kobe, and Shanghai, in addition to the Japanese refusal to permit the Polish contingent to reside in Hongkou, one would be led to assume that several thousand Polish refugees were about to descend on Shanghai. This was, however, hardly the case. Although accurate figures are hard to come by, according to one report, 4,664 refugees came to Japan between July 1940 and the end of May 1941. The report lists 1,962 as having come from Poland, 2,498 from Germany, and 204 from various other countries. Of these 2,797 left Japan; 1,563 went to America; and approximately 1,000 went to other countries. By June 1941 there would have been 1,867 refugees in Japan who were candidates for Shanghai.[16] Another report mentions the arrival of 4,413 refugees between July 1, 1940 and June 1, 1941. Of these, 3,092 departed, leaving 1,321 in Japan.[17] The latter figure seems more plausible, and we may assume that a little over one thousand Polish refugees eventually came to Shanghai.

In New York the Joint worried about having to deal with two committees, Eastjewcom and CAEJR; in Shanghai the CAEJR was concerned with where to

---

13  YIVO, Hias-Hicem, I, MKM, 15.57, 15-B24, J. Epstein, The Jewish Community of Kobe, Committee for Assistance to Refugees, Kobe, to Lisbon, August 18, 1941.

14  Daljewcib, 72.4, J. Epstein, Hicem to Polish Jewish Relief Committee, East Brunswick, Vic. Australia, June 4, 1941.

15  Harry Schneiderman, ed., *The American Jewish Yearbook, 5702*, September 22, 1941 to September 11, 1942, Philadelphia: The Jewish Publication Society of America, 1941–5702, Vol. 43, p. 336.

16  YIVO, Hias-Hicem, I, MKM, 15.57, 15-C7, Moise Moiseff, "Jewish Transients in Japan," n. d., 3 pp. from *Congress Weekly*, July 25, 1941.

17  The report by J. Epstein, 15-B24, cited above. See also JDC, RG 33–44, file 462, "Summary of Important Recent Communications Regarding Overseas Developments." However, according to the Polish Ambassador, Tadeusz Romer, 950 Polish refugees remained in Shanghai. Tadeusz Romer, "Uchodzcy żydowscy z Polsku na dalekim Wschodzie (Jewish refugees from Poland in the Far East)," National Archives of Canada Reel C-10451, MG31, O-68, Vol. 2, file #3.

put the Polish Jews once they started arriving; in Kobe the Polish refugees wondered how to resist living in the shelters. Meanwhile the Joint was preparing to dispatch Laura Margolis (1903–1997), a social worker, to Shanghai. Her task, as defined by the U.S. State Department was to obtain American visas for would-be immigrants.[18] The emigration task seems not to have taken much of her time and she was, therefore, increasingly involved in refugee affairs, feeling profoundly sorry for the treatment they received from the committee in charge. Her letters, regularly dispatched to Robert Pilpel at the Joint, express not only her growing frustration – indeed, futility – with the Shanghai refugee situation, but also with most of the men in charge. In a long letter which she wrote before leaving the quarrelsome Shanghai scene for a rest in Manila, she described each of the men in rather unflattering terms. Speelman, she believed, was becoming senile; Ellis Hayim was sadistic; Mr. and Mrs. Abraham are nice enough, but absolutely blind where Jewish religion was concerned.[19] Despite being thoroughly discouraged about being able to make a contribution to both U.S. visa problems and refugee relief, Margolis returned to Shanghai from Manila in September 1941, and from then on the Eastjewcom problem began to be discussed in her letters.

A cable from Robert Pilpel had informed her that the Joint could not possibly deal with two committees as well as preferential standards for the Kobe refugees. To this Margolis responded by stating that there was no way Eastjewcom and the CEAJR could work together. Nonetheless, money should not be disbursed to the former directly, but channeled through the latter. As to equality of maintenance that was of prime importance to the Joint, she seems to have preferred evading the issue, writing merely that there were inequalities of treatment within Eastjewcom also, some being more kosher and others less so.[20] The following month she wrote again complaining this time that the CEAJR had made absolutely no arrangements for housing the Kobe refugees, and she was especially incensed about the treatment accorded the yeshivoth group together with their rabbis. She declared categorically that the Mir Yeshiva (238 persons) must be housed together; the Klecker (22), Telser (12), Lublin (35), and Lubow (29) groups could be housed in a smaller building. For the remaining 73 persons individual accommodations could be found.[21]

---

**18** JDC, RG 33–44, file 60, "500 Refugees Transferred to Shanghai from Japan," pp. 6–7.

**19** JDC, RG 33–44, File 462, Margolis to Robert Pilpel, August 11, 1941.

**20** JDC, RG 33–44, file 462, Margolis to Robert Pilpel, September 10, 1941.

**21** JDC, RG 33–44, file 462, Margolis to Robert Pilpel, October 26, 1941. Margolis's figure of 409 for the religious group is probably fairly accurate.

Appended to Laura Margolis's long letter was a "Memorandum" by Inuzuka that he had sent to Captain Herzberg, as the latter had been entrusted with the business management of all refugee affairs. (Margolis respected Herzberg, but did not like his German manner or the way he spoke to the refugees.) The Memorandum is a plaintive sort of document, complaining that the Japanese have treated the refugees very generously, allowing them to reside in Hongkou, yet the Jewish authorities have always refused to cooperate with the Japanese authorities. Indeed, some Jews have "openly engaged in anti-Japanese activities. The Japanese authorities have now a very bad impression of the Jewish people."[22] Although Inuzuka's memorandum was not all that strongly worded, he clearly indicated that a further influx of Jewish refugees into Hongkou – after all, to a large extent populated by Japanese – was not desirable. Places elsewhere would have to be found.

From the correspondence it emerges that apparently the Joint had not given Margolis the authority to deal with refugee relief when she first arrived in Shanghai in 1941. After she returned from Manila in summer 1941, however, matters were entirely different and by October she was fully in charge. Now she was the one who determined how Joint funds would be allocated. The men of both committees understood this soon enough and apparently the relationship between them and Margolis improved. It is difficult to know to what extent she was being manipulated by one side or the other for, above all, it was important to preserve a façade of equanimity in Shanghai. By October, Speelman reported to New York that the Polish problem had been settled. The Polish refugees will receive US $ 5.00/month, whereas the German and Austrian refugees will be fed on US $ 3.00/month.[23] In short, the CEAJR and Joint were led to accept unequal treatment, no doubt, because of Margolis's intervention, who, as was shown above, was not troubled by inequality.

However, her important role as conduit to American money was short lived. On December 8, 1941, the Japanese bombed Pearl Harbor and the Pacific War broke out. All remittances from the United States ceased, and funds to feed the refugees had to be found locally. Throughout 1942, Margolis and her assistant, Manuel Siegel, who had arrived from the U. S. in November 1941, brought ingenuity and inventiveness to the problem of raising funds. By the time both were interned at the beginning of 1943, food for the refugees – even if hardly adequate – was available. It is to the war years that we must turn next in order to understand the vast changes experienced by Shanghai's Jewish communities.

---

**22** JDC, RG 33–44, Ibid., September 17, 1941, handed to Herzberg September 22, 1941.
**23** JDC, RG 33–44, file 462, Speelman to the secretary of the American Joint, October 4, 1941.

## The Pacific War and the Jewish Communities

On December 8, 1941 (Pearl Harbor time it was December 7), at about 3:30 a.m. a huge explosion was heard. As noted by John Potter,

> There on the river stretch just before the [American] club was a vivid scene of war. Along the Bund just under the window were brilliant explosions as field pieces fired and shells struck their target up the river. Reddish streaks made by tracer bullets chase one another in low curves. Then came the bursts of flame from the target.

The target, the British gunboat *Petrel*, "Quickly ... burst into flames, was battered to pieces. She sank. Her lifeboats drifted away, afire, and floated downstream."[24] Thus began the war in Shanghai.

But it did not last long. Proclamations went up everywhere that business was to continue as usual. And while Japanese troops poured into the International Settlement, shopkeepers gradually opened stores, trams and buses began to run, rickshaws appeared as usual.[25] The outbreak of war led to the occupation of the International Settlement, but not of the French Concession. There a council appointed by the Vichy government ruled until July 1943 when the Concession was handed over to the Wang Jingwei[26] government, ending extraterritoriality at the same time.

Whereas, on the one hand, war put an end to the fragmentation of Shanghai when first the International Settlement and then the French Concession were abolished,[27] the British and French influence and presence, on the other, did not end all at once. Throughout 1942, until their internment in February and March 1943, the British continued to run affairs in the International Settlement and they continued actively in the Shanghai Municipal Police. As Robert Bickers observes, "Wartime relations in the International Settlement between national communities did not necessarily mirror the political alliances operating worldwide."[28] It seems hardly a coincidence that the Japanese did not arrest the British at once, but began to intern them about a year later, ordering

---

**24** Edna Lee Booker, with John S. Potter, *Flight from China*, New York: The Macmillan Co., 1945, pp. 131,132.

**25** Ibid., pp. 132–134.

**26** Wang Ching-wei (1883–1944) established his Japan sponsored puppet government in Nanjing in 1940.

**27** Robert Bickers, "Settlers and Diplomats, the End of British Hegemony in the International Settlement, 1937–1945," in Henriot and Yeh, *In the Shadow of the Rising Sun, Shanghai*, p. 229.

**28** Ibid., p. 243. The SMC functioned until August 1943.

stateless persons confined to a specific area in Hongkou at the same time. Throughout 1942, however, life in Shanghai seemed almost normal.

Yet, for many refugees the Pacific War was the final blow. Their sense of isolation and of abandonment deepened. Now, it was felt, they were truly cut off from all contact. Shoshana Kahan wrote in her diary:

> What will be now? We are again in the fire of war. God in heaven, haven't we suffered enough? The Pacific War... began today in the morning. No longer can one find a piece of earth in God's world where there is peace. All our friends are running around like poisoned mice ... The last hope has disappeared, [we are] without any help. Abandoned in an Asian country, who knows what will now happen to us ... [29]

The theme of abandonment predominated also in Simcha Elberg's (E. Simkhoni) poem,

"My God, My God, Why Hast Thou Forsaken Me."
Why God, have You abandoned me
And extinguished Your light.
Rain outside
and all rooms are locked with no key
if not You, who can answer me outright?
When night fell
you and all others mocked me.


In back of the book the mite eats till full.
The worm sleeps quietly in its terrestrial bed.
To me You gave as a friend the street
where it is dark, full of sleet.

In Your holy books it is written:
"Heaven for God, earth for men."
So why must I remain forsaken?[30]

All doors are closed now, says the poet in despair, God has abandoned the unfortunates, indeed, makes fun of their misery. Only worms still exist in peace, for others darkness has fallen. Interestingly, an announcement of the

---

**29** Kahan, *In fajer un flamen,* p. 289, entry December 8, 1941.
**30** *Undzer Lebn,* no. 39 (January 30, 1942). Elberg took the title from Psalm 22:1, "Eli, Eli, lamah azavtani."

war did not appear in the official publication of the German refugees. Instead they had a warning. The Jüdische Gemeinde, it stated, requests that all immigrants obey the directives of the Japanese authorities and refrain from public discussions because quiet and discipline are the foremost requirements at this time. Whoever goes against these basic principles injures our community.[31]

Perhaps it was just as well that the refugees did not know how grim the situation was in Shanghai. Since money was no longer arriving from America, Shanghai's local Jewry was reluctant to assume responsibility for those refugees who had no incomes of any kind. A revealing report about events in 1942 by Laura Margolis tells a distressing tale of hardships exacerbated by petty animosities.[32]

One major problem that Margolis and the CEAJR had to face after Pearl Harbor was that without American money the problem of refugee maintenance would have to be solved locally. Authorized by the New York Joint to arrange for loans in Shanghai, to be redeemed whenever this became feasible, Margolis and Manuel Siegel pursued this course energetically, keeping Inuzuka Koreshige informed about their activities. The latter had demanded that loans should be only from neutrals and not from "enemy nationals."[33] Where money matters were concerned, Margolis had high praise for Joseph Bitker and his astute financial advice; he was especially helpful in averting a financial catastrophe in June 1942. At that time the Nationalist currency (*fabi*) was withdrawn and CRB notes (Central Reserve Bank of the Nanjing government) were put in circulation at a rate of two to one.[34] The loss would have been horrendous had purchases of goods not been made before the devaluation.

Another major problem concerned the reorganization of existing committees. The CEAJR was for all practical purposes defunct by the early months of 1942; members had either resigned, were arrested, or, except for Michel Speelman, were unacceptable to the Japanese. Anyone serving in a public capacity had to have the stamp of approval of the Japanese authorities.

The "Kitchen Fund" was formed in August or September 1942 with the aim of raising money on the so-called "*Patenschaft*" basis, regular monthly

---

31 *Juedisches Nachrichtenblatt*, no. 25, December 19, 1941.

32 JDC, RG 33–44, file 463, Margolis, "Report of Activities in Shanghai, China, from December 8, 1941, to September 1943," is not dated. It can be assumed, however, that it was written shortly after her release from Japanese internment and repatriation to the United States in September 1943. I thank Bernard Wasserstein for making the "Report" available.

33 Margolis, "Report," pp. 2–6, and JDC, RG 33–44, file 376 (2), "Refugees in the Far East," in *The Rescue of Stricken Jews in a World at War*, pp. 17–18.

34 Margolis, "Report," p. 7.

contributions by Russian Jews and refugees who had arrived with money. In addition, a local Joint Distribution Committee was set up to act as a controlling body.[35] When it was suggested in the spring of 1942 that the Russian (Ashkenazi) community also use the Patenschaft plan to support German refugees, a violent quarrel broke out between those who were for helping the German refugees and those who were against it. This led to the appearance of yet another committee, Centrojewcom (Central European Refugee Committee) in favor of aiding the German refugees,[36] in distinction to Eastjewcom, which did not want to have anything to do with them. Finally – although this is getting somewhat ahead of the story and will be discussed in greater detail below – because the Japanese authorities only wanted to work with members of the Russian Jewish community, SACRA (Shanghai Ashkenazi Collaborating Relief Association) was organized in February 1943. The Japanese were in contact with SACRA, and SACRA dealt with the Kitchen Fund and the Shanghai Joint.[37]

In an attempt to clarify the relationship among the various committees to Edward Egle of the International Red Cross Committee, members of the Shanghai Joint wrote that: The Joint is an independent organization. Its function is to carry out relief work among the refugees. The Kitchen Fund is a local organization that administers refugee camps and is supervised by the Shanghai Joint. SACRA is a separate organization established in connection with the February 18 Proclamation.[38] Not stated in the letter was the obvious fact that through SACRA the Japanese controlled both the Kitchen Fund and the Shanghai Joint and that, in fact, none of the three organizations was independent.

Laura Margolis and Manuel Siegel were arrested and confined to internment camps at the beginning of 1943. But the fundraising and the organizational framework that they had set up continued to function throughout the war years. Several major figures, long time Shanghai residents, played an increasingly prominent role in refugee affairs, among them a Mr. Brahn. Perhaps because of his connection to highly placed persons in the Japanese army, or

---

**35** YVA, reel 16, 11.728, M. Siegel to Leavitt, August 26, 1945, pp. 4–5; Margolis, "Report," pp. 12, 15; YIVO, XV, C-10, Birman to Hicem, Lisbon, November 12, 1942. Birman apparently sent reports regularly to neutral European destinations like Portugal, Sweden, and Switzerland. Unfortunately, the reports are mostly illegible; they were typed on poor paper with worn typewriter ribbons.

**36** Margolis, "Report," p. 13. According to Birman, the Russian members of the "Kitchen Fund" organized Centrojewcom. See YIVO, XV, C-10, Birman to Hicem, Lisbon, November 12, 1942.

**37** Margolis, "Report," p. 20.

**38** YVA, reel 16, 11.728, D. M. and Gluckman, Shanghai Jewish Joint Distribution Committee to Edward Egle, International Red Cross Committee, Shanghai, September 14, 1944.

the fact that he had a Japanese friend, a Mrs. Nogami, who was an interpreter in the *Gendarmerie* (the military police), Margolis decided to appoint him chairman of the Shanghai Joint. Although feared and considered sadistic, he kept his position until asked to resign in August 1945.[39]

Shanghai in 1942 was, however, not like Warsaw or any other wartime European capital. To be sure, the Japanese presence in the International Settlement and in the Chinese portions of the city was apparent to all. There was real hunger and the Chinese refugee problem was all too obvious. Nor could the rampant inflation be ignored. By 1943 prices of consumer goods had risen approximately forty-five times above what they had been in 1940.[40] Nevertheless, refugee restaurants continued to do business. There were the Taverne; Kuenstlinger, and the famous Roy Roof Garden on Wayside Road; the Café Eastern Garden on Ward Road; Café Gloria at 321 Kungping Road; and others along the main roads of Hongkou.[41]

Art exhibits and theatrical performances, even if reduced in number, continued. Between May 31 and June 15, 1942, for example, the gifted painter-poet, Yoni Fayn (b. 1914) from Poland, exhibited 53 paintings at the Jewish Club. The paintings were divided into four themes: Japanese, Bible, Jewish subjects, and terrible times.[42] Canvasses or paper and paints were expensive and one wonders how Fayn raised the money to purchase these. Theatrical performances and variety shows were popular. A benefit program for the Shanghai Joint was featured in the Doumer Theatre on January 25, 1942, and there were benefit programs with such well known performers as Gerhard Gottschalk (1899–1974) and Raja Zomina July 19, 1942 and August 2, 1942.[43] A light opera (with music by popular composers), *Hänsel und Gretel*, was performed at the Eastern Theatre on March 18, 1942.[44] Comedies were, however, more in demand than serious theater, and two by Hans Schubert (1905–1965) were performed in December

---

**39** Margolis, "Report," p. 15 and YVA, reel 16, 11.728, M. Siegel to Leavitt, August 26, 1945, p. 5. According to Margolis, Mrs. Nogami was "sympathetic to the refugees, and she was Mr. Brahn's "personal friend," p. 3.
**40** Wang Ke-wen, "Collaborators and Capitalists: The Politics of 'Material Control' in Wartime Shanghai," *Chinese Studies in History*, Vol. 26, no. 1 (Fall 1992), p. 51.
**41** Advertisements in *Shanghai Woche*, no. 12 (August 29, 1942), and no. 17 (October 3, 1942). The last has a list of Shanghai restaurants and cafes together with brief biographies of their owners.
**42** YIVO, (no catalogue no.), "Exhibition of Paintings" by J. Fein, Catalogue, 1942, Shanghai, 31, 5–15, 6, Jewish Club. For a brief biography of Yoni Fayn, see Eber, *Voices from Shanghai*, p. 98.
**43** Handbills of these performances are reproduced on the Rickshaw Express Web.
**44** Ralph Harpuder, "The Theater in Shanghai Hongkew," The Rickshaw Express Web.

1942 and January 1943.[45] Performances might take place in movie theaters like the Eastern or Doumer, but more often than not they were staged successfully in the shelters.

Yiddish theater was, as in previous years, performed in the Jewish Club. Shoshana Kahan describes an extremely successful performance of *Mirele Efros* on February 18, 1942.[46] *Tevye, the Milkman* was equally successful on May 10th. She writes that she played Golda to a full house, despite the fact that she and her husband Layzer had to write the script, there not being one available in Shanghai.[47] Shoshana Kahan also performed in a variety show, written and performed by the refugees and called "Hamentashen with Rice." As always, they played to a full house, but she remarks regretfully that the Japanese censor cut many numbers.[48] Yiddish theater declined after the Jewish Club was taken over by the Japanese authorities at the end of November 1942, as noted above, and the facilities were moved to a different location.

There were, of course, also concerts, considering the large number of refugee musicians and conductors in Shanghai. But, as the editor of the *Almanac, Shanghai 1946–47*, Ossi Lewin, perceptively remarks, "Operetta performances enjoyed far more popularity than concerts ... For after the daily grind, the emigrants ... longed for humorous fare and a number of excellent artists did their part to enthrall their audience."[49]

## Anti-Semitism, The Proclamation, and The "Designated Area"

At the beginning of August 1942, an article appeared in *Nasha Zhizn*, written by the editor, David Rabinovich, warning against the spreading of rumors. He

---

**45** Michael Phillip, *Nicht einmal ein Thespiskarren, Exiltheater in Shanghai 1939–1947*, Hamburg: Hamburger Arbeitstelle für deutsche Exilliteratur, 1996, pp. 89, 91. For a brief biography of Schubert, see p. 179. I thank Dr. Hartmut Walravens for making the book available to me.

**46** Kahan, *In fajer un flamen*, p. 290, entry for February 20, 1942. The "Mirele Efros" script was written by the playwright Jacob Gordin (1853–1909). It was performed a second time after the war and received a glowing review from Alfred Dreifuss, "Mirele Efros, von Jacob Gordin," *The Shanghai Herald*, May 7, 1946, p. 3.

**47** Kahan, *In fajer un flamen*, pp. 292–293, entry for May 10, 1942.

**48** Ibid., p. 291, entry for March 8, 1942. Hamentashen are a kind of filled cookie (literally: pockets of Haman), usually poppy seeds, and eaten for the Purim festival. Here rice signifies China.

**49** YVA, 078/54, Ossi Lewin, ed., *Almanac, Shanghai 1946–47*, Shanghai: Shanghai Echo, n. d. See also, Xu Buzeng and Tess Johnston, "The Legacy, the Influence of

did not say what these rumors were, but he reminded his readers that the Japanese authorities had given the refugees asylum in Shanghai and that they were the recipients of an "exceptionally humane attitude."[50] Was Rabinovich's rumor the same as that mentioned by Shoshana Kahan July 20, 1942, in her diary, namely that the refugees were to be incarcerated in a concentration camp?[51] According to Laura Margolis's "Report" of about one year later, "something was brewing among the Japanese authorities with regard to 'segregation' plans for the refugees."[52]

Sometime later, Margolis does not specify exactly when, a meeting took place at Michel Speelman's house at which Ellis Hayim, Fritz Kaufmann, Boris Topaz, Joseph Bitker, Robert Peretz, and Shibata Mitsugi (Margolis mistakenly wrote Mr. Katawa) were present. The meeting presumably was called by Peretz and Shibata to inform the others of Japanese plans to segregate the Jews and to consider steps to dissuade the Japanese from undertaking such a move. (Margolis believed, however, that the men met in order to decide how to pay the Japanese off. Peretz and Shibata were planning to earn a percentage from the payoff. It was decided to have Fritz Kaufmann get in touch with Mr. Brahn and have the latter verify the story with army authorities. Brahn did, indeed, do as he was charged and told all he knew, whereupon all seven men were arrested and imprisoned in the notorious Japanese jail, the Bridge House.[53] Margolis's account is the earliest mention of this episode. It would surface time and again in subsequent accounts with various accretions and embellishments.

Thus, for example, Fritz Kaufmann, one of the participants in the meeting, blames the arrests on the Gestapo and, in particular on the Gestapo agent, Joseph Albert Meisinger (1899–1947),[54] who, according to Kaufmann's account, had arrived in Shanghai in a submarine. All Japanese authorities, said Kaufmann, came under Gestapo influence thereafter. The German plan was to load the 40,000 Shanghai Jews on old ships and sink them in the open sea, or to unload them on Chongming Island, a large island located at the mouth of the

Jewish Refugees on the Musical and Intellectual Life of Shanghai," The Rickshaw Express Web, p. 2.

**50** David Rabinovich, "More Self Control and Calm," *Nasha Zhizn*, August 7, 1942, p. 1.

**51** Kahan, *In fajer un flamen*, p. 294, entry for July 20, 1942.

**52** Margolis, "Report," p. 14.

**53** Margolis, "Report," pp. 14–15. Aside from Shibata, the six men were leaders in the Baghdadi community, the Jüdische Gemeinde (Jewish Community of Central European Jews) and the Russian Ashkenazi Community.

**54** Meisinger is also known as the "butcher of Warsaw" for his part in the German occupation of the city in 1939.

Yangzi, where they would starve to death. It was Shibata who had gotten wind of the plan and had prevailed on Ellis Hayim to call the emergency meeting. Kaufmann, according to his account, was charged with contacting the Japanese military through Brahn, which he did. But Brahn confessed all and the seven were arrested. After the war, added Kaufmann, documents were found in Japan that showed that Shanghai Jewry was to be exterminated. The protest of the seven men prevented the tragedy from occurring.[55]

Rather than Kaufmann, according to Marvin Tokayer and Mary Swartz, the real hero of this episode was Shibata Mitsugi, vice-consul at the Shanghai Japanese consulate, who informed the Jewish leaders of the plans the Gestapo had in store for them. He had participated in a meeting in the course of which Meisinger outlined three possible solutions to Shanghai's Jewish problem. One was to load them on unseaworthy ships, to set these adrift, and to have the Jews die of hunger and thirst. The second solution was to put them to work in salt mines where they would not last long. And the third solution was to build a concentration camp on Chongming Island where the Jews would undergo medical experiments. Shibata was horrified upon hearing this and asked Ellis Hayim to call a meeting. This Hayim did, and it was decided to inform the chief of the Japanese military police (the Kempeitai) through Brahn's very close Japanese lady friend. Presumably Tokyo would then have to be involved, and Tokyo would not want such a plan carried out. The men also proposed having Boris Topaz get in touch with Dr. Abraham Cohn, who knew Kubota Tsutomu, director of refugee affairs.[56]

Increasingly, we see, the villain of this story becomes the evil Meisinger and the Gestapo, whereas Shibata is intent on saving the Jews. According to Alfred Dreifuss, a refugee in Shanghai, plans were afoot to erect gas chambers on Pudong Island. Humanitarian reasons did not prevent the Japanese from carrying out the evil designs of the "Butcher of Warsaw." Rather, it was fear of American revenge against the Nisei (Japanese) population in the United States.[57]

---

**55** Fritz Kaufmann, "Die Juden in Shanghai im 2. Weltkrieg," Leo Baeck Institut, 73 (1986), pp. 12–23. This essay is, no doubt, based on the earlier, 1963, version used by David Kranzler. See Kranzler, *Japanese, Nazis and Jews*, pp. 478–479, 601.

**56** Marvin Tokayer and Mary Swartz, *The Fugu Plan, The Untold Story of the Japanese and the Jews During World War II*, New York–London: Paddington Press, Ltd., 1979, pp. 223–234. The authors tell a gripping story. Unfortunately, documentation is not provided.

**57** Alfred Dreifuss, "Schanghai – eine Emigration am Rande," in *Exil in den USA, mit einem Bericht "Schanghai –eine Emigration am Rande,"* Frankfurt/Main: Röderberg, 1980, p. 480. The book was reprinted in Leipzig: Philipp Reclam jun., 1983.

Finally, Ernest Heppner's memoir indicates that even Zyklon B, the gas used in the gas chambers of the extermination camps, was available in Shanghai. Presumably, Meisinger together with Hans Neumann and Adolph Puttkammer, traveled to Tokyo, trying to convince the Japanese to exterminate the Jews. As they did not find a receptive hearing, they went by submarine to Shanghai carrying the Zyclon B canisters. After the war the gas canisters were found in the warehouses of Shanghai's Siemens and Bayer firms. After he had attended a meeting at the Japanese consulate where the three Germans had outlined their plan, Shibata, in a hastily convened meeting in July 1942, alerted the Jewish community leaders to the danger facing them.[58] Heppner's information about the Zyklon B canisters is based on a 1946 article by M. Elbaum, who does not mention the submarine journey, but instead suggests that extermination camps had been readied. Chinese partisans, writes Elbaum, had seen suspicious buildings being erected on Pudong and Jiangwan. Strange machinery was brought to these buildings, and the buildings were visited daily by Japanese and civilians. "Were these work – or extermination camps? Who can ascertain this definitely?" asks Elbaum.[59]

Most likely we shall never know exactly what took place in Shanghai in the summer of 1942; why a meeting of Jewish community leaders was called; what role the Gestapo had in these events; or why the participants at the meeting were arrested. I cannot but agree with the Japan expert, Gerhard Krebs, that the documentary evidence is too flimsy for concluding that Meisinger and others came to Shanghai to convince the Japanese authorities to construct installations for Jewish extermination.[60] What seems certain is that Meisinger and six other Gestapo agents arrived in Japan early in October 1941, and that later in the month Meisinger was in Shanghai.[61] Was he also in Shanghai one year later?

---

**58** Ernest G. Heppner, *Shanghai Refuge, A Memoir of the World War II Jewish Ghetto.* Lincoln–London: University of Nebraska Press, 1994, pp. 104–105. With minor variations this story is also told by Chaim U. Lipschitz, *The Shanghai Connection*, New York: Maznaim Publishing, 1988, pp. 88–89.

**59** M. Elbaum, "18. Februar 1943, die Geschichte des Hongkewer Ghettos," *The Shanghai Herald*, Sondernummer, April 1946, pp. 24–25. (Donated by Howard Levin).

**60** Gerhard Krebs, "Antsemitismus und Judenpolitik der Japaner," in Georg Armbrüster, et.al., eds., *Exil Shanghai, 1938–1947*, Teetz: Hentrich and Hentrich, 2000, p. 72.

**61** "Gestapo Agents Reported to have Arrived in Japan," *The China Press*, October 8, 1941, p. 1, and Joseph C. Grew, *Ten Years in Japan*, New York: Simon and Schuster, 1944, p. 458, diary entry, October 17, 1941. However, according to Bernard Wasserstein, Meisinger was in Shanghai in May 1941 where Trebitsch Lincoln had an interview with him. See Bernard Wasserstein, *The Secret Lives of Trebitsch Lincoln*, London: Penguin Books, 1989, p. 312. In his interrogation by the Americans, Meisinger stated that he was in Shanghai August–

There can be no certainty regarding these issues, nor can there be any certainty about plans for the Jews the Japanese authorities may or may not have had. It can be assumed, however, that the decision to concentrate state- less Jews in one part of the Shanghai area was not hastily undertaken and seems to have evolved over a period of time, as will be suggested below. The Proclamation of February 1943, announcing its implementation, was, further- more, issued in conjunction with other events, most notably with the intern- ment of British and American civilians.[62]

But were the confinement and subsequent acts anti-Semitically motivated? Were the Japanese naval authorities or the notorious secret military police anti- Semites? A clear cut answer is impossible. In 1939 and 1940, as was shown above, a number of anti-Semitic articles appeared in the Japanese-censored newspaper, the *Xin Shenbao*. Furthermore, "Jewish experts," like army colonel Yasue Norihiro (1886–1950) and navy captain Inuzuka Koreshige, were culti- vated, and their views were enlisted on various occasions. But Yasue and Inuz- uka "combined an ideological anti-Semitism with a practical friendship for Jews."[63] The anti-Semitism that they expressed and accepted in others differed from German anti-Semitism; it warned of Jewish power; it believed in Jewish plans for world domination; it was certain about Jewish aggressive aims.[64] But it did not advocate ridding the world of Jews, annihilating or exterminating them. Following the outbreak of war, on the occasion of a banquet for both Yasue and Inuzuka, the former indicated what the nature of the Japanese rela- tionship to the Jews was. Jews "will not be persecuted for being Jewish" as long as they are loyal to Japan and do not act contrary to Japanese interests. If, however, the Japanese authorities will have to undertake measures against the Jews, these "measures [will have been] caused by the Jews themselves."[65]

November 1941 and June 1, 1944–June 14, 1944. National Archives, Washington, D.C., RG 226, entry 182A, Box 8, folder 62, "CI Final Interrogation Report (CI-FIR), no. 113, July 13, 1948.

**62** Marcia R. Ristaino, *Port of Last Resort, The Diaspora Communities of Shanghai*, Stanford: Stanford University Press, 2001, p. 188. The internment process had begun in November 1942.

**63** Ben-Ami Shillony, *The Jews and the Japanese, The Successful Outsiders*, Rutland– Tokyo: Charles E. Tuttle Co., Inc., 1991, p. 187.

**64** David G. Goodman and Masanori Miyazawa, *Jews in the Japanese Mind, The History and Uses of a Cultural Stereotype*, New York-Singapore: The Free Press, 1995 is a useful study of the complex phenomenon identified as anti-Semitism.

**65** "Banquet in Honor of Colonel N. Yasue and Captain K. Inuzuka in the Shanghai Jewish Club," *Nasha Zhizn*, no. 34, December 26, 1941, p. 1,3,5. No doubt to demonstrate their loyalty, the Jewish Harbin community and the Shanghai Ashkenazi community donated sums of money to the Japanese cause. See *Nasha Zhizn*, no. 36, January 2, 1942, p. 4 and no. 37, January 16, 1942, p. 1.

In Shanghai, neither before nor after the outbreak of the Pacific War, was there an official anti-Semitism, despite the sporadic publication of anti-Semitic articles, similar to earlier ones. The fact that anti-Semitic incidents were certainly not the order of the day can be seen by the brief articles in the *China Weekly Review*, which noted the sudden occurrence of anti-Semitism when propaganda leaflets denouncing local Jewry were released in the vicinity of Bubbling Well Road.[66] Like an ominous sign of things to come, two days before the Proclamation, on February 16, 1943, an especially virulent article appeared in the *Shanghai Times*. Written by Wang Jingwei's staunch supporter, Tang Leangli (1901–1970), the Jews were said to strive for "world domination and world rule." Having lost their own culture as well as moral scruples, he said, Jews are associated with anarchism and communism. Their nefarious activities began in Shanghai long before the arrival of the "latest horde" and, therefore, the most immediate problem is how to prevent the Jews from getting Shanghai into "Jewish clutches."[67]

No doubt, the plan to confine the Jews was taken for political considerations. But to the refugees it was the final blow. "That which has frightened us, has now finally happened. Today the official notice appeared that all who came after 1937 must move into a special area." We are about to be locked up in a ghetto, wrote Shoshana Kahan bitterly, and for this "we had to run thousands of miles to fall into a ghetto here."[68] Only "stateless refugees" were mentioned, not Jews, and they were ordered into the area by May 18. The Proclamation was signed by the Commander-in-Chief of the army and his counterpart in the navy.

As indicated earlier, concentrating the Jews in a specific area in Shanghai was not a spur of the moment idea. The establishment of a "special zone" had been discussed in 1939 and 1940 in Tokyo as well as in committees in which Yasue and Inuzuka were participants.[69] Despite the fact that German authorities noted apprehension among Russian immigrants about possible confine-

---

**66** "Anti-Semitism makes Appearance in S'hai," *The China Weekly Review*, November 1, 1941, and "Nazis Continue Anti-Jewish Campaign Despite Their Denial of Circular," *The China Weekly Review*, November 8, 1941. (I thank Bernard Wasserstein for making a photocopy available to me).

**67** Tang Leangli, "Shanghai, Hunting Ground of Thriving Jewish Racketeers," *Shanghai Times*, February 16, 1942.

**68** Kahan, *In fajer un flamen*, p. 298, entry for February 18, 1943. For the complete text of the Proclamation, see Kranzler, *Japanese, Nazis and Jews*, pp. 489–490.

**69** I thank Professor Avraham Altman for making his notes on this subject available to me. However, according to Fritz Wiedemann (1891–1970), at the time German Consul General in Tianjin, in an official statement declared that the Germans had convinced the Japanese to establish the ghetto. Robert M. W. Kempner, "Nazis errichteten das

ment of stateless Russians as well, it was felt that the Proclamation was the first Japanese anti-Jewish measure. Not taken because of military necessity (as claimed by the Japanese), its purpose was to combat foreign influence.[70] But concentrating a troublesome segment of Shanghai's population in a specific area was also a means of controlling them. Moreover, that American and British citizens were finally interned at about the same time was not a coincidence. Lest the Japanese be accused of anti-Semitism, Kubota Tsutomu, Chief Director of the Shanghai Bureau for Stateless Refugees, reiterated in April 1943 that because "certain elements of the stateless refugees hampered the Japanese in conducting the great East Asian war" this measure had, regrettably, to be taken.[71]

For many refugees who had established businesses in parts of Shanghai, the order to move into Hongkou was a catastrophe, especially when they had to sell their businesses for a pittance. Although the Eisfelders were able to open a second Café Luis on the ghetto's Ward Road, for example, they had to hand over their thriving establishment in the International Settlement for a small sum of money. Dr. A. Cohn, the recipient, gave it to a Japanese person.[72] Al Zunterstein's father was fortunately contacted by a Chinese man willing to exchange houses. His father paid a small sum and acquired a house on Tongshan Road that even had an indoor toilet.[73]

Refugees could petition to remain outside the Hongkou designated area, or they could request remaining outside past the deadline. It is impossible to know how many requests were granted or what reasons may have been claimed.[74] It seems, however, that people moved, but slowly, into the ghetto and by the end of April there were still 7.352 persons outside. Three weeks later only 90% had moved.[75]

Shanghai Ghetto," *Aufbau*, January 16, 1953. See also, Gerhard Krebs, "The 'Jewish Problem' in Japanese-German Relations, 1933–1945," in E. Bruce Reynolds, ed., *Japan in the Fascist Era*, New York: Palgrave Macmillan, 2004, p. 122. Krebs negates Fascist involvement.

**70**  German General Consulate Shanghai, to the German Embassy Nanking, March 10, 1943, signature illegible, and YVA, 078/73A, telegram, Fischer, Shanghai, February 20, 1943.

**71**  *Nasha Zhizn*, no. 100, April 2, 1943.

**72**  YVA, 078/21, Eisfelder, "Chinese Exile," p. 54.

**73**  YVA, 078/70, Al Zunterstein tape, "Shanghai 1938–1949," p. 14.

**74**  See YVA, 078/64. Lipot and Elisabeth Kardos claimed they had identity cards issued by the Royal Hungarian Legation in Tokyo, Eva Hamburger wrote that her husband, Otto Hamburger, was a Chinese national and had lived in China since 1934. Dr. Bernard Silberstein had permission to practice medicine as of April 22, 1935 from Tianjin.

**75**  "Amendment," *Our Life*, April 30, 1943, and YVA, 078/78a, SMP Report, May 22, 1943, Signature illegible.

The Polish group gave the most trouble, claiming that they were not stateless and had, in fact, a government in London. They were supported in their refusal by the General Council of the Polish Residents' Association in China, which submitted a list of names in April 1943 certifying that all were Polish citizens and, therefore, exempt from the Proclamation.[76] Of the 932 Polish refugees, 400 – less than half – had moved to Hongkou by August 1943.[77]Kubota did not mince his words when he stated in a public address that the Polish refugees are all lawbreakers. They are most certainly stateless, he added, "since they actually have no state," otherwise they would be enemy nationals and their property would be confiscated. Although the Japanese authorities treat them most leniently, their conduct is most unsatisfying.[78]

The Polish group's rebelliousness was, however, not politically motivated. Whatever political activity there was – and there was precious little – seems to have been mostly among German-speaking leftist-oriented persons and communists. Of the latter there were very few in Shanghai; according to Alfred Dreifuss, perhaps fifty party members in all. He, Dreifuss, believes that there were more, but that many did not want to admit membership for fear of arrest.[79] Whether before the move into the ghetto or after (roughly the area called *Tilanqiao*), the major function of the small group of party members was to explain to themselves and to others what was happening, to somehow convey to the refugees not to lose hope.[80] Thus political activity seems to have consisted mainly of discussions and was the work of a man named Grzyb (1896–1941), who had come to China in 1925 and again in 1932 as a Comintern delegate.[81]

Al Zunterstein describes a Shanghai underground that seems to have been similarly inactive. Their work consisted in "observing the success of air raids,

---

**76** YIVO, Y2300–1854.1–10, folder 40, letter from Dr. Stan. Tomaszewski, Chairman and Marian Krzyżanowski, secretary, April 9, 1943.

**77** Central Zionist Archives, 1125, Polish Ministry for Foreign Affairs to I. Schwarzbart, August 20, 1943.

**78** "First General Meeting of the Reorganized SACRA Committee, Important Speech by Mr. T. Kubota," *Nasha Zhizn*, no. 152, May 5, 1944, p. 2.

**79** Alfred Dreifuss, "Schanghai – Eine Emigration am Rande," in *Exil in den USA*, p. 475.

**80** Ibid., p. 477. See also Gerd Kaminski, *General Luo Genannt Langnase, das abenteuerliche Leben des Dr. med. Jakob Rosenfeld*, Vienna: Löcker Verlag, 1993, p. 48, who mentions that the German speakers met once a week to discuss political issues.

**81** Günter and Genia Nobel, "Als politische Emigranten in Shanghai," *Beiträge zur Geschichte der Arbeiterbewegung*, Vol. 21, no. 6 (June 1979), p. 886. According to Kaminski, p. 46, Grzyb's first name was Gregory, and in China he was known as Heinz Schippe. Actually, Grzyb went by several names. He was probably born as Moses Wolf Grzyb. I thank Yitzhak Shichor for the information about the man.

reporting parachutists, committing sabotage as well as guerilla tactics, coordination with other resistance groups ..." Presumably, various nationalities had such resistance groups, but he cannot say much about them.[82] After the war, non-Jewish Germans too claimed to have organized a "Free German Movement" (*Frei- Deutschlandbewegung*) in 1940. Under the leadership of Karl Heinz Hinzelmann, they produced anti-Nazi and anti-Japanese flyers and posters. This group was, so they claimed, instrumental in having Meisinger arrested after the end of war.[83]

The outbreak of war created a new situation for the foreign and Jewish communities. The Chinese population was, of course, affected as well. But by that time, we must remember, it had been under Japanese occupation for more than four years. During those years and thereafter economic problems mounted, in addition to political difficulties under successive Chinese puppet governments. Japan was not at war with Russia so that the Russian Jewish community did not have to be concerned about possible moves against it. However, by 1943, as we shall see, the Russian leadership, would be forced to become a puppet governing body for the Central European refugees. Although the small Baghdadi community, many of whom were British passport holders, was at first left alone, by the time the Proclamation was published most had been rounded up and interned. But those who had passports of neutral countries continued normal lives.[84] For all practical purposes, the Baghdadi community ceased to exist during the Pacific War. Between February 1943 and the end of war the major concern of the Japanese in Shanghai would be how to create organizations for controlling the refugee community, and the concern of the refugees would be how to make a living and live as normally as was possible under wartime conditions.

## Life in the Ghetto

The occupation of large parts of China and of Shanghai by Japanese forces, however, did not lead to active and universal Chinese resistance. Quite the

**82** YVA, 078/70, Al Zunterstein tape, "Shanghai 1938–1949," p. 29.

**83** "Untergrundarbeit in Shanghai," *Aufbau*, May 17, 1946, p. 29. Five months earlier, another German group had surfaced, calling itself "Association of Democratic Germans in Shanghai" (Gemeinschaft der demokratischen Deutschen in Shanghai), *Aufbau*, January 11, 1946, p. 28.

**84** Central Archives of the History of the Jewish People (CAHJP), DAL 83, Birman to Hicem, Paris, January 31, 1940. According to Birman, Russians without passports are helped by the Russian Emigrants' Committee together with the Jewish Communal Association. Among Baghdadis, Sassoon Jacoby, for example, had a Portuguese

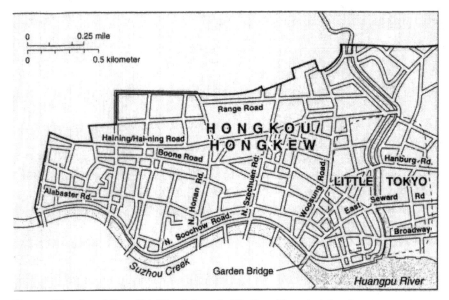

**Map 3:** "Hongkou." From Yeh Wen-hsin, ed., *Wartime Shanghai*, London–New York: Routledge, 1998.

contrary as Lloyd Eastman points out, along with a strong nationalism among intellectuals, there was also "an astonishing degree of peaceful interaction" with the Japanese, and there were day-to-day relations. Trade, moreover, was carried on between ports and was in most cases controlled by Chinese agents who acted for the Japanese.[85]

The relatively smooth functioning of the economy and society were by no means due to the benevolent rule or the pervasive control of the Japanese authorities. No doubt, the fact that puppet agencies, loyal to the conqueror (and concerned, of course, with their self-interest) came into existence, must have accounted in large measure for the Japanese "success." The experiences the Japanese had gained in other parts of China and in Shanghai after July 1937 were now also applied to control the refugee population. In addition to concentrating the Jewish refugee population in a roughly forty block area, or

---

passport and continued to work in his profession as a journalist. I. Eber interview with Sassoon Jacoby, June 6, 1976, in the Oral History Division, Institute of Contemporary Jewry, The Hebrew University.

**85** Lloyd E. Eastman, "Facets of an Ambivalent Relationship: Smuggling, Puppets, and Atrocities during the War, 1937–1945," in Akira Iriye, ed., *The Chinese and the Japanese, Essays in Political and Cultural Interaction*, Princeton: Princeton University Press, 1980, pp. 275–281.

one square mile of Hongkou, the Japanese created new Jewish organizations for carrying out their directives. Thus a situation came into being that minimized direct contact between the refugees and the occupation authorities and maximized the control of proxy organizations, including the control of funds needed to keep the shelters functioning and the destitute refugees alive.

The major organization created – quite probably together with the appearance of the Proclamation – was SACRA (Shanghai Ashkenazi Collaborating Relief Association),[86] headed by Dr. A. J. Cohn, a Rumanian Jew who was fluent in Japanese. Honorary chairman of SACRA was Kubota Tsutomu and in this capacity he presided over the newly appointed committees. Consisting of eighteen members, each with a specific function, SACRA's immediate task was to speed up the move into Hongkou, thus assuring SACRA's bad reputation. Shoshana Kahan noted in her diary that SACRA was hated by all the refugees for assuming this ugly job of forcing the refugees into the ghetto.[87] SACRA, however, did not work directly with the refugees either. For this the help of the Jüdische Gemeinde was needed. By order of the Shanghai Bureau for Stateless Refugees the Jüdische Gemeinde was dissolved because its work in connection with the Proclamation was unsatisfactory, according to Cohn. A new organization was created, headed by L. M. Rogovin, a Russian emigrant and chairman of Centrojewcom.[88] The new organization was announced on the front page of the *Juedisches Nachrichtenblatt*, April 17, 1943. The reorganization was clearly aimed at creating a centralized command and ending the process of decision making by several bodies with no clear distinction of hierarchy. A similar process of centralizing command was also carried out on the Japanese side. In 1940, before Inuzuka was transferred, he had set up the Bureau for Jewish Affairs, but left Shanghai in March 1942. (He was temporarily replaced by Captain Saneyoshi.) When Kubota was appointed in his place, the Shanghai Bureau for Stateless Refugees was transferred to the Ministry for Greater East Asia, thus becoming subordinate to the Japanese Consulate General, as well as to both the military and naval authorities.[89]

---

**86** See Kranzler, *Japanese, Nazis and Jews*, pp. 522, 536, note 2, and YIVO, RG 243, Shanghai Folder 12, "Memorandum," March 15, 1944.

**87** Kahan, *In fajer un flamen*, p. 299, entry for March 30, 1943.

**88** YIVO, RG 243, Shanghai file 13, "Minutes no. 7," April 1, 1943 and YVA, 078/78A, April 12, 1943, added note to "Report," April 5, 1943. The Community of Central European Jews had begun unofficially in June 1939. In elections held July 29, 1941, twenty one representatives were elected and a board of seven representatives was created. See Anna Ginzbourg, "Activities of the Jewish Community of German Immigrants in Shanghai," *Nasha Zhizn*, no. 23, October 10, 1941, p. 10.

**89** "The Bureau for Stateless Refugees Included in the Ministry for Greater East Asia," *Nasha Zhizn*, no. 108, June 7, 1943, p. 2.

**Fig. 11:** An alley in the ghetto, 1944. Courtesy H. P. Eisfelder Photography Collection (4801-4648). Now housed at Yad Vashem Archives, Jerusalem.

In addition to a police force, the organizational structure on which the Japanese authorities could rely was now in place. The police force was important because it would prevent the refugees from leaving the area without passes and would enforce law and order within the area. Called Foreign *Bao-jia*, perhaps "auxiliary police force," it had been organized already in September 1942. Starting October 1, 1942, all males between the ages of 20 and 45 were required to serve. The episode was considered a shameful chapter in refugee life. After the war Elbaum called it a blemish on refugee history.[90]

---

**90** M. Elbaum, "18. Februar 1943, die Geschichte des Hongkewer Ghetto," *The Shanghai Herald,* Sondernummer, April 1946, p. 25.

A major function of this police force was to guard the exits of the designated area and to ascertain that everyone leaving had a pass and that those who returned did so at the time specified by the pass. Passes to leave the ghetto were apparently considered of major importance by the Japanese authorities and provided the only instance (other than arrests) in which direct contact between the refugees and the occupying power occurred. The person in charge of issuing passes was the infamous Ghoya Kanoh who, without exception, earned the hatred of all the refugees. He was apparently a brutal and sadistic person, a man given to psychotic behavior, who arbitrarily issued or denied issuing a pass and who used physical violence whenever it suited him.[91] Ghoya's colleague, Okura, also in charge of issuing passes, was equally if not more sadistic. Both men seemed to take special pleasure in the long waiting lines formed by the refugees requiring passes. As described by Shoshana Kahan,

> I and Layzer stand already the second day in line [waiting] for the murderer Okura in order to get special permission to travel to the city. Today I came at six in the morning to get a number [to see Okura]. At 12 o'clock we were notified that we can go home, Okura will not receive anyone before afternoon. I again stood, but I did not even receive a number.[92]

But why were the refugees in need of passes? In 1943 and thereafter people continued to transact business in the International Settlement or French Concession. Others may have been employed outside the designated area. Often visits had to be made to acquaintances who had not had to move into the ghetto. Hospital visits were sometimes necessary. Musicians tended to play outside; Shoshana Kahan performed at the Jewish Club, which was not in the ghetto. But aside from the unpleasant business of obtaining a pass, as remarked by Siegel after the war, "The Japanese Authorities apart from segregating and issuing passes did very little else to regulate refugee life in the district or to interfere with the refugees managing their own affairs."[93]

Turning now to what life was like in the ghetto, it was clearly difficult, unpleasant, pervaded by hardships; the ghetto was unbelievably crowded, and people lived under conditions that in many cases bordered on inhuman. Hunger, starvation, vitamin deficiencies, and decline in caloric intake that brought

---

**91** The actor Herbert Zernik composed a long satiric poem in 1945 about Ghoya. For the English translation of Zernik's poem see Eber, *Voices from Shanghai*, pp. 104–106.
**92** Kahan, *In fajer un flamen*, pp. 309–310. Entry for April 22, 1943.
**93** YVA, reel 16, 11.728, M. Siegel to Leavitt, August 26, 1945, p. 3.

on various illnesses were common occurrences.[94] There was the ever present fear of infectious diseases. No matter how hard people tried to keep surroundings clean, wash food, boil water or purchase boiled water, diseases that had been brought under control in Western European countries lurked everywhere. Hospital facilities that at first suffered the lack of money when American funds ceased to arrive, eventually had to close down, and medicines were always in short supply.[95]

Anxieties took their toll. News was nearly impossible to come by, the many newspapers that had appeared before the Pacific War had closed down. There was still the highly censored *Shanghai Jewish Chronicle*, the *Juedisches Nachrichtenblatt*, or *Nasha Zhizn* for Russian readers and, for those who had connections to the non-Jewish Russian community, news about the war raging in Europe could be obtained from the Russian news services. The absence of information about the course of war and about the fate of the families left behind, together with the unrelenting struggle for existence, must have created a sense of insecurity hard to imagine.

Yet, despite the enormous hardships, life went on, and places of entertainment and restaurants, even if fewer, continued to attract clientele. As before, there was the Taverne at 291 Wayside Road, Café Gloria, Café Atlantic and Eastern Garden, as well as Café Roy and Café Ohio Bar on Ward Road. *Zum Weissen Roessl* continued to serve lunch and dinner with dance music featured Sunday evenings after relocating to the corner of Ward and McGregor Roads.[96]

Although far fewer now, theatrical performances and concerts could still be attended. According to Alfred Dreifuss, the Japanese censor forbade altogether thirty-three plays, among them a number written by playwrights in Shanghai.[97] There is no evidence that Chinese theatergoers came to see plays performed in German, except for a brief mention by Dreifuss that a Chinese

---

**94** Dr. T. Kunfi, "Die medizinische Betreuung der Immigranten," *Shanghai Herald*, Sondernummer, April 1946, pp. 9–10.

**95** Aid was requested from the SMC and was granted when it was decided that the Jews "must now be considered to be permanent residents." See YVA, 078/97, Speelman to SMC, May 15, 1942, SMC, Circular no. 253, and J. H. Jordan, Commissioner for Public Health, May 26, 1942.

**96** Advertisements in *Shanghai Woche*, no. 12 (August 29, 1942). See also list of restaurants and brief biographies of some of the café owners in *Shanghai Woche*, no. 17 October 3, 1942). Also *Juedisches Nachrichtenblatt*, Vol. 5, no. 40 (November 12, 1944) and Arthur Kornik, "Interview with Hans Zelinka, Chairman of Proprietors of Bars, Cafes and Restaurants' Association in Designated Area," *Our Life*, no. 58 , August 12, 1943, p. 8.

**97** Alfred Dreifuss, "Unser Theater," *The Shanghai Herald*, Sondernummer, April 1946, p. 14.

public also came to the performance of Franz Molnar, *Delila*.[98] Performances were staged at the shelters and at the Eastern Theater on Muirhead Road, or at the Broadway Theater. Light operas were favorites and Shaw's *Pygmalion* and *The Merry Widow*, for example, received glowing reviews.[99]

Charity performances were popular and Raja Zomina, a dancer and Yiddish folksinger, was a favorite. Even the predominantly German-speaking refugee population in the shelters apparently liked an evening of Yiddish humor and cheerful sketches. At these, not only Zomina but also Shoshana Kahan (using the name R. Shoshano) would perform.[100] Not as often as in previous years, Kahan also performed at the Jewish Club. On November 21, 1943, for example, she had a highly successful evening in the Sholem Aleichem play *Competitors*.[101] A gala concert attended by the Japanese dignitaries, Kubota, Ghoya, and others was presented by the Foreign Baojia at the Eastern Theater. It received, as one might expect, raving reviews.[102] Mention should be also made of the two art exhibits held in 1944 by the Artists' Association at which members of the Japanese authorities put in an appearance.[103]

Yet the importance of restaurants, performances, and exhibits must not be exaggerated. There remained a semblance of cultural life; it had not ceased altogether with the establishment of the ghetto, but it was minimal. Still, there is much we don't know. For example, were the performances sold out? How many people did the theaters hold? How much did tickets cost? Who could afford to attend performances? What kind of audience appreciated *Pygmalion*, for example? Was it an intellectual elite that attended?

Whereas it is not easy to discuss the performing arts in terms of success or failure, the matter is quite different where three educational institutions are concerned: one of these is Willy Tonn's Asia Seminar, the other is ORT, and the third is Gregg Business College. All three must be considered supremely successful during the cruel weeks and months of the war. Willy Tonn (1902–1957) was a remarkable individual, the son of a well-to-do German Jewish

---

**98** Alfred Dreifuss, "Shanghai – eine Emigration am Rande," p. 492.

**99** *Our Life*, no. 72, November 26, 1943; no. 78, January 7, 1944, p. 2; no. 85, March 3, 1944.

**100** Tang Yating, "Reconstructing the Vanished Musical Life of the Shanghai Jewish Diaspora: A Report," *Ethnomusicology Forum*, Vol. 13, no. 1 (January 2004), pp. 114–115.

**101** Kahan, *In fajer un flamen*, p. 325, entry for November 21, 1943.

**102** "Gala-konzert der Foreign Pao Chia," *Juedisches Nachrichtenblatt*, Vol. 4, no. 44 (December 3, 1943), p. 2.

**103** Alfred Dreifuss, "First Jewish Artists' Exhibition in the Designated Area," *Our Life*, no. 86, March 10, 1944, p. 2, and "Arta's Second Exhibition," *Our Life*, no. 96, May 26, 1944, p. 2.

family. He had studied Chinese and other Asian languages in Berlin and had published works on Chinese history while still in Germany.[104] Tonn arrived in Shanghai in April 1939, not so much as a refugee fleeing from the Nazi regime but "driven by a longing for the East," as he put it.[105] Weiyan Meng, who has written a brief biography of the man, states that, "No one seemed to equal Tonn in bridging the cultural gap between the Jewish refugees and the Chinese environment. In his writing he endeavored to draw profound impulses from the immediate Chinese world and to incorporate, with great subtlety, the Chinese culture into the Western culture ..."[106]

Although Tonn began planning the Asia Seminar as an adult education "People's University" in 1939, the project did not get under way until September 1943, after the establishment of the ghetto. Initially the students met in totally inadequate quarters, but in fall 1944, he was able to use the facilities of the S.J.Y.A. school. His lecture courses and seminars were taught by about thirty lecturers and offered such language courses as Japanese, Sanskrit, and Hebrew, aside from Chinese. The last included Chinese for doctors and Chinese for lawyers. Lectures on the Vedas and Upanishads were held as well as on Chinese history and culture. Nor was science neglected, and in 1944 there were courses on the sociology of medicine and the science of atoms.[107] Courses were well attended, and the Asia Seminar continued to function for five years, until 1948, when the refugee exodus from Shanghai was well under way. Not only an imaginative teacher, Tonn was also a skillful and tireless writer. Although he was unable to publish much during the war years because there were not many papers left during the Japanese occupation, the *Shanghai Evening Post and Mercury, Shanghai Sunday Times,* and *Shanghai Jewish Chronicle* carried dozens of his articles in 1941 and 1942. Tonn came to Israel in 1949. Unfortunately, the young country, refuge of the remnants from war torn Europe, was not ready to receive hospitably the talented man whose longing for the east had brought him to the shores of China. Tonn died eight years later.[108]

---

104  The impressive bibliography of Tonn's writings was compiled by Hartmut Walravens, "Martin Buber and Willy Tonn und ihre Beiträge zur Kenntnis der chinesischen Literatur," *Monumenta Serica,* 42 (1994), pp. 465–481.

105  "American Seminary to Ready Local Jews for Life in the U. S.", *The China Press,* August 31, 1946, pp. 5, 12.

106  Weiyan Meng, "Willy Tonn: 'The Fighting Scholar' of Shanghai," *Sino-Judaica, Occasional Papers of the Sino-Judaic Institute,* Vol. 2 (1995), p. 113.

107  E. Lebon, "Refugee University," *Our Life,* no. 125, December 22, 1944, p. 2; no. 112, September 18, 1944; no. 87, March 17, 1944, p. 2.

108  The other lonely genius at the time in Israel was Martin Buber. For the brief collaboration of the two men in the 1950s see I. Eber, "Martin Buber and Taoism," *Monumenta Serica,* 42 (1994), p. 450.

ORT (initials for the Russian Obshtchestvo Remeslenovo Truda, Society for the Encouragement of Handicraft), or trade vocational school, was established comparatively late, but flourished during the war years.[109] Toward the end of April 1941, an ORT delegate had arrived in Shanghai with the aim of organizing a training center. Before it could actually begin to function properly, however, the Pacific War broke out and funds from the American JDC were no longer available. Until remittances via Switzerland began to arrive again in mid-1944, the school nonetheless continued to function and did not close its doors until 1945. In the four years of its existence 1185 students attended. Its beginnings were modest; for men courses were offered in locksmithing, carpentry, electro-fitting; for women there was machine knitting and dressmaking. Engineering courses were offered in the evening including civil, mechanical, and electrical engineering.[110]

The largest group attending ORT was between the ages of 21 and 35, and was equally divided between those who had finished elementary and those who had completed secondary school.[111] Both the ages and education may indicate that young people believed that acquiring a skill – whether it would be used in Shanghai or elsewhere if and when the war ended – offered some security that they could make a living. It is doubtful whether anyone in their early twenties thought about a university education then. Although there was at least one foreign university in Shanghai, St. John's, few if any could aspire to an university education in wartime.

The Gregg Business College came into being when the Deman family was evicted from their premises on 9 Monkham Terrace where they had run a successful business school until September 1942. The relocated College on 369 Kwenming Road offered, among others, courses in shorthand, typing, languages, and bookkeeping.[112] After the war ended in 1945, the skills acquired were usefully applied in employment with the American army.

Actors and actresses contributed to raising flagging spirits in performances in the shelters and in the few theaters in Hongkou. Tonn's Asia Seminars helped maintain a semblance of intellectual life. The possibility of acquiring a useful skill in the ORT program and Gregg College provided hope that some-day the war would end and life would be resumed in Shanghai or elsewhere.

---

**109** ORT was founded in Russia in 1880. A network of vocational schools was created in many countries thereafter.

**110** YVA, 078/14B, "Four Years of 'ORT' Activities in Shanghai, 1941–1945," *The Shanghai Herald*, n. d. Booklet prepared by M. Rechenberg, director ORT Training Center, Shanghai, 85 pp.

**111** Ibid., p. 81.

**112** YVA, 078/56B, Deman, "Ein verlorenes Jahrzehnt," pp. 137–137a.

**Fig. 12:** Yeshiva men in the Hongkou district. Courtesy H. P. Eisfelder Photography Collection (4901-4648). Now housed at Yad Vashem Archives, Jerusalem.

The spiritual dimension was not neglected and, no doubt, rabbis and religious students saw themselves as those who made sure that Jewish spirituality would not disappear entirely even in Shanghai. Rabbi Mandelbaum expressed this idea forcefully:

> A Yeshiva in Shanghai! Museum Road is an oasis in the Shanghai spiritual desert. When one enters there, one stops in deferential astonishment at that mighty forge of Judaism called the 'Mirrer Yeshiva' which stands iron-strong on its post. [For] indeed, it will be marked with golden letters in the Jewish history of the present

period, that the spiritual giant called 'Mirrer Yeshiva' has undergone and survived the fire-test of today's world-cataclysm. [And] Happy is the nation, that has such a youth ...[113]

Rabbi Mandelbaum had good reasons for expressing positive if not optimistic views. In Shanghai, between the years 1941–1946 (with the exception of 1944), the rabbis were able to make lithographic prints of 104 different titles important for study in the rabbinic schools. These included prayer books, books of the Bible and of law, and rabbinic writings. Such books were hardly available in Shanghai and had to be reproduced from volumes the students and rabbis had brought with them.[114]

Like most of Shanghai's Chinese population, the refugees suffered great hardships during the years of war. The leadership selected and approved by the Japanese authorities was not always able to work in the best interests of the refugees. However, it is doubtful that most were aware of the pressure these men were subject to under the Japanese occupier. Nor would many have been aware that to the Japanese authorities the refugees were merely another group of foreigners that had to be controlled and kept in check by men deemed reliable. That many of the leaders were unsuitable and not equal to their assigned tasks goes without saying. Yet, the communities, Russian, Central European, and Polish, even if divided against one another, carried on, attempting to maintain a semblance of cultural life. We cannot help but admire the strength of spirit that many among them maintained and manifested. The end of war came late to Shanghai, following Japan's capitulation in August 1945, and presented the refugees, as well as the other Jewish communities to whom Shanghai was home, with new and complex choices.

---

113 YIVO, Y2003, 1854.7,B. Mandelbaum, "The Mirrer Yeshivah in Galuth-Shanghai," *The Jewish Almanac, Dedicated to the Jewish Religious Thought* (Der yiddisher almanakh, 194–?, zamelheft farn religyezn gedank), pp. 13–14. [In Yiddish, Russian, and English].

114 Avishai Elboim, "Defusei Shanhai ve'she'arit ha'plitah (Printing in Shanghai and the refugee remnants [Holocaust survivors]," *Ha'ma'ayan*, 1999–2000, pp. 75–86. Elboim's comparison volume by volume of those printed in Germany after WWII and during the war in Shanghai is instructive.

# Chapter 6:
# End of War and the Jewish Exodus

Whereas the war in Europe ended with the German capitulation in May 1945, Asia and Shanghai did not see the war's conclusion until August. By then Japan had suffered the experience of the catastrophe of the atom bomb, and Shanghai and Hongkou – the latter unexpectedly – had not escaped one last disastrous bombardment by American planes.

The end of war in August was greeted with jubilation by the refugees as well as the Chinese. Whether the men who had cooperated with the Japanese for more than two years were concerned about their future is not known. It is to the credit of the refugees that they did not initiate reprisals against members of the several wartime organizations. New worries, however, surfaced immediately. There were the problems of how to continue feeding the destitute thousands and how to keep soup kitchens going. Slowly news about the Nazi crimes began to appear in Shanghai. Then lists of survivors were posted and the desperate search for loved ones and friends began. Anxieties mounted as the months went by: Where to after Shanghai? Return to Germany? Or Austria? Or Poland?

**Fig. 13:** Refugees check lists for names of survivors. Courtesy H. P. Eisfelder Photography Collection (4801-4648). Now housed at Yad Vashem Archives, Jerusalem.

Most had reconciled themselves to there no longer being a "home" – so, if one cannot return home, where else can one go? Would the gates of countries that had once been closed now be open? Remain in Shanghai perhaps, where after the war greater opportunities beckoned?

But when the Chinese civil war between the Communist and Nationalist forces spread after 1945, the latter was no longer an option and Jews, old-timers as well as refugees, tried to leave China as quickly as possible. Today the erstwhile Shanghailanders are spread over several continents. Increasingly, some of the older, but mostly the younger generation that grew into teenage and young adulthood in Shanghai are writing memoirs to tell how they remember their lives in the great metropolis. Over the years a number of documentaries have been produced relating the memories of their experiences. These documentaries, but especially memoirs, are useful materials because they give us glimpses not only of past events, but also of how the memoirist thinks about those events years later. Events experienced in youth, they had been for many of the memoir writers, are often fondly remembered and integrated in various ways in adult life.

## The Disaster of July 1945

Air raid alerts in and around Shanghai had been frequent as the war neared its end, but occurred more often in July 1945. Air raid shelters were few and far between due to ground water which was only 1 or 1½ meters below street level.[1] Whenever an alert was sounded, the population usually went into the streets. July 17 was a Tuesday, a hot and humid day, as described by Ernest Heppner. He worked at a bakery in a crowded lane and decided to go home at noon. As it turned out, this saved his life when the American bombs started falling at about 2 pm. In the lane where he and his wife lived, fronting Dong-shan Road, houses collapsed and were burning as they ran outside. Casualties were heavy and the bakery was completely demolished.[2] The eyewitness, Hugo Burkhard, reported that what occurred during those terrible hours is difficult to describe in words. Body parts, legs, arms, hands, could be seen everywhere in the streets. It was an unbearably hot day, and weeping and screams were

---

1 Arthur Kornik, "Das Rettungswerk," *Juedisches Nachrichtenblatt*, Vol. 6, no. 29 (July 27, 1945), pp. 3–4
2 Ernest G. Heppner, *Shanghai Refuge, A Memoir of the World War II Jewish Ghetto*, Lincoln–London: University of Nebraska Press, 1993, pp. 123–125.

heard from all sides. The help of physicians to alleviate the human misery was exemplary.[3]

Shoshana Kahan was in the French Concession on that fateful day, where she was having lunch with friends. When she heard of the catastrophe, she rushed home in a rickshaw. "The whole way from the Bund to Hongkou was in a terrible [state, clogged] with the wounded ... passes were not controlled at the [ghetto] entrance." Fortunately, her husband was unharmed, but bombs continued to fall on Shanghai, though not on Hongkou, even on subsequent days.[4] Thousands of Chinese were killed in the bombing raids. Among the refugees were 31 dead and 190 wounded; 703 persons were left homeless. Thirty-four homes were completely destroyed and 180 damaged.[5] Were the American bombs dropped on Hongkou inadvertently or by design? It was generally believed that a Japanese radio transmitter close to Dongshan Road was the reason. There may also have been ammunition factories in Hongkou, as Shoshana Kahan claimed.[6]

After the tragedy came the funerals. Shoshana has left a moving description of one of these.

> The heat was terrible. Awful lamentations began when the trucks carrying the dead bodies arrived. They were covered with bloody rags and swarms of flies crawled on the bodies on which the blood had dried. The trucks had left the synagogue quickly because the bodies were already becoming bloated. Mrs. Kushnir was given an injection before going to the cemetery [and as a result] she had absolutely no idea what was happening. When her husband and son were lowered into the double grave, the poor woman watched as if it had no connection to her. People wept uncontrollably and the woman just stood there nonchalantly, not aware of her misfortune. Tired and broken-hearted we returned from the cemetery.[7]

There was sorrow, but also anger. A German Jew confronted Meir Birman on a walk to the ruins and accused him of being a mass murderer. "The Jewish organizations are responsible for this misfortune," said the German Jew, "because they did not give any money toward emigration." Yehoshua Rapoport, who accompanied Birman on the walk, agreed with this accusation. He and

---

**3** Hugo Burkhard, *Tanz Mal Jude! Von Dachau bis Shanghai,* Nürnberg: Richard Reichenbach, n. d. [1967].

**4** R. Shoshana Kahan, *In faier un flamen, tagebukh fun a yidisher shauspilerin* (In Fire and Flames, Diary of a Jewish Actress), Buenos-Aires: Central Association of Polish Jews in Argentina, 1949, entry for July 17, 1945, pp. 337–338.

**5** "The Bombed Out," *Our Life,* no. 136, October 26, 1945, p. 3.

**6** Kahan, *In faier un flamen,* entry for July 17, 1945, p. 337.

**7** Ibid., entry July 18, 1945, pp. 339–340.

his family could have left for Burma, a country for which visas were not required, but Birman would not permit it. Now he understands, writes Rapoport, because three tickets for ship passage would have been required.[8]

Still, other events soon overshadowed the tragedy that had occurred. Gradually, the atrocities perpetrated by the Nazis became known in Shanghai, quite likely by means of Soviet reports. The first article mentioning death camps and Treblinka (though not gas chambers) appeared in *Our Life* on June 22, 1945.[9] Rumors began to circulate about Japan's defeat and surrender even before emperor Hirohito capitulated on August 15. It is doubtful that many people paid much attention to the Japanese proclamation issued on the same day that warned the population to maintain peace and order and cooperate with the Japanese forces in "view of the new situation."[10] The end was greeted at first with disbelief, then with jubilation.

> Crowds gathered everywhere. Practically nobody stays at home, can stay at home. Discussing, shouting, howling. Songs are springing up, German, Jiddish, Polish, Russian. Sights experienced once or twice in a lifetime ... complete strangers congratulating, embracing each other. Spontaneous celebrations ...[11]

In her diary Shoshana Kahan wrote, "One is drunk from the mere word peace! We have waited so many years for this one small word: peace. Dreamt about it in our sleep ... breathed 'peace', and now I hear the word from all sides."[12]

The euphoria of peace did not vanish, but after some time a new set of concerns was felt. Among these were questions of whether and how to mete out justice to those who had been in power during the war years; whether to leave Shanghai; and where, finally, to end the years of exile. Above all was the need to rid the community of the dishonest and corrupt elements who had assumed leadership positions while the Japanese were in power. Calling them yes-men and lackeys, Philip Kohn demanded ridding the administration of the Jüdische Gemeinde of these men and for arranging for new elections.[13] Similarly, the Kitchen Fund came under attack and the Polish refugees demanded

---

**8** Arc. 4°, 410, Yehoshua Rapoport Diary, Jewish National and University Library Archive, Jerusalem.

**9** "War Criminality," *Our Life*, no. 130, June 22, 1945.

**10** YVA, 078/56C, Wilhelm Deman, "Ein verlorenes Jahrzehnt, Shanghai 1939–1940, Tagebuchblätter eines Heimatvertriebenen." (Document pages are not paginated).

**11** Joc.[undus], "How Refugees Took It," *Our Life*, no. 133 , September 7, 1945, pp. 3–4.

**12** Kahan, *In faier un flamen*, entry for August 11, 1945, p. 346.

**13** Philip Kohn, "1933 und neues Leben blueht ... 1941–1945," *Juedisches Nachrichtenblatt*, Vol. 6, no. 34, August 31, 1945), p. 4.

that the responsible Japanese be prosecuted as war criminals.[14] Apparently no further steps were taken and aside from naming the Japanese, the writers of articles generally abstained from naming people they believed had worked together with the Japanese.

Nonetheless, it was easier to get rid of the culprits (although by January 1946 Ghoya was still wandering around freely)[15] than to establish a viable administration that would see to the daily needs of the refugees, especially in the shelters. Inflation was catastrophic and finding capable managerial staff was a herculean task. Between the summer of 1945 and spring 1946, committees came and went, until finally the Joint took over directly. Manuel Siegel, newly released from the internment camp, summarized the situation for the New York office. "Selfishness, suspicion, personal enmities and hostility characterize the whole mentality of the refugee community." Cliques had formed that did not have good words for one another.[16]

In view of these and other difficulties it is perhaps not surprising that the Jewish press showed no particular interest in the Nazi trial taking place in 1946 in Shanghai. An additional reason may have been that the so-called Bureau Erhardt ring was only charged with continuing spying activities against the Americans despite the German surrender months earlier. Thus the ring still furnished the Japanese with military intelligence between May 8 and August 16, 1945.[17]

It should be mentioned also that, the war having ended and Chinese rule re-established, the refugees became aware of the ambiguity of their legal status. The Chinese government had published an announcement in November 1945 which called for the repatriation of all German and Austrian nationals as enemy aliens, regardless of their refugee status. "So the incredible has happened ..." was the horrified response, "the victimizers and the victimized, the robbers and the robbed are being meted out the same treatment."[18] Although this may have been an inadvertent slip-up by the Chinese government, to the

---

**14** The Speaker, "Kitchen Fund Presidium Must Go!," *Our Life*, no. 134, September 21, 1945, p. 3 and "Polish Refugees Demand Punishment of Kubota, Okura, Ghoya and Kano as Chief War Criminals in Shanghai," *Our Life*, no. 134, September 21, 1945, p. 4, signed by The Executive Committee of Polish War Refugees in Shanghai.

**15** "Ghoya in Hongkew verpruegelt," *Shanghai Echo*, Vol. 1, no. 30 (January 29, 1946), p. 4.

**16** YVS, reel 16, 11.728, M. Siegel to Leavitt, August 26, 1945, p. 1.

**17** See United States Army, Military Commission, "Review of the Record of a Trial by a Military Commission, U. S. Army, of Lothar Eisengraeger [i. e. Eisentraeger], alias Ludwig Erhardt," Shanghai 1947. The accused were sentenced January 1947.

**18** "A Bolt out of the Blue," *Our Life*, no. 140, December 21, 1945, p. 1.

refugees it was a clear sign that they were no longer welcome in China. A subsequent announcement was less strongly worded, stating that each case will be dealt with individually. Should continued residence be useful to China, a person can remain and acquire Chinese citizenship.[19]

## Leaving China

Leaving China was not a simple matter. On the one hand, ships for civilian transport were simply not available at the end of war. Nor did diplomatic representation get under way immediately. The American Consulate General, for example, did not open until December 1945, and the American quota system continued in force, although people of any nationality could apply. On the other, was the dilemma of the refugees expressed succinctly in German "weiterwandern oder zurückwandern" (continue emigrating or return). Many of the older generation, the forty to sixty group,[20] were reluctant to move on to a third country to begin life anew, believing that it might be easier to rebuild their lives in familiar surroundings. This despite the warning of the widely read *Shanghai Echo* that conditions were not all that marvelous elsewhere. Germany was in ruin and America was troubled by strikes and unemployment.[21] In addition there was the rather complex situation of the approximately 4.780 Austrian refugees. After the 1938 incorporation into Germany, Austrians had become German citizens and in 1941 they became stateless, together with the German Jewish refugees. At the end of war, not wanting to be stateless any longer, they were anxious to reclaim their Austrian citizenship, possibly unaware that for those who wished to emigrate to the United States, the Austrian quota was nearly nonexistent.[22]

Those who under no circumstances wanted to return to Austria, like the Demans, became increasingly desperate. In response Deman founded an Association of Small-Quota Committee, which included in addition to Austrians also Hungarians, Rumanians, Lithuanians, Yugoslavs, and Turks – all nationalities for which the American quota was very small.[23] Meanwhile those counted within

---

**19**  YIVO, reel Y-2003-1854.1, "Refugees keine Feinde," *The Shanghai Herald*, no. 11, March 12, 1946.

**20**  "The Case for the Middle Aged," *Our Life*, no. 144, March 1, 1946, p. 3. This age group, the article stated, was disproportionately high, which presented a unique problem in arranging emigration.

**21**  "Schlaraffenland?," *Shanghai Echo*, Vol. 1 no. 20 (January 19, 1946), p. 1.

**22**  YVA, 078/56C, Deman, "Ein verlorenes Jahrzent," p. 190.

**23**  Ibid., p. 201.

the German quota continued to leave and Deman noted with considerable dismay the changes in Hongkou. Rickshaws and pedicabs filled with luggage now crowded the streets. All were headed toward the Hongkou wharves where the giant American steamers of the "President" line were waiting. Hongkou was gradually emptying out and the Gregg business school that had assured many a young person a livelihood now stood empty. Both students and teachers had either already left or were about to depart.[24] Their feelings of being stranded, hopeless, and abandoned were expressed in a poem by Alla Maria Maass:[25]

Song of the 5000
Ten years we stood and minutes three
on river's bank a homeless army
while yellow Wangpoo's waves they roll
into the unconcerned sea ...

Ten years of typhus and malaria misery
and on Point Road a grave so cold
while yellow Wangpoo's waves they roll
into the unconcerned sea.

Although the America quota for Germans was more favorable, some families did decide to return to Germany, perhaps not fully realizing the extent to which exile had estranged them from their native country. No longer were there homes to return to. These had vanished together with their families and their possessions. If they had fled to Shanghai with teenage children, these had grown into young adults abroad and their formative years had been spent in the metropolis. Upon returning they were not always welcomed with open arms, either by the new government or by the population.[26]

Aside from the refugees, the Baghdadis and Russians too had to make hard decisions. This was especially true for the Russian Jews who owned properties and businesses and who had not suffered confiscations of their assets by the Japanese as had the Baghdadis. Many waited, even after Mao's armies marched into Shanghai in May 1949. But the hoped for accommodation did not materialize under the new regime. Private property ceased to exist and heavy taxes were levied that had to be cleared before a family could leave China. The

---

24  Ibid., p. 208.
25  Ibid., p. 202. These are the first two verses of a longer poem.
26  Gabriele Anderl, "Der Weg Zurück," *Zwischenwelt*, Vol. 18, no. 2 (August 2001), p. 50. This was especially true of the reception in Austria.

**Fig. 14:** Shanghai Harbor, December 1947. Farewell to refugees departing for America. Courtesy H. P. Eisfelder Photography Collection (4801-4648). Now housed at Yad Vashem Archives, Jerusalem.

process might take several years and many Russian Jews did not leave until the early years of the 1950s. The Moshinsky family, for example, was finally able to depart in 1952.[27]

For the Baghdadis, Pearl Harbor in December 1941, the subsequent occupation of Shanghai by the Japanese, and the internment in 1943 of numerous British passport-holding Baghdadis signaled the beginning of the end of the Jewish diaspora. Sassoon Jacoby summed it up well when he said that he did not doubt that both Germany and Japan will be defeated. But Shanghai then must again become Chinese as it should be. What options would be open to Jews when that happened? According to Jacoby, only Zionism. "I started reading Jabotinsky and a lot of things began to make sense and fall into place," he said.[28] When the state of Israel was established in May 1948, Jacoby and many Russian Jews, especially those who had been strongly pro-Zionist earlier, took advantage of the new opportunity. If they had hesitated to emigrate to

---

**27** Sam Moshinsky, *Goodbye Shanghai, A Memoir*, Australia: Mind Film and Publishing, 2009, p. 187.
**28** The Hebrew University of Jerusalem, Institute for Contemporary Jewry, Eber interview with Jacoby, May 23, 1976, p. 42.

Palestine before, they felt now that the time had come.[29] Unlike the refugees, those with money and connections simply got on a plane and came to the newly established state. Although accurate figures are hard to come by, according to one estimate as many as 10.000 Jews went to Israel from Shanghai and other Chinese cities in the second half of 1952.[30]

Some refugees, like the Eisfelders and Charles Bliss,[31] considered Australia a viable option, and were encouraged to think of emigrating to that country, since a group had been able to sail on the *Javanese Prince* as early as March 1946.[32] At the end of the year a much larger group departed for Australia on the *Hwa Lian*. Although not very seaworthy, the ship arrived without serious mishaps. However, the hoped-for breakthrough did not occur and in subsequent years anti-refugee sentiments prevailed. In the end only about 2.500 Shanghai refugees were able to get Australian visas.[33]

## Shanghai Remembered

The memory of Shanghai is expressed in many different ways. The children or teenagers from Central Europe, adults today, remember Shanghai differently from those who were born in Shanghai of Russian or Baghdadi parents. Religious youngsters and rabbis experienced the city still differently, and those who came as adults and had to cope with life's vicissitudes saw even something else in the city. Memories of Shanghai are preserved in various kinds of writing: a small number of diaries, mostly unpublished; journalistic reports of persons who lecture about their experiences; collections of articles based on interviews, autobiographies and memoirs.

How to distinguish between the latter two? James Cox reminds us that the term autobiography emerged only recently and began to be used widely only

---

**29** Georg Armbrüster and Steve Hochstadt, "Rückkehr aus Shanghai," *Aktives Museum, Mitgliederrundbrief*, 57, July 2007, p. 12.

**30** Nehemia Robinson, "Oifleyzong fun di Yidishe kehilos in Chine (Dissolution of the Jewish Communities in China)," New York: Institute of Jewish Affairs, Jewish World Congress, 1954, p. 10. Typewritten copy.

**31** YVA, 078/52, Charles Bliss, "Semantography, My Life in China and Afterwards," p. 18.

**32** Heinz Ganther, "36 Emigranten verlassen Shanghai," *The Shanghai Herald*, no. 17, March 18, 1946, p. 3.

**33** Suzanne D. Rutland, "'Waiting Room Shanghai': Australian Reactions to the Plight of the Jews in Shanghai After the Second World War," *Leo Baeck Yearbook XXXII*, 1987, pp. 407–433.

toward the middle of the nineteenth century in place of memoir.[34] Yet the two terms, autobiography and memoir, are not interchangeable and in discussing one or the other the literary value of either must not be neglected. Cox suggests that a memoir does not allow the imaginative to obtrude, whereas autobiography will relate to the "inner world of self-reflection."[35] We might also consider that some memoirs are largely autobiographical and that there is a memoir-mode of writing autobiography as well.[36] This brief digression is relevant to our enterprise below to show not only the relative complexity, if not ambiguity of the subject, but also to define my own usage. When a narrative is largely concerned with exploring the self, or presenting a certain kind of self, in reference to external events, I shall use the term autobiography and in some cases autobiographical memoir. When, on the other hand, a narrative is more concerned with external events, placing the self in reference to them, as need be, I shall call it a memoir.

Compared to German and Austrian writers, Russians in Shanghai and their descendants have barely tried their hand at autobiographical accounts. The autobiographical memoir by Judith Ben-Eliezer, *Shanghai Lost, Jerusalem Regained* (1985) is a rare exception.[37] Born in Shanghai of Russian parents, she describes her charmed childhood in an opulent household against the background of the turbulent events then occurring in China. Her father lost his wealth and she had to take a job instead of being able to attend university. In due course, Judith became a successful businesswoman dealing in coal. In addition, throughout this 445-page account her activities in the Zionist Revisionist Party in Shanghai and in Betar are documented in detail.[38]

The Sino-Japanese War of July 1937 and the outbreak of the Pacific War in December 1941 did not end her activities either in business or in the Party. She carried on despite close brushes with the Japanese authorities. Subjected to unpleasant interrogations, she reproduces these verbatim and affects a cinema

---

**34** James M. Cox, "Recovering Literature's Lost Ground Through Autobiography," in James Olney, ed., *Autobiography, Essays Theoretical and Critical,* Princeton: Princeton University Press, 1980, pp. 123–124.

**35** Ibid., pp. 125, 143.

**36** Louis A. Renza, "The Veto of the Imagination: A Theory of Autobiography," in Olney, Ibid., p. 280. He uses the latter phrase in juxtaposition to the memoir-prone autobiographer.

**37** Full bibliographical data is supplied in Appendix 4, where additional works not discussed in the text are also listed.

**38** The Revisionist Party refers to the party founded by Vladimir Jabotinsky in 1925, which was opposed to the official Zionist policy. It eventually seceded from the World Zionist organization. Among Russian Jews in China, the Revisionist Party was singularly successful. Betar was the youth organization of the Revisionist Party.

style description that has the Japanese interrogators sputter and lose their composure while she remains cool and collected.

She deals briefly with the crucial war period between 1942 and the summer of 1945 and devotes most of the second half of the book to her business, the American suitors who court her, and Zionist activities, which culminate in the organization of an Irgun branch in Shanghai.[39] The establishment of the state of Israel is the decisive moment in her life and she realizes she can no longer remain in China. Judith and her mother depart for Israel where at last she meets the love of her life. The book ends with her marriage to Aryeh Ben-Eliezer.

The kind of self the narrator seeks to present is that of an idealist and a committed person. Her idealism is, however, not devoted to China's struggle with the Japanese invader, though she works briefly on behalf of the Chinese underground. Her commitment is to Zionist goals and to contributing in whatever way she can toward the establishment of a homeland. What she would have said of herself, she puts in the mouth of one of her American admirers. "You have always lived in two worlds. Physically you are still in China but spiritually and mentally you have completely drifted away. That tiny spot on earth ... has drawn you like a magnet" (p. 369). Born in China and yet not part of its destiny, only a small handful of Jews identified their fate with that of the country of their sojourn. For Shanghai, although she was born there, Ben-Eliezer expresses no special attachment. The emphasis in this autobiographical memoir is on the political activity on behalf of Zionist goals, rather than on the rare opportunity Shanghai offered to carry on such activity. Her work thus differs markedly from those of the exiles discussed below, who tended to underscore Shanghai's uniqueness, either positively or negatively.

In his autobiographical memoir Yaakov (Yana) Liberman, *My China, Jewish Life in the Orient, 1900–1950*, (1998), also born in China, explains that to him China is a milieu and not a second country. He never made an attempt to become part of China. Nor would the Chinese have wanted him to. He attributes this to the fact that "we were living in permanent exile separate from the centers of Jewish life" (p. 11). Therefore, unlike Judith Ben-Eliezer, he does not see himself as having lived in two worlds.

Born in Harbin, he was early attracted to Revisionist Zionism and became an active member in the Betar movement with its athletic activities, and in time assumed a leadership position. His parents were determined to give him a good education, meaning a foreign education, and the young Liberman at-

---

**39** The full name is Irgun Tzevai Leumi, National Military Organization, which was founded in 1937. During the war years, the organization attempted to organize illegal immigration into Mandatory Palestine. The organization was dismantled in1948.

tended an English school in Shanghai, a foreign school in Korea, and Sophia University in Japan where he earned both a BA and an MA degree. Thus in his adult years he manifested the kind of cosmopolitanism, so characteristic of a large segment of upper class Russian Jews in China, that made their existence pleasant and comfortable in Shanghai. Liberman's life from Harbin to Shanghai, furthermore, demonstrates the extent to which Shanghai's Russian Jewish community had ties to Harbin, as mentioned earlier.

Unlike the refugees who suspected Japanese involvement in Shanghai affairs and even rumored that the Germans together with the Japanese were plotting their demise, discussed in an earlier chapter, Liberman makes no such mention. Indeed, he remembers not being affected by the war in Europe. In 1941, dog racing and horse racing alike drew crowds, cinemas and nightclubs were filled to capacity, and the local theaters offered outstanding Russian and English plays and musicals, operas and ballets (p. 132). Even after Pearl Harbor and the start of the Pacific War as well as internment of friends considered "enemy nationals" by the Japanese, Jewish life retained surprising strength. In Hongkou, he reminds us, European Jews built a haven no longer in evidence in Europe.

Finally the day came for Liberman and others with a commitment to Zionism to leave for the new state of Israel. He tells the reader that people left China not under threat to their lives. They were leaving a diaspora voluntarily, dismantling their institutions, synagogues, and schools. "Jews could leave or stay, the choice was theirs." (p. 226) A unique chapter of Jewish wandering was closed.

Liberman realizes in this memoir that he and other upper-class Russian Jews occupied a privileged position in Shanghai. To them the Chinese did not matter, were hardly noticed except as servants. He and Judith Ben-Eliezer wanted to be perceived as idealistic young people, committed to the establishment of the State. His idealism, like hers, did not extend to the Chinese and their aspirations, despite the fact that even under Japanese occupation they enjoyed a degree of freedom not possible anywhere else at the time. The reader will not find in Liberman's pages a nostalgic backward look to Shanghai. It was a good place to be for a time, but his sojourn there had ended and, now that the Zionist dream was realized, it was time to move on.

Although members of several rabbinic seminaries (yeshivoth) landed in Shanghai, only the Mir Yeshiva managed to arrive intact with its rabbis and students. According to Rabbi Elhanan Yosef Hertsman's memoir, *Escape to Shanghai* (1981)[40] the hand of the Almighty guided the rabbis and students the

---

40 A briefer account in Yiddish is, *Mirer Yeshiva in goles* (Mirer Yeshiva in Exile), Amherst: National Yiddish Book Center, 1999, Steven Spielberg Digital Yiddish Library, no. 04595. First published in 1950.

entire way. Sugihara was dispatched to Kovno only in order to save the yeshiva students (p. 29). That the rickety boat on which they crossed from Vladivostok to Tsuruga did not sink is seen by Hertsman as another miracle. They escaped "in the grace of Torah and with the force of Torah" (p. 51). They ended up in Shanghai's Beit Aharon Synagogue that had not been used before because no Jews lived in that area. The magnificent building waited just for them for fifteen years. But there were dangers, and Rabbi Hertsman repeats the well-known story about Germans trying to persuade the Japanese to exterminate the Jews. "A great miracle" saved them from the gas chambers (p. 105). In Shanghai the students studied and engaged in doing good works, bringing *Yiddishkeit* (Jewishness) to the refugees and establishing a chain of Torah institutions. Unlike others, the Mir Yeshiva students had no difficulties getting passes to leave the ghetto after moving to the Ohel Moishe synagogue. Indeed, a Japanese brought the required passes to the yeshiva (p. 96). Dr. Cohen of SACRA was not regarded with suspicion. To the contrary, he was "a special messenger of G-d sent to be at our side in a time of crisis." (p. 97)

Shanghai or the Chinese barely figure in this narrative. The yeshiva might have been anywhere in this world because what mattered ultimately was a life of study and the existence of Jewish life in this far flung place. Shanghai is remembered as another one of the Almighty's miracles, "It is G-d's wonder that in the farthest corner of the Far-East existed a vibrant Jewish community ..." (p. 86)

Sigmund Tobias's autobiography, *Strange Haven* (1999) also deals with the Mir Yeshiva, however, as a student and as an adolescent. He arrived with his Polish-born parents from Germany in 1938 as a six-year old and left when he was not quite sixteen for the United States. Of the ten years he spent in Shanghai, four were in the Mir Yeshiva, and the reader must perforce assume that these years had a formative role in his future life.

His memory of Hongkou, the lane houses, and the tradesmen-letter writers, shoe repair men, who plied their trade there is sharp. He first attended the Kadoorie School where he was quite unhappy and received poor grades. Despite his parents' objections, he switched to the Mir Yeshiva and the warm friendships the religious students offered him there. He was not the only one to do so. Some of his friends, Tobias tells his readers, also decided on the change and, "Those of us who dropped out of the Kadoorie School and switched to the yeshiva full-time received some money every two weeks ..." (p. 79). The school routine, Shabbat prayers, holiday celebrations, all these are described in considerable detail. Talmudic studies gave him confidence in his intellectual capabilities that he so obviously needed and had not received in the Kadoorie School. Like others, he remembers the Hongkou bombing of July

17 and the end of war soon thereafter. The joy over Japan's surrender is soon dampened, however, by the tragic news from Europe.

The Mir Yeshiva departed for the United States in mid-1947 leaving him at loose ends. When criticisms began to be heard about the yeshivoth, namely that they lived well while others starved and were ill, the teenager became increasingly confused. He felt ashamed, but also angry with the critics. "Now it became even more difficult to remain religious when I heard what was being said about the people I had admired so much" (p. 113). It comes as no surprise that ultimately he decided not to return to the yeshiva after arriving in America, and instead embarked on a successful academic career.

The years he spent studying in the Mir Yeshiva may have been no more than an interlude in a long and productive life that followed. Nonetheless, it was an important interlude – a haven in a world of shifting sands in which a sensitive youngster looked for and found stability and an anchor. In 1988, Tobias returned to Shanghai to give a series of lectures. And it was during the journey to familiar places he had once known that he began drafting this autobiography. The Shanghai he encountered was vastly changed, yet in some ways the same, he tells his readers. But then, he too had changed, yet re-mained the same person. To be sure, Shanghai was a way station, but undenia-bly one that played a major role in his life. Tobias's parents cushioned the hardships of those years and, therefore, his fond recollections of Shanghai are understandable.

The autobiography of Ellis Jacob, *The Shanghai I Knew* (2007) is a very different kind of work.[41] It does not deal with catastrophes or major cataclysms. The author, about the same age as Tobias, did not suffer major displacement at a young age. Born of Iraqi parents, Jacob wrote this book, as he tells in the introduction, "from the point of view of a young boy and then a teenager" as well as a person raised in a cosmopolitan environment. (p. 17). His was a happy childhood in a large family. Like the narratives described earlier, the outbreak of WW II in Europe did not affect the nine- year-old boy and he continued to attend the cosmopolitan British school until the outbreak of the Pacific War. As Iraqi subjects were not at war with Japan, his and other Iraqi families were not interned, and he switched to the Shanghai Jewish school. To be sure, there were "shortages, [but] life went on pretty much as usual during the war" (p. 85). The major change in his life occurred when the Red Army arrived in Shanghai in May 1949. It was then that an anti-foreign attitude in the Chinese population became dominant and he and his mother left China.

---

41 My thanks to Dr. Maisie Meyer for making this work available to me.

Almost wistfully, he concludes his account, "But in a sense I will always be a Shanghailander – it was my home town, and it was part of me ..." (p. 130).

Shanghai is remembered as variously by the refugees as the narratives described so far. There are those who, like Ursula Bacon, think of Shanghai as an "unforgettable experience," whereas to Franziska Tausig in *Shanghai Passage* (1987), who was over forty years old when she came to Shanghai, these were "bitter years." The age a person was when he or she came to the metropolis determined in large measure what the experience would be like. In addition to memories that reflect the direct experience, there are also "second hand" memories, as it were, by children too young to remember experiences and who, therefore, narrate their parents' memories.

An example of the latter is Vivian Jeanette Kaplan, *Ten Green Bottles* (2002). Kaplan was born in Shanghai after WWII and left at two years of age. Although a first person account, the book is based on her remembering her mother's stories, and she calls it a memoir "in the creative non-fiction genre." The book begins like most memoirs of this kind with a happy childhood of the author's mother. By the time of the Austrian Anschluss, she is a young adult and, after encountering great difficulties, the family leaves for Shanghai. Life is not treating them too badly; the author's mother is married to her sweetheart from Vienna; they take a partnership in a bar. After the war ends, they open a fur salon, but by 1949 it is clear they should leave China. "The sights and smells have become familiar, but we were never a part of this land ..." (p. 277).

The self that emerges in this book is a daughter's perception and understanding of her mother and her memories. In these, Shanghai is a grim place; even the good times are soon submerged under the dread of the everyday. The author conveys the mother's fearfulness of what happens and what may yet happen. But this, the reader must remember, is written by the daughter, who has never experienced war and its terrors.

Like Kaplan's *Ten Green Bottles*, Evelyn Pike Rubin, *Ghetto Shanghai* (1993 and 2nd edition, 2000)[42] is a tribute to her mother. Her happy childhood changed at once with Kristallnacht when her father was arrested. As soon as he was released the family left for Shanghai. The father died soon thereafter leaving her mother to support herself and her young daughter. Rubin writes on the last page, "She [her mother] demonstrated monumental fortitude and ingenuity in keeping the two of us alive during our years of deprivation" (p. 199). For these mothers no sacrifice was too great to give their daughters some semblance of normalcy.

---

**42** The German edition, published in 2002, is a shorter version and includes an account of her return visit to Shanghai.

Ursula Bacon's *The Shanghai Diary* (2002) is an autobiography that tells a rather different story. With a Chinese partner her father started a painting business that provided the family with income and with contacts among Chinese. Thus she meets sing-song girls when she helps her father get painting estimates, and they teach her how to count in Chinese and how to eat with chopsticks. She gives English language lessons to three concubines of a Chinese general. When the family has to move into Hongkou, she writes "and in between all the misery, I [nonetheless] managed to have a good time." (p. 164)

Ursula Bacon is a person who finds a positive side even in the most unpleasant of situations. Above all she is interested in the people around her, an interest confirmed by her friendship with Yuan Lin, a Buddhist monk with a Chinese father and an English mother and an Oxford degree in economics. "Life was not about events, but about people," (p. 228) he tells her. The book seems to assert that the Shanghai years are not lost years – a past to be regretted. Rather they were an "unforgettable experience," Shanghai was a safe haven, "exotic, eccentric, and exciting," as she tells the reader in her foreword.

This brief survey of memoirs and autobiographies reveals the various kinds of responses and destinies of those born in China and those who came there as refugees. Some struggled against all odds to make a living, to pursue a religious life; others found romance and married or strove to live up to political ideals. Writers of fiction have as yet barely appropriated the richly woven fabric of these lives to further transform rapidly fading memories. Among novels, I might briefly mention the German novel by Alfred W. Kneucker, *Zuflucht in Shanghai* (1984), who completed this fictionalized account toward the end of his China years. When he passed away in 1960 it was found among his papers and was published posthumously. The novel by Jerome Agel and Eugene Boe, *Deliverance in Shanghai* (1983) is by two authors who were never in Shanghai. They make use of the rich refugee materials by weaving together many different and disparate lives. Finally, there is a recent Chinese novel by Bei La, *Mozhou gangqin* (2007, A magic piano, the Chinese translation is "Jewish Piano"). This is a love story between a Polish-Jewish pianist and a Chinese Red Army orphan. Unlike other novels, Bei La's extends into the 1980s. But are novels important? And need they be considered by the historian? I cannot but agree here with Yosef Hayim Yerushalmi, who writes that the image of the Holocaust (the Shanghai exile included) "is being shaped, not at the historian's anvil, but in the novelist's crucible."[43]

---

43 Yosef Hayim Yerushalmi, *Zakhor, Jewish History and Jewish Memory*, New York: Schocken Books, 1989, p. 98.

These final years of euphoria over the end of war, then mounting grief, and finally anxieties as to their uncertain future are little understood. The American Hongkou bombardment was soon eclipsed by information about the monumental catastrophe of Jews murdered in Europe. But there was little time for mourning and often illusory hope co-existed with despair. Meanwhile decisions had to be made and, while some might have preferred remaining in Shanghai, the threat of yet another war convinced all but the few to leave. Return to Europe was not an option for most, yet countries like America or Australia were not exactly eager to throw their gates open. By the beginning of 1948 only a little over half of the Central Europeans, Baghdadis, and Russians had left.[44] Jews of all persuasions were not unaware that the Chinese communist armies were scoring one victory after another and would soon approach Shanghai. Indeed, by May 1949 Mao Zedong's army had entered the metropolis. Like the European Holocaust survivors, it took several decades before Shanghai refugees were able to translate experience into memory and write memoirs and autobiographies. They do not yet tell us enough about how those years of another time and place are remembered.

---

**44** Harry Schneiderman and Morris Fine, eds., *American Jewish Year Book*, Vol. 50, 1948–1949, Philadelphia: The Jewish Publication Society of America, 1949, p. 710, and Ernest Strauss, "The Far East," Maurice Spector and Maurice Basseches, eds., *American Jewish Year Book*, Vol. 49, 1947–1948, Philadelphia: The Jewish Publication Society of America, 1947, p. 482.

# Some Final Remarks

Escape to Shanghai was for most of the Central Europeans escape into the unknown. Although works about China and translations of Chinese works into German were available between the wars, only few would have read these and most were addressed to scholarly circles. Some might have gained their impressions of Shanghai together with its ill and opium-smoking Chinese from such novels as Vicki Baum's *Hotel Shanghai* (1939), but these would have only confirmed their view of the unwholesomeness of the place. It took much courage and a great deal of desperation for these middle class merchants and pampered bourgeois daughters to decide to leave comfortable homes, families, and friends.

On the other hand, I want to suggest that perhaps the Yiddish speakers from Poland might have been better informed about China. Included in this group, arriving in 1941 from Kobe, was a considerable number of so-called "intelligentsia," writers, journalists, and scholars. These would have been newspaper readers, in addition to readers of Yiddish publications about Chinese philosophy and poetry. The latter were available in inexpensive editions and such papers as *Haynt* and *Der Moment,* published in Warsaw, carried articles about current Chinese events. A history of modern China was published in Vilnius, Lithuania as late as 1940.[1] Although we have no evidence who might have read this book, it is entirely possible that, say, a scholar like Yehoshua Rapoport would have picked it up to find out more about China.

Still, not many among the refugees would have been aware that they were fleeing to a country at war, large parts of which were under Japanese occupation. Nor would most of them, as we saw, have been able to relate compassionately and sympathetically to Chinese among whom millions endured incredible hardships. This was not only because they too were in dire straits, but also because, no matter how badly off, for the most part they considered themselves superior to the unwashed "yellow" kuli. It was, therefore, highly unusual when Yiddish writers like Yosl Mlotek or Jacob Fishman in Shanghai pointed out the plight of Chinese fellow human beings in their poetry and prose. Of course not all of Shanghai's Chinese were poverty stricken. There was a sizeable middle class, wealthy entrepreneurs and industrialists; students, intellectuals, and writers. Similar to the Chinese, however, who were largely unable to distin-

---

1 This is the book by Layzer Boimgarten, *Khine* (China), Vilna: Farlag Tamar, 1940. There is no information about the quantity printed. However, an earlier modern history of China by J. Raymon, printed in Kiev in 1927, for example, was published in an edition of 3.000 copies, a not inconsiderable quantity.

guish one Westerner from another, Westerners could not easily differentiate various kinds of Chinese unless they were the abject poor.

Nonetheless, and this is of great importance, the absence of anti-Semitism on the part of the city's Chinese population made Shanghai truly a refuge. Contrary to their experience under the Nazi hordes, in Shanghai these Jews could be free, at least until 1943, when stateless Jews were confined to the ghetto by the Japanese occupation. Indeed, one might say, Shanghai's Chinese received them hospitably and the memoirs tell frequently of Chinese-Jewish cooperation in business enterprises and work situations. It would be good to know more about these interactions as well as about Chinese concert goers and Chinese audiences at dramatic performances. Might young people have had opportunities for forming friendships? Unfortunately, evidence for all this is lacking. Whatever interaction there was between refugees and Chinese seems to have ended with the establishment of the ghetto in February 1943,[2] and at the end of war there were new problems for both Chinese and refugees. Yet even then, when anti-imperialist sentiments were running high, anti-Semitism was not in evidence and it must have been a genuine relief for the refugees to encounter a society that may not have exactly loved them, but that did not despise them for what and who they were.

But should active interaction between Jews and Chinese, friendships – whether between Baghdadis or refugees and Chinese – be expected? Or is this a fallacious assumption? To answer these questions, we must first and foremost remember that Shanghai was like a mosaic, consisting of many variegated pieces that all somehow fit together, despite the pervasive inequality between colonialists and colonized. Not only was the Chinese population divided by social and native place differences, but the foreign population too was divided by national origin differences. As far as the Jews were concerned there was not one Jewish community but, in fact, five – Sephardic, Russian, German, Austrian, and Polish. Linguistic differences between groups militated against close social relationships even where Germans and Austrians were concerned. To be sure, German speakers made efforts to learn English, though more for purposes of earning a livelihood than for establishing social relations. Adapting to Shanghai, therefore, did not necessitate reaching out beyond one's familiar group. It did not mean adapting to a Chinese environment. It meant adapting

---

2 After the war in Germany, acknowledgment of the Shanghai ghetto and offering of compensation for depriving thousands of freedom was slow in coming. A series of articles in the *Aufbau*, Vol. 21, no. 13 (April 1955), p. 14A; no. 17 (April 29, 1955), p. 1; no. 19 (May 13, 1955), p. 6; no. 25 (June 24, 1955), p. 16; no. 31 (August 5, 1955), p. 19 makes this clear.

to the specific and unique environment of Shanghai. It was the mosaic-like structure of Shanghai society that eased the settling-in process of newcomers, be they Chinese or Europeans. For the refugees from Central Europe a second advantage was that they had become estranged from their native countries before becoming strangers in Shanghai.[3]

To return then to the questions posed above, except in rare instances neither Chinese nor foreigner would have found it necessary to establish friendships among the "other." Linguistic and cultural barriers were formidable and the outbreak of the Pacific War confronted both peoples with a new situation. New barriers were created.

The departure of the Jews from Shanghai, Tianjin, and Harbin after WWII closed a chapter on Jewish life in modern China. I hesitate calling them Diaspora or exile communities – except for the German and Austrian communities. Such terms obscure the real differences and make them appear monolithic. These terms also do not allow us to see that for some China had become home, whether they were born there or were families like the Baghdadis who had lived in Shanghai for several generations. Had it not been for war and revolution, some would have elected to remain. Even the establishment of the state of Israel would not have changed that. As it was, they departed and it took more than thirty years for a Jewish presence to make itself felt once more in China.

But how different are these people who arrive today! Businessmen, single or with families, come for longer or shorter periods of time. They come from many parts of the world: Europe, America, Israel, and they are vastly different from the Jewish population of seventy years ago. Today's Jews are not refugees, nor are they associated with colonialist enterprises. They are free men and women then as now hospitably received by their Chinese hosts; then as now suffering no discrimination for what they are and cannot help being. Although synagogues are no longer in evidence, except here and there as monuments of a bygone era, religious observances take place, and in 2008 a wedding was at last celebrated in Shanghai's Ohel Rachel, even if the synagogue is no longer used for religious purposes.

Finally, Chinese interest in Jews and Israel as well as in Jews who once lived among them is widespread today. Not only scholarly works, but also a number of recent popular publications support this interest. Several universi-

---

**3** Mulan Ahlers, "Die Emigranten kämpfen mit Shanghai wie Jacob mit dem Engel," *Exilforschung, ein Internationales Jahrbuch*, Vol. 5, 1987. Fluchtpunkte des Exils und andere Themen, p. 117. Her perceptive article stresses the importance of better understanding the issue of adaptation.

ties have Jewish Studies institutes and visiting professors teach courses on Jewish topics. Translation work is flourishing and books on Jewish topics and fiction by major Israeli novelists are being translated. A new and very different chapter in Chinese-Jewish relations has begun.

# Appendices

## Appendix 1: Old and New Street Names Mentioned in Text

| | | |
|---|---|---|
| Alcock Road | Anguo Lu | 安國路 |
| Avenue Road | Beijing Xi Lu | 北京西路 |
| Avenue Joffre | Huaihai Zhong Lu | 淮海中路 |
| Baikal Road | Huimin Lu | 惠民路 |
| Bubbling Well Road | Nanjing Xi Lu | 南京西路 |
| Chaoufoong Road | Gaoyang Lu | 高陽路 |
| Chusan Road | Zhoushan Lu | 舟山路 |
| Jessfield Road | Caoyang Lu | 曹楊路 |
| Kingchow Road | Jingzhou Lu | 荊州路 |
| Kweichow Road | Guizhou Lu | 貴州路 |
| Kwenming | Kunming Lu | 崐明路 |
| Mohawk Road | Huangpin An Lu | 黃皮南路 |
| Museum Road | Hu Qiu Lu | 虎丘路 |
| Nanking Road | Nanjing Dong Lu | 南京 東路 |
| Peking Road | Beijing Lu | 北京路 |
| Pingliang Road | Pingliang Lu | 平涼路 |
| Rou de la Tour | Xiangyang Nan Lu | 襄 陽南路 |
| Route Pichon | Fenyang Lu | 汾陽路 |
| Seward Road | Changzhi Dong Lu | 長治東路 |
| Seymor Road | Shanxi Bei Lu | 陝西北路 |
| Tibet Road | Xizang Lu | 西藏路 |
| Tongshan Road | Tangshan Lu | 唐山路 |
| Ward Road | Chang Yang Lu | 長陽路 |
| Wayside Road | Huoshan Lu | 霍山路 |
| Whashing Road | Xuchang | 許昌路 |
| Yu Yuen Road | Yu Yuan Lu | 愚園路 |
| Yuhang East Rd | Dong Yuhang Lu | 東余杭路 |

## Appendix 2: Journals and Newspapers Published in Shanghai for the Jewish Communities 1939–1946

This list is incomplete. It contains only the papers and journals that I have seen, but there may be additional items as well. Also, except for *Israel's Messenger*, I was able to locate only scattered issues. In most cases, therefore, it was impossible to ascertain how long a run each paper or journal had.

*8-Uhr Abendblatt* (Eight o-clock Evening Paper), ed. Philipp Kohn, 1939–1941.

*Der Mitarbeiter* (The Co-worker), weekly, ed. Arthur Kornik, 1940–1941.

*Der Queerschnitt* (The Cross Cut), weekly, ed. Egon Varro, 1939.

*Di Yiddishe Stime fun vaitn Mizrakh* (The Jewish Voice From the Far East), Aguda publication with Russian and English pages, 1942, also 1946.

*Die Laterne* (The Lantern), Unabhängige Wochenschrift für freies geistiges Schaffen, weekly, ed. Heinz Ganther, 1941.

*Dos Vort, Vokhnshrift for dem religezen gedank oyfn Vaytn Mizrakh.* (The Word), A Jewish Weekly for the Religious Revival in the Far East, Yiddish and English, 1941.

*Gelbe Post* (Yellow Post), Ostasiatische Monatsschrift, ed. Adolph J. Storfer, 1939.

*Gemeindeblatt der Jüdischen Kultusgemeinde*, weekly, 1939.

*In Veg* (On the Way), Zamelheft, aroisgegeben durch der Vereinikung fun di Yiddishe Schreiber un jurnalistn, plitim fun Poiln (published by the Association of Jewish Writers and Journalists, refugees from Poland), 1941.

*Israel's Messenger*, Official Organ of the Shanghai Zionist Association, fortnightly, ed. N. E. B. Ezra, 1904–1910, 1918–1941.

*Juedisches Nachrichtenblatt*, Offizieles Organ der juedischen Gemeinde [the subtitle changed several times in the course of the five years], ed. Philipp Kohn, 1940–1945.

*Journal of the Association of Central European Doctors* (Mitteilungen der Vereinigung der Emigranten-Aerzte), bilingual ed. J. Bogard 1940–1942, Th. Friedrichs, as of March 1942.

*Medizinische Monatshefte Shanghai* (Shanghai Medical Monthly), Organ of the C.A.E.J.R. – Medical Board, eds. Paul Salomon, Egon Goldhammer, 1940–1941.

*Me'or Torah* (Torah Light), Journal for the renewal of Torah concerning Halakha. Published by the Committee of Torah Light, 1944–1946, Hebrew, eds. Rabbis Ephraim Mordechai Ginzburg and Abba Zonitz(?).

*Nasha Zhizn* (*Our Life*, English page, *Undzer lebn*, Yiddish page), weekly, ed. David. B. Rabinovich, 1941–1946.

*The Shanghai Herald*, German supplement, daily, 1945–1946. April 26, 1946 title changed to *China Daily Tribune*.

*Shanghai Jewish Chronicle*, Tageszeitung fuer die Juden im Fernen Osten, English and German, daily, ed. Ossi Lewin, 1939–1945.

*Shanghai Medical Journal*, English, German, Chinese, Th. Friedrichs, ed., 1942–1943.

*Shanghai Woche* (Shanghai week), ed. Wolfgang Fischer, 1939, 1942–1943.

*Undzer Velt* (Our World), weekly, ed.?, 1946.

*Unzer Vort* (Our word), Zamelheft 1945, also Zamelheft 1946.

*Yedies*, Wokhenblat far di interesn fun di Poilishe krigs-pleytim (Weekly for the Interests of the Polish War Refugees), 1941.

# Appendix 3: Documentary Films about Shanghai

(1) *Flucht nach Shanghai, Erinnerungen an ein jüdisches Ghetto am Ufer des Wangpoo*, ein Bericht von Lutz Mahlerwein. (German)

Norddeutscher Rundfunk (video, author)

Photography: Frank-Joachim Arnold and Rainer Schäffer
Producer: Horst Bennit
Editor: Ludwig Schubert
Time: 60 minutes
1982

Synopsis:
A group of erstwhile Germans and Austrians from Los Angeles who survived WWII in Shanghai, return to Hongkou. Mahlerwein interviews them in their homes, and they relate their experiences. The men and women interviewed are Gerhard Heimann, Max Krupstein, Kurt Pollak, Jenny Rausnitz, and Trixie Wachsner. Of special interest is the interview with Jenny Rausnitz who was an actress and gives a first-hand account of what it was like to act under adverse conditions. Also interesting is a brief interview with Erwin Wickert, who was attaché at the German Embassy. The documentary contains some excellent footage from occupied Shanghai. The source of this footage is not indicated.

(2) *Shanghai Youtai Ren* (Chinese) (video, author)

Narrator: Xu Zheping (Shula) 徐哲平
Director: Du Lihua 杜櫟華
Photography: Du Lihua
Script: Gai Chenguang 蓋晨光
Time: 15 minutes
n. d.

Synopsis:
A leisurely walk with Xu Zheping through Shanghai; she points out the mansions where rich Baghdadis lived; high rises; spruced-up Kadoorie Marble Palace; site of Ohel Moishe; the interior of Ohel Rachel without lighting. There is

only present-day footage and the photography is not very good. Interviews with Chinese. Quite puzzling is a visit to a cemetery with Gubbay's gravestone. Where is the cemetery? From where has the Gubbay gravestone been brought?

(3) *Round Eyes in the Middle Kingdom*

Producer: Ronald Levaco
Time: 52 minutes
1995

Synopsis:
Levaco was born in China of Russian-Jewish parents. His father's best friend was Israel Epstein. The film is about Epstein and the kind of life he has led in China.

(4) *Escape to the Rising Sun* (English)

Les Films de la Memoire
Written and directed: Diane Perelsztejn
Photography: Guido Van Rooy
Editor: Ewald Wels
Time: 95 minutes
1989

Two short films, one about Chinese antiquities and another about Japanese paintings are included. I thank Professor Yitzhak Shichor for making the film available.

Synopsis:
Most of the film deals with the Polish group of refugees. Starting with the invasion of Poland, the time spent in Vilna, Yukiko Sugihara relates her husband's role in procuring transit visas after presumably 1600 visas for Curacao or Surinam were issued. Good discussion about problem of obtaining Soviet exit visas. The quality of the film is not the best, but there are many valuable stills. Among the various narrators are Zorah Wahrhaftig, Kalmanowicz, Nathan Gutwirth, Yosl Mlotek, Mrs. Yasue Inuzuka, Anna Frankel-Ginsbourg, and Laura Margolis. Narratives are translated into English. Good description of the long journey on the Trans-Siberian Railway and arrival in Vladivostok, arrival

in Kobe, greeting by Alex Triguboff of the Kobe Jewish Committee. Great admiration of Kobe is expressed, interesting shots from Japanese archives, and the sorrowful departure for Shanghai. The Shanghai portion is very short. There is a brief discussion by Margolis about Heime and the problem of German refugees, Pearl Harbor, and the 1943 Ghetto. The film ends with a brief recapitulation of what happened to the people who narrated in the film. The film makes good use of archival footage from YIVO, Beit Hatefutsoth, Spielberg Film Archives, and others.

(5) *Another Time ... Another Moses*

Time: 25 minutes

Synopsis:
Interview with Shanghai survivor Martin Moses. Available from Oakton Community College, 1600 Golf Road, Des Plaines IL 60016

(6) *The Port of Last Resort, Zuflucht in Shanghai* (English with Hebrew subtitles)

Pinball Films/Extrafilm

Producers and directors: Joan Grossman and Paul Rosdy
Time: 79 minutes
1998

Synopsis:
Excellent narration and very good use of archival footage. There are no shots from present-day Shanghai. Four people are interviewed and tell the story of the refugees' arrival in Shanghai. The stories of their everyday lives are woven around those four persons. Pictures of what they looked like as young people are interspersed with the narration. The viewer sees Nazi Germany, Annie Witting's letters, the ship on which refugees arrived, bombed out Hongkou, Garden Bridge, starving Chinese, Heime, Little Vienna, entertainment, theater. The ghetto, foreign *baojia*, and the end of war with American bombs on Hongkou, the initial postwar years, jobs, and search for emigration are also shown. The interviewees give brief reflections of what kind of experience Shanghai had been.

(7) *A Place to Save Your Life* (video, English)

The Ontario Film Development Corporation

Producer, director: Karen Shopsowitz
Photography: Antonin Lhotsky
On-line Editor: Dave Nesbitt
Time: 52 minutes (video, The Spielberg Archive, The Hebrew University, Jerusalem)
1992

Synopsis:
The film describes the arrival of German and Austrian refugees in Shanghai and tells how they viewed their lives in the city after their arrival and during the war. Shopsowitz has used far too many interviews and, while the list of names is given at the end of the documentary, there is no way of knowing who is talking at what time. Some of the interviewees speak only once. Among the names given at the time of viewing are those of Leo Hardoon and David Kranzler, who is a historical commentator. A large number of *North China Daily News* clippings are shown, some stills, and some archival footage. The former refugees also speak about the difficulty of leaving Shanghai, and cast a retrospective glance at their years in Shanghai. Most praise the communal spirit of the refugee community and praise the Chinese who allowed them to live there as well as the Japanese.

(8) *"Shanghai Ghetto"* (English)

Rebel Child Productions

Producers: Dana Janklowicz-Mann and Amir Mann
Time: 95 minutes (video, author)
2002

Synopsis:
Interviews with people who were in Shanghai as children. One of the major persons interviewed is Harold Janklowicz, the producer's father. Skillful narration by Martin Landau, interspersed with comments from experts who have done research on the subject. Comments by Laura Margolis, who was in Shanghai at the outbreak of WWII. Good photography of present day Shanghai and archival footage from the 1930s. Betty Grebenschikoff and Janklowicz's return visit to Shang-

hai and the apartments where they lived is recorded. Arrival and departure from Shanghai, as well as one of the reunions are shown. This is an intelligently produced film presenting a variety of points of view.

(9) '*Zerakh', palit vesarid bashoah* ('Zerakh', A Refugee and Survivor in the Holocaust)" (Hebrew)

Director: Adir Zik
Producer: Moshe Aphil
Editor: Jan Claude Aviv
Time: 60 minutes (video, author)
1999?

Synopsis:
The film deals primarily with Zerakh Wahrhaftig and the Polish group that traveled from Warsaw to Kovno to Japan and from there to Shanghai. The 90-year old Wahrhaftig returns to Lithuania; Zwartendijk and Sugihara are remembered, as are the visas, the Trans-Siberian to Validostok, and the reception by the Jewish Committee. Japanese-Jewish friendship is stressed. Also useful are the pictures of rabbis of the various Yeshivoth and anecdotes told. Avraham Kotsuji, Japanese convert to Judaism and Bible scholar is buried in Jerusalem; his daughters are shown, and the film begins with Izumi Sato placing flowers on his grave. Wahrhaftig travels next to Shanghai, and there are useful shots of Hongkou. Ohel Rachel, and Ohel Moishe (which is the museum today). This is followed by Mrs. Sugihara, her book, brief interviews with various people all of whom remember that Sugihara was ordered not to issue visas. Between 4000–5000 visas were issued.

(10) *Visas that Saved Lives* (Japanese with Hebrew subtitles, feature film)

Fuji Television Network, Inc.

Producer: Naonori Kawamura
Actor as Chiune Sugihara: Go Kato
Actress as Yukiko Sugihara: Kumiko Akiyoshi
[Names supplied by Ellis Tinios]
Time: 60 minutes
1992

Synopsis:
A fictional film about Sugihara, his wife, and children in Kovno from October 1939 to August 1940. It is a very moving feature film, well acted, emphasizing Sugihara's dilemma of political loyalty and of human concern for the plight of the refugees who besiege the consulate in July 1940. The family, wife and even children, are invariably supportive, emphasizing the human condition. The famous train scene is enacted in much detail, Sugihara still signing visas as the train is pulling out of the station.

(11) *Exil Shanghai*

Ulrike Ottinger Film Production/Berlin in cooperation with Transfax Film, Tel Aviv, Shanghai Film Studio.

Director and script: Ulrike Ottinger
Photography: Ulrike Ottinger
Production: Erica Marcus
Editing: Bettina Boehler
Time: 275 minutes
1997

Synopsis:
Ottinger's film does not deal exclusively with the refugees, but with the Jewish communities in Shanghai in general. Various people who once lived in Shanghai tell their stories at great length: Rena Krasno, Georges Spunt, Inna Mink. Extensive use of stills and long sequences of present-day Shanghai. No archival footage. Poorly edited, has no focus, and is far too long.

(12) *The Last Refuge: The Story of Jewish Refugees in Shanghai.*

Producer: Noxi Productions, Xiaohong Cheng and Noriko Sawada
Script by Xiaohong Cheng
Ergo Media Inc., Teaneck N.J.
2003, 2004

Synopsis:
Personal accounts of survivors with some scholarly analysis, and archival footage.

**Films with Partial Shanghai Content**

*Dissolution-Resettlement, 1945–1950* (English)

Written, directed, and produced by Judith E. Doneson
Editor: Braha Zisman-Cohen
Narrator: Bernard Stevens
Jerusalem, Tel Ad Studios
Time: 30 minutes
1987

Synopsis:
The film deals with the end of WWII, the emergence of Israel, and the period of movement of peoples. Shown are DP camps in Europe and the Kielce massacre of 1946. Shanghai is dealt with in a 10 minute segment consisting mainly of an interview with Sassoon Jacoby. This is probably the earliest documentary film that includes Shanghai.

**Jewish Communities Elsewhere in China**

*Tientsin Diaries*

Written and directed by Serge Gregory
Digital Video, Black and White
Vashino Films
Time: 30 minutes
2006

Synopsis:
This is a fictionalized documentary about Misha and Natasha's courtship in Tianjin. The film recreates the vanished world of Russian émigrés against the disintegrating world of China as a result of the outbreak of WWII.

## Appendix 4: Partial List of Published German and English Language Memoirs and Autobiographies

Armbrüster, Georg, Michael Kohlstruck, Sonja Mühlberger, eds., *Exil Shanghai, 1938–1947: Jüdisches Leben in der Emigration*, Teetz: Hentrich and Hentrich, 2000.

Bacon, Ursula, *The Shanghai Diary: A Young Girl's Journey from Hitler's Hate to War-Torn China*, Seattle: Hara Publishing, 2002.

Ben-Eliezer, Judith, *Shanghai Lost Jerusalem Regained*, Jerusalem: Steimatzky, 1985.

Burkhard, Hugo, *Tanz mal Jude! Von Dachau bis Shanghai*, Nürnberg: Richard Reichenbach, n. d. [1967].

Eisfelder, Horst Peter, *Chinese Exile, My Years in Shanghai and Nanking*, Victoria/Australia: Makor Jewish Community Library, 2003.

Epstein, Israel, *My China Eye-Memoirs of a Jew and a Journalist,* San Francisco: Longer River Press, 2005.

Finanne, Antonia, ed., *Far from Where: Jewish Journeys from Shanghai to Australia*, Carlton: Melbourne University Press, 1999.

Foster, John, ed., *Community of Fate, Memoirs of German Jews in Melbourne*, Sydney-Boston: Allen and Unwin, 1986.

Grebenschikoff, Betty, *Once My Name was Sara. A Memoir,* Ventnor, N.J.: Original Seven Publishing Co., 1995.

Heinemann, Headly Hannelore, *Blond China Doll: A Shanghai Interlude, 1939–1953,* St. Catharines, Ont.: Triple H Publishing, 2004.

Hemming, Heinz, Recorded, "Hier sind meine Wurzeln, hier bin ich zu Haus, das Leben der Gerti Meyer-Jorgensen geborene Salomon," Mainz: *Sonderheft der Mainzer Geschichtsblätter*, 2010.

Heppner, Ernest G., *Shanghai Refuge: A Memoir of the World War II Jewish Ghetto,* Lincoln–London: University of Nebraska Press, 1993.

Hertsman, Elhanan Yosef, *Escape to Shanghai*, New York: Maznaim Pub. Corporation, 1984.

Hutton, Esther Robbins, *Sojourn, A Family Saga,* Vashon, Washington: Esfir Books, 1997.

Jacob, Ellis, *The Shanghai I Knew: A Foreign Native in Pre-Revolution*, Margate, N.J.: ComteQ Publishing Co., 2007.

Kaplan, Vivian Jeanette, *Ten Green Bottles: The True Story of One Family's Journey from War-Torn Austria to the Ghetto of Shanghai*, New York: St. Martin's Press, 2005.

Kelly, L.J.H., ed., *To Wear the Dust of War, From Bialistok to Shanghai to the Promised Land, An Oral History, by Samuel Iwry*, New York: Palgrave Macmillan, 2004.

Klotzer, Charles, *Shanghai Remembered: Stories of Jews who Escaped to Shanghai from Nazi Europe*, Royal Oak, Mich.: Momentum Books, 2005.

Krasno, Rena, *Strangers Always: A Jewish Family in Wartime Shanghai*, Berkeley: Pacific View Press, 1992.

Liberman, Yaacov (Yana), *My China: Jewish Life in the Orient, 1900–1950*, Berkeley: Judah L. Magnes Museum and Jerusalem–New York: Gefen Publishing House, Ltd., 1998.

Maynard, Isabelle, *China Dreams, Growing up Jewish in Tientsin,* Iowa City: University of Iowa Press, 1996.

Moshinsky, Sam, *Goodbye Shanghai, A Memoir*, Australia: Mind, Film, and Publishing, 2009.

Mühlberger, Sonja, *Geboren in Shanghai als Kind von Emigranten: Leben und Überleben (1939–1947) im Ghetto von Hongkew*, Teetz: Hentrich and Hentrich, 2006.

Rubin, Evelyn Pike, *Ghetto Shanghai*, New York: Shengold Publishers, 1993.

Rubin, Evelyn Pike, *Ghetto Shanghai, von Breslau nach Shanghai und Amerika, Erinnerungen eines jüdischen Mädchens, 1943–1947, 1995 und 1997*, Konstanz: Hartung-Gorre Verlag, 2002.

Reinisch, George, *Shanghai Haven*, Cheltenham: Standard Commercial Printers, n. d.

Tausig, Franziska, *Shanghai-Passage. Flucht und Exil einer Wienerin*, Vienna: Verlag für Gesellschaftskritik, 1987.

Tobias, Sigmund, *Strange Haven, A Jewish Childhood in Wartime Shanghai*, Urbana-Chicago: University of Illinois Press, 1999.

Witkowski, Lutz, *Fluchtweg Shanghai: über China nach Israel und zurück nach Deutschland: eine jüdische Biographie*, Frankfurt/Main: Peter Lang, 2006.


### Shanghai Memoir Fiction

Agel, Jerome and Eugene Boc, *Deliverance in Shanghai*, New York: Dembner Books, 1983.

Kneucker, Alfred Walter, *Zuflucht in Shanghai: Aus den Erlebnissen eines Oesterreichischen Arztes in der Emigration 1938–1945*, Vienna-Graz: Herman Böhlaus Nachfolger, 1984.

Wagenstein, Angel, Elisabeth Frank and Deliana Simeonova, trans., *Farewell Shanghai*, New York: Handsel Books, 2007.


### Fiction

Bei La 貝拉, *Mozhou Gangqin* 魔咒鋼琴 (A Jewish Piano), Shanghai: Renmin chubanshe, 2007.

Rozan, S. J., *The Shanghai Moon*, New York: Minotaur Books, 2010.


# Appendix 5: A Biographical Sketch of the Karfunkel Family

Although the story of the Karfunkel family can be told only in the barest outlines, it is nonetheless worthwhile to preserve these fragments. Theirs is a highly unusual story of how a family of seven souls adapted itself to living under conditions and circumstances that must have seemed strange to them, if not bizarre.

The family consisted of the dentist Dr. Leo Karfunkel (born in Berlin, 1879–?), and his wife Friedel; his son, the physician Viktor (1906–?), his daughter-in-law Sendi (surnamed Shao, Hangzhou, 1915–?, later called Diana); Leo's brother, the physician Hans Karfunkel (?–1948), his son Wolfgang and daughter-in-law Sulan (?–1986). This appendix is based on an interview conducted by Professor

Avraham Altman and myself, January 16, 2001 in Nahariya and the account by Wolfgang Karfunkel sent to me in 23 typewritten pages. Viktor Karfunkel was present at the interview but did not speak. He was then 94 years old.

According to Diana Karfunkel, Leo ran afoul of the Nazi regime in 1933 when he wrote an anti-Hitler poem. He was denounced by his nurse and imprisoned for nine months. Released, by claiming to have contracted cancer, he at once boarded a train for Czechoslovakia, instead of reporting to the police as instructed. From Czechoslovakia Leo went to Paris, then to Moscow. From there he went by Trans-Siberian to Harbin. He did not remain in Harbin, however, and in 1935 apparently opened a dental practice in Mukden (Shenyang). Whereas another physician, Dr. Silberstein, was eventually granted a permit by the Japanese authorities to practice medicine legally, Leo was not. Since without a permit he could neither advertise nor put up a signboard,[1] he apparently decided to leave Manchukuo and move on, eventually ending up in Nanjing.

In January 1936, Leo was granted Chinese citizenship, presumably because he would then find it easier to open a dental practice.[2] While in Nanjing in 1936, his nephew Wolfram Neumann, considered joining him as a druggist, but nothing came of it and the young man, together with wife and baby, managed to get to Palestine.[3] Meanwhile, also in 1936, his son Viktor, having been dismissed from his position at Berlin's University hospital, decided to leave Germany. He went first to Amsterdam where Leo's first wife (Viktor's mother) lived, and then to Genoa where he boarded a ship for Shanghai. Viktor joined his father in Nanjing where he was also granted Chinese citizenship, and then went on to Hangzhou. In Hangzhou he practiced medicine and taught German at two high schools.

But neither Nanjing nor Hangzhou were destined to become a permanent refuge for the Karfunkels. In July 1937, the Sino-Japanese war broke out and Viktor went to Kunming in Yunnan province. At some point Leo joined him there. Many Chinese had made the long trek from China's occupied areas to Yunnan – then under Chiang Kai-shek's control – among them the entire Qinghua University of Beijing, reestablished in Kunming as Lianda.[4] Diana, who had been a student of

---

1 CAHJP, DAL 55, letters from Birman to HICEM Paris, dated May 9, May 30, and June 10, 1935.

2 YVA, JM 11701, letters from Trautmann, L. von Plessen, and M. Fischer to the Foreign Office in Berlin, the Prussian Interior Ministry, and German Consulate General Hankow, February 17, 1936, April 20, 1936, September 17, 1937.

3 CAHJP, DAL 61, Letter from Birman to Leo Karfunkel, September 24, 1936.

4 The stirring history of the Qinghua odyssey and its rebirth as Lianda is told by John Israel, *Lianda: A Chinese University in War and Revolution*, Stanford: Stanford University Press, 1999.

English literature at Qinghua, met Viktor in Kunming, became the interpreter in his medical practice, and eventually married him.

The Karfunkels did not remain long in Kunming. After the Nationalist government under Chiang Kai-shek was established in Chongqing, Sichuan province in 1938, they decided to go there. Leo Karfunkel's brother Hans, a widower and also a physician, finally left Germany in August 1940. According to his son Wolfgang, Leo had arranged for the visa to inland China. He and Wolgang traveled on a German airline via Russia to Alma-Ata and then to Urumchi, on to Zhengtu, and then to Chongqing. Once there, however, they searched in vain for Leo because he had gone meanwhile to Beibei in the vicinity of Chongqing to escape the constant bombardment of Chongqing. Beibei may have been a backwater, a small village with rice paddies and fields among the mountains, but many educational institutions had fled there to escape the ravages of war.[5]

According to Wolfgang's account, when Hans and Leo finally met up, Leo at once told his brother and nephew a dirty joke. Although the joke is not reproduced, one gains the impression of a man somehow both lighthearted and inventive. This impression is confirmed by a letter he wrote to Hans, still in Germany, in 1938 that is fortunately preserved in the files of the Berlin Hilfsverein. Leo suggested in the letter that the Chinese island of Hainan be used for a Jewish settlement of 20,000–30,000 persons. A university should be established there, he wrote, so that Chinese students need not attend European universities. Land in China is cheap and only Chinese are allowed to purchase land. But, since he and Viktor are Chinese citizens, he argued, they can buy as much land as they want.

The family did not remain long in Beibei. Viktor and Diana returned to Chongqing where he again opened a medical practice. A brief note by Viktor in 1940 mentions that he helped a Mr. Landau, who tried to commit suicide, and the German consulate thanked him for his efforts.[6] In 1941, however, Viktor and Diana moved once again, this time to Luxian, a small town on the Yangzi where there was a government hospital and where he opened a private practice as he was the only European doctor in the area. They remained in Luxian until 1948, finding congenial friendships among the Catholic and Protestant missionaries in town. Hans and Wolfgang lived in Chongqing, while Leo may have remained in Beibei longer, but he eventually joined Viktor in Luxian.

Wolfgang was sixteen in 1940 when he and his father arrived in China. He learned some Chinese, interpreted for his father, and eventually began driving a

---

5  Robert Payne, *Chinese Diaries, 1941–1946*, New York: Weybright and Talley, 1970, pp. 103–105. In 1942, Payne had gone to Beibei to teach at one of the universities.
6  YVA, RG JM.M. 29 P/11677. Viktor's note is dated March 14, 1940, A. Hürter's to Viktor, March 11, 1940.

truck between Chongqing and Kunming. It was on one of these trips on the famous Burma Road that he met Sulan. They were married in 1949. Hans had died in Chongqing in 1948, and Wolfgang might have wanted to remain with Sulan's family in Kunming, but that was not to be. Becoming the despised foreigner after Liberation, he was finally told by the authorities to leave.

The Karfunkels, one after another, came to Israel. Leo died in Nahariya and is buried in the town's cemetery. Sulan died in Germany in 1986 on the way to her first visit with her Kunming family. Wolfgang brought her body back to Israel. Viktor's medical instruments from China were deposited in the Kfar Veradim museum. Diana visited her family for the first time in 1987, traveling with a German tourist group. At the time of the interview she still lived in Nahariya and was the author of three novels and two collections of short stories, published in Taiwan under the name of Jin Xin. In addition to fiction, she has written widely for a number of journals. In 1974, she won a prize for her short stories that were published in German translation in 1988.

## Appendix 6: List of German Refugees Entering Shanghai Since 1937, Registration Made by Zangzou Police Station

The statistics presented below are derived from a list dating from 1941 that was prepared either by or for the Japanese authorities. The list consists of twenty eight pages, one of which is unreadable. It also reveals a sad truth: the closing of Shanghai's gates to refugees. In 1939, 377 people arrived, while in 1941 only 32 were able to come.

The list reveals an interesting demographic profile.[7] However, it should be kept in mind that this is a list of only one police precinct in the French Concession and cannot be considered representative. It shows a cross section of refugees able to pay rent and who had achieved a measure of independence. Hence a similar list from a Hongkou precinct may vary considerably. Nonetheless, the list allows today's historian to see that Shanghai provided a refuge for entire families, sometimes of two or three generations. It also consisted of an older age group who by coming to Shanghai escaped annihilation.

There were 513 men and 422 women, with 257 families, totaling 935 people in this police precinct. The larger number of men was due to the fact that at that time men were being incarcerated in Nazi Europe and continued to be more vulnerable at the time. There were 118 unmarried women. There were relatively few children: 23 teenagers between the ages 15 and 19 and 43 children under the age

---

7 YVA, 078/78A, Shanghai Municipal Police, Box 79, file 826/3/2.

of 14. The few young children were probably due to the fact that this was an older age group, with most women well past child-bearing age. The average age for men was 42.9 years and the average for women was 44.3. Some were in their seventies, like Arnold Goetz who was born in 1874, or Hans Eyck, born in 1877. A sizeable number of men and women were born in the 1880s.

Professions varied, with merchants predominating among the men. Women generally had no professions, and when they did it was as secretaries or typists. Thirteen men listed their professions as musicians – among them 3 pianists – and 12 professors. There were several dentists and physicians. In sum, this was a middle class group of people and not a highly educated one, similar to those in other precincts in Hongkou.

## Glossary of Chinese Names and Terms

| | |
|---|---|
| bao jia | 保甲 |
| Beibei | 北被 |
| Chen Jie | 陳介 |
| Congming Island | 崇明 |
| Da dao | 大道 |
| *Dagong Bao* | 大公報 |
| Ding Ling | 丁玲 |
| *Dongfang Zazhi* | 東方雜誌 |
| fabi | 法幣 |
| Fu Xiao'an | 傅筱庵 |
| Gonggong zujie | 公共租界 |
| He Fengshan | 何鳳山 |
| Hongkou | 虹口 |
| Huang Fu | 黃孚 |
| Huangpu (jiang) | 黃埔江 |
| Huang Tienmai | 皇天邁 |
| Jiang Jieshi (Chiang Kai-shek) | 蔣介石 |
| Jin Xin | 金鑫 |
| Kung H.H. (Kong Xiangxi) | 孔祥熙 |
| Lilong fangzi | 里弄房子 |
| Long Yun | 龍雲 |
| Mao Dun (Shen Yanbing) | 茅盾 (沈雁冰) |

| | |
|---|---|
| Pudong | 浦東 |
| Shanghairen | 上海人 |
| Shanghai tebieshi shehui ju | 上海特別社會侷 |
| *Shen* Bao | 申報 |
| Sun Fo | 孫佛 |
| Tang Leangli | 湯良禮 |
| Tilanqiao | 提籃橋 |
| Wang Jingwei | 汪精衛 |
| tongxianghui | 同鄉會 |
| xiao shimin | 小市民 |
| *Xinshen Bao* | 新申報 |
| Yao Keming | 姚克明 |
| Zhabei | 閘北 |

# Bibliography

## Archives

Central Archive for the History of the Jewish People, Jerusalem
Public Record Office, London
Yad Vashem Archive, Jerusalem
Shanghai Municipal Archives
Joint Distribution Committee, New York
National Archives of Canada. Manuscript Division, Toronto

## Newspapers

Aufbau
The China Press
Dagongbao 大公報
Japan Times
Nasha Zhizn (Russian title), Our Life (English page), Undzer Lebn (Yiddish page)
North China Herald
Shanghai Evening Post and Mercury
Shanghai Times
Xin Shenbao 新申報

## Interviews

Eber interview with Howard Levin, Institute for Contemporary Jewry, Jerusalem, October 14, 1988.
Eber interview with Sassoon Jacoby, Institute for Contemporary Jewry, Jerusalem, May 23, 1976.

## Books

— *300 Jahre Juden in Halle, Leben, Leistung, Leiden, Lohn*. Halle: Mitteldeutscher Verlag, 1992.
— *The Battle of Muddy Flat*. Shanghai: Printed and Published at the North China Herald Office, 1904. Pamphlet.
Adler, Samuel N. *Against the Stream*. Jerusalem, 2001.

Akira Iriye, (ed.). *The Chinese and the Japanese: Essays in Political and Cultural Interaction.* Princeton: Princeton University Press, 1980.

Arad, Yitzhak, Yisrael Gutman, Abraham Margaliot. (eds.). *Documents on the Holocaust.* Jerusalem: Yad Vashem, 1981.

Armbrüster, Georg, Michael Kohlstruck, Sonja Mühlberger, (eds.). *Exil Shanghai, 1938–1947.* Teetz: Hentrich and Hentrich, 2000.

Barnett, Robert W. *Economic Shanghai: Hostage to Politics, 1937–1941.* New York: Institute of Pacific Relations, 1941.

Barkai, Avraham. *Das Wirtschaftssystem des Nationalsozialismus: Ideologie, Theorie, Politik 1933–1945.* Frankfurt/Main: Fischer Taschenbuch Verlag, 1988.

Bauer, Yehuda. *American Jewry and the Holocaust: The American Jewish Joint Distribution Committee. 1939–1945.* Detroit: Wayne University Press, 1981.

Ben-Eliezer, Judith. *Shanghai Lost, Jerusalem Regained.* Israel: Steimatzky, 1985.

Bentwich, Norman. *Wanderer Between Two Worlds.* London: Kegan Paul, Trench, Trubner and Co., Ltd., 1941.

Berenstein, Tatiana, A. Eisenbach, a. Rutkowski (comps., eds.). *Eksterminacja Żydów na ziemiach Polskich w okresie okupacji hitlerowskiej* (The extermination of Jews on Polish soil during the Nazi occupation). Warsaw: Żydowski Instytut Historyczny, 1957.

Bickers, Robert and Christian Henriot (eds.). *New Frontiers: Imperialism, New Communities in East Asia 1842–1943.* Manchester-New York: Manchester University Press, 2000.

Bloch, Michael. Ribbentrop. New York: Crown Publishers, Inc., 1992.

Boelcke, Willi A. *Die deutsche Wirtschaft, 1930–1945.* Düsseldorf: Droste Verlag, 1983.

Broszat, Martin and Norbert Frei (eds). *Das dritte Reich im Überblick: Chronik, Ereignisse, Zusammenhänge.* Munich–Zurich: Piper, 1989.

Browning, Christopher, R. *Nazi Policy, Jewish Workers, German Killers.* Cambridge: Cambridge University Press, 2000.

Booker, Edna Lee, with John S. Potter. *Flight from China.* New York: The Macmillan C., 1945.

Burkhard, Hugo. *Tanz mal Jude! Von Dachau bis Shanghai.* Nürnberg: Richard Reichenbach, n. d. [1967].

Cairis, Nicholas T. *Era of the Passenger Liner.* London–Boston: Pegasus Books Ltd., 1992.

Cheng Naishan, Britlen Dean, (trans.). *The Banker.* San Francisco: China Books and Periodicals, Inc., 1992.

Coble, Parks M. *The Shanghai Capitalists and the National Government, 1927–1937.* Cambridge: Cambridge University Press, 1980.

Coble, Parks, M. *Facing Japan: Chinese Politics and Japanese Imperialism, 1931–1937.* Cambridge: Council of East Asian Studies, Harvard University, 1991.

Cornwall, Claudia. *Letter from Vienna: A Daughter Uncovers Her Family's Jewish Past.* Vancouver–Toronto: Douglas and McIntyre, 1995.

Cressey, George B. *China's Geographic Foundations: A Survey of the Land and Its People.* New York–London: McGraw-Hill Book Co., Inc., 1934.

Davidson-Houston, J. V. *Yellow Creek: The Story of Shanghai.* London: Putnam, 1962.

Deutschkron, Inge. *Ich trug den Gelben Stern.* Köln: Verlag Wissenschaft und Politik, 1978.

Dirksen, Herbert von. *Moskau, Tokio, London: Erinnerungen und Betrachtungen zu 20 Jahren deutscher Aussenpolitk, 1919–1939*. Stuttgart: W. Kohlhammer, 1949.

Döscher, Hans-Jürgen. *Das Auswärtige Amt im Dritten Reich. Diplomatie im Schatten der "Endlösung"*. Berlin: Siedler Verlag, 1987.

Drechsler, Kurt. *Deutschland–China–Japan 1933–1939: das Dilemma der deutschen Fernostpolitik*. Berlin: Akademie Verlg, 1964.

Duus, Peter, Ramon H. Myers, Mark R. Peattie. *The Japanese Informal Empire in China, 1895–1937*. Princeton: Princeton University Press, 1989.

Eber, Irene. *The Jewish Bishop and the Chinese Bible: S. I. J. Schereschewsky (1831–1906)*. Leiden–Boston: Brill, 1999.

Eber Irene. *Chinese and Jews: Encounters Between Cultures*. London–Portland: Valentine Mitchell, 2008.

Eber, Irene, (ed., trans.). *Voices from Shanghai: Jewish Exiles in Wartime China*. Chicago–London: University of Chicago Press, 2008.

Fairbank, John K., Edwin O. Reischauer, Albert M. Craig. *East Asia: The Modern Transformation*. Boston: Houghton Mifflin, 1965.

Feingold, Henry L. *The Politics of Rescue: The Roosevelt Administration and the Holocaust, 1938–1945*. New Brunswick, N.J.: Rutgers University Press, 1970.

Fox, John P. *Germany and the Far Eastern Crisis 1931–1938: A Study in Diplomacy and Ideology*. Oxford: Clarendon Press, 1982, reprint 1985.

Frey, Paul W. *Faschistische Fernostpolitik: Italien, China und die Entstehung des weltpolitischen Dreieckes, Rom–Berlin–Tokio*. Frankfurt/Main: Peter Lang, 1997.

Friedlander, Saul. *Nazi Germany and the Jews: The Years of Persecution 1933–1939*. New York: Harper-Collins, 1997. Vol. 1.

Friedman, Philip, Ada J. Friedman (ed.). *Roads to Extinction: Essays on the Holocaust*. New York-Philadelphia: The Jewish Publication Society of America, 1980.

Fu Pao-jen, "The German Military Mission in Nanking 1928–1938, a Bridge Connecting China and Germany," Ph.D. Dissertation, Syracuse University, 1989.

Furuya Keiji, Chung-ming Chang. *Chiang Kai-shek: His Life and Times*. New York: St. John's University, 1981.

Ganther, Heinz and Günther Lenhardt (eds.). *Drei Jahre Immigration in Shanghai*. Shanghai: Modern Times Publishing House, 1942.

Goldstein, Jonathan (ed.). *The Jews of China*. Armonk–London: M. E. Sharpe, 1999, 2 vols.

Goodman, David G. and Masanori Miyazawa. *Jews in the Japanese Mind: The History and Uses of a Cultural Stereotype*. New York-Singapore: The Free Press, 1995.

Grew, Joseph C. *Ten Years in Japan*. New York: Simon and Schuster, 1944.

Griese, John William. "The Jewish Community in Manila." MA Thesis, University of the Philippines, 1955.

Gutman, Yisrael (ed.). *Rescue Attempts during the Holocaust*. Proceedings of the Second Yad Vashem International Historical Conference, Jerusalem, April 8–11, 1974, Jerusalem: Yad Vashem, 1977.

He Fengshan, 何鳳山. *Waijiao Shengya Sishi Nian* 外交生涯四十年 [My forty-year diplomatic career]. Hong Kong: The Chinese University Press, 1990.

Henriot, Christian, Wen-hsin Yeh, (eds.). *In the Shadow of the Rising Sun: Shanghai under Japanese Occupation*. Cambridge: Cambridge University Press, 2004.

Heppner, Ernest G. *Shanghai Refuge: A Memoir of the World War II Jewish Ghetto*. Lincoln–London: University of Nebraska Press, 1993.

Herman, Stewart W. Jr. *It's Your Souls We Want*. New York–Boston: Harper and Brothers, 1943.

Hilberg, Raoul. *The Destruction of the European Jews*. New York–London: Holmes and Meier, 1985, rev. ed., 2 Vols.

Hildesheimer, Esriel. *Jüdische Selbstverwaltung unter dem NS-Regime: der Existenzkampf der Reichsvertretung und Reichsvereinigung der Juden in Deutschland*. Tübingen: J. C. B. Mohr (Paul Siebeck), 1994.

Hoster, Barbara, Roman Malek and Katharina Wenzel-Teuber (eds.). David Ludwig Bloch, *Holzschnitte Woodcuts, Shanghai 1940–1949*. Sankt Augustin: China-Zentrum and Monumenta Serica Institute, 1997.

Hsiung, James C. and Steven I. Levine (eds.). *China's Bitter Victory: The War with Japan, 1937–1945*. Armonk-London: M. E. Sharpe, Inc., 1992.

Iriye, Akira (ed.). *The Chinese and the Japanese: Essays in Political and Cultural Interaction*. Princeton: Princeton University Press, 1980.

Isaacs, Harold R. *Re-Encounters in China: Notes of a Journey in a Time Capsule*. Armonk, N.Y.-London: M. E. Sharpe, Inc., 1985.

Johnston, Tess and Deke Erh. *God and Country: Western Religious Architecture in Old China*. Hong Kong: Old China Hand Press, 1996.

Johnstone, William C. *The Shanghai Problem*. Stanford: Stanford University Press, 1937.

Jordan, Roger W. *The World's Merchant Fleets 1939: The Particulars and Wartime Fates of 6000 Ships*. Annapolis: Naval Institute Press, 1999.

Kahan, R. Shoshana. *In Faier un Flamen: Tagebukh fun a Yiddisher Shoishpilerin* [In Fire and Flames, Diary of a Jewish Actress]. Buenos Aires: Central Association of Polish Jews in Argentina, 1949.

Kaminski, Gerd. *General Luo genannt Langnase: das abenteuerliche Leben des Dr. med. Jakob Rosenfeld*. Vienna: Löcker Verlag, 1993.

Kirby, William C. *Germany and Republican China*. Stanford: Stanford University Press, 1984.

Knipping, Franz and Klaus-Jürgen Müller (eds.). *Machtbewusstsein in Deutschland am Vorabend des zweiten Weltkrieges*. Paderborn: Ferdinand Schöning, 1984.

Kounin, I. I., (comp.). *Eighty-five Years of the Shanghai Volunteer Corps*. Shanghai: The Cosmopolitan Press, 1938.

Kranzler, David. *Japanese, Nazis and Jews: The Jewish Refugee Community of Shanghai, 1938–1945*. New York: Yeshiva University Press, 1976.

Kuo Heng-yu (ed.). *Von der Kolonialpolitik zur Korporation: Studien zur Geschichte der Deutsch-Chinesischen Beziehungen*. Munich: Minerva Publikation, 1986.

Lang, H. *Shanghai Considered Socially: A Lecture*. Shanghai: American Presbyterian Mission Press, 1875, 2nd ed.

Lee, Leo Ou-fan. *Shanghai Modern: The Flowering of Urban Culture in China, 1930–1945*. Cambridge: Harvard University Press, 1999.

Levine, Hillel. *In Search of Sugihara: The Elusive Japanese Diplomat who Risked His Life to Rescue 10.000 Jews from the Holocaust*. New York–Singapore: The Free Press, 1996.

Lu Hanchao. *Beyond the Neonlights: Everyday Shanghai in the Early Twentieth Century.* Berkeley–Los Angeles: University of California Press, 1999.

Malek, Roman (ed.). *Jews in China, from Kaifeng ... to Shanghai.* Sankt Augustin: Monumenta Serica Institute, 2000.

Martin, Brian G. *The Shanghai Green Gang: Politics and Organized Crime, 1919–1937.* Berkeley: University of California Press, 1996.

Mendelsohn, John (ed.). *The Holocaust: Selected Documents in Eighteen Volumes.* New York–London: Garland, 1982.

Meskill, Johanna M. *Hitler and Japan: The Hollow Alliance.* New York: Atherton Press, 1966.

Meyer, Maisie. *From the Rivers of Babylon to the Whangpoo.* Lanham–New York: University Press of America, Inc., 2003.

Midell, Eike. *Exil in den USA.* Leipzig: Verlag Philipp Reclam jun., 1983.

Moore, W. J. *Shanghai Century or 'Tungsha Flats to Soochow Creek'.* Ilfracombe, Devon: Arthur H. Stockwell, Ltd., n. d.

Nellist, George F. M. *Men of Shanghai and North China: A Standard Biographical Work.* Shanghai: Oriental Press, 1933.

Ofer, Dalia. *Escaping the Holocaust: Illegal Immigration to the Land of Israel, 1939–1944.* New York: Oxford University Press, 1990.

Olney, James (ed.). *Autobiography: Essays Theoretical and Critical.* Princeton: Princeton University Press, 1980.

Oxaal, Ivar, Michael Pollak, Gerhard Botz (eds.). *Jews, Anti-Semitism and Culture in Vienna.* London-New York: Routledge and Kegan Paul, 1987.

Pannell, Clifton W. and Laurence J. C. Ma. *China: The Geography of Development and Modernization.* New York: John Wiley and Sons, 1983.

Pauker, Arnold (ed.). *Die Juden im national-sozialistischen Deutschland, 1933–1943.* Tübingen: J. C. B. Mohr, 1986.

Pehle, Walter (ed.). *November 1938: From 'Reichskristallnacht' to Genocide.* New York: Berg, 1991.

Philipp, Michael. *Nicht einmal einen Thespiskarren: Exiltheater in Shanghai 1939–1947.* Hamburg: Hamburger Arbeitsstelle für deutsche Exilliteratur, 1996.

Powell, John B. *My Twenty-Five Years in China.* New York: The Macmillan Co., 1945.

Quested, Rosemary. *The Russo-Chinese Bank: A Multi-National Financial Base of Tsarism in China.* Birmingham: Birmingham Slavonic Monographs, 1977.

Rankin, Mary B. *Early Chinese Revolutionaries: Radical Intellectuals in Shanghai and Chekiang, 1902–1911.* Cambridge: Harvard University Press, 1971.

Ratenhof, Udo. *Die Chinapolitik des deutschen Reiches, 1871 bis 1945: Wirtschaft – Rüstung – Militär.* Boppard am Rhein: Harald Boldt Verlag, 1987.

Ravitch, Meylekh. *Kontinentn un Okeanen: Lider, Baladn, un Poeme* [Continents and oceans: songs, ballads, and poems]. Warsaw: Literarishe Bletter, 1937.

Richarz, Monika (ed.). *Bürger auf Wiederruf: Lebenszeugnisse deutscher Juden 1780–1945.* München: C. H. Beck, 1989.

Ristaino, Marcia R. *Port of Last Resort: The Diaspora Communities of Shanghai.* Stanford: Stanford University Press, 2001.

Rosenkranz, Herbert. *Reichskristallnacht, 9. November 1938 in Oesterreich.* Vienna: Europa Verlag, 1968.

Robinson, Marc. *Altogether Elsewhere*. San Diego–London: Harcourt Brace and Co., 1994.

Robinson, Nehemia. *Oifleyzung fun di Yidishe Kehilos in Chine* [Dissolution of the Jewish Communities in China]. New York: Institute of Jewish Affairs, Jewish World Congress, 1954.

Ross, James R. *Escape to Shanghai: A Jewish Community in China*. New York: The Free Press, 1994.

Rothke, Claus. *Deutsche Ozean-Passagierschiffe 1919 bis 1985*. Berlin: Steiger, 1987.

Schneiderman, Harry (ed.). *The American Jewish Yearbook, 5702, September 22, 1941 to September 11, 1942*. Philadelphia: The Jewish Publication Society of America, 1941–5702, Vol. 43.

Schlögel, Karl (ed.). *Der grosse Exodus: die russische Emigration und ihre Zentren 1917 bis 1941*. München: C. H. Beck, 1994.

Schrecker, John E. *Imperialism and Chinese Nationalism: Germany in Shantung*. Cambridge: Harvard University Press, 1971.

Schubert Hans, Mark Siegelberg. *"Die Masken fallen": "Fremde Erde": Zwei Dramen aus der Emigration nach Shanghai 1939–1947*. Hamburg: Hamburger Arbeitsstelle für deutsche Exilliteratur, 1996.

Seywald, Wilfried. *Journalisten im Shanghaier Exil 1939–1949*. Salzburg: Wolfgang Neugedauer, 1987.

Shillony, Ben-Ami. *The Jews and the Japanese: The Successful Outsiders*. Rutland–Tokyo: Charles E. Tuttle Co., Inc. 1991.

Shirer, William L. *Berlin Diary: The Journal of a Foreign Correspondent 1939–1941*. New York: Alfred A. Knopf, 1941.

Simpson, John Hope. *Refugees: A Review of the Situation Since September 1938*. New York: Oxford University Press, 1939.

Sommer, Theo. *Deutschland und Japan zwischen den Mächten, 1935–1940*. Tübingen: J. C. Mohr (Paul Siebeck), 1962.

Spence, Jonathan D. *The Search for Modern China*. New York–London: W. W. Norton and Co., 1990.

Spitzer, Leo. *Hotel Bolivia: The Culture of Memory in a Refuge from Nazism*. New York: Hill and Wang, 1998.

Strauss, Herbert A. *International Biographical Dictionary of Central European Emigres 1933–1945*. München: K. G. Saur, 1983, 4 Vols.

Tobias, Sigmund. *Strange Haven: a Jewish Childhood in Wartime Shanghai*. Urbana–Chicago: University of Illinois Press, 1999.

Tokayer, Marvin and Mary Swartz. *The Fugu Plan: the Untold Story of the Japanese and the Jews during World War II*. New York–London: Paddington Press, Ltd., 1979.

Trapp, Frithjof, Werner Mittenzwei, Henning Rischbieter. *Handbuch des deutschsprachigen Exiltheaters, 1935–1945*. München: K. G. Saur, 2 Vols.

Tupper, Harmon. *To the Great Ocean: Siberia and the Trans-Siberian Railway*. London: Secker and Warburg, 1965.

Twitchett, Dennis and J. K. Fairbank (eds.). *The Cambridge History of China*. Cambridge: Cambridge University Press, 1978.

Vogel, Rolf. *Ein Stempel hat gefehlt: Dokumente zur Emigration deutscher Juden*. München–Zürich: Droemer Knaur, 1977.

Wakeman, Frederic Jr. and Wen-hsin Yeh (eds.). *Shanghai Sojourners*. Berkeley: East Asian Studies, University of California, 1992.

Wakeman, Frederic Jr. *Policing Shanghai*. Berkeley: University of California Press, 1995.

Wakeman, Frederic Jr. *The Shanghai Badlands: Wartime Terrorism and Urban Crime 1837–1941*. New York: Cambridge University Press, 1996.

Wasserstein, Bernard. *Secret War in Shanghai*. London: Profile Books, 1999.

Wasserstein, Bernard. *The Secret Lives of Trebitsch Lincoln*. London: Penguin Books, 1989.

Wei, Betty Peh-T'i. *Shanghai: Crucible of Modern China*. Hong Kong–Oxford: Oxford University Press, 1987.

Wilbur, Martin C. and Julie Lien-ying How (eds.). *Documents on Communism, Nationalism, and Soviet Advisers in China 1918–1927*. New York: Columbia University Press, 1956.

Wolff, David. *To the Harbin Station: The Liberal Alternative in Russian Manchuria, 1898–1914*. Stanford: Stanford University Press, 1999.

Woodhead, H. G. W. (ed.). *The China Yearbook*. Shanghai: China Daily News, 1939.

Wright, Arnold (ed.). *Twentieth Century Impressions of Hongkong, Shanghai, and Other Treaty Ports of China: Their History, People, Commerce, Industries and Resources*. London: Lloyd's Greater Britain Publishing Co., Ltd., 1908.

Wyman, David S. *The Abandonment of the Jews: America and the Holocaust, 1941–1945*. New York: Pantheon Books, 1984.

Xu Zhucheng, 徐鑄成 。 *Hatong Waizhuan* 哈同外傳 [Hardoon's unofficial history]. Hong Kong: Wuxing jishu baoshe, 1982.

Yeh Wen-hsin. *The Alienated Academy Culture and Politics in Republican China, 1919–1937*. Cambridge–London: Council on East Asian Studies, Harvard, 1990.

Yeh Wen-hsin (ed.). *In the Shadow of the Rising Sun: Shanghai under Japanese Occupation*. Cambridge: Cambridge University Press, 2004.

Zhou Xun. *Chinese Perceptions of the Jews and Judaism: A History of the Youtai*. Richmond: Curzon, 2001.

*Zhonghua Minguo Daxue* Shi 中華民國大學史 [History of Chinese National Universities]. Taibei: Wenhua, 1952, 2 Vols.

Zuroff, Efraim. *The Response of Orthodox Jewry in the United States to the Holocaust: the Activities of the Vaad-Ha-Hatzala Rescue Committee, 1939–1945*. New York: Yeshiva University Press and Hoboken: Ktav Publishing House, Inc., 2000.

# Articles

A Bolt Out of the Blue. *Our Life* no. 140 (December 21, 1945): 1.

A New Homeland in China. *Shanghai Evening Post and Mercury* (June 26, 1939): 3.

All Shanghai Now Closed to Emigres. *The China Press* (August 15, 1939): 18.

American Seminary to Ready Local Jews for Life in U. S. *The China Press* (August 31, 1946): 5, 12.

Anti-Semitism Makes Appearance in S'hai. *The China Weekly Review* (November 1, 1942).

Arta's Second Exhibition. *Our Life* no. 96 (May 26, 1944): 2.

Banquet in Honor of Colonel N. Yasue and Captain K. Inuzuka in the Shanghai Jewish Club. *Nasha Zhizn* no. 34 (December 26, 1941): p. 2.

Biancamano with 841 Jews Due Tomorrow. *China Press* (February 21, 1939): 1, 4.

The Case for the Middle Aged. *Our Life* no. 144 (March 1, 1946): 3.

China Plans Special Area for Emigres. *China Press* (March 1, 1939).

Chise Youtairen lai Huhou, bai E shangji beiduo 赤色猶太人來滬後白俄生機被奪 [After red Jews come to Shanghai, White Russians are deprived of their livelihood]. *Xin Shen Bao* 新申報 (December 18, 1938): 2.

Dr. Quo Tai-chi Condemns Axis Recognition of Wang. *Shanghai Evening Post and* (July 3, 1941): 1, 3.

Dr. Yotaro Sugimura Discusses World Jewish Problems. *Israel's Messenger* (November 3, 1933): 9.

Election and War Fevers Compete in Shanghai. *North China Daily News* April 11, 1940): 1.

562 German Emigres Due in Port Today. *China Press* (December 20, 1938): 1.

524 German Emigres Land in Shanghai. *China Press* (December 21, 1938): 1.

Four Hundred Emigres Arrive Here Eve of Passover. *Israel's Messenger* 36, no. 2 (May 5, 1939): 10.

Gala-Konzert der Foreign Pao Chia. *Juedisches Nachrichtenblatt* 4, no. 44 (December 3, 1944): 2.

German-Manchu Trade Accord Concluded. *North China Herald* (July 27, 1938): 153.

Germany May Buy More Soya Beans from Manchoukuo. *Japan Times* (February 24, 1936): 1.

Gestapo Agents Reported to Have Arrived in Japan. *China Press* (October 8, 1941): 1.

Ghoya in Hongkew verpruegelt. *Shanghai Echo* 1, no. 30 (January 29, 1946): 4.

Japan Supplies Food to Germany; Sends 1.500 Tons Daily Via Russia. *The New York Times* (June 4, 1941): 3.

Japanese Authorities Explain Policy of Emigrants in Hongkew. *Nasha Zhizn* (September 12, 1941) 11.

Japanese Bribing Emigres for Votes, Relatives Getting Landing Permits. *Shanghai Evening Post and Mercury* (April 3, 1940): 2.

Japanese Seize Jewish Paper. *North China Daily News* (April 9, 1940): 2.

Jewish Emigres Due Here Today. *China Press* (January 15, 1939): 1.

Jewish Influx Being Studied by Japanese. *Shanghai Times* (May 24, 1939).

Kitchen Fund Presidium Must Go!. *Our Life* no. 134 (September 21, 1943): 3.

Last Group of German Jewish Refugees Brought to Shanghai. *China Press* (September 13, 1939): 3.

List of Commercial Houses, Agents, etc. *Chinese Repository* 15, no. 1 (January 1846): 1–8.

M.S.E., Frau Dr. Sun Yat Sen auf dem deutschen General Konsulat: Haende Weg von der deutschen Innenpolitik!. *Deutsche Shanghai Zeitung* (May 16, 1933).

Manchukuo Fades as Centre of German Jewish Settlement. *Israel's Messenger* 31, no. 7, (October 5, 1934): 8.

More Jewish Refugees Reach Shanghai from Germany and Austria. *China Press* (October 19, 1938): 3.

Nazis Continue Anti-Jewish Campaign Despite Their Denial of Circular. *The China Weekly Review* (November 8, 1941).

New Émigré Group of 400 Arrives Here. *China Press* (January 1, 1939): 1.

N.Y. Committee Planning for Jewish Colony in West China. *China Press* (September 22, 1939): 3.

Notices of Shang-hai: Its Position and Extent; Its Houses, Public Buildings, Gardens, Population, Commerce, Etc. *Chinese Repository* 15, no. 9 (September 1846): 466–472.

One Hundred Thousand Jews May Find Homes in China. *Israel's Messenger* 36, no. 4 (July 14, 1939): 14.

1,400 Emigres to Greet New Year in City. *China Press* (December 31, 1938): 2.

Refugee Held in Fake Pass Charges Here. *Shanghai Evening Post and Mercury* (October 10, 1940): 2.

Refugees from Germany Go to the Far East. *Israel's Messenger* 33, no. 3 (June 5, 1936): 10.

Refugees Urged to Remain Neutral. *North China Daily News* (April 4, 1940): 2.

Reich Emigres in Shanghai Placed at 500. *China Press* (November 26, 1938): 3.

Reich-Manchukuo Trade End: Year Favorable for Puppets. *China Press* (August 7, 1939): 7.

Ri De xieding yu Zhongguo 日德協定與中國 [The Japan-German agreement and China] *Da Gongbao* 大公報 (November 27, 1936): 2.

Schlaraffenland?, *Shanghai Echo* 1, no. 20 (January 19, 1946): 1.

Serious Sino-Japanese Disturbances. *North China Herald* (January 26, 1932).

The Triple Alliance. North China Herald (October 2, 1940): 5–6.

Two Arrested on Fake Pass Count. *Shanghai Evening Post and Mercury* (August 13, 1940): 2.

Untergrundarbeit in Shanghai. *Aufbau* (May 17, 1946): 29.

Wohin koennen wir wandern? *Shanghai Echo* 1, no. 27 (January 26, 1945): 1.

Youtai nanmin rujing wenti, benshi ponan rongna, geguolingshi yicheng bao zhengfu 猶太難民入境問題本市頗難容納各國領事已呈報政府 [The Jewish refugees are a regional problem, the city has considerable difficulty accommodating them, consuls of other countries have already notified their governments]. *Xin Shenbao* 新申報 479 (February 19, 1939): 7.

Youtai nanmin xuxiang Ri, shenqinhou ke juliu, fouze lingqi tuichu jingbeiqu 猶太難民須向日申請後可居留否令其退出警備區 [Jewish refugees must now request from the Japanese to go on living in the special area, otherwise they will be ordered to leave it]. *Xin Shenbao* 新申報 671 (August 12, 1939): 7.

Zhongguo he Youtairen wenti 中國和猶太人問題 (China and the Jewish problem). *Xin Shenbao* 新申報 (September 29, 1939): 2.


Altman, Avraham and Irene Eber. Flight to Shanghai, 1938–1940: The Larger Setting. *Yad Vashem Studies* 28 (2000): 65–82.

Anderl, Gabriele. Der Weg zurück. *Zwischenwelt* 18, no. 2 (August 2001): 47–53.

Arendt, Hannah. We Refugees. In *Altogether Elsewhere*, Marc Robinson (ed.), 110–119. San Diego–London: Harcourt Brace and Co. 1994.

Armbrüster, Georg and Steve Hochstadt. Rückkehr aus Shanghai. *Aktives Museum*, Mitgliederrundbrief 57 (July 2007).

Bergere, Marie-Claire. The Other China: Shanghai from 1919 to 1949. In *Shanghai, Revolution and Development in an Asian Metropoplis,* Christopher Howe (ed.), 1–34. Cambridge: Cambridge University Press, 1981.

Bernd, Martin. Das deutsche Militär und die Wendung der deutschen Fernostpolitik von China auf Japan. In *Machtbewusstsein in Deutschland am Vorabend des zweiten Weltkrieges*, Franz Knipping and Klaus Jürgen Müller (eds.), Paderborn: Ferdinand Schöning, 1984.

Betta, Chiara. From Orientals to Imagined Britons: Baghdadi Jews in Shanghai. *Modern Asian Studies* 37, no. 4 (2003): 999–1023.

Betta, Chiara. Myth and Memory. Chinese Portrayals of Silas Aron Hardoon, Luo Jialing and the Aili Garden Between 1924 and 1925. In *Jews in China, from Kaifeng ... to Shanghai*, Roman Malek (ed.), 375–400. Sankt Augustin: Monumenta Serica Institute, 2000.

Bi Chunfu and Ma Chendu (eds.), Di Jin, Diane Rabinowitz and Michael Rabinowitz, trans. A Plan to Settle Jewish Refugees in China. *Sino-Judaic Occasional Papers* 2 (1945): 67–84.

Bickers, Robert. Settlers and Diplomats, the End of British Hegemony in the International Settlement, 1937–1945. In *In the Shadow of the Rising Sun: Shanghai under Japanese Occupation*, Christian Henriot and Yeh Wen-hsin (eds.), 229–256. Cambridge: Cambridge University Press, 2000.

Botz, Gerhard, The Jews of Vienna from the Anschluss to the Holocaust. In *Jews: Anti-Semitism and Culture in Vienna*, Ivaar Oxaal, Michael Pollak, Gerhard Botz (eds.), 185–204. London–New York: Routledge and Kegan Paul, 1987.

Bresler, Boris. Harbin's Jewish Community, 1898–1958, Politics, Prosperity and Adversity. In *The Jews of China*, Jonathan Goldstein (ed.), 200–215. Armonk–London: M. E. Sharpe, 1999, Vol. 1.

Brown, Mendel. The Modern Jews of China – Shanghai II. *Israel's Messenger* (December 4, 1936): 10–11.

Calder, A. Bland. Shanghai Trade. *Israel's Messenger* 34, no. 10 (January 14, 1938): 23, 19.

Ceng Xubai 曾虛白. Sili sheng Yohan daxue 私立 哟翰大學 (Private St. John's University), 397–403. In *Zhonghua minguo daxue shi* 中華民國大學 (Record of Chinese National Universities). Taibei: Wenhua, 1952, Vol. 2.

Chen Jian 陳兼. Shijie dongluan yu Youtaizhi guoji yinmou 世界動亂與猶太之國際陰謀 (World Disorder and the Jewish National Conspiracy). *Zhongguo Gonglun* 中國公論 2, no. 5 (February 1940): 13–24.

Darwin, John. Afterword: A Colonial World. In *New Frontiers: Imperialism's New Communities in East Asia, 1842–1953*, Robert Bickers and Christian Henriot (eds.), 250–260. Manchester-New York: Manchester University Press, 2000.

Davis, Douglas. Ho Fengshan: The Chinese Oskar Schindler. *The Jerusalem Post* (February 20, 2000): 2.

Di Jin, Diane Rabinowitz, and Michael Rabinowitz, trans. A Plan to Settle Jewish Refugees in China. *Sino-Judaica Occasional Papers*, Vol. 2 (1995), pp. 67–84.

Dreifuss, Alfred. First Jewish Artists' Exhibition in the Designated Area. *Our Life* 86 (March 10, 1944): 2.

Dreifuss, Alfred. Shanghai – eine Emigration am Rande. In *Exil in den USA*, Eike Midell (ed.), 449–517. Leipzig: Verlag Philipp Reclam Jun., 1983.

Dreifuss, Alfred. Mirele Efros, von Jacob Gordin. *The Shanghai Herald* (May 7, 1946): 3.

Dreifuss, Alfred. Unser Theater. *The Shanghai Herald*, Sondernummer (April 1946): 14.

Eastman, Lloyd E. Facets of an Ambivalent Relationship: Smuggling, Puppets, and Atrocities During the War, 1937–1945. In *The Chinese and the Japanese, Essays in Political and Cultural Interaction*, Akira Iriye (ed.), 275–285. Princeton: Princeton University Press, 1980.

Eber, Irene. Martin Buber and Taoism. *Monumenta Serica* 42 (1994): 445–464.

Elliot, Mark C. The Limits of Tartary: Manchuria in Imperial and National Geographies. *Journal of Asian Studies* 59, no. 3 (August 2000): 603–646.

Elbaum, M. 18. Februar 1943, die Geschichte des Hongkewer Ghettos. *The Shanghai Herald*, Sondernummer (April 1946): 24–25.

Ekboim, Avishai. Defusei Shanhai ve'she'arit ha'plitah [Printing in Shanghai and the refugee remnants]. *Ha'ma'ayan* (1999–2000): 75–86.

Embacher, Helga and Margit Reiter. Schmelztiegel Shanghai? – Begegnungen mit dem Fremden. *Zwischenwelt* 18, no. 1 (February 2001): 40–50.

Fairbank, John K. The Creation of the Treaty System. In *The Cambridge History of China*, D. Twichett and J.K. Fairbank (eds.), 213–263 Vol. 10. Cambridge: Cambridge University Press, 1978.

Fogel, Joshua A. 'Shanghai-Japan': The Japanese Residents' Association of Shanghai. *Journal of Asian Studies* 59, no. 4 (November 2000): 927–950.

Ganther, Heinz. 36 Emigranten verlassen Shanghai. *Shanghai Herald*, 17 (March 18, 1946): 3.

Garver, John W. China's Wartime Diplomacy. In *China's Bitter Victory, The War with Japan, 1937–1945*, James C. Hsiung and Steven I. Levine (eds.), 3–32. Armonk–London: M. E. Sharpe, Inc., 1992.

Goodman, Bryna. New Culture, Old Habits: Native-Place Organization and the May Fourth Movement. In *Shanghai Sojourners*, Frederic Wakeman, Jr. and Wen-hsin Yeh (eds.), 76–107. Berkeley: Institute of East Asian Studies, University of California, 1992.

Griggs, Joseph. Japan Joins Axis in Military Pact. *Shanghai Evening Post and Mercury* (September 28, 1940): 1, 3.

He Pingsong, 何燏 松. Shangwu yin shuguan beihui jilue 商務印書館被燬紀略 (General account of the destruction by fire of the Commercial Press). *Dong fang Zazhi*, 東 方雜誌 29, no. 4 (October 16, 1932): 3–9.

Henriot, Christian. 'Little Japan' in Shanghai: An Insulated Community, 1875–1945. In *New Frontiers, Imperialism's New Communities in East Asia, 1842–1953*, Robert Bickers and Christian Henriot (eds.), 146–169. Manchester–London: Manchester University Press, 2000.

Henriot, Christian. Shanghai Industries under Japanese Occupation: Bombs, Boom, and Bust. In *In the Shadow of the Rising Sun, Shanghai under Japanese Occupation*, Christian Henriot and Yeh Wen-hsin (eds.), 17–45. Cambridge: Cambridge University Press, 2004.

Henriot, Christian. Shanghai and the Experience of War: The Fate of Refugees. *European Journal of East Asian Studies* 5, no. 2 (September 2006): 215–245.

Jennings, Eric. Last Exit from Vichy France: The Martinique Escape Route and the Ambiguities of Emigration. *The Journal of Modern History* 74, no. 2 (June 2002): 289–324.

Kahan, Layzer. Nisim oif unzer vanderveg (Miracles On Our Journeys). *In Veg* (November 1941): 1–9.

Kaim, Julius R. Neugierig auf Yunnan. *Gelbe Post* 6 (July 1939): 122–123.

Kaufmann, Fritz. Die Juden in Shanghai im 2. Weltkrieg. *Leo Beck Institute* 73 (1986): 12–23.

Kornik, Arthur. Das Rettungswerk. *Juedisches Nachrichtenblatt* 6, no. 29 (July 27, 1945): 3–4.

Krasno, Rena. History of Russian Jews in Shanghai. In *Jews in China, from Kaifeng … to Shanghai*, Roman Malek (ed.) 331–344. Sankt Augustin: Monumenta Serica Institute, 2000.

Krebs, Gerhard. Antisemitismus und Judenpolitik der Japaner. In *Exil Shanghai, 1938– 1947*, Georg Armbrüster, Michael Kohlstruck, Sonja Mühlberger (eds.), 58–76. Teetz: Hentrich und Hentrich, 2000.

Krebs, Gerhard. The 'Jewish Problem' in Japanese-German Relations, 1933–1945. In *Japan in the Fascist Era*, Bruce E. Reynolds (ed.), 107–132. New York: Palgrave Macmillan, 2004.

Kohn, Philipp. 1933 und neues Leben blueht … 1941–1945. *Juedisches Nachrichtenblatt* 34 (August 31, 1945), 4.

Kornik, Arthur. Interview with Hans Zelinka, Chairman of Proprietors of Bars, Cafes and Restaurants' Association in Designated Area. *Our Life* 58 (August 12, 1943): 8.

Kunfi, T. Die medizinische Betreuung der Immigration. *Shanghai Herald* Sondernummer (April 1946): 9–10.

Lahnsen, Thomas. Remembering China, Imagining Israel: The Memory of Difference. *The South Atlantic Quarterly* 99, 1 (Winter 2000): 253–272.

Lebon, E., Refugee University. *Our Life* 125 (December 22, 1944): 2.

Leong Yuen Sang, Regional Rivalry in Mid-Nineteenth Century Shanghai: Cantonese vs. Ningpo Men. *Ch'ing-shih Wen-t'i* 4, 8 (December 1982): 29–50.

Lin Han-sheng. Wang Ching-wei and Chinese Collaboration. *Peace and Change* 1 (Fall 1972): pp. 17–35.

Liu James T.C. German Mediation in the Sino-Japanese War, 1937–1938. *Far Eastern Quarterly* 8, 2 (February 1949): 157–171.

Lu Hanchao. Away from Nanking Road: Small Stores and Neighborhood Life in Modern Shanghai. *The Journal of Asian Studies* 54, 1 (February 1995): 95–123.

Mandelbaum, B. The Mirrer Yeshivah in Galuth – Shanghai. *The Jewish Almanac, Dedicated to the Jewish Religious Thought* (Der Yidisher Almanakh, 194?, Zamelheft farn religyezn gedank) 13–14. [In Yiddish, Russian and English].

Margaliot, Abraham. Emigration – Planung und Wirklichkeit. *Die Juden im national-sozialistischen Deutschland, 1933–1943*, Arnold Pauker (ed.), 303–316. Tübingen: J. C. B. Mohr, 1986.

Margaliot, Abraham. The Problem of the Rescue of German Jewry during the Years 1933–1939; the Reasons for the Delay in their Emigration from the Third Reich. In *Rescue Attempts during the Holocaust*, Yisrael Gutman (ed.), 247–265, Proceedings of the Second Yad Vashem International Historical Conference, Jerusalem, April 8–11, 1974, Jerusalem: Yad Vashem, 1977.

Martin, Bernd. Das deutsche Militär und die Wendung der deutschen Fernostpolitik von China auf Japan. In *Machtbewusstsein in Deutschland am Vorabend des zweiten Weltkrieges*, Franz Knipping und Klaus-Jürgen Müller (eds.), 191–207. Paderborn: Ferdinand Schöningh, 1984.

Martin, Bernd. Das deutsche Reich und Guomindang-China, 1927–1941. In *Von der Kolonialpolitik zur Kooperation, Studien zur Geschichte der deutsch-chinesischen Beziehungen,* Kuo Heng-yu (ed.), 325–375. Munich: Minerva Publikation Saur Inc., 1986.

Maurer, Trude. The Background of Kristallnacht: The Expulsion of Polish Jews. In *November 1938, from 'Reichskristallnacht' to Genocide,* Walter Pehle (ed.), 44–72. New York: Berg, 1991.

Merker, Peter. Israel in Yunnan – zu den Plänen der GMD-Regierung, in Südwestchina ein jüdisches Siedlungsgebiet einzurichten. *Newsletter, Frauen in China* 9 (August 1995): 10–12.

McKinnon, Stephen R. Toward a History of the Chinese Press in the Republican Period. *Modern China* 23, 1 (January 1997): 5–11.

Meng Weiyan. Willy Tonn: 'The Fighting Scholar of Shanghai' *Sino-Judaica, Occasional Papers of the Sino-Judaic Institute,* Vol. 2 (1995): 111–128.

Menzel, Johanna M. Der geheime deutsch-japanische Notenaustausch zum Dreimächtepakt. *Vierteljahrheft für Zeitgeschichte* 5 (1957): 182–193.

Nobel, Günter and Genia. Erinnerungen: als politische Emigranten in Schanghai. *Beiträge zur Geschichte der Arbeiterbewegung* 21, no 6 (June 1979): 882–894.

Pałusz-Rutkowska, Ewa and Andrzej T. Romer. Współpraca Polsko-Japońska w czasie II Wojny Światowey. *Zeszyty* Historiczne 110 (1994): 43. (English translation: Polish-Japanese cooperation during World War II. *Japan Forum* 7 no. 2 (Autumn 1995): 285–316.

Peattie, Mark. R. Japanese Treaty Port Settlement in China, 1895–1937. In *The Japanese Informal Empire in China, 1895–1937,* Peter Duus, Ramon H. Myers, Mark R. Peattie (eds.). 166–209. Princeton: Princeton University Press, 1989.

Pollak, Ernst. Menschen die uns halfen. *Shanghai Jewish Chronicle,* Special Number (March 1940).

Rabinovich, David. More Self Control and Calm. *Nasha Zhizn* (August 7, 1942): 1.

Ristaino, Marcia R.The Russian Diaspora Community in Shanghai. In *New Frontiers, Imperialism's New Communities in East Asia, 1842–1953,* Robert Bickers and Christian Henriot (eds.), 192–210. Manchester–New York: Manchester University Press, 2000.

Rosenstock, Werner. Exodus 1933–1939: A Survey of Jewish Emigration from Germany. *Leo Baeck Institute Yearbook* 1 (1956): 373–390.

Rutland, Suzanne, D. 'Waiting Room Shanghai': Australian Reactions to the Plight of the Jews in Shanghai After the Second World War. *Leo Baeck Institute Yearbook* 32, 1987: 407–433.

Selmanson, Ephraim. Liza Hardoon, die Geschichte der reichsten Erbin Asiens. *Shanghai Morgenpost* (November 16, 1941): 7.

Skidelsky, Robert. A Chinese Homecoming. *Prospect* (January 2006): 36–41.

Stein, Joshua B. Britain and the Jews of Danzig, 1938–1939. *The Wiener Library Bulletin* 32, 49–50, n.s. (1979): 29–33.

Tang Leangli. Shanghai Hunting Ground of Thriving Jewish Racketeers. *Shanghai Times* (February 16, 1942).

Tang Yating. Reconstructing the Vanished Musical Life of the Shanghai Jewish Diaspora: A Report. *Ethnomusicology Forum* 13, 1 (January 2004).

Tennenbaum, Joseph. The Crucial Year 1938. *Yad Vashem Studies* 2 (1958): 49–77.

Wagner, Rudolf G. The Role of the Foreign Community in the Chinese Public Sphere. *The China Quarterly* 142 (June 1995): 423–443.

Wakeman, Frederic, Jr. Policing Modern Shanghai. *The China Quarterly* 115 (September 1988): 408–440.

Wakeman, Frederic Jr. Licensing Leisure: The Chinese Nationalists' Attempt to Regulate Shanghai, 1927–49. *The Journal of Asian Studies* 54, 1 (February 1995): 19–42.

Walravens, Hartmut. Martin Buber und Willy Tonn und ihre Beiträge zur Kenntnis der chinesischen Literatur. *Monumenta Serica* 42 (1994): 465–481.

Wang ke-wen. Collaborators and Capitalists: The Politics of 'Material Control' in Wartime China. *Chinese Studies in History* 26, 1 (Fall 1992): 42–62.

Weinberg, Gerhard L. German Recognition of Manchoukuo. *World Affairs Quarterly* 28 (1957): 149–164.

Wolff, Reinhard. Hässliches Mobiliar im schönen Volksheim. *Taz-mag* (Tageszeitung, Berlin) (February 5/6, 2000): 4–5.

Xu Jie 許. Hongkou Ribenren juzhuqu shulun 虹口日本人居住區 論 (Collected presentation of the Japanese quarter in Hongkou). *Shanghai yenjiu luncong*上海研究論叢 (Shanghai studies papers) 10 (1996): 278–298.

Xu Xin. Sun Fo's Plan to Establish a Jewish Settlement in China During World War II Revealed. *Points East* 16, 1 (March 2001): 1,7–8.

# Index of Persons

Made in the USA
Lexington, KY
01 September 2018